Refugees and Gender

Law and Process

Refugees and Gender
Law and Process

Heaven Crawley

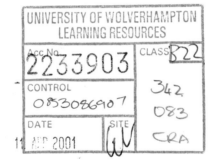

JORDANS
2001

Published by
Jordan Publishing Limited
21 St Thomas Street
Bristol BS1 6JS

British Library Cataloguing-in-Publication Data
A catalogue record for this book is available from the British Library.

ISBN 0 85308 690 7

Typeset by Mendip Communications Ltd, Frome, Somerset
Printed by MPG Books Ltd, Bodmin, Cornwall

PREFACE

The Refugee Women's Legal Group (RWLG) was established by individuals and organisations concerned about the impact of changes in immigration law on refugee women in the UK. Central among its aims is the development of a gendered perspective on refugee law and policy. In 1997 the RWLG, with ILPA and Refugee Action, published *Women as Asylum Seekers: A Legal Handbook* by Heaven Crawley as part of a long-term strategy to advance standards of representation and decision-making and to increase awareness of the gendered experiences of refugee women fleeing persecution. In 1998, the RWLG produced *Gender Guidelines for the Determination of Asylum Claims in the UK* similar to those adopted in other refugee-receiving countries. The *Gender Guidelines* draw upon a wide range of legal and other expertise from solicitors, barristers, practitioners, academics, refugee community organisations, women's groups, human rights groups and non-governmental organisations working with refugees and asylum seekers in the UK as well as refugees and asylum-seeking women themselves. The *Gender Guidelines* have been widely endorsed, including by the UNHCR, but they have yet to be adopted by the government.

This book provides a substantial theoretical and legal update on the interpretation of women's experiences in the asylum determination process and is essential reading for all those working with refugee and asylum-seeking women in the UK.

Dr Heaven Crawley studied for her BA (Hons) in Geography with African Studies and MA in Gender and Development at the University of Sussex and Institute of Development Studies, before moving to Nuffield College, Oxford to undertake research on the experiences of refugee women seeking asylum in the UK. She was awarded her DPhil by the University of Oxford in 1999. The work for this book was completed before Heaven started work with her current employer, the Research Development and Statistics Directorate of the Home Office (London).

The production of this book would not have been possible without the contributions of members of the RWLG.

We would also like to thank the following organisations and individuals for generously supporting the production of this book: The Joseph Rowntree Charitable Trust, Oxfam, Eleanor Rathbone Charitable Trust, Tooks Court Barristers Chambers, Immigration Law Practitioners' Association, Bindman and Partners, Coker Vis Partnership, Fran Webber, Julia Onslow-Cole, Hugh Southey, Wilson & Co and Ian MacDonald QC.

RWLG
January 2001

CONTENTS

TABLE OF CASES

TABLE OF STATUTES

References are to paragraph numbers and Appendices.

TABLE OF STATUTORY INSTRUMENTS

References are to Appendices.

TABLE OF HOUSE OF COMMONS PAPERS

References are to paragraph numbers.

TABLE OF STATUTORY ETC MATERIALS FROM OTHER COUNTRIES

References are to paragraph numbers and Appendices.

TABLE OF INTERNATIONAL MATERIALS

References are to paragraph numbers and Appendices.

TABLE OF ABBREVIATIONS

ADIs	Asylum Directorate Instructions
ADIMA	Australian Department of Immigration and Multi-Cultural Affairs
AIR	Asylum Interview Record
ALO	Airline Liaison Officer
ALU	Asylum Liaison Unit
APC	All People's Congress
ARC	Asylum Rights Campaign
BIA	Board of Immigration Appeals (US)
CA	Court of Appeal
CAT	Convention Against Torture
CCR	Canadian Council for Refugees
CEDAW	Convention on the Elimination of All Forms of Discrimination against Women
CIO	Chief Immigration Officer
CIRB	Canadian Immigration and Refugee Board
CLA	Immigration (Carriers' Liability) Act (1987)
CRDD	Canadian Refugee Determination Division (the initial decision-making part of the CIRB)
CRLP	Centre for Reproductive Law and Policy
DAS	Detention Advisory Service
DHS	Demographic and Health Survey
DSI	Dublin Screening Interview
ECHR	European Convention on Human Rights
ECRE	European Council on Refugees and Exiles
ELE/R	Exceptional Leave to Enter/Remain
EXCOM	Executive Committee of UNHCR
FGM	Female Genital Mutilation
HOPO	Home Office Presenting Officer
IAA	Immigration Appellate Authority
IAS	Immigration Advisory Service
IAT	Immigration Appeals Tribunal
ICCPR	International Covenant on Civil and Political Rights
ICD	Integrated Casework Directorate
ICESCR	International Covenant on Economic, Social and Cultural Rights
IFA	Internal Flight Alternative
IGLHRC	International Gay and Lesbian Human Rights Commission
ILPA	Immigration Law Practitioners' Association

Imm AR	Immigration Appeal Reports ('Green Books')
IND	Immigration and Nationality Directorate (UK)
INS	Immigration and Naturalization Service (US)
IO	Immigration Officer
IPPF	International Planned Parenthood Federation
JCWI	Joint Council for the Welfare of Immigrants
LTTE	Liberation Tamil Tigers of Eylam
MRG	Minority Rights Group
NGO	non-governmental organisation
QBD	Queen's Bench Division
Refugee Convention	1951 Convention and 1967 Protocol relating to the Status of Refugees
RFR	Reasons for Rufusal
RIS	Resource and Information Service
RLC	Refugee Legal Centre
RLG	Refugee Legal Group
RRT	Refugee Review Tribunal (Australia)
RWLG	Refugee Women's Legal Group
SBS	Southall Black Sisters
SCQ	Self-Completion Questionnaire
SEF	Statement of Evidence Form
SP	Short (now Standard) Procedures
SSHD	Secretary of State for the Home Department
TA	Temporary Admission
UDHR	Universal Declaration of Human Rights
UNHCR	United Nations High Commission(er) for Refugees
USC	United Somali Congress
Vienna Convention	Vienna Convention on the Law of Treaties
WAF	Women Against Fundamentalism
WAR	Women Against Rape
WHO	World Health Organisation
WOAT	World Organisation Against Torture

GLOSSARY

adjudicator	arbiter at first level of appeal structure
Appellate Authority	the name given to the Court structures that are specifically set up to deal with immigration appeals
asylum seeker	a person who has applied for asylum
asylum appellant	a person whose asylum claim has been refused but has an appeal pending
bail	release from detention by order of the appellate authorities following a hearing
chador	a large sheet wrapped around the body and held together by one hand; if the woman is a very strict Muslim it will be held under the eyes, otherwise under the chin. Literally means a tent
deportation order	an order signed by the Secretary of State that a person be deported
exceptional leave to enter/remain	given to people who have sought asylum in the UK, who have not been granted refugee status but who have been allowed to remain outside the normal provisions of the Immigration Rules
hejab*	Islamic modest dress for women (also referred to as *hijab*). It literally means a partition or curtain, and describes a type of women's clothing that protects her body from the eyes of men who are forbidden to her. The exact form of *hejab* varies, but it is regarded in its current usage to include a headscarf, a loose and long dress that is high at the neck and has long sleeves and a pair of trousers under it to cover the legs. *Chador* (see above) is a more strict form of *hejab*
Judicial Review	Divisional Court proceedings to challenge an administrative decision by an authority. In immigration cases it is used to challenge a Home Office decision that a person is an illegal entrant or to challenge the final decision in an asylum case
mullahs	Islamic clerics
mut'a	the Arabic term for *singheh* which is used as both name and verb for temporary marriage. It is a practice that is confined to the Shii branch of Islam, in which every man is entitled to have as many *singheh* wives as he wishes
port	point of arrival in the country
Quran*	Islamic holy book (also referred to as the *Koran*)

---

*   For the sake of consistency, *hejab* and *Quran* are used throughout this book.

sharia   Islamic canon law

zina   adultery or sexual intercourse between men and women
                who are not married to each other. *Zina-bil-habr* refers
                to rape. In the Islamic Republic of Iran *zina* is a crime
                punishable by flogging or stoning to death

Chapter 1

REFUGEE WOMEN AND THE ASYLUM DETERMINATION PROCESS

1.1 INTRODUCTION

There has typically been no gender attached to the term 'refugee' and limited attention has been focused on the protection needs of women as asylum seekers. This is reflected in the fact that statistics regarding the proportion of asylum seekers who are female are often inaccurate, misleading[1] or unavailable. Until recently, gender-differentiated statistics were available for those claiming asylum in the UK but not for the outcome of the decision-making process. The absence of such information reflects in part an implicit assumption by some of those involved in the refugee determination process that gender does not make a difference to the experience of being a refugee. There is increasing evidence, however, that refugee women may be unable to benefit equitably from protection and assistance efforts. Although some countries have begun to recognise the specific needs of refugee women and have taken appropriate measures to ensure their access to protection and material assistance, much more still needs to be done in the UK to respond to the ways in which gender shapes the experience of seeking asylum. These concerns, which are both procedural and substantive, have been the driving force behind this book.

On the basis that women may experience persecution differently from men, this book considers how those representing asylum seekers can best approach claims where gender has implications for the kind of persecution or harm suffered and the reasons for it:

> 'Even where gender is not the central issue, giving conscious consideration to gender-related aspects of a case will assist representatives in understanding the totality of the environment from which an applicant claims fear of persecution or abuse of their human rights.'[2]

There is increasing concern that the failure to gather full information about the basis of the claim at the initial stages, and to consider fully all aspects of the claim in the light of the UK's international obligations, leads to poor quality initial decision-making and increases the pressures on the appeals system. This is not only expensive and inefficient but has significant implications for the lives of individual asylum seekers.

NOTE References in the text are given using only the author's name and publication date. For full details, the Bibliography at the end of the book should be consulted.

1   An example of this is the statement that 80 per cent of the world's refugees are women and children. This statistic is misleading because around 60 per cent of the world's refugees are children, and the remaining 40 per cent is divided between adult males and adult females (ie 20 per cent of each).

2   ADIMA 1996, para 2.15.

Accordingly, this book is intended to help representatives to consider fully the extent to which the gender of the asylum applicant has implications for the procedural and substantive considerations of the claim.

Chapter 1 sets out the issues to be considered. Chapter 2 provides a detailed theoretical overview of the ways in which gender influences women's relationship to politics, nationalism and the State in the countries from which they flee, and considers the implications of the public/private dichotomy within asylum law for the ways in which these experiences are subsequently interpreted in the determination process. Chapter 3 provides a gendered framework for the analysis of asylum claims. This draws upon the framework developed by Hathaway (1991) and provides a systematic overview of the key elements of the refugee definition and the current state of national and international jurisprudence in relation to each of these. The remaining chapters systematically apply the gendered framework which is developed in Chapter 3 to a range of issues which arise in the asylum claims of women. These include: women's political participation and resistance; gendered social mores and the concept of honour; violence within the family; reproductive rights including forced sterilisation and abortion; sexual orientation; and female genital mutilation (FGM). Although there is some overlap between the issues which are discussed in each chapter, the material is presented thematically in order to assist representatives in constructing their arguments. At the end of the book, further readings and sources of information and support in relation to the topic addressed are provided. The book concludes with an overview of procedural and evidential issues and the gender-specific implications of these.

The aim of this book is to ensure that all aspects of a woman's asylum claim are properly presented and considered. It should be noted, however, that it is not intended that the book is regarded as a substitute for existing sources used by representatives. Instead, it is intended to give representatives, and ultimately decision-makers, an additional level of understanding of the particular needs of women within existing policy frameworks for refugee and humanitarian applications. As such, it does not replace other relevant advice, but complements it. Whilst every effort has been made to include relevant information from a wide range of sources and to provide an overview of existing case-law on gender-related asylum claims in the UK, the situation is a constantly evolving one and representatives should ensure that they keep up to date with developments subsequent to publication.

1.2 THE EXPERIENCES OF REFUGEE WOMEN

Refugee women suffer the same deprivation and hardship which is common to all refugees and they are frequently persecuted for reasons which are similar to their male counterparts. Many are targeted because they are political activists, community organisers, members of women's movements or persist in demanding that their rights or those of their relatives or community members are respected. In many cases, however, the experiences of women differ significantly from those of men because women's political protest, activism and resistance may manifest itself in different ways. For example:

- women may hide people, pass messages or provide community services, food, clothing and medical care;
- women who do not conform to the moral or ethical standards imposed on them may suffer cruel or inhuman treatment;
- women may be targeted because they are particularly vulnerable, for example, those who are young, elderly or disabled or those with caring responsibilities;
- women may be subjected to human rights violations simply because they are the wives, mothers or daughters of people whom the authorities consider to be 'dangerous' or 'undesirable';
- women may be persecuted by members of their family and/or community.

Women, along with their dependants, are often the first victims of political, economic and social repression in significant part because of laws and social norms which dictate gender-related behaviour and treatment. In addition, the authorities in some countries exploit family relationships to intensify harm. Women may be threatened, held as substitutes for their relatives, tortured or even killed as governments attempt to exert their will over those closely connected to them. An attack on women may also represent an attack on their ethnic group; because they have a reproductive role, women may be viewed as the embodiment of a given ethnic identity's maintenance.

> 'In conflicts between different political or religious groups, sexual violence against women has been used as a means of aggression towards an entire section of the community or as a means of acquiring information about the activities and location of family members.'[1]

In many of these scenarios, gender-specific forms of harm are inflicted by the persecutor. Rape is a common method of torture inflicted on women, but sexual abuse takes many forms in addition to rape including sexual contact falling short of rape, verbal humiliation, threats of violent attack or forced acts intended to degrade. This kind of abuse constitutes a particularly humiliating assault and one which often carries traumatic social repercussions which range from shame and social stigma to reprisals by relatives. Sexually abused women may be ostracised by their communities and rejected by their families. Refugee women who have been sexually abused often blame themselves for their tragedy. Such gender-specific forms of persecution are additional to non-gender-specific abuses and can have significant implications in the refugee determination process, both procedurally and substantively. As a result, they form an important focus for this book. However, a further issue related to the protection of women has emerged in the international arena more recently, and concerns the need to recognise as Convention refugees those who suffer persecution in their own country because of their sexual status. In many parts of the world, women who do not live up to the moral or ethical standards imposed on them by their societies can suffer cruel or inhuman treatment. Refusing to marry, having sexual relations outside marriage, providing unsatisfactory dowry, or even wearing certain dress can result in persecution, and even death. Because of social and economic constraints, relatively few of these women manage to flee to other countries for protection yet,

---

1   Siemens 1988, p 22.

when they do, their experiences tend to be interpreted as discriminatory as opposed to persecutory.

There is considerable evidence that the principles of international law impinge differently on men and women. A significant, and growing, proportion of this evidence focuses on the legal problems facing asylum-seeking women who are able to reach western countries. This evidence suggests that women are refused refugee status for reasons that seem to have less to do with refugee law than with the gender of the asylum applicant. In most western countries, including the UK, about one-third of asylum seekers are female yet statistics show that in some countries women are less likely than men to be granted refugee status. As Spijkerboer (1994) suggests, the authorities in these countries might justify this by claiming that women are less deserving, or that women qualify as refugees less often than men as they are less involved in political activities. However, this kind of reaction begs a number of questions: for example, do women participate in political activities less often than men, and what precisely constitutes 'politics' in different countries and contexts?

1.3 THE INTERNATIONAL FRAMEWORK FOR PROTECTION

The international community's obligation to asylum seekers is based on the 1951 Convention and 1967 Protocol relating to the Status of Refugees ('the Refugee Convention') and the principle of *non-refoulement*. According to Article 1A of the Refugee Convention, the term 'refugee' shall apply to any person who:

> '... owing to a well-founded fear of being persecuted for reasons of race, religion, nationality, membership of a particular social group or political opinion, is outside [her] country of origin and is unable or, owing to such fear, is unwilling to avail [herself] of the protection of that country; or who, not having a nationality and being outside the country of [her] former habitual residence as a result of such events, is unable or, owing to such fear, is unwilling to return to it.'[1]

Protection is at the heart of the responsibility that the international community bears towards refugees. In order to be granted protection, individuals have to show that they have a well-founded fear of persecution on account of their race, religion, nationality, political opinion or membership of a particular social group. Acts of persecution or feared persecution must also be committed by the State or by groups or individuals which the State either cannot or will not control.[2] It is assumed that international law is objective and that international law norms directed at individuals within States are universally applicable and gender-neutral. However, Convention refugee law, as it is currently interpreted, presents considerable difficulties for women whose fears of persecution arise out of forms of protest or ill-treatment not considered 'political' or deserving of international protection. Whilst international refugee instruments make no distinction

---

1   UNHCR 1979, p 11.
2   Goodwin-Gill 1983; Hathaway 1991; Macdonald and Blake 1995.

between male and female refugees,[1] their interpretation by the State, at both the national and international level, reflects and reinforces gender biases.

Women are unable to benefit equitably from international protection available under the Refugee Convention. The reasons are two-fold.

(1) **In interpreting the Refugee Convention, women's experiences have been marginalised**. For example, whilst overt expression of a political opinion through conventional means, such as involvement in a political party, may be considered as a basis for political asylum, less conventional forms of political resistance, such as refusal to abide by discriminatory laws or to follow prescribed rules of conduct, are often wrongly categorised as personal conduct. Women are also more likely to be involved in so-called 'low-level' political activities or in providing supporting roles, so that what appears to be a non-political activity by women may, on more careful inspection, turn out to be a form of political protest or activism. Many refugee women face similar problems with regard to establishing the failure of the State to provide protection when the harm to which they are subjected takes place within the home or community.

(2) **Procedural and evidential barriers** often inhibit women's access to the determination process and may serve to limit the quality of the information which is gathered about the claim and, in turn, the quality of the decision-making process.

In many respects, the failure to incorporate the gender-related claims of refugee women seeking asylum is a product of the general failure of refugee and asylum law to recognise social and economic rights and its emphasis instead on individual targeting and specific deprivation of civil and political rights. This is despite the fact that social and economic rights may be violated for political reasons. However, it is also related to a larger criticism of human rights law and discourse: that it privileges male-dominated 'public' activities over the activities of women, which take place largely in the 'private' sphere. As a result, the key criteria for being a refugee are drawn primarily from the realm of public sphere activities dominated by men.[2] Although the refugee definition incorporated into the Refugee Convention is gender-neutral: 'the law has developed within a male paradigm which reflects the factual circumstances of male applicants, but which does not respond to the particular protection needs of women'.[3] Bhabha (1993) and Goldberg and Kelly (1993) similarly suggest that refugee law has evolved through an examination of male asylum applicants and their activities: men have been considered the agents of political action and therefore the legitimate beneficiaries of protection for resulting persecution. Greatbach summarises the criticism: 'by portraying as universal that which is in fact a male paradigm, it is argued, women refugees face rejection of their claims because their experiences of persecution go unrecognised'.[4] In the context of a largely male-oriented body

---

1   Johnsson 1989 notes, however, that to the extent that gender is revealed in these legal texts, the masculine language used suggests that the male refugee was in the mind of the drafters.
2   Indra 1987.
3   Kelly 1993, p 674.
4   Greatbach 1989, p 518.

of law, women's cases are often formulated in ways which reflect the advocate's understanding of the law rather than the reality of the applicant's experiences.

Much of this literature also points to the fact that the Refugee Convention does not specifically refer to gender as one of the grounds upon which an individual can be recognised as a refugee and given protection.[1] It is the lack of an appropriate ground to explain *why* women are persecuted which has largely been seen as the basis of women's marginalisation. This has led some to call for the refugee definition to be rewritten and for 'gender' to be added to the Refugee Convention grounds alongside race, nationality, religion, social group and actual (or imputed) political opinion, an approach which is potentially dangerous given current efforts by States to limit their obligations under the existing definition. It has also led to calls for women to be recognised as 'members of a particular social group' within the meaning of the Refugee Convention and offered protection on this basis. As is shown in this book, extent to which this is an appropriate ground is heavily dependent upon the particular circumstances of the individual case and the political, social and economic context from which the applicant fled.

Efforts to ensure adequate protection for women asylum-seekers may be undermined where practitioners and decision-makers do not properly comprehend the concept of gender or understand what is meant by gender-related persecution. Generalisations about the experiences of women may not serve the best interests of women themselves. This issue is discussed in detail throughout the book with reference to the experiences of women and international and national case-law developments.

1.4 THE CONCEPTS OF 'GENDER' AND 'GENDER-RELATED PERSECUTION'

The existing literature on the experiences of refugee and asylum-seeking women has undoubtedly been important in highlighting women's marginalisation within current interpretations of international refugee law. However, it is also problematic because of its tendency to be grounded in an analysis of 'sex' as the key factor accounting for the differential experiences of refugee and asylum seeking women rather than the construction of gender identity in specific geographical, historical, political and socio-cultural contexts. There has been a tendency for the term 'gender' to be used synonymously with the term 'sex'. However, 'gender' is not the same as biological 'sex' and cannot be equated solely with women because it is a key *relational* dimension of human activity and thought. The term 'gender' as used in this book refers to the social construction of power relations between women and men, and the implications of these relations for women's (and men's) identity, status, roles and responsibilities (in other words, the social organisation of sexual difference). Gender is not static or innate but acquires socially and culturally constructed meaning because it is a primary way of

---

1   It should be noted, however, that in some countries, for example the Republic of Ireland, 'gender' has been recognised as an additional ground for providing protection under the Refugee Convention.

signifying relations of power. Gender relations and gender differences are therefore historically, geographically and culturally specific, so that what it is to be a 'woman' or 'man' varies through space and over time. Any analysis of the way in which gender (as opposed to biological sex) shapes the experiences of asylum-seeking women must therefore *contextualise* those experiences.

Box 1.1   Definitions

Gender – refers to the social construction of power relations between women and men, and the implications of these relations for women's (and men's) identity, status and roles. It is not the same as 'sex' which is biologically defined.

Gender-related persecution – refers to the experiences of women who are persecuted *because* they are women, ie because of their identity and status as women.

Gender-specific persecution – refers to forms of serious harm which are specific to women.

The focus on *women* as opposed to gender in forced migration research and practice replicates and reinforces the marginalisation of women's experiences within the dominant discourse. While it is a significant conceptual advance over not considering gender at all, gender is not usefully equated simply with women because it can lead to a number of unnecessary conceptual limitations and political dead ends. Perhaps most significantly, in the context of the analysis presented in this book, it can lead to a tendency to generalise about the experiences of women as asylum seekers. This tendency is problematic for several reasons.

First, it leads to confusion about what is meant by the term 'gender-related persecution'. In order to comprehend, and appropriately respond to, the role of gender in shaping women's experiences of persecution, it is important that interviewers and decision-makers understand clearly the relationship between gender and the elements of the refugee definition. As Macklin (1995) suggests, the concept of women being persecuted as women is not the same as women being persecuted *because* they are women. The concept of women being persecuted *as* women addresses forms of persecution that are gender-specific including, for example, sexual violence, female genital mutilation, forced abortion and sterilisation and the denial of access to contraception. Understanding the ways in which women are violated as women is critical to naming as persecution those forms of harm which only or mostly affect women. To say that a woman fears persecution *because* she is a woman addresses the causal relationship between gender (as socially constructed) and persecution. For example, sexual activity outside a socially condoned relationship may result in persecution. Gender-specific persecution is therefore a term used to explain 'serious harm' within the meaning of persecution. Gender-related persecution is used to explain the basis of the asylum claim (ie the grounds of the persecution). A woman may be persecuted as a woman (eg raped) for reasons unrelated to gender (eg activity in a political party), not persecuted as a woman but still because of gender (eg flogged for refusing to wear a veil), and persecuted as and because she is a woman (eg female genital mutilation). Gender-specific violations do not necessarily constitute persecution because of gender. For example, if a man's genitals are subjected to electric shocks, he is certainly being tortured in a gender-specific way, but it does not follow that he is being persecuted because of his gender.

A second problem, but one which is closely related to the first, concerns the need to recognise that whilst there are often significant differences between the experiences of women and men, there are also *critical differences between women* within and between particular countries and contexts. Gender is a social relation that enters into, and partly constitutes, all other social relations and identities. Women's experiences of persecution, and of the process of asylum determination, will also be shaped by differences of race, class, sexuality, age, marital status, sexual history and so on. The tendency of academics, practitioners and policy-makers to treat 'women' as a homogeneous category, in order to emphasise the ways in which the experiences of women generally have been marginalised within the dominant discourse, means that critical differences between women have often been ignored. This approach inhibits any examination of the significance of heterogeneity for the persecution suffered or feared.

The problem with such an approach, therefore, is that it counter-poses the 'male experience' of persecution with a 'female model'. This model tends to generalise about women's experiences of 'gender-related persecution' and to over-emphasise sexual violence at the expense of other forms of resistance and repression that are experienced by women in their countries of origin. However, differences between women have significant implications for their experiences of both persecution and the process of asylum determination. For example, because nationalist agendas are more open to incorporating some groups of women than others, or view certain groups of women as particularly threatening to the nationalist agenda itself, the apparatus and institutions of the State may establish differential policies towards them. One unintended but very serious effect of merely adding 'women' to existing analyses without an understanding of the differences between women, is that women appear in the story only as victims. Refugee women are presented as uniformly poor, powerless and vulnerable, while western women are the reference point for modern, educated, sexually liberated womanhood.[1] This in turn leads to the depoliticisation and decontextualisation of women's experiences of persecution and their conceptualisation as passive victims of, for example, 'male oppression' or 'oppressive cultures, religions or traditions'. However, gender identity itself is (and can be) a mobilising category for political action. Women are neither a homogenous group nor are they passive victims of patriarchal domination, rather they are fully fledged social actors, bearing the full set of contradictions implied by their class, racial and ethnic locations as well as their gender. This was recognised in *Shah and Islam* in the House of Lords:

---

1   Parpart 1993.

'Generalisations about the position of women in particular countries are out of place in regard to issues of refugee status. Everything depends on the evidence and findings of fact on the particular case.'[1]

This contrast between the realities of women's experiences of persecution and the dominant discourse is perhaps nowhere more evident than in the prevalence of stereotypes which currently prevail about Islamic societies. As Parpart (1993) suggests, Arab women are often presented as passive pawns, trapped in a world of hopelessly outdated and retrogressive religious traditions. Yet, in countries such as Iran, where the politicisation of gendered identities has been facilitated by an ideological understanding of Islam which has demolished the *de facto* divide between public and private, women have actually been at the centre stage of politics. Since the Revolution, whatever concerns women – from their private to their most public activities, from what they should wear and what they should study to whether and where they should work – are issues that have been openly debated and fought over by different factions, always in highly charged and emotional language. Not only in Iran but also in countries such as Afghanistan and the Sudan, the articulation of prevalent ideologies with policies have proved particularly detrimental to women. Whilst the material presented in this book suggests that many women experience severe hardship and oppression as a consequence of their gender identity as women, women's agency and resistance should not be underestimated.

This book therefore examines the ways in which gender shapes women's experiences, whilst avoiding generalisations about their experiences as 'women' which negate critical aspects of resistance and oppression. The framework for asylum determination needs to be transformed to accommodate an inclusion of women not as a special case deviating from the norm, but as one of many different groups in an open and heterogeneous universe. The theoretical focus is not on women per se but in the ways in which socially and culturally constructed ideas around 'gender' have conditioned the normative structures of international refugee law. This approach to the politics of protection suggests that the 'problem' is not so much the actual invisibility of women but rather how their experiences have been 'represented and analytically characterised'.[2] The development of this approach is important to ensure that the asylum claims made by women are properly and consistently considered by decision-makers and that the legal and theoretical arguments are coherent and able to stand the test of time. Looking at gender as opposed to sex enables an approach which can accommodate specificity, diversity and heterogeneity. It also ensures that the asylum claims of women are not routinely dismissed as culturally relative and therefore outside the mechanisms for protection available under the Refugee Convention.

---

1   *Islam v SSHD; R v IAT ex parte Shah* [1999] INLR 144, Imm AR 283 (HL).
2   See also Indra 1989 and Indra (ed) 1999.

1.5 RECONCILING UNIVERSAL HUMAN RIGHTS AND CULTURAL RELATIVISM

One of the key themes which runs through both academic analysis and case-law relating to the experiences of women as asylum seekers concerns the relationship between women's human rights and the issue of cultural relativism. Representatives should be aware that a differential and profoundly gendered understanding of human rights is often applied to women's asylum claims. This understanding raises critical questions about the basic concept of 'human rights' itself and about how the enforcement of universal human rights standards can be reconciled, in a non-ethnocentric way, with an understanding of, and respect for, cultural difference.[1]

The debate about cultural relativism and women's human rights has polarised between two extremes, both of which are problematic. On the one hand there are those who argue that women's human rights are systematically violated by oppressive 'cultures' and 'traditions'. Well-meaning attempts to highlight the experiences of women in the so-called 'less-developed' areas of the world have often tended to reproduce Western hegemony. As has been suggested by both Spijkerboer (1994) and Macklin (1995), this feeds into a protection discourse which is already highly imbued with (and in many senses based upon) notions of political, economic, social and cultural superiority. Spijkerboer notes that 'in the great majority of writings on the relevance to refugee law of non-compliance by women with social mores, one gets the impression that social mores are a phenomenon particular to third world countries, and, more specifically, to Muslim countries'.[2] He suggests that most authors on social mores and refugee law tend to construct a 'third world' or even an 'Orient' in which gender oppression is subtly explained as symptomatic of an essential, non-western barbarism. A particularly clear example of this is the article by Cipriani (1993) who describes the 'horrific practices' and 'institutionalised misogyny' which exists in Pakistan and Iran (Islamic law), India (Hinduism), Africa ('tribal custom') and Brazil, Argentina and Peru ('machismo policies and practices'). Macklin is concerned at what she regards as 'a distressing degree of cultural hyperopia regarding local conditions for women', and notes with regard to Cipriani's 'survey of world misogyny' that 'in each case, the source of the persecution is located in a religion other than Christianity, customs of non-white societies, or "cultural norms" about women that are portrayed as locally specific'.[3] These associations of 'third world women' with 'culture' and 'tradition' have implications for both asylum-seeking women and the discourse of protection more generally. Spijkerboer (1994), for example, suggests that this way of framing an argument on refugee women can actually serve to reproduce

---

1   There is currently considerable debate about whether human rights can be universal or are culturally relative. However, it is important that representatives are aware that this debate is not only taking place in the countries of the so-called 'developed' world. In many other countries, academics and practitioners alike have campaigned extensively to ensure that standards of human rights are not set at a lower standard in order to comply with past or present culturally specific practice.

2   Spijkerboer 1994, p 33.

3   Macklin 1995, p 287.

the dehumanising structures from which some of them have suffered. Such approaches infer that a woman comes from an inferior marginal culture to a superior core culture: 'it brands her as an alien of her own culture because she rejects a particular view of it, in a way that resembles what she may have experienced from the authorities in her own culture ... Thus, the banishment of women who refuse to conform to norms they find oppressive may be re-enacted'.[1] Such discourses may, ironically, actually serve to further undermine women's access to protection from persecution because they further depoliticise their experiences and marginalise them from the normatively masculine interpretation of international refugee law.

There are also fundamental problems with approaches which argue that human rights are not universal but should be viewed in relation to the cultures to which they are applied. Representatives should be aware that this association between human rights and culture is specific to women, and that it has been used by decision-makers to argue *against* the protection of women. As Bhabha (1996) suggests, this association gives fertile soil for claims and counterclaims about universalism, cultural relativism and cultural imperialism. Human rights arguments are supposed to 'trump' sovereign States' justifications for oppressive or restrictive behaviour and the international refugee system is supposed to be a mechanism for translating this theory into practice. However, in the asylum context, where restrictionist immigration pressures and partisan foreign agendas have a clear bearing on the decision-making process, the content of protected rights has often been relativised in line with practices prevailing in different States. This process is reflected in the use of 'culture' to exclude women from protection under the Refugee Convention:

> 'decisions upholding an asylum applicant's claim of persecution may contain culturally arrogant, even racist descriptions of the state of origin's policies. Conversely judgements that dismiss the asylum application may adopt the language of cultural sensititivity or respect for state sovreignty as a device for limiting refugee admission numbers.'[2]

This process can be seen in several UK cases. For example, in *Islam* the IAT commented that 'we do not think that the purpose of the Convention is to award refugee status because of a disapproval of social mores or conventions in non-western societies'.[3] The use of this approach is particularly evident in cases involving female genital mutilation, and is discussed in more detail in Chapter 9.

Representatives should be aware of the theoretical difficulties inherent in reconciling the concepts of universal human rights and cultural relativism. However, it is both necessary and possible to find a way of reconciling, in a non-ethnocentric way, the enforcement of universal human rights standards with an understanding of, and respect for, cultural difference. 'Culture' and 'tradition' cannot be used to defend human rights abuses because cultural values and cultural practices are as legitimately subject to criticism from a human rights

---

1   Spijkerboer 1994, p 33.
2   Bhabha 1996, p 11.
3   *Islam and Others v SSHD* (unreported) 2 October 1996 (13956) (IAT). This case was subsequently re-examined in the House of Lords in *Islam v SSHD; R v IAT ex parte Shah* [1999] INLR 144, Imm AR 283 (HL).

perspective as any other structural aspect of society. In this context, it is important to consider what is meant by 'culture' when it is used to defend violations of women's human rights. The concept of culture is a dynamic notion, not a static one, and may be appropriated by those with power to justify an otherwise untenable position. The approach taken in this book tries to bridge the gap between the view that human rights are non-existent, or completely relative to different cultures, and the view that they are universal, simply derived from a basic human nature we all share. Respect for international human rights law does not require that every culture use an identical approach, but it does require that human rights be defined and protected in a manner consonant with international principles. In this sense it is possible to reconcile the two. As James suggests:

> 'To argue that human rights are universal is not equivalent to saying that their understanding or interpretation is self-evident or immutable, or to deny the various cultural contexts in which human rights must be embedded. Rejecting radical cultural relativism does not preclude flexibility in the conceptualisation, interpretation and application of human rights within and between different cultures. Human rights are universal but not absolute (in the sense of pure, unalloyed, completely uniform) in their application to various cultures. In this way, the relativist "truth" about enculturation can be accommodated within [a] human rights framework.'[1]

1.6 NATIONAL AND INTERNATIONAL INITIATIVES

Following years of neglect of the needs of refugee and asylum-seeking women, a new awareness and willingness to take gender into account in policy development and implementation has emerged and there have been many encouraging recent developments legitimising the factual basis for women's asylum claims. Human rights groups in particular have increasingly focused their attention on gender-specific human rights abuses and human rights abuses inflicted on women because of their gender. Meanwhile, the United Nations High Commission for Refugees (UNHCR) has also begun to turn its attention to gender-related persecution, and Canada, the US and, most recently, Australia have extended their interpretation of the Refugee Convention to women making claims on this basis. In the UK, the Refugee Women's Legal Group has produced its own *Gender Guidelines for the Determination of Asylum Claims in the UK* which were launched in the House of Commons in 1998.[2] The approaches and recommendations made in the existing guidelines on refugee women and protection have been substantially incorporated into this analysis. It is important that representatives and others within the asylum determination process keep pace with, and where possible utilise, these developments.

1.6.1 UNHCR

The Executive Committee (EXCOM) of the UNHCR has issued a number of notes and conclusions relating specifically to refugee women.[3] The UNHCR has also issued several publications of interest to those representing refugee women

---

1   James 1994, p 4.
2   See Appendix 3.
3   See Appendix 1.

as asylum seekers. These include *Guidelines on the Protection of Refugee Women* (1991) and *Sexual Violence Against Refugees; Guidelines on Prevention and Response* (1995a). Both sets of guidelines address gender-related persecution and recommend procedures to make the asylum determination process more accessible to women. The information they contain about the gendered experiences of women asylum applicants is of considerable use to representatives and reference is made to these publications throughout this book. Although the UNHCR materials do not have the force of law or form part of the Refugee Convention and therefore cannot override express terms of the Immigration Acts or Rules, they can provide guidance and are aids to interpretation of the Refugee Convention and may be relevant to the exercise of a broad discretion.[1]

1.6.2 Canada

On 9 March 1993, the Canadian Immigration and Refugee Board[2] issued its ground-breaking *Guidelines on Women Refugee Claimants Fearing Gender-Related Persecution* which were developed after extensive consultation with interested governmental and non-governmental groups and individuals. The guidelines were issued because of a strong conviction among decision-makers themselves that a fair and effective refugee determination system should be gender inclusive, and that guidelines are the best method of achieving that goal.[3] The guidelines attracted considerable interest internationally because they were the first national guidelines to formally recognise that women fleeing persecution because of their gender could be recognised as Convention refugees. Eight years after their release, the Canadian guidelines remain a model for gender-sensitive asylum adjudication and the CIRB released an updated version in November 1996, necessitated by the volume of jurisprudence that had emerged in the field of gender-related refugee claims since the original guidelines were issued.[4] One of the most important changes reflected in the *Update* resulted from the 1993 Supreme Court decision in *Ward*[5] to which reference is made in this book. The *Update* also provides a framework for analysis which is useful for representatives. This book draws heavily on the information provided by the CIRB, not least because the Immigration Appeal Tribunal (IAT) has given clear guidance that such guidelines should be considered by decision-makers where they are relevant to the appellant's claim:

> 'Whilst not themselves binding they are a tool to ensure that vital issues are objectively canvassed in weighing refugee claims where gender is a factor ... we would commend the use of the Canadian Guidelines to adjudicators.'[6]

---

1 Macdonald and Blake 1995, p 337.
2 Unlike the Home Office, the Canadian Immigration and Refugee Board (CIRB) is an independent administrative tribunal performing quasi-judicial functions. The CIRB is made up of three divisions, the most important of which for the purposes of this book is the Convention Refugee Determination Division (also referred to as the CRDD or Refugee Division). Because the CRDD provides lengthy quasi-judicial determinations in all cases, its decisions are often cited in this book.
3 Comments made by Nurjehan Mawani, Chairperson of the CIRB at a Seminar on Women and Asylum, Copenhagen, Denmark, 3 March 1997.
4 See Appendix 2.
5 *Canada (Attorney General) v Ward* [1993] 2 SCR 689.
6 *Gimhedin v SSHD* (unreported) 1 October 1996 (14019) (IAT).

1.6.3 United States

In June 1995 the Immigration and Nationality Service (INS) issued its *Considerations for Asylum Officers Adjudicating Asylum Claims From Women* which were designed to assist asylum officers in interviewing women refugees and in making asylum decisions in light of well-established international human rights and refugee law principles. In so doing, the US became the second country to adopt formal guidelines recognising that the persecution of women based on their gender could be the grounds for political asylum. The guidelines give specific instructions to decision-makers that recognise rape and other forms of sexual violence as persecution and also recognise that women who are beaten, tortured, or subject to other such treatment for refusing to renounce their beliefs about the equal rights of women may be considered for asylum protection. The INS guidelines also emphasise the importance of creating a 'customer-friendly' asylum interview environment that allows women claimants to discuss freely the elements and details of their claims.

1.6.4 Australia

Australia's refugee and humanitarian intake has two components: an 'off-shore' or overseas programme and an 'on-shore' programme. There is a special category in the off-shore programme that offers protection to 'women-at-risk' in addition to standard Refugee Convention obligations. Responding to concerns about gender bias in both the definition of a refugee and in procedures for processing applications, the Australian Department of Immigration and Multi-Cultural Affairs (ADIMA) issued *Guidelines on Gender Issues for Decision-makers* in July 1996 which are perhaps the most comprehensive of all those which so far exist, and are referred to throughout this book.[1]

1.6.5 Europe

In 1984, the European Parliament adopted a resolution calling upon States to consider women who have been the victims of persecution as belonging to a 'particular social group' within the definition of the Refugee Convention and therefore qualifying for refugee status. Since that time, however, there appears to have been very little progress on this issue although there have been calls for gender guidelines to be adopted. A European Parliament Resolution of 14 November 1996 urged all Member States to adopt guidelines on women asylum seekers as agreed by the UNHCR Executive Committee, and emphasised that it is 'crucial that sexual violence be recognised as a form of torture, particularly given the use of rape as a weapon of war and the cultural traditions of certain countries which involve gender persecution'. In December 1997, ECRE published its *Position Paper on Asylum Seeking and Refugee Women* which called for European States to develop best practice guidelines on the determination of asylum claims from women.[2]

---

1   See Appendix 4.
2   Available on-line at http://www.ecre.org

Currently, the process of asylum determination continues to vary significantly between EU States. This was reflected in the written responses of governments to the questionnaire issued by the UNHCR concerning gender-based persecution in general and the social group issue in particular, which provided the basis for discussion at the Symposium on Gender-Based Persecution held in Geneva in February 1996. In addition, moves towards harmonisation suggest that standards for protection are being reduced to the lowest common denominator.[1] Representatives should ensure that they are up to date with these developments and with the ways in which moves towards temporary and subsidiary forms of protection and efforts to further narrow the interpretation of the Refugee Convention, particularly with regard to persecution by non-State agents and the construction of particular social groups, may disproportionately affect women who seek asylum. With the adoption of minimum standards and the incorporation of asylum into binding agreements as a result of the Amsterdam Treaty, such developments will gain in significance.

One important aspect of the European system is the fact that it has its own European Convention on Human Rights (ECHR) with a European Court of Human Rights which has the aim of ensuring compliance.[2] The right of individual petition is important. Although Article 3 of the ECHR is most often referred to, asylum seekers may also invoke a number of other Articles in support of their claim for protection from persecution, and representatives should ensure at an early stage that they are fully aware of the additional protection that may be available to some refugee women through the ECHR.[3]

1.6.6   United Kingdom

In contrast with other refugee-receiving countries, the Home Office has not accepted that gender guidelines can assist both the quality and consistency of the decision-making process. This is reflected in the UK government's response to a questionnaire for governments participating in a symposium on gender-related persecution held by UNHCR in 1996:

> 'Each set of circumstances, individual and collective, is addressed on its merits ... casework experiences suggests that in practice few, if any, asylum claims made by women in the UK turn solely on the question of gender-based persecution ... we have not yet identified a need to issue *separate* guidance on dealing with female asylum seekers in the UK.'[4]

In this context, *Gender Guidelines for the Determination of Asylum Claims in the UK* were produced by the Refugee Women's Legal Group (RWLG) and launched in the House of Commons in 1998.[5] The guidelines drew upon the experience and knowledge of solicitors, barristers, practitioners, academics, non-governmental

---

1   UNHCR 1995b; Guild 1996.
2   See Appendix 5.
3   Contact the AIRE Centre for further information on how representatives can utilise the protection mechanisms available through the ECHR (Appendix 5).
4   UK response to the questionnaire issued by UNHCR for its Symposium on Gender-Based Persecution which was held in Geneva (22 and 23 February 1996). See *International Journal of Refugee Law* (Special Issue) Autumn 1997, 71.
5   See Appendix 3.

organisations and refugee women themselves and have been widely endorsed, including by the UNHCR. They were recently cited by the House of Lords in the case of *Shah and Islam*,[1] and the Immigration Appellate Authorities (IAA) launched their own guidelines in November 2000 to ensure that the experiences of women as asylum seekers are fully and properly taken into account during the decision-making process.[2] In addition, the incorporation of the ECHR into domestic jurisdiction through the Human Rights Act 1998 in October 2000 will have significant implications for the determination of asylum claims in the UK.[3]

---

1   *Islam v SSHD; R v IAT ex parte Shah* [1999] INLR 144, Imm AR 283 (HL).
2   See Appendix 6.
3   See Appendix 5. Following entry into force of the Human Rights Act 1998, decision-makers will be obliged to take the ECHR into account. For further information see Sarmer 1999.

Chapter 2

A THEORETICAL OVERVIEW

2.1 FEMINIST CRITIQUES OF INTERNATIONAL REFUGEE LAW

The aim of this chapter is to expose some of the underlying gendered assumptions upon which international refugee law is based and to consider some of the implications of such assumptions for the interpretation of women's experiences of persecution. Feminists have referred to this approach as asking 'the woman question' which involves examining how the law fails to take into account the experiences and values which seem more typical of women than men, for whatever reason, or how existing legal standards and concepts might disadvantage women. In recent years, feminist jurisprudence has emerged as a systematic critique of the practice and profession of law, with its central theme that law is an inherently gendered system which serves to reinforce male domination.[1] Feminist jurisprudence asks questions about where the law fits with women's experiences, what its role is in perpetuating gendered systems and how law might be a vehicle for change. It exposes the gender bias of apparently neutral systems to reveal underlying assumptions and value judgements made by, and in the interests of, men.

Central to the gendered critique of international law, including refugee law, has been an analysis of the public/private dichotomy. The terms 'public' and 'private' are used to refer both to the distinction between State and society, and to the distinction between non-domestic and domestic life. In both dichotomies, the State is conceived of as public, and the family, domestic and intimate life are conceived of as private.[2] This distinction is ideological in the sense that it presents society from a male perspective and enables theorists and practitioners alike to ignore the political nature of the family, the relevance of justice in personal life and, as a consequence, a major part of the inequalities of gender. Breaking down the dichotomy between the public and the private has important implications for research on the experiences of women seeking protection in the UK, because it ensures that the analysis is not limited to a narrow range of 'women's issues' or to areas where women are present. Women's activities within the geographically and conceptually 'private' sphere of the home can be recovered from their usual invisibility. Most significantly, it questions the ways in which boundaries work to define some people (and practices) as being 'in bounds' while others are located 'out of bounds'.

The ways in which the asylum claims of women are represented and analysed reflects the way dominant concepts of gender have become embedded and accepted as the norm in the interpretation and implementation of refugee law.

---

1   See, eg, Roach Anleu 1992, MacKinnon 1993, Binion 1995.
2   Okin 1998.

Charlesworth et al (1991) maintain that it is this which enables issues of particular concern to women to be either ignored or undermined, and which has depoliticised and legitimised gender-specific and gender-related persecution. In particular, modern international law, including asylum law, rests upon and reproduces various dichotomies between the public and private spheres and between political and apolitical concerns and forms of resistance. A distinction is made, for example, between matters of international 'public' concern and matters 'private' to States which are considered within their domestic jurisdiction, and in which the international community has no recognised legal interest. Feminist critiques of these dichotomies suggest that at a deeper level this public/private dichotomy is highly gendered. The two spheres are accorded asymmetrical value with greater significance being attached to the public, male world than to the private, female one. They reveal not only the centrality of this masculinist approach in excluding women from the public realm, but also the politics of defining public and private. The power to define and create classifications is neither a disinterested nor an un-gendered one. Categories such as those inherent in the Refugee Convention are social constructs which need to be examined in order to understand the larger political contexts of their creation.

2.2 THE PUBLIC/PRIVATE DICHOTOMY

The process of challenging knowledge and understanding of the experiences of women has increasingly focused on the gendered construction of dichotomies and the binary categories (eg male/female, public/private, political/apolitical) which arise from them. The use of these binary categories is so widespread, and their common sense meaning so embedded in our lives, that we often take them for granted. Binary categories appear to offer the possibility of describing and analysing the world in a way which appeals to ideas of stability, completeness and authority. However, these dichotomies and the binary oppositions which stem from them have very significant implications for the ways in which we think about, and organise our analysis of, the concepts of time and space:

> 'Binary categories often suggest the existence of discrete spaces, that is spaces associated with different types of activities. In this respect, then, they could be said to appeal to the idea of absolute space, and they often depend on the drawing of sharp lines between the two halves within the binary category. These lines are like boundaries, or fences; they are put up between the two sides which comprise the binary category. So, for example, the public/private distinction works by establishing a boundary between the public and private sphere, and by drawing a line between public and private space.'[1]

Binary categories are frequently presented as if they are fixed and immutable. However, these categories, and the boundaries which divide them, are actually political and ideological constructions which are both gendered and have gendered consequences. The boundary between the public and the private is not, and never has been, anything like as distinct as it is often presented, rather there is a continuum between the two. Boundaries are contested and undecided. They

---

1   Laurie et al 1997, p 112.

are not stable. They fluctuate and are subject to challenge. They move and change across space and time. They are geographically and historically situated.[1] Questions therefore need to be asked about what both the content of various categories and the boundaries which are drawn between them tell us about the construction of knowledge and the relations of power that it reflects.

Distinctions which are drawn between the public and the private are responsible, in significant part, for the current mismatch between women's experiences of persecution and their interpretation in asylum policy and practice. Although international law is gender-neutral in theory, in practice it interacts with gender-based domestic laws and social structures which relegate women and men to separate spheres of existence. In the context of international asylum law, 'the consequences for women of this dichotomous perspective are fundamental and profound'.[2]

Although the basis of the public/private distinction has been thoroughly attacked and exposed as a culturally constructed ideology, it continues to have a strong grip on legal thinking. As Indra suggests, 'this dichotomy of private and public spheres remains deeply grounded in discourse about refugees and leads to many ironies concerning notions of rights, privacy and culture'.[3] For example, it can lead to the tendency to idealise family life through reference to an idealised, historical traditional culture, even when it encodes profound gender and other disparities. An interesting example of such a tendency can be found in the paper by Spijkerboer (1994), who points out that the issue of 'derivative persecution' related to family membership poses less of a problem for women in refugee law than that of direct persecution where the applicant has to demonstrate not only that she has suffered persecution but that there is a persecution ground. This conclusion may appear to be fundamentally at odds with the simplistic notion of a public/private dichotomy in the normative structures of international refugee law – the family is, after all, a sphere which in most analysis is regarded as 'private'. The analysis here, however, suggests that the issue of the 'family' only becomes relevant because it enables women who are persecuted because of the activities of their husbands to be perceived of as being persecuted in their capacity as defenceless women. Therefore, because women in such a situation somehow elicit the chivalrous impulse to save them, 'it should not be surprising that refugee law practice and doctrine come to their rescue'.[4] Thus, in this example, women are perceived to be victims not of something 'natural' (as in the case of sexual violence) but of something fundamentally 'unnatural' – the wish to harm the family which, as stated in the Universal Declaration on Human Rights, represents the 'natural and fundamental group unit of society'. These provisions ignore the fact that, to many women, the family may be a unit for abuse and violence. Hence, the protection of the family also preserves the power structure within the family, which can lead to subjugation and dominance by men over women and children.[5]

---

1   Okin 1998, Philips 1998, Indra (ed) 1999.
2   Binion 1995, p 519.
3   Indra 1993, p 14.
4   Spijkerboer 1994, p 53.
5   Charlesworth et al 1991.

Whilst the refugee definition does not intrinsically exclude women's experiences, in practice the public/private distinction is used in such a way that what women do and what is done to them is often seen as irrelevant to refugee law. It should also be acknowledged, however, that reconceptualising gender in forced migration through an analysis of the ways in which asylum-seeking women are positioned with existing discourse and practice is not without its problems. First, there is a tension in dealing with both the universal and the specific.[1] In focusing on the experiences of refugee and asylum-seeking women in the UK, this book inevitably makes generalisations about these experiences whilst simultaneously attempting to highlight difference. Despite the enormous observable variation in understandings of what the categories 'men' and 'women' mean, certain notions about gender are common to a wide range of societies: the public/private dichotomy is frequently reflected in categories or dichotomies which are commonly used to distinguish and order gender differences. However, the meaning and the associated characteristics of each side of the categories are historically, geographically, socially and culturally specific. As a result, an analysis of refugee law that uses the public/private distinction has to be on its guard.[2] This gives rise to a second, and possibly irresolvable, tension, namely that the deconstruction of both the public/private dichotomy and the categories associated with each simultaneously relies upon both the dichotomy and the categories themselves. This problem is not unique to the analysis in this book. For example, in the volume edited by Indra (1999) every author (Indra included) ultimately depends at least in part on the simplifying characterisations which they challenge. This is, in part at least, a reflection of the fact that the ideological use of the public/private dichotomy continues to structure and mould gender experiences and expectations. The terms still have a certain meaning with respect to access, agency and interest, notwithstanding the fact that the reality of women's and men's lives may not exactly correspond, either historically or in the present, to such polarised categories.[3]

In challenging the validity of the public/private dichotomy, this book does not dispute the existence of such distinctions or even their value for clarification and analysis, but argues that conceiving of the boundaries as fixed and rigid and confining inquiry and analysis within the limits of the boundaries can serve to reinforce the existing power relations, including those which are exclusionary and oppressive. Although there is no such thing as a private or a public act per se, such distinctions form the basis of decisions which are made about whether or not an asylum seeker can be protected under the Refugee Convention. Despite the problems which are inherent to any critique of the public/private dichotomy, this theoretical approach remains necessary because the assumption that underlies all law, including international refugee law, is that the public/private distinction *is* real. Human society, human lives can, it is implied, be separated into two distinct spheres. Only by challenging this dichotomy can it be demonstrated that this division is an ideological construct rationalising the exclusion of women from the sources of power. Most feminists now query the tendency to dissolve *all* distinctions between public and private but all argue that

---

1   See also Indra (ed) 1999.
2   Spijkerboer 1994.
3   Kofman and Peake 1990.

the boundaries are more permeable than is often assumed. Re-examining the boundaries gives new insights into the processes of exclusion and marginalisation.[1] In this context, the argument presented in this book supports Greatbach's proposal (1989) for a gendered critique which takes account of historical and cultural context, and places the question of gender within a broader analysis of the limitations of the refugee definition. Women are less likely than men to be granted asylum, not because of the absence of explicit recognition of gender-related persecution, but because of the social and political context in which the claims of women are adjudicated. Whilst the definition of 'refugee' contained in the Refugee Convention does not specifically name gender as one of the bases upon which asylum can be granted, the problem lies primarily in the fact that decision-makers, in applying the refugee definition, have typically failed to acknowledge and respond to the gendering of politics and of women's relationship to the State.

2.3 THE CONCEPT OF 'POLITICS'

'Political opinion' is probably the least disputed of all the grounds included in the Refugee Convention definition, not least because it implies some direct relationship to the State. This is reflected in the tendency for commentators to refer, in general terms, to the concepts of 'political asylum' and 'political refugee' despite the existence of other enumerated grounds. It has been suggested that because women are much less likely than men to be involved in politics, the concept of 'political opinion' is unlikely to be central in the claims of women seeking asylum.[2] However, it is the dominant conceptualisation of 'politics' as relating primarily to the public sphere which serves to undermine the validity of women's experiences. As Indra suggests, 'the key criteria for being a refugee are drawn primarily from the realm of public sphere activities dominated by men. With regard to private sphere activities where women's presence is more strongly felt, there is primarily silence – silence compounded by an unconscious calculus that assigns the critical quality "political" to many public activities but few private ones'.[3]

Perhaps nowhere are the effects of the public/private dichotomy on the understanding of women's experiences more evident, therefore, than with regard to the concept of 'politics'. As Philips (1998) suggests, the politics portrayed to us via the daily newspapers and television accounts remains overwhelmingly masculine in style. Although the character of formal politics (eg elections, parties, parliaments and unions) is diverse, the traditional subject matter of political analysis, 'high politics', involves areas typically dominated by men.[4] 'Politics' is viewed largely as men's 'territory', based on masculine assumptions and with a strongly masculine identity. This is reflected in an assumption that the 'big' issues

1 Philips 1998.

2 See, eg, Stairs and Pope 1990 and Castel 1992. This understanding is also implicit in those analyses which focus upon 'membership of a particular social group' as the most appropriate, or indeed only, basis on which women can be protected under the Refugee Convention.

3 Indra 1987, p 3.

4 Waylen 1996a.

of traditional political science – boundaries, State structures, international conflicts – have little to do with gender. However, gendered analyses of women and politics, such as that by Siltanen and Stanworth (1984), interrogate the assumptions and explanatory frameworks underlying these 'male-stream' accounts, so as to lay the foundations for a clearer understanding of the political capacities of both women and men. Existing definitions are saturated with gender and this saturation has worked in such a way as to legitimate women's lack of political power. They also suggest that 'politics' is about power and those forces and ideologies which maintain and alter the use and distribution of power. Gender, as a primary way of signifying relationships of power, is therefore critical to the study of politics.

Political scientists, particularly in the West, have generally failed to acknowledge women's extensive participation in political processes. Women's political activities have typically been seen as marginal, peripheral or non-existent: 'the Western-centred academic analysis of politics that has evolved ignores women and places them at the peripheries of political processes'.[1] Gendered analyses of women's marginalisation within both politics and political thought suggest that much of this process depends on a particular way of conceiving of the public/private divide. Afshar and others argue that this reflects the fact that most of the political theory which underlies Western liberal democracy and liberal democratic theory has its roots in the separation of the public and the private.[2] Beginning with Locke, the public sphere was seen as the arena where the individual was incorporated as a citizen into the political world. The private domestic sphere was seen as lying outside the proper realms of investigation and interference by the State or other and therefore assumed to be irrelevant to social and political theory. As Okin (1998) suggests, much of the mainstream continues to use these concepts as if relatively unproblematic. Sometimes explicitly, but more often implicitly, the idea is perpetuated that these spheres are sufficiently separate, and sufficiently different, that the public or political can be discussed in isolation from the private or personal. Because Western political thought continues to rely to a significant extent on binary oppositions, which are both hierarchical and closed, it is often unable to provide any insights into the content, form and representation of political protest carried out by women in different parts of the world.[3]

Gendered critiques of politics and political participation challenge dominant models and analyses of politics and open up the notion of politics, its forms and its practices. Two key themes are central to this critique. First, that gender differences in political participation have been exaggerated and, secondly, that women's participation in political processes has been misrepresented.

(1) Gender differences in political participation have been exaggerated

Within 'male-stream' analyses of politics, women are said to participate in politics less than men. This is reflected in a tendency to assume that politics is more 'natural' for men than women, and that women are more concerned with

---

1   Afshar (ed) 1996, p 1.
2   See, eg, Peterson 1992; Waylen 1996a; Philips 1998.
3   Waylen 1996b.

'moral' or 'social' than political issues.[1] Where women are politically active, their political orientation is argued to be less authentic than that of men and based on a relatively unsophisticated political understanding. There is an assumption, for example, that the attention that women give to the political is underpinned by concerns and objectives which are distinctive to their sex. Moreover, women are generally considered as inherently more conservative than men.[2] Feminist analyses of the relationship between gender and politics suggest that although we cannot simply 'pretend away' the differences between women and men in terms of their political participation, sexual differences are often over-emphasised and based on assumptions and stereotypes rather than empirical evidence. For example, Siltanen and Stanworth (1984) suggest that gender differences have been exaggerated as a result of the dubious assumption that 'political environments' (political parties, trade unions and the organisational and policy imperatives which shape their operation) are neutral as to sex or gender-blind. Challenging the tendency within the dominant discourse to essentialise differences between women and men, *and* among women, the authors suggest that the political environment is less responsive to women than to men, and it is this rather than a uniquely feminine ambivalence to politics which underlies women's political profile. The marginalisation of particular groups from politics is not simply a reflection of their social position and purported innate proclivities. Rather, we need to seek alternative explanations which would question the distribution of roles, status and power, as well as the very definition of politics itself.

(2) Women's participation in political processes has been misrepresented

Feminist analyses of politics are not just about 'filling the gaps' but raise critical questions about the meaning of 'politics', and often involve a self-consciously irreverent disruption of existing conceptual and analytical norms.[3] Such analyses have not only examined structural constraints which limit the extent of women's participation in formal politics associated with the public sphere but have also suggested that the public/private dichotomy is itself constructed through political processes onto which a whole series of dualities, such as apolitical/political and female/male have been mapped. As Waylen suggests, because of the dominance of a narrow view of politics which includes only the institutional echelons of the public sphere and concentrates on the actions of political elites, those activities outside the conventional political arena in which women participate are excluded: 'politics appears to be a largely male activity, as women are not part of the political elites in any great numbers and therefore appear as politically inactive in this vision of the world'.[4] This point has been made particularly strongly by Brown, who argues that:

> 'More than any other kind of human activity, *politics* has historically borne an explicitly masculine identity. It has been more exclusively limited to men than any

---

1   Bourque and Grossholtz 1998.
2   Siltanen and Stanworth 1984.
3   See, eg, Philips 1998.
4   Waylen 1996a, p 118. Peterson and Runyan 1993 similarly suggest that when the activities associated with masculinity are examined it appears simply that men are present and women are absent.

other realm of endeavour and has been more intensely, self-consciously masculine than most other social practices' (emphasis in original).[1]

The relationship between women and 'politics' reflects the way in which politics is analysed as opposed to the reality of women's experiences: 'by taking the male experience as the norm and privileging it as the most important to know about, we find ourselves focusing on some activities at the expense of others'.[2] Although it is important to bring women back into the study of formal politics, a narrow view of politics, which includes only the institutional echelons of the public sphere and concentrates on the actions of political elites, rests upon a restricted vision of democracy simply as a institutional arrangement rather than the wider distribution of power (or its lack) in society.[3] It also results in research which implicitly supports a patriarchal hierarchy of values.[4] We therefore need to move away from conventional notions of the exercise of power as something that has to be within a formal institutional framework and away from the distinctions between private and public orientations as being strictly correlated with non-political spheres of activity. This is perhaps particularly important in contexts where access to institutionalised political power is limited more generally. As Siltanen and Stanworth suggest, 'by questioning the taken-for-granted boundary of the political, which operates such that women's expertise and concerns are often excluded, feminists offer an alternative interpretation of women's relation to political life'.[5]

This book therefore challenges the criteria by which 'politics' is defined through its association with the 'public' sphere in order to highlight the ways in which these gendered assumptions both underestimate and misrepresent women's political contributions. This is particularly important in the context of the asylum determination process because women often participate as political subjects in different ways than men, and the predominant emphasis on participation within formal, constitutional, government-oriented institutions or procedures provides a misleading view of women's political identity. A satisfactory account of politics, as well as a comprehensive picture of women as participants, includes ad hoc politics not fully integrated into the formal political protests and *protest* activity directed against the existing regime. In many contexts, women's political resistance is less formal than that of men and it often takes place within the geographically and conceptually 'private' sphere of the home. The political activities which women are involved in are, in many instances, not as 'public' as making speeches, attending demonstrations and writing publications but, instead, include informal organisations and meetings, providing food, clothing and medical care, hiding people, passing messages from one political activist to another and so on. All of these activities may be essential for the on-going existence of the political organisation, and the knowledge women gain through these activities puts them in danger and at risk. Indeed, the evidence presented in Chapter 4 suggests that women who participate at a so-called 'low level' in supportive roles may actually be at greater risk of persecution than their male

---

1   Brown 1988, p 4.
2   Peterson and Runyan 1993, pp 43–44.
3   Waylen 1996a.
4   Jones 1988.
5   Siltanen and Stanworth 1984, p 98.

counterparts, partly because, as women, they should not be politically active at all, but also because it may be more effective to target low level political activists and undermine political resistance from below. Moreover, in many contexts, women's identities, beliefs and status are subsumed under those of their male kin. There may be a societal assumption that women defer to men on all significant issues and that their political views are aligned with those of the dominant members of the family.

Women are not without power in their non-public roles and nor are they non-political beings. Only by examining these experiences can we address the issue of the political participation of women from within a conceptual framework which does more than fit women into the categories and value systems which consider men and male experience as the measure of significance, and understand why women seeking asylum in the UK have fears of persecution which are grounded in their political identity. In this context, Spijkerboer (1994) argues that whilst one can say that refugee law is gendered on the basis that the very notion of a refugee is thought of as a 'public' phenomenon, it is not *necessarily* gendered. Activities are not inherently political or apolitical. Whether or not activities are 'political' depends on their context; whether or not they can give rise to sustainable claims to refugee status depends on the reaction of the authorities or non-State actors in the woman's country of origin:

> 'The public/private distinction ... cannot be considered as something out there. Human activities can shift from one sphere to another. Private talk in itself can be subversive, and therefore a political act ... In the context of refugee law, cooking will normally be a private act and therefore irrelevant. This may change however if the food is given to a political opponent of the authorities, or if the cooking is done communally by relatives of "disappeared" persons. There is political talk and private talk – as we know. But there is also private cooking and political cooking.'[1]

Activities commonly associated with women and occurring in the 'private' sphere of the home and community or at the boundaries between the public and private spheres are not inherently any less political than those taking place in the public sphere. The danger, however, is that 'women's activities' – and, more importantly, women's *actions* – are taken less seriously in refugee law practice because they are assumed to be 'private' and therefore not of relevance to refugee law which is concerned only with the 'public'. The 'boundaries' between the public and private spheres are, conceptually and in reality, far more fluid than is typically assumed in the process of asylum determination. The theoretical analysis and supporting empirical evidence presented in this book therefore suggests the need for alternative approaches to the conceptualisation of 'politics' which take account of the fluidity of boundaries between the public and private spheres and which are grounded in the reality of women's experiences. Such approaches should do more than simply consider women individually as political actors. As Jones and Jonasdottir suggest, they need to reformulate the basic categories of political thinking in order to allow gender to infect the ways we conceptualise political reality with a feminist vision: '... it means, materially and metaphorically, conceptualising the political arena in terms of gender'.[2] Such

---

1   Spijkerboer 1994, p 58.
2   Jones and Jonasdottir 1988, p 5.

approaches must also recognise that women's experiences of 'politics', the State and political conflict are highly varied. As Waylen (1992) suggests, there is a need to find ways of examining both the role played by different groups of women in conventional politics, and the part played by different groups of women in political activity outside of conventional politics, which can accommodate specificity, diversity and heterogeneity. Gender should not be 'added in' to the analysis of political processes at the expense of other forms of social relations because women's experiences of persecution cannot be analysed separately from their specific context of class and ethnic differences, of national history or purpose, and of cultural tradition.

It is clear from the gendered critique of 'politics' and the public/private dichotomy that political/apolitical cannot be mapped onto the public/private in any straightforward way. 'Politics' has both private and public dimensions as reflected in, on the one hand, the extent to which the private domain is implicated in the political process and, on the other, the lack of fit between the public sphere and the boundaries of the political. 'Politics' is not the prerogative of the public sphere and nor are women located firmly in the private sphere and men in the public. In addition, feminists have reclaimed the formal side of the formal/ informal political dichotomy through showing that there are other, less obvious, ways in which political discourses are gendered. Redefining the concept of 'politics' necessarily challenges the assumed division of the public and private into two geographically and conceptually isolated realms, and in so doing has considerable explanatory potential. It begins to account for, and helps us to understand, the persecution claims of many women seeking asylum in the UK. An understanding of women's political identity in the context of the asylum determination process must take account of the fluidity of politics in different contexts and leave room for historical shifts in the definition of the political related to the changing 'frames of meaning' or forms of consciousness by which social relations are understood. This requires the analysis of women and politics to focus not solely on the 'private' sphere per se but rather on the relationship between the public and private spheres and, in particular, the crucial role of the State and governments in structuring sex/gender systems. It must take account of the ways in which the public currently constitutes and narrows private options in many contexts.

2.4 GENDER, NATIONALISM AND THE STATE

A critical issue related to the protection of women which has emerged in the international arena in recent years concerns the need to recognise as Convention refugees those who experience persecution in their own country because of institutionalised discrimination against women. Although women are on the whole under-represented in formal politics, this does not mean that the policies made and implemented in the political process do not have a huge impact on the lives of different groups of women and on gender relations in general.[1] Indeed, in the context of growing struggles over national identity, prevalent ideologies have

---

1   Waylen 1996b.

articulated with policies that have proved particularly detrimental to women because the role of gender in the construction of national identity becomes reflected in policies which the State adopts.[1]

Perhaps the most obvious example of this is the imposition of dress codes in a number of countries. Pettman (1996) argues that, since independence, almost all 'third-world' States have been concerned to control women's sexuality and fertility, and that 'the status of women' often signals priorities in State and nation-building agendas. This process can be seen not only in policies which are aimed specifically at women but also, and perhaps more typically, in policies which deal with relations between men and women, particularly property rights, sexuality and family relations, and areas where power relations between men and women and therefore sets of gender relations are institutionalised. The laws and regulations around these issues frequently become an area of struggle, and for women in particular, the penalty for non-compliance may be disproportionately severe. As Moghadam suggests, 'it is in the context of the intensification of religious, cultural, ethnic and national identity . . . that we see *the politicisation of gender, the family and the position of women*'[2] (emphasis added).

The failure to recognise the gendering of political identity is reflected in the fact that women are usually 'hidden' in the various theories and analyses of nationalist phenomena, even though the significance of gender in the construction of national collectivities and political identities goes far beyond the symbolic use of women's bodies as a metaphor for the body politic and place.[3] As was noted by Hall et al, the editors of a special issue of *Gender and History* focusing upon 'Gender, Nationalism and National Identities' in 1993, nationalism is one of the most powerful forces in contemporary political life. Yet whilst 'national identity' and what that means has become an important topic for discussion, how national identity might relate to gender is rather less central. Very little has been said, for example, about gender hierarchies, about laws around women and the family or about the significance of the concepts of masculine and feminine, or about how these gendered discourses might impact upon the experiences of women and men. This is despite a general interest in the differential participation of various social groups in nationalist agendas[4] and despite increasing evidence that 'laws and discourses pertaining to gender are central to the self-definition of political groups and, indeed, signal the political and cultural projects of movements and regimes'.[5] Sharp (1996) suggests that the silencing of gendered identities within nationalism is due in part to the taken-for-granted nature of national identity in the contemporary world system. The explanation proposed by Yuval-Davis (1993), (1997) is perhaps most salient – women are hidden from analyses of nationalism for the same reasons that women are hidden from analyses of

---

1   Afshar (ed) 1996.
2   Moghadam 1994b, p 16.
3   This criticism of existing analyses of nationalism and nationalist struggles has also been made by, amongst others, Jayawardena 1986, Anthias and Yuval-Davis (eds) 1989; Hall et al (eds) 1993; Yuval-Davis 1993, 1997; Radcliffe 1993; Dalby 1994; Moghadam (ed) 1994a, 1994b; Ashfar (ed) 1996; Sharp 1996; Waylen 1996b; and McDowell and Sharp (eds) 1997.
4   Hall et al 1993; Moghadam (ed) 1994a.
5   Moghadam 1994a, p 2.

'politics', namely the ideological division of society into public and private spheres. Because women (and the family) are located in the private domain, which is not seen as politically relevant, women (and gender) are assumed to have no relevance to debates about nationalism and national identity: 'as nationalism and nations have usually been discussed as part of the public political sphere, the exclusion of women from that arena has effected their exclusion from that discourse as well'.[1]

The failure to recognise the gendered construction of nationalism therefore reflects a particular set of assumptions about women's relationship to both the 'State' and the 'nation'.[2] In order to understand the gendering of nationalism both in academic theories of national identity and in the operation of nationalism in everyday life, we need to 'bring the State back in' to the analysis of women's experiences.[3] However, before examining the relationship between women and the State in the context of nationalism, it is important to be clear about what we mean when we refer to 'the State' and to acknowledge the difficulties inherent in the concept itself.

Many of the theoretical and empirical difficulties involved in specifying the State are noted by Anthias and Yuval-Davis (eds) (1989), who acknowledge both that State processes can be more delineated than national processes, and that the State can extend beyond the boundary of the nation. They also raise a particular concern about the tendency to conflate the boundaries of 'the State' with the boundaries of 'the nation'. The concept of 'nation-State' frequently assumes a complete correspondence between the boundaries of the nation and the boundaries of those who live in a specific State. Although this has been the basis of nationalist ideologies and is frequently replicated in academic (and other) discourses, it is virtually everywhere a fiction. There are always people living within particular societies and States who are not considered to be (and often do not consider themselves to be) members of the hegemonic nation, and there are nations which never had a State (like the Palestinians) or which are divided across several States (like the Kurds). In this context, Anthias and Yuval-Davis suggest that whilst it is useful to retain the concept of 'the State' it is important to be clear about what we are referring to when we use the term:

> 'The term refers to a particular "machinery" for the exercise of "government" over a given population, usually territorially and nationality defined, although the definitions of what constitutes these boundaries etc. will shift and change depending on what is being managed or negotiated. Hence we can specify the state in terms of a body [of] institutions which are centrally organised around the intentionality of control with a given apparatus of enforcement at its command and basis. Coercion and repression are then to be seen both as forms of control and as a back-up ... Using this formulation, the state can harness a number of different processes, including ideological ones, through judicial and repressive mechanisms at its command.'[4]

Waylen similarly rejects any simplistic or straightforward conceptualisation of either 'the State' or women's relationship to it:

---

1   Yuval-Davis 1997, p 3.
2   Waylen 1996b.
3   Rai 1996; Kandiyoti (ed) 1991.
4   Anthias and Yuval-Davis 1989, p 5.

'The state can rarely if ever be seen as a homogenous category. It is not a unitary structure but a differentiated set of institutions and agencies, the product of a particular historical and political conjuncture. It is far better to see the state as a site of struggle, not lying outside of society and social processes, but having, on the one hand a degree of autonomy from these which varies under particular circumstances, and on the other, being permeated by them.'[1]

The conclusions drawn by Anthias and Yuval-Davis (1989) and Waylen (1996b) that the State is a battleground arena in which different social forces articulate their interests, is critical when considering women's relationship to the State and, in turn, their experiences of persecution during periods of nation-building. On the one hand, women are acted upon as members of collectivities, institutions or groupings and as participants in the social forces which give the State its given political agendas in any specific social and historical context. On the other hand, they are a specific focus of State concerns as a social category with a specific role (particularly human reproduction), although the way in which this articulates in policy and practice varies widely.

One of the critical ways in which States are able to maintain control over a given population is, as Peterson suggests, through normalising practices which mask the State's coercive power by effectuating rule indirectly: 'crucial to the State's ability to rule effectively is a claim to legitimacy, a means by which politically organised subjection is simultaneously accomplished and concealed'.[2] In this way, domination practices are legitimated, reproduced and institutionalised within States by rendering them 'natural' and therefore not political. It is therefore important to move away from simply looking at the way the State *treats* women in relation to men (although this may be of particular concern in some contexts), towards an approach which focuses, instead, on the ways in which particular States act to construct gendered State subjects and the public/private divide in different contexts. Through these processes the State plays a critical role in reconfiguring individual and collective identities, 'new' histories, and 'imagined communities'. This approach, which is clearly very strongly influenced by the work of Benedict Anderson (1983), challenges the narrow history of nationalism which focuses primarily on the making of States and on definitions of citizenship, and calls for a recognition of the political and, above all, cultural factors that allow 'the nation' to emerge as 'an imagined community':

'[Nations] are systems of cultural representation whereby people come to imagine a shared experience of identification with an extended community . . . As such, nations are not simply phantasmagoria of the mind, but are historical and institutional practices through which social difference is invented and performed. Nationalism becomes, as a result, radically constitutive of people's identities, through social contests that are frequently violent and always gendered.'[3]

Yuval-Davis (1994) similarly suggests that the exclusionary/inclusionary boundaries which form collectivities tend to focus around a myth (which may or may not be real) of a common origin or a common destiny. However, it is also important to remember that both the imagined boundaries which form

1   Waylen 1996b, p 16.
2   Peterson 1992, p 5.
3   McClintock 1993, p 61.

collectivities and the symbols which define 'membership' of the collectivity are historically specific. Nations, nationalism and national identities are always in a process of evolution, never fixed and stable, although often drawing on a repertoire of traditions, myths and representations which are constantly reworked and rearticulated to different national agendas.[1] Moreover, because the struggle for power takes place, at any specific moment, not only between collectivities but also within them, different and sometimes conflicting cultural resources can be used simultaneously by different members of the collectivity.

Anderson's description of 'the nation' as the product of the imaginations of the citizens of a territory has proved to be a useful insight into the origin and spread of modern nationalism. The invented nature of nationalism has found wide-spread theoretical currency as a consequence. However, both Yuval-Davis (1993), (1994) and McClintock (1993) are highly critical of Anderson's failure to recognise that the imagined bonding between individuals and the nation in narratives of national identification is differentiated by gender. As McClintock suggests, there is no single narrative of the nation. Different genders (and also different classes, ethnicities and generations) do not identify with, or experience the myriad of national formations in the same way. Feminist analyses have uncovered the gender dynamics of these processes of social change, transition and political struggle to reveal nationalism as profoundly and intrinsically gendered. Women and men may imagine (and be imagined within) such communities, identify with nationalist movements and participate in State formations in very different ways. Most notably, perhaps, even a cursory look at nationalism's construction and politics reveals the significance of women in *'marking the boundaries of difference'*:

> 'Both nation and nationalism are constructed on and through gender. Women are constructed as mothers of the nation, and markers of its boundaries ... Interrogating nationalism means recognising women's roles and the uses made of terms in both constructing and reproducing nationalism.'[2]

In this context, Anthias and Yuval-Davis (1989) suggest a number of different (although not exclusive) ways in which women have tended to participate in ethnic and national processes and State practices on different terms to men. Although the distinctions between the processes they identify are often more complex and inter-related than such a framework might suggest, at least two key themes emerge:

(1) women have a relationship as biological reproducers of members of particular collectivities, as 'mothers of the nation', and are held responsible for the reproduction of 'the nation';
(2) women play a critical role in the ideological reproduction of the collectivity, as transmitters of its culture and as signifiers of ethnic/national differences.

Anthias and Yuval-Davis also suggest that various forms of population control are the most obvious policies which relate to women as biological reproducers of members of collectivities. As Yuval-Davis (1997) suggests, the right of women to choose whether to have children, as well as how many to have and when, has been seen by many feminists as the basic 'touchstone' of feminist politics. The

---

1   Hall et al 1993.
2   Pettman 1996, p 45.

pressures on women to have or not to have children may relate to them not as individuals, workers and/or wives, but as members of specific national collectivities. This is reflected in three main discourses:

(1) a 'people as power' discourse which sees maintaining or enlarging the population of the nationalist collectivity as vital for the nationalist interest;
(2) a eugenicist discourse which aims at improving the 'quality of the national stock';
(3) a Malthusian discourse which, in contrast to the first discourse, sees the reduction of the number of children as the way to prevent future national disaster.

The encouragement or discouragement of women to bear children is determined to a significant extent by the specific historical situation of the collectivity. Notions like 'population explosion' or 'demographic balance' are expressions of various ideologies that can lead controllers of national reproduction towards different population control policies. These policies are rarely, if ever, applied in a similar manner to all members of a civil society. According to different national agendas, therefore, under specific historical circumstances, some or all women of childbearing age might be called upon, sometimes bribed, and sometimes even forced to have more, or fewer, children as reflected, for example, in the one-child policy most commonly associated with China. In this way the reproductive process becomes intensely politicised.

This understanding of the context and politics of coercive/compulsory population policies has very significant implications for the conceptualisation and representation of the asylum claims which are made on this basis, and is discussed in detail in Chapter 7. Seen in the context of gendered nationalism outlined here, it would seem more appropriate, as Spijkerboer (1994) suggests, that a woman who refuses to comply with a population control policy is expressing her political opinion about the legitimacy of a State policy or, at the very least, that such an opinion will be attributed to women who are pregnant without (effective) authorisation. As the biological reproducers of members of collectivities and of the boundaries of ethnic/national groups, women are therefore affected by a series of State measures which men are not. These relate not just to reproductive processes themselves, but also to institutions associated with childbearing.

Women's relationship to the nation and to national identity cannot (and should not) be reduced to biological reproduction alone. Women are controlled not only by being encouraged or discouraged from having children, but also in terms of the 'proper' way in which they should engage in these processes. Nationalist discourse often contains a strong defence of the family (and of women's traditional role within it). Familial language, ordering gender relations, are frequently at the heart of the 'imagined community'.[1] As Moghadam (1994b) suggests, crisis and transition seem to bring about an exaggerated reliance on the home and family as refuge for the assaulted identity. This point is made by Baron (1993) with reference to Egyptian nationalism, who suggests that, through the use of the metaphor of the nation as a family, popular notions about family

---

1   Hall et al 1993; Rai 1996.

honour and female sexual purity were elevated to a national ideal, leading to the construction of the concept of family honour. Within this process women are often not 'imagined' as part of the nation, but rather they are used as subjects and symbols around which to rally male support. In the Iranian context, similarly, not only have women been directed towards domesticity but the family and motherhood have come to be defined as the kernel of 'nationhood'. When group identity becomes intensified, women are elevated to the status of symbol of the community and are compelled to assume the burden of the reproduction of the group: 'their roles as wives and especially mothers are exalted, indeed fetishized. Women's place in the home and in the family is lauded. It is Woman as Wife and Mother – not women as workers, students, citizens – who is ideologically constructed in the discourse and program of the movement'.[1]

These two aspects of national identity (re)construction – biological and symbolic – mean that the nationalist agenda increasingly assigns to women the rather onerous responsibility for the reproduction of the group – through family attachment, domesticity and maternal roles – with particular consequences for women who refuse, fail or are unable to conform to such norms. Moreover, women are often particularly affected by legislation aimed at the institution of the family itself. Far from being an enclave, the family is vulnerable to the State, and the laws and social policies which impinge upon it undermine the notion of a dichotomy between the public and private spheres. As Mertus (1995) suggests, nearly all States restrict access to legally sanctioned family life through marriage regulation, defining acceptable and unacceptable forms of union and the social and political costs of unacceptable unions. For example, the State may adopt policies to prevent women from marrying outside a particular ethnic or religious 'group' through preventing Muslim women from marrying non-Muslim men because within Islamic law any resultant children would then take their father's name and religious identity. Such policies do not apply to Muslim men marrying non-Muslim women.[2] Similarly, nationality laws generally discriminate against women by limiting their rights in situations in which men's nationality rights are not limited. A common form of discrimination is the failure to extend to women the legal ability to confer on 'foreign' husbands certain rights that men can confer on their 'foreign' wives. For example, in Kenya, under section 91 of the Constitution, a Kenyan man who marries a 'foreigner' is able to pass his citizenship to his 'foreign' wife, but a Kenyan woman who marries a 'foreigner' cannot do the same.[3] If a woman's decision to marry a national of another country results in her losing citizenship or his having an uncertain right to reside in her country, her fundamental right to marry and found a family is restricted. Alternatively, a woman who goes ahead and marries a 'foreign' national and is then denied her own citizenship or is punished as a result, is being persecuted because in choosing to marry outside the boundaries she undermines the nationalist agenda. She is, therefore, seen to be challenging the regime, even if her choice of marriage partner did not have this as an intended effect.[4] Laws frequently regulate rights and responsibilities *within* family units by, for example,

---

1   Moghadam 1994b, p 18.
2   El Saadawi 1997.
3   Mertus 1995.
4   Freeman 1995.

specifying the responsibilities of family members to each other, and respective rights (or their lack) upon dissolution or death, for example, laws with regard to adultery within marriage, consent to and conditions of divorce and issues of child custody and inheritance. The laws of many regions of the world grant the father the right to custody and control over children. Freeman (1995) notes that in many legal systems women must establish more dramatic grounds for divorce than men, for example, Uganda, Uruguay, Argentina. For instance, under *sharia*, which (to varying degrees) regulates family laws in Muslim countries, even when children live with their mother, fathers are considered the legal guardians and maintainers. In this way, family law becomes an important mechanism for interventions which serve larger political and social goals. Indeed, Mertus (1995) goes further when she suggests that the State has such an instrumental approach towards women and the family that it intrudes upon family life *only* in order to exploit and support images of women that strengthen its own goals.

In order to understand the gendering of nationalist discourse and its implications for women, it is therefore critical to recognise that women participate in nationalist struggles not only through their role in the biological reproduction of members of collectivities and its boundaries, but also in the ideological reproduction of the collectivity and transmitters of its culture, and as signifiers of ethnic/national differences; in other words, as a focus and symbol in ideological discourses used in the construction, reproduction and transformation of ethnic/national identities. This is the second, and perhaps most important, theme which emerges from the framework developed by Anthias and Yuval-Davis (1989) and which has subsequently been developed by Yuval-Davis:

> 'The "proper" behaviour of women is often used to signify the difference between those who belong to the collectivity and those who do not; women are also seen as the "cultural carriers" of the collectivity and transmit it to the future generation; and *being properly controlled in terms of marriage and divorce ensures that children born to those women are not only biologically but also symbolically within the boundaries of the collectivity*' (emphasis added).[1]

Women are often viewed as cultural reproducers because of their role in transmitting group values and traditions as agents of socialisation of the young.[2] But as Yuval-Davis (1997) suggests, the relationship between gender and culture in the context of nationalism is more complex than might be assumed because of women's simultaneous role as symbolic 'border guards' in identifying people as members or non-members of a specific collectivity. This symbolic role is often closely linked to specific codes of style of dress and behaviour (particularly as it relates to sexuality) because women's behaviour and appearance are often manipulated by male-controlled religio-political institutions.

Nationalist struggles are often profoundly gendered because they involve the manipulation of gendered identities and symbols as well as gender divisions of power, labour and resources,[3] although as Sharp (1996) suggests, the use of such symbols may take on an apparently 'natural' presence so that they become difficult to identify and/or challenge (national identity itself becomes natural-

---

1   Yuval-Davis 1994, p 413.
2   Moghadam 1994.
3   Peterson and Runyan 1993, Dalby 1994.

ised). A similar point is made by Peterson (1996) who notes how nationalist ideologies attempt to legitimate particular forms of rule in the name of (invented) collective identities. Their moral/normative power often lies in claims to cultural superiority.

In order to understand the centrality of gender relations and identities to nationalist agendas, it is therefore necessary to analyse 'culture' as a dynamic contested resource which can be used differently in different agendas and by people who are differentially positioned in the collectivity. 'Culture' remains a conceptually ambiguous term, difficult to operationalise, and with a number of different usages. The revival of cultural analysis reflects in part the influence of interpretative research and of discourse analysis. A central proposition in these new approaches is that identities are not shared but exist in competition; competing loyalties may be manipulated both by the State and by social forces purporting to represent those identities. Seen from this perspective, gender identity is symbolic, ideological and profoundly political:

> 'Women frequently become the sign or marker of political goals and of cultural identity during processes of revolution and state-building, and when power is being contested or reproduced. Representations of women assume political significance, and certain images of women define and demarcate political groups, cultural projects, or ethnic communities. *Women's behaviour and appearance – and the acceptable range of their activities – come to be defined by, and are frequently subject to, the political or cultural objectives of political movements, states, and leaderships*' (emphasis added).[1]

The centrality of gender identity and roles to the construction of 'the nation' and of national identity go some way towards explaining the potential threat to the entire nationalist agenda (as reflected in resultant accusations of disloyalty) which women who refuse, fail or are unable to conform to the symbolic order represent. Although women are often under-represented in political institutions and silenced in public debates, they are, at the same time, the *embodiment* of national identity in many contexts, whether in its progressive or regressive guises. This can have profound implications and frequently forms a key aspect of asylum claims made by women in the UK and elsewhere.

---

1   Moghadam 1994a, p 2.

Chapter 3

A GENDERED FRAMEWORK FOR THE ANALYSIS OF ASYLUM CLAIMS

3.1 CONTENT VERSUS INTERPRETATION

The failure of representatives and decision-makers to recognise and respond appropriately to the experiences of women stems not from the fact that the Refugee Convention does not refer specifically to persecution on the basis of gender, but rather because it has often been approached with a partial perspective and interpreted through a framework of male experiences. The main problem facing women as asylum seekers is the failure of decision-makers to incorporate the gender-related claims of women into their interpretation of the existing enumerated grounds. In interpreting the Refugee Convention, decision-makers have largely failed to recognise the political nature of seemingly private acts of harm to women. For example, because rape is frequently viewed as a sexual act rather than as an act of violence, the rapist, even when a government official or a member of an anti-government force, is perceived as acting from personal motivation. The sexual nature of the harm may serve to personalise the event in the eyes of the adjudicator.

This book demonstrates the need for a *proper interpretation* of the Refugee Convention to include victims of oppression and discrimination on the basis of their gender. Both actual (and imputed) political opinion and 'membership of a particular social group' within the meaning of Article 1A of the Refugee Convention can provide a legal basis for the recognition of women as Convention refugees. Furthermore, the concept of 'persecution' itself must take into account harm inflicted upon women which is both specific to their gender and/or takes place at the hands of non-State agents. The need for a proper interpretation of the Refugee Convention, which takes into account its overall purpose and the general human rights context, is consistent with the general rule of interpretation of treaty provisions which appears in Article 31 of the Vienna Convention on the Law of Treaties ('Vienna Convention')[1]:

> 'A treaty shall be interpreted in good faith in accordance with the ordinary meaning to be given to the terms of the treaty in their context and in the light of its object and purpose.'

This is also reinforced by a number of decisions in the UK courts which have dismissed the idea that the Refugee Convention is outdated and instead called for a reinterpretation of its elements which accurately reflects current circumstances.[2] Some of these decisions have arisen in claims involving gender-related

---

1   Vienna Convention, Article 31, para 1.
2   See, eg, *Islam v SSHD; R v IAT ex parte Shah* [1999] INLR 44, Imm AR 283 (HL) and *SSHD ex parte Adan, Subaskaran and Aitseguer* [1999] INLR 1362, Imm AR 521 (CA).

persecution. For example, in considering the issue of whether women from Pakistan constitute a particular social group within the meaning of the Refugee Convention in *Shah*,[1] Mr Justice Sedley, as he then was, emphasised the dangers of a prescriptive approach to the Refugee Convention definition. Unless it is seen as a living instrument, adopted by civilised countries for a humanitarian end which was constant in motive but mutable in form, the Refugee Convention will eventually become an anachronism. The fact that the Refugee Convention has, in recent times, been exploited by the unscrupulous or is being genuinely invoked by a previously unimaginable volume of asylum seekers, calls for scrupulous attention to every claim but cannot redefine its meaning. Mr Justice Sedley also emphasised the importance of examining the context and particular circumstances of every application:

'Its adjudication is not a conventional lawyer's exercise of applying a legal litmus test to ascertained facts; it is a global appraisal of an individual's past and prospective situation in a particular cultural, social, political and legal milieu, judged by a test which, though it has legal and linguistic limits, has a broad humanitarian purpose.'

The need to constantly bear in mind this broad humanitarian purpose, as outlined in the Preamble, has been referred to in a number of other important decisions which have dealt with the interpretation of key elements of the Refugee Convention's definition of a refugee, including persecution by non-State agents and the construction of particular social groups. It has been accepted that the preambles provide an insight into the purpose of the Refugee Convention. For example, in *Adan, Subaskaran & Aitseguer*[2] the Court of Appeal referred to the Preamble and the general human rights context in which an individual's need for protection should be assessed:

'It is clear that the signatory States intended that the Convention should afford continuing protection for refugees in the changing circumstances of the present and future world. In our view the Convention has to be regarded as a living instrument: just as, by the Strasbourg jurisprudence, the European Convention on Human Rights is so regarded. Looked at in this light, the Geneva Convention is apt unequivocally to offer protection against non-State agent persecution, where for whatever cause the State is unwilling or unable to offer protection itself.'

Lord Steyn in *Islam*[3] made the following observations:

'The relevance of the preambles is two-fold. First they expressly show that a premise of the Convention was that all human beings shall enjoy fundamental rights and freedoms. Secondly, and more pertinently, they show that counteracting discrimination, which is referred to in the first preamble, was a fundamental purpose of the Convention.'

Efforts to ensure that the interpretation of the Refugee Convention includes issues of gender should be seen in this general context.

The object and purpose of the Refugee Convention is to provide protection but it has often failed to do so in many claims made by women because of the current

---

This has also been recognised elsewhere, eg Australia. See *A v Australia (MIEA)* [1998] INLR 1 (High Court of Australia).

1   *R v IAT ex parte Shah* [1997] Imm AR 145 (QBD).
2   *R v SSHD ex parte Adan, Subaskaran and Aitseguer* [1999] INLR 1362, Imm AR 521 (CA).
3   *Islam v SSHD; R v IAT ex parte Shah* [1999] INLR 144, Imm AR 283 (HL).

gendered interpretation of its key elements. In this context, this chapter provides a gendered framework for the analysis of asylum claims based on that developed by Hathaway (1991). This framework ensures that the Refugee Convention is *properly* interpreted to include the experiences of women. As Hathaway has noted, 'gender-specific claims to refugee status are, in fact, no different than any other claims to refugee status. You don't need a new definition. You don't need to manipulate the current definition. Gender-specific claims to refugee status ought to be assessed on exactly the same grounds as every other claim to Convention refugee status'.[1]

3.2 FRAMEWORK FOR THE ANALYSIS

As is noted in UNHCR (1979) at para 42, the phrase 'well-founded fear of persecution' is central to the definition of a refugee and is said to exist if the applicant can establish, to a reasonable degree, that her continued stay in her country of origin has become intolerable. This fear may be based on personal experience, or on the experiences of persons similarly situated (para 43). However, because there is no universally accepted definition of 'persecution' the courts in the various jurisdictions have defined persecution on a country by country basis.[2] According to well-recognised commentators, this omission of a precise definition was deliberate so as to permit a case-by-case determination of whether any given conduct constitutes a persecutory act.[3] Yet the lack of any intrinsic meaning is also highly problematic in terms of objective assessment of individual refugee women's claims for asylum.

Given the problems of interpretation associated with the refugee definition as it currently exists, and in particular surrounding the central concept of persecution, a gendered critique is needed of all of its aspects. Following Hathaway (1991), the framework outlined in this book divides the Refugee Convention definition of a refugee into its six essential elements:

(1) alienage;
(2) genuine risk;
(3) 'serious harm';
(4) failure of State protection;
(5) grounds for the persecution;
(6) needs and deserves protection.

The concept of alienage has attracted comment elsewhere,[4] although neither it nor the cessation and exclusion clauses contained within Article 1C(1)–(6), 1D, 1E and 1F of the Refugee Convention will be examined in detail here. Rather the

---

1   Hathaway 1990, p 1.
2   The leading case in the UK on the definition of persecution is *Gashi v Nikshiqi* [1997] INLR 96 (IAT).
3   Grahl-Madsen 1966; Goodwin-Gill 1983; Hathaway 1991.
4   See, eg, Castel 1992; Goldberg 1993; Kelly 1993, 1994. Castel 1992 makes a general point about the concept of alienage from a gendered perspective. Noting that the majority of the world's refugee claimants are men, she suggests that for women facing persecution, travelling to potential countries of asylum to make a claim for refugee status is particularly

analysis in this book centres around the concept of 'persecution' and the enumerated Refugee Convention grounds. Hathaway (1991) suggests that in order to understand whether persecution exists it is useful to examine two key issues. First, the issue of whether harm apprehended by the claimant amounts to persecution, ie whether it constitutes 'serious harm' within the meaning of persecution, and secondly, whether there has been a failure of State protection.

'Persecution' = 'Serious harm' + 'The Failure of State Protection'

The use of this framework to consider whether an individual applicant should be recognised as a refugee within the meaning of the Refugee Convention has been examined in both *Shah and Islam*[1] and *Horvath*.[2]

In cases of persecution by non-State agents the failure of the State to 'deter and inhibit' was found to illustrate the State's tacit acceptance of the threat to the appellants in *Shah and Islam*.[3] The violence perpetrated by husbands upon their wives would not have amounted to persecution on its own, nor would a generalised inadequacy in the protection offered by the State of Pakistan against violence. It was the fact that the State was discriminatory in the protection it afforded to a particular group of its citizens, namely women, which turned those women into refugees within the definition. In other words, the two elements were not treated separately from one another but were linked in determining whether a fear of persecution existed.

By contrast, in *Horvath*,[4] it was argued by the appellant that the IAT were in error to introduce the element of the State's ability to provide protection into the question of whether what the appellant feared was persecution. The Court of Appeal was divided over the principal issue of law; whilst Ward and Hale LJJ agreed with Lord Hoffmann in *Shah and Islam* that the existence or otherwise of State protection is relevant to the question of whether 'mistreatment' amounts to persecution, Stuart-Smith LJ reasserted Hathaway's original framework that there are six conditions that the appellant must satisfy to establish status as refugee. These elements are separate and discrete and each should be addressed logically and sequentially:

> 'I can see no reason or advantage in importing into the consideration of one issue, matters which logically fall to be considered under another. On the contrary, it seems to me to be likely to lead to confusion.'

At the time of writing, these issues had been re-examined by the House of Lords in *Horvath*.[5] In the leading judgment, Lord Hope held that in cases of persecution by non-State agents, there is a relationship between whether the harm experienced or feared rises to the level of persecution and the existence or

---

difficult owing to their responsibility for the care of their children, their lack of financial resources, and cultural and other restrictions.

1   *Islam v SSHD; R v IAT ex parte Shah* [1999] INLR 144, Imm AR 283 (HL).
2   *Horvath v SSHD* (unreported) 6 July 2000 (HL).
3   *Islam v SSHD; R v IAT ex parte Shah* [1999] INLR 144, Imm AR 283 (HL).
4   *Horvath v SSHD* [2000] INLR 15 (CA).
5   *Horvath v SSHD* [2000] 3 WLR 379 (HL).

otherwise of effective mechanisms for protection by the State in the country of origin:

> 'Where the allegation is of persecution by non-state agents, the sufficiency of state protection is relevant to a consideration of whether each of the two tests – the "fear" test and the "protection" test – is satisfied. The proper starting point, once the tribunal is satisfied that the applicant has a genuine and well-founded fear of serious violence or ill-treatment for a Convention reason, is to consider whether what he fears is "persecution" within the meaning of the Convention. At that stage the question whether the state is able and willing to afford protection is put directly in issue by a holistic approach to the definition which is based on the principle of surrogacy.'

By contrast, Lord Lloyd's judgment makes it clear that the two elements should be addressed separately. In other words, it should be established whether there is a fear of persecution in the ordinary meaning of the word ('serious harm') before addressing the failure of the State to protect against such harm:

> 'It is surely simpler, and therefore better from every point of view ... that the fact-finding tribunal should first assess the ill-treatment and answer the question whether it amounts to persecution for a Convention reason, and then, as a separate question, evaluate the protection available to the applicant. I can see no advantage in running these two questions together ... it follows that ... the absence of state protection is not a relevant ingredient in the definition of persecution.'

According to the judgment by Lord Clyde, where 'serious harm' is directly related to agents of the State, the second part of the equation is automatically satisfied:

> 'Where the state is itself through its agents the persecutor, the question does not acquire to arise. Active persecution by the state is the very reverse of protection. In that context it is sufficient to proceed simply upon dictionary definitions ...'

3.3 THE MEANING OF 'SERIOUS HARM'

Women are frequently subjected to forms of harm which are similar to those of their male counterparts, but they also face physical harm or abuse which is specific to their gender including sexual violence and rape, discriminatory social mores, female genital mutilation, bride burning, forced marriage, violence within the family, forced sterilisation and forced abortion. There is growing concern that the concept of persecution has not been widely interpreted to include these generally female-specific experiences.

A key problem in these cases is the definition of 'serious harm'. Does the treatment to which the applicant was subjected in the past or which the applicant fears amount to persecution? The UNHCR Handbook (1979) recognises that there is no universally accepted definition of 'persecution', but from para 33 of the Handbook it may be inferred that a 'threat to life or freedom' on one of the five enumerated grounds is always persecution. The Handbook further acknowledges at para 51 that 'other serious violations of human rights, for the same reasons, would also constitute persecution'. Meanwhile, in an important Canadian case, the judge concluded that 'underlying the Convention is the international community's commitment to the assurance of basic human rights. . . .'[1] Given that all existing definitions of persecution share the notion that violations of basic human rights constitute persecution, it is necessary to examine the human rights protected under international law. The process of assessing harm against internationally agreed standards of human rights allows proper consideration of all forms of serious harm a person may face including those harms that are gender-specific.

In this context, Hathaway (1991) proposes that we move away from any intuitive reasoning about what persecution is and try to substantiate our reasoning by basing it on very objective indicators. Arguing that basic international legal obligations are the appropriate common denominators, Hathaway (1991) grounds his definition of 'serious harm' in human rights agreements containing standards accepted as legitimate by virtually all States.[2] On the basis of these international agreements he establishes a hierarchy of rights (see Box 3.1). According to Hathaway (1991), persecution is most appropriately defined in relation to the core entitlements which have been recognised by the international community. The types of harm to be protected against include the breach of any right within the first category, a discriminatory or non-emergency abrogation of a right within the second category, or the failure to implement a right within the third category which is either discriminatory or not grounded in the absolute lack of resources.

Box 3.1

Examples of Level 1 Rights: freedom from arbitrary deprivation of life; protection against torture or cruel, inhuman or degrading punishment or treatment; freedom from slavery; freedom of thought, conscience and religion;

Examples of Level 2 Rights: freedom from arbitrary arrest or detention; equal protection of the law; fair criminal proceedings; family privacy; freedom of internal movement; freedom of opinion, expression, assembly, and association; rights to vote; access to public employment;

Examples of Level 3 Rights: right to work; right to essential food, clothing and housing; health care; basic education; cultural expression;

Examples of Level 4 Rights: private property; protection from unemployment.

For the purposes of this book, therefore, the definition of 'serious harm' follows Hathaway who defines persecution within a human rights paradigm as 'the sustained or systemic violation of basic human rights demonstrative of a failure of State protection'.[3] Within this framework, certain human rights are considered

---

1　　*Canada (Attorney General) v Ward* [1993] 2 SCR 689.
2　　The Universal Declaration of Human Rights, the International Covenant on Civil and Political Rights and the International Covenant on Economic, Social and Cultural Rights.
3　　Hathaway 1991, pp 104–105.

so fundamental as to be non-derogable, such that any violation of those rights is considered egregious. Genocide, slavery, assassination, torture, arbitrary arrest and detention are among the human rights violations that are the most widely accepted as prohibited conduct. In addition to the human rights instruments identified above, it may be possible to invoke various Articles of the ECHR, most particularly Articles 3, 5, 8 and 14, to ensure that applicants are not returned.[1]

The concept of 'serious harm' within the meaning of persecution has been variously interpreted in the different jurisdictions. In the **US**, persecution has been defined as a threat to life or freedom, or the infliction of suffering or harm upon those who differ in a way regarded as offensive.[2] The harm or suffering could consist of confinement or torture.[3] Harsh conditions shared by others does not amount to persecution.[4] Persecution does not include every type of treatment that our society regards as offensive.[5] Rather, the harm or suffering has to have been inflicted on an individual so as to punish the individual for possessing a belief or characteristic.[6] The courts in **Australia** have been consistent in their interpretation of the term persecution, and physical harm, even amounting to an abuse of human rights, may not be enough. They have held that 'persecution involves the infliction of harm, but it implies something more: an element of an attitude on the part of those who persecute which leads to the infliction of the harm, or an element of motivation (however twisted) for the infliction of the harm. People are persecuted for something perceived about them or attributed to them by their persecutors'.[7] More recently, in *A and Another v MIEA and Another*,[8] the courts referred to the primary meaning of the term 'persecution' in ordinary usage as being the action of persecuting or pursuing with enmity and malignity; especially the infliction of death, torture, or penalties for adherence to a religious belief or an opinion as such, with a view to the repression or extirpation of it.

Hathaway's framework for the assessment of 'serious harm' has been accepted in the **UK**. In *Jonah*,[9] it was held that 'persecution' in the context of Article 1A of the Refugee Convention should be given its ordinary meaning of 'to pursue with malignancy or injurious action'. In *Gashi and Nikshiqi*,[10] the IAT conducted a rigorous intellectual enquiry into the meaning of 'persecution'. The Tribunal adopted a teleological approach to the interpretation of the Refugee Convention, drawing on its object and purpose as set out in the preamble, which refers explicitly to the affirmation of the Universal Declaration of Human Rights. In allowing the appeals of both appellants, the IAT explicitly used Hathaway's framework to assess the level of harm and concluded that 'there seems to be no

---

1   See, eg, *Soering v United Kingdom* 14038/88 [1989] 11 EHRR 439 (ECtHR) and *Chahal v United Kingdom* (1997) 23 EHRR 413 (ECtHR).
2   *Matter of Acosta* 19 I&N Dec citing *Kovac v INS* 407 F.2d 102, 107 (9th Cir) (1969).
3   *Blazina v Bouchard* 286 F.2d 507, 511 (3rd Cir) (1961).
4   *Fatin v INS* 12 F.3d 1233 (9th Cir) citing *Matter of Acosta* 19 I&N Dec.
5   *Fatin v INS* 12 F.3d 1233 (9th Cir).
6   *Matter of Diaz* (1963) US BIA.
7   *Ram v MIEA and Another* (1995) 57 FCR 565, 568.
8   *A v Australia (MIEA)* [1998] INLR 1; *A and Another v MIEA and Another* [1997] 142 ALR (High Court of Australia).
9   *R v IAT ex parte Jonah* [1985] Imm AR 7 (QBD).
10   *Gashi v Nikshiqi* [1997] INLR 96 (IAT).

doubt that [persecution] includes not only the first category but the second category as well and some aspects of the third category'. The submissions by the UNHCR and, in particular, its recognition that there is an important link between persecution and the violation of fundamental human rights, appear to have been significant for the IAT's determination on this issue. Hathaway's framework was also referred to extensively by the IAT in *Horvath*,[1] which again held that whether harm amounts to persecution should be assessed on the basis of internationally recognised human rights standards, and has been adopted in other jurisdictions.[2]

Despite growing acceptance of the use of Hathaway's framework, however, several important problems remain in the interpretation of serious harm, which have implications for the way in which the asylum claims of women are currently determined. The first of these relates to a general theme in recent literature centred around the idea that human rights, for a variety of reasons, have not always been women's rights. The second concern relates to the hierarchical nature of Hathaway's framework and, in particular, the distinction which is commonly drawn between persecutory and discriminatory treatment.

3.3.1 Women's human rights and sexual violence

Gender-specific violence may include rape, sexual violence and abuse, female genital mutilation, marriage related harm, violence within the family, forced sterilisation and forced abortion. Whilst these forms of violence do not, in theory, differ analytically from other forms of ill-treatment and violence that are commonly held to amount to persecution, in practice the approach of decision-makers has been more ambiguous. This is particularly evident in cases involving rape and sexual violence, as can be seen throughout this book.

Sexual violence is a major factor in forced migration and occurs in a variety of different contexts. It can also take a variety of different forms. These include, but are not limited to:

–   rape;
–   mechanical or manual stimulation of the erogenous zones;
–   the insertion of objects into the body openings (sometimes with objects made of metal to which an electrical current is later connected);
–   the forced witnessing of sexual acts;
–   forced masturbation or to be masturbated by others;
–   fellatio and oral coitus;
–   a general atmosphere of sexual aggression and threats of the loss of the ability to reproduce and enjoyment of sexual relations in the future.[3]

Examples from UK cases also include the use of high-power water jets directed at the vagina, being forced to watch others (including children) being sexually abused or raped, being watched by others, and forced prostitution.

---

1   *Horvath v SSHD* [1999] INLR 7 (IAT).
2   Eg in *Re MN*, Refugee Appeal No 2039/93, Refugee Status Appeals Authority, 12 February 1996 the New Zealand Refugee Status Appeals Authority termed it an 'elegant and comprehensive theory of persecution based on international human rights instruments'.
3   UNHCR 1991, para 59.

Sexual violence including rape has serious physical, social, intellectual and psychological consequences. Physical consequences can include HIV infection, STDs, mutilated genitalia, pregnancy, miscarriage of an existing foetus, menstrual disorder, severe abdominal pain and self-mutilation as a result of psychological trauma. The UNHCR (1995a) also notes in its publication entitled *Sexual Violence Against Refugees; Guidelines on Prevention and Response* that where women have undergone extreme forms of female genital mutilation, they may suffer extensive injuries if their genitalia are reopened by a sharp instrument or by the force of penetration itself.[1] Even if physical injury is minimal, all victims experience psychological trauma. This may lead to difficulties for the representative in 'finding out' about the harm itself.[2] It may also carry traumatic social repercussions, which may be affected by a woman's cultural origins or social status. In some countries, women who have been sexually abused in custody are unwilling to report the abuse. Some may feel degraded or ashamed, or fear that they would suffer social stigma should they disclose what has been done to them. The social consequences of sexual violence can range from rejection by the spouse and immediate family members, to stigmatisation or ostracism by the wider community to severe punishment and/or deprivation of education, employment and other types of assistance and protection which may in themselves rise to the level of serious harm.

It has been suggested that the key to understanding the injury of sexual violence including rape is to recognise that, although in many cases the insult may have been intended for men through women, it is internalised by women.[3] This happens in three ways. First, women bear the physical injury. Secondly, they blame themselves for being raped and feel ashamed. Thirdly, in cultures where men view rape as a stain on their honour and that of the family, women internalise this guilt.[4] In many cultural contexts, therefore, the experience of sexual violence may lead to the woman being ostracised by both her family and the community. She may be unable to marry or stay married or may be 'married off'. In some societies, a woman who has been raped may also be perceived as a culprit and consequently may be liable to punishment by the State. Where a rape victim may be killed or banished, or considered to have no alternative but to marry her attacker or become a prostitute, these should be considered as additional human rights violations. According to the UNHCR (1995a), in cases where the harm has occurred after the applicant has left the country of origin and where return to that country would have one of these results, the applicant may be considered a refugee *sur place*.

Sexual violence including rape should be one of the least controversial examples of 'serious harm' in the context of a definition of persecution. However, this has not always been the case. As Macklin suggests, 'some decision-makers have proven unable to grasp the nature of rape by State actors as an integral and tactical part of the arsenal of weapons deployed to brutalise, dehumanise, and

---

1   UNHCR 1995a, p 6.

2   This issue is examined in more detail in Chapter 10.

3   Thompkins 1995.

4   Many of these processes are not unique to women but also affect men who have been subjected to sexual violence. However, it could be argued that the effects are exacerbated for women because of gendered social norms and mores.

humiliate women and demoralise their kin and community'.[1] This is reflected in
the fact that such violence has often been characterised as the random expression
of spontaneous impulses by a military officer toward a woman, or as the common
(and by implication acceptable) fate of women caught in a war zone. The
UNHCR (1995a) suggests that this shows a lack of awareness and maintains that
it is important to understand that sexual violence is a serious violation of an
individual's personal security and integrity. The point is also made by the INS in
the gender guidelines that have been produced for decision-makers in the United
States.

> 'Severe sexual abuse does not differ analytically from beatings, torture, or other
> forms of physical violence that are commonly held to amount to persecution. The
> appearance of sexual violence in a claim should not lead adjudicators to conclude
> automatically that the claim is an instance of purely personal harm.'[2]

There is no difference between the sexual violence used against women and the
other forms of violence inflicted on men. Hathaway finds that 'the threat of rape,
for example, is a sufficient basis for persecution' and cites a Canadian precedent
which labels rape as 'persecution of the most vile sort'.[3] There can be no doubt,
therefore, that sexual violence and rape fulfil the necessary criteria for 'serious
harm' in a human rights framework. This unanimity seems to be inescapable in
the light of international law (see Box 3.2).

Box 3.2

Sexual violence including rape is a grave violation of the right not to be
subjected to torture or other cruel, inhuman or degrading treatment or
punishment. This right has been laid down in, inter alia:

Articles 3 and 5 of the Universal Declaration of Human Rights (General
Assembly Resolution 217A (III));

Article 7 of the International Covenant on Civil and Political Rights
(General Assembly Resolution 2200 A (XXI));

The Convention against Torture and Other Cruel, Inhuman or Degrading
Treatment or Punishment (General Assembly Resolution 39/46).[4]

These rights are so fundamental that no circumstance whatsoever justifies their
derogation under international law.[5] Refugee law doctrine is unanimous
therefore in its opinion that sexual violence, including rape, constitutes an act of
serious harm and there is solid support for this position in the gender guidelines
which have been produced by Canada, the US and Australia:

---

1   Macklin 1995, p 226.
2   INS 1995.
3   Hathaway 1995, p 112.
4   See, eg, Kisoki 'Committee Against Torture (CAT)' 16th Session Communication No
       41/1996, 13 May 1996. Contact the AIRE centre for further information.
5   See, eg, the UNHCR's *Note on Certain Aspects of Sexual Violence Against Refugee Women*
       [A/AC.96/822] 1993.

'The fact that violence, including sexual and domestic violence, against women is universal is irrelevant when determining whether rape, and other gender-specific crimes constitute forms of persecution.'[1]

'Rape and other forms of sexual assault . . . clearly come within the bounds of torture as defined by the Convention Against Torture (CAT). Furthermore, sexual violence amounts to a violation of the prohibition against cruel, inhuman or degrading treatment, the right to security of person and in some instances the right to life, as contained in a variety of national instruments.'[2]

Rape and other forms of sexual abuse violate the prohibitions of violence to person, cruel treatment and torture, and degrading treatment contained in the four Geneva Conventions of 1949. International humanitarian law also explicitly prohibits rape. Article 27 of the Fourth Geneva Convention of 1949 states that 'women shall be especially protected against any attack on their honour, in particular against rape, enforced prostitution, or any other form of indecent assault'. This provision is reiterated in Additional Protocols I and II:

'Sexual violence is a gross violation of fundamental human rights and, when committed in the context of armed conflict, a grave breach of humanitarian law.'[3]

3.3.2 Discrimination as 'serious harm' within the meaning of persecution

Violations of rights which might be seen to constitute discrimination and which, conceivably, might be more likely to affect women are often placed lower in the hierarchy of human rights which is used to assess whether what an individual fears can be said to rise to the level of persecution. This lends support to the conclusions of Charlesworth et al (1991) that human rights law on which the definition of persecution may be based is cast in terms of violations of rights and offers more limited redress in cases where there is pervasive, structural denial of rights. This may be particularly problematic for the asylum claims of women because gender-related persecution is sometimes more subtle than other forms. It can take the form of restrictions on the way a woman behaves or it can involve forcing her to act in a certain way. In many countries, women are subjected to discriminatory treatment and social mores which are enforced through law or through the imposition of cultural or religious norms which restrict their opportunities and rights. Discrimination or social mores as 'serious harm' is particularly clear in cases where the level of punishment for violating gendered discriminatory norms violates international human rights standards and there-fore rises to the level of persecution. In some cases, the penalty imposed by the State for non-compliance with a discriminatory law might be disproportionately severe. There are many examples where women are punished for transgressing social mores or for finding themselves in circumstances deemed socially and culturally unacceptable. Neal (1988) cites Iranian law that makes women's failure to wear the veil a criminal act punishable by 74 lashes as an example of this.

---

1   CIRB 1996, section B.
2   ADIMA 1996, para 4.6.
3   UNHCR 1995a, p 1.

A further example is where women who have been sexually abused face harsh punishment because it is a condition of marriage that a woman be a virgin. The inability to fulfil this condition seriously jeopardises her honour and that of her family. To save face, the family may disown the woman or she may be killed by a family member ('honour killing'). Although such practices may not be officially sanctioned by the State, the authorities may be unable or unwilling to stop them. Similarly, women who are divorced or separated, whether or not by agreement, may be subjected to a whole range of discriminatory measures which can amount to 'serious harm'.

In some cases, the 'serious harm' experienced or feared arises not from any punishment that may be sustained for violating the norm, but rather the imposition of the law or norm in and of itself.[1] Although the legal obligation to eliminate all forms of discrimination against women is a fundamental tenet of international human rights law, the level of discrimination sufficient to rise to the level of 'serious harm' is not a point on which States readily agree. The UNHCR Handbook (1979) at paras 54–55 specifically addresses the issue of discrimination in the context of the definition of 'persecution'. If measures of discrimination lead to consequences of a substantially prejudicial nature for the person concerned then 'serious harm' can be said to have occurred:

> 'Where measures of discrimination are, in themselves, not of a serious character, they may nevertheless give rise to a reasonable fear of persecution if they produce, in the mind of the person concerned, a feeling of apprehension and insecurity as regards [her] future existence. Whether or not such measures of discrimination in themselves amount to persecution must be determined in the light of all the circumstances. A claim to fear of persecution will of course be stronger where a person has been the victim of a number of discriminatory measures of this type and where there is thus a cumulative element involved.'

The UNHCR Handbook (1979) at para 55 cites the examples of serious restrictions on the right to earn a livelihood, the right to practise his or her chosen religion, and his or her access to normally available educational facilities as examples of discrimination rising to the level of persecution.

The UNHCR *Guidelines on the Protection of Refugee Women* (1991) does not clarify this issue any further insofar as it does not distinguish persecution from discrimination. Other authors, by contrast, are very much clearer and locate discrimination within Hathaway's framework. For example, in addition to the punishment inflicted for failing to abide by social mores, it can be argued that a policy compelling women to wear the veil violates her 'first order' freedom of religion or conscience. The premise is that if the law discriminates by selectively abrogating fundamental human rights of designated groups, the law itself persecutes. In principle, it should not matter that it would be relatively 'easy' for the claimant to obey the law (and thus avoid prosecution) by wearing a veil, if in doing so she must forsake a protected freedom.[2] More often, however, the wearing of the veil constitutes only one element in a plethora of rules, policies and customs circumscribing the lives of women from particular countries. Therefore, in a claim based on discriminatory treatment and/or social mores, the decision-

---

1   Kelly 1993.
2   Macklin 1995.

maker must evaluate all the circumstances, including the type of right or freedom denied, the manner in which the right is denied, the seriousness of the harm to the applicant, and any non-persecutory justification for the discriminatory treatment. Any harm to a right lower than level 1 or 2 may be persecutory if the harm is systematic or cumulative and seriously affects the integrity of the applicant.[1]

The courts in **New Zealand** have explicitly recognised gender-based discrimination as 'serious harm' within the meaning of the Convention:

> 'The Authority should ... consciously strive both to recognise and to give proper weight to the impact of discriminatory measures on women.'[2]

> 'Discrimination can affect gender-based groups to different degrees ... various acts of discrimination, in their cumulative effect, can deny human dignity in key ways and should properly be recognised as persecution for the purposes of the Convention.'[3]

In the **UK**, case-law relating to discrimination as 'serious harm' is clearer in cases of persecution which are not gender-specific. For example, in *Chiver*[4] the IAT ruled that discrimination could constitute 'serious harm' where the respondent, a Romanian, had suffered serious discrimination in being barred from employment and State benefits because of his political opinions. In *Gashi and Nikshiqi*, the IAT accepted that human rights violations below level 1, can also constitute 'serious harm' within the meaning of 'persecution':

> 'We do not think that when the Convention was drafted it was intended to include the right to be free of arbitrary deprivation of property or to be protected against unemployment (Professor Hathaway's fourth category) ... However there seems to be no dispute that it includes not only the first category but the second category as well and some aspects of the third category.'[5]

Most recently, the issue of whether discrimination constitutes serious harm rising to the level of persecution has again been addressed in *Horvath*.[6] This case concerned a Roma from Slovakia who was harassed by skinheads and whose father died as a result of being beaten. He had been unable to find employment. The IAT had found what Horvath feared – acts of discrimination and breaches of third category rights – were not sufficiently serious to constitute persecution. It was the view of the IAT that it was the failure of the State to provide protection that converts discriminatory acts into persecution, and on that approach it was held that the case failed. However, the Court of Appeal considered that certain acts of discrimination affecting the ability of the applicant to find work, and denial of normal public facilities including marriage and education for his child, considered separately or in conjunction with the persecution by non-State agents, could amount to persecution. In the House of Lords, the emphasis was on whether there had been a failure of State protection and the issue of surrogacy. However, as was discussed above, their Lordships also gave some consideration

---

1   Hathaway 1991.
2   New Zealand Refugee Status Appeals Authority, Appeal No 1039/93 (13 February 1995).
3   New Zealand Refugee Status Appeals Authority, Appeal No 2039/93 (12 February 1996).
4   *SSHD v Chiver* (unreported) 24 March 1994 (10758) (IAT).
5   *Gashi and Nikshiqi v SSHD* (unreported) 22 July 1996 (13695) (IAT).
6   *Horvath v SSHD* [1999] INLR 7 (IAT); *Horvath v SSHD* [2000] INLR 15 (CA); *Horvath v SSHD* [2000] 3 WLR 379 (HL).

to whether the word 'persecution' denotes merely sufficiently severe ill-treatment, or sufficiently severe ill-treatment against which the State fails to provide protection.

By contrast, in cases of gender-specific discrimination, there has sometimes been a failure on the part of decision-makers to recognise general human rights as women's right. For example, in *Islam*,[1] the IAT stated that 'we do not think that the purpose of the Convention is to award refugee status because of disapproval of social mores or conventions in non-western societies'. However, in both the earlier case of *Gilani*[2] and case of *Fathi and Ahmady*,[3] there has been recognition that gender-specific treatment of women in the Iranian context rises to the level of 'serious harm':

> 'We accept the penalties which can be imposed for transgressing against the "social mores" of dress and behaviour can amount to persecution and indeed in Iran may amount to persecution.'[4]

> 'The next question then is whether the treatment amounts to persecution. I think that the cumulative effect of her being arrested because of her failure to observe the dress laws, the fact that she has been dismissed from her employment for the same reason and that she has been harassed on occasions by security forces might well amount to persecution.'[5]

This issue was finally resolved in the House of Lords in *Shah and Islam*[6] where the position taken in *Fathi and Ahmady*[7] was accepted.

3.4 THE FAILURE OF STATE PROTECTION

There is a difference between a failure of State protection under international refugee law and the notion of State responsibility in human rights law. This is important because the aim of the Refugee Convention is not to hold States responsible but to ensure that effective surrogate protection is available. It is the failure to address this distinction and the confusion between the two which has given rise to the current confusion over the respective role of the State in the country of origin. Representatives need to establish that there has been a failure of State protection and *not* that the State is accountable or culpable for the harm sustained or feared. This is particularly important in cases involving non-State agents. This approach to the failure of State protection in the UK, as reflected in *Adan, Subaskaran & Aitseguer*,[8] is different to that adopted in other European

---

1   *Islam and Others v SSHD* (unreported) 2 October 1996 (13956) (IAT). This case was subsequently heard in both the Court of Appeal and House of Lords.
2   *Gilani v SSHD* (unreported) 3 June 1987 (5216) (IAT).
3   *Fathi and Ahmady v SSHD* (unreported) 1 December 1996 (14264) (IAT).
4   *Gilani v SSHD* (unreported) 3 June 1987 (5216) (IAT).
5   *Fathi and Ahmady v SSHD* (unreported) 1 December 1996 (11544) (IAT). This comment was made by the initial adjudicator who had refused her appeal on the grounds that the persecution suffered was not for a Convention reason.
6   *Islam v SSHD; R v IAT ex parte Shah* [1999] INLR 144, Imm AR 283 (HL).
7   *Fathi and Ahmady v SSHD* (unreported) 1 December 1996 (11544) (IAT).
8   *R v SSHD ex parte Adan, Subaskaran & Aitseguer* [1999] INLR 1362, Imm AR 521 (CA).

countries where persecution is generally interpreted more narrowly as relating solely to the actions of State agents.

The concept of State responsibility, as outlined clearly elsewhere,[1] defines the limits of a government's accountability for human rights abuses under international refugee law, which was formulated as a back-up to, and not a replacement of, the State machinery for protection. It is meant to come into play only in situations where that protection is unavailable. In this context, refugee law reinforces the primacy of the State.[2] Insofar as it is established that meaningful State protection is available to the claimant, a fear of persecution cannot be said to exist. A person seeking to establish eligibility for asylum must therefore demonstrate more than a well-founded fear of 'serious harm'. In order to constitute persecution, such harm must be at the hands of the State or a force that the State cannot or will not control. A failure of State protection exists in the following situations:

(1) if 'serious harm' has been inflicted by the authorities or by associated organisations, groups or individuals;
(2) if 'serious harm' has been committed by others and the authorities are *unwilling* to give effective protection, because they support the actions of the private persons concerned, because they tolerate them or because they have other priorities;
(3) if 'serious harm' has been committed by others, and the authorities are *unable* to give effective protection.

Representatives should be aware that in recent years a number of countries have narrowed their interpretation of the Refugee Convention and have restricted their application of the concept of agents of persecution.[3] In some cases, it has been wrongly considered that there has been a failure of State protection only where the State's designated agents are directly implicated in persecutory measures. States have not been considered responsible if they have maintained a legal and social system in which violations of physical and mental integrity are endemic. This approach, which is fundamentally flawed, can be seen in an Act adopted by the Member States of the EU pursuant to Title VI of the Treaty setting out their Joint Position as at 4 March 1996 on the meaning of the term 'refugee'. Although this Act does not supersede the Refugee Convention, it may be used by governments to limit their international obligations. Section 5.2 deals specifically with persecution by third parties (non-State agents):

> 'Persecution by third parties will be considered to fall within the scope of the Geneva Convention where it is based on one of the grounds in Article 1A, is individual in nature and is encouraged or permitted by the authorities. Where the official authorities fail to act, such persecution should give rise to individual examination of each application for refugee status, in accordance with national judicial practice, in the light in particular of whether or not the failure to act was deliberate.'[4]

---

1 See, eg, Thomas and Beasley 1993.
2 Goldberg 1993.
3 See UNHCR 1995b.
4 Council of the European Union Joint Position defined by the Council on the basis of Article K3 of the Treaty on European Union on the *Harmonised Application of the Definition of the Term 'Refugee' in Article 1 of the Geneva Convention of 28 July 1951 Relating to the Status of Refugees.*

In order to respond to the experiences of women as asylum seekers, the assessment within the determination process of whether there has been a failure of State protection must reflect existing international obligations to protect against systematic abuse based on gender. Demanding that international refugee law reconceptualise human rights abuse to include that which has largely been deemed 'private' may face opposition from States trying to narrow the existing interpretation. However, some States, most notably Canada, the US and Australia, and latterly the UK in *Shah and Islam*,[1] have explicitly recognised that there is a failure of State protection in relation to private actions and this is reflected in their case-law. There are a number of other human rights documents such as the UN Convention on the Elimination of All Forms of Discrimination Against Women and the UN Platform for Action which explicitly articulate an obligation on the part of the State to protect against the conduct of private actors.[2]

In this context, the argument that there has been 'a failure of State protection' for refugee women fearing serious harm which is not directly at the hands of the State is clear. It will be necessary, however, for the representative to prove that State protection was not available for his or her client through research and through the use of expert evidence to substantiate the claim. In some cases, State protection may appear to be available, but the efficiency of such protection may be questionable:

> 'In determining whether the State is willing or able to provide protection to a woman fearing gender-related persecution, decision-makers should consider the fact that the forms of evidence which the claimant might normally provide as "clear and convincing proof" of State inability to protect, will not always be either available or useful in cases of gender-related persecution.'[3]

> 'In assessing gender-based persecution it is important to research the accepted norms of the relevant societies to determine how they operate both through legislation and in terms of actual practice in order to determine the degree of protection available to women.'[4]

3.4.1 Persecution by the State or an agent of the State

The UNHCR Handbook (1979) comments at para 65 that 'persecution is normally related to action by the authorities of the country'. According to Macdonald and Blake (1995) at p 390, the authorities of a country will include regional or local government or parties which control the State. Cases of sexual violence (including rape) against women often involve the security forces or other public officials yet such is the extent of the public/private dichotomy in the interpretation of refugee law, that even acts committed by the authorities are not attributed to them and are dismissed as 'private'.[5] It is also evident that there are a variety of situations in which 'serious harm' in a form other than direct physical

---

1   *Islam v SSHD; R v IAT ex parte Shah* [1999] INLR 44, Imm AR 283 (HL).
2   See Appendix 8.
3   CIRB 1996, section C.
4   ADIMA 1996, para 4.11.
5   Spijkerboer 1994.

attack is inflicted upon women by gender-based discrimination enforced through law.

The representative must establish whether a reasonable basis exists for regarding the act of persecution as one that can be attributed directly to the State. If they do not consider the State to be directly implicated, then they must determine whether the State has been unwilling or unable to provide protection.

3.4.2 Gender-based discrimination enforced through law

Serious harm need not take the form of direct attacks on the physical integrity of women. Gender-based discrimination is often enforced through law as well as through social practices. In cases of legislated discrimination, a woman will have to prove that the nature of the discrimination was sufficient to rise to the level of serious harm within the meaning of persecution. It should be noted that a woman's claim to Convention refugee status cannot be based solely on the fact that she is subject to a national law or policy to which she objects.[1] As is suggested in the Canadian guidelines, the claimant will need to establish one of the following.

(1) The law or policy is inherently persecutory

An example of legislated discrimination which could be construed as persecutory is Pakistan's *Hudood* laws. The *Hudood* laws affect all citizens of Pakistan, but are applied to women with particularly disastrous effects. Women are discriminated against by law. They find it extremely difficult to prove rape and may face criminal prosecution if they fail to do so. Women who behave in ways their husbands or fathers dislike, or who seek to divorce and re-marry, or who choose to marry against the will of their parents, or who happen to be related to a man wanted by the authorities and thus get wrongly accused of *Hudood* offences as a means of intimidating their relatives, all risk criminal prosecution under the *Hudood* laws, often with no basis in fact.

(2) The policy or law, although having 'legitimate' goals, is administered through persecutory means

An example of a discriminatory policy with a 'legitimate' end pursued through persecutory means is the 'one-child policy' in the People's Republic of China.[2] While the goal of population control might be defensible, forced sterilisation and abortions are each persecutory means of achieving the objective. Whilst the Chinese government maintains that forced abortion and sterilisation are strictly prohibited by Chinese law and offenders will be punished according to the law, the reality is very different.[1]

---

1   CIRB 1996.
2   Representatives should note that the Asylum Policy Unit has given specific instructions to decision-makers that forcible abortion and sterilisation constitute torture. See Asylum Policy Unit Internal Memo ATP 13/96 and House of Lords considerations of Lords amendments 15 July 1996, Hansard cols 822–825. See also Baroness Blatch, House of Lords Reports 20 June 1996, Hansard cols 476–477. These statements can also be found in *The Asylum and Immigration Act 1996: A compilation of ministerial statements made on behalf of the government during the Bill's passage through Parliament* (ILPA 1996).
3   See, eg, *China: One-Child Policy Update* produced by the Research Directorate of the CIRB (June 1999) and available on-line at http://www.irb.gc.ca

(3) The penalty for non-compliance with the law or policy is disproportionately severe

This approach to the issue of whether there has been a failure of State protection is particularly relevant in cases from countries such as Iran, where those in contravention of the dress code are subject to punishment which may range from a verbal reprimand, to a fine, to 74 strokes of the lash, to a prison sentence of up to one year. Women are regularly harassed and arrested or detained under legal pretexts for wearing make-up or being improperly veiled. Meanwhile, sexual segregation means that any form of friendship or association between the sexes outside the marriage contract is punishable by flogging, imprisonment, forced marriage or stoning to death. A similar argument could also be made with regard to Pakistan's *Hudood* laws and was discussed in the case of *Shah and Islam*.[1]

3.4.3 Persecution by non-State agents

'A Convention refugee is someone who is at risk because their country of nationality has failed to protect them from persecution. A failure to protect can occur in several ways. It may be that the authorities themselves are the perpetrators of persecution. However, it may be that the perpetrator is another party from whom the authorities do not protect the person either because they are unwilling or unable to do so. Claims of gender-based persecution often involved persecution committed by non-state agents.'[2]

Exposing the gendered harms that women endure may not always be sufficient to sustain a finding of persecution. Because violence against women often assumes the form of a social or cultural norm, it is frequently not recognised as a violation of women's human rights for which the State is accountable. Whilst there is no shortage of episodes where women are directly victimised by the State or by agents of the State, much of the violence committed against women is committed by non-State agents. It is perpetrated by husbands, fathers, boyfriends, in-laws, and, in the case of female genital mutilation, women in the local community:

'For most women, indirect subjection to the state will almost always be mediated through direct subjection to individual men or groups of men.'[3]

As a result, the problem for many female applicants may lie not in demonstrating that the abuse constitutes 'serious harm', but rather that the State is implicated in, or has failed to protect them from, that harm. In this context, and assuming that, except in situations where the State is in a condition of complete breakdown, States are presumed capable of protecting their citizens, it is necessary to determine whether the State is liable for failing to protect against the acts of private individuals which violate protected human rights and, if so, when.

Although there is no universally accepted definition of persecution in refugee law, the conclusion that State complicity in persecution is not a prerequisite to a valid refugee claim is supported in the drafting history of Article 1A of the Refugee Convention, the prevailing authorities and academic commentary.

---

1   *Islam v SSHD; R v IAT ex parte Shah* [1999] INLR 44, Imm AR 283 (HL).
2   ADIMA 1996, para 4.11.
3   Wright 1992, p 249, cited in Macklin 1995, p 232.

According to the UNHCR Handbook (1979), persecution can take the form of government inaction as well as government action:

> 'Where serious discriminatory or other offensive acts are committed by the local populace, they can be considered as persecution if they are knowingly tolerated by the authorities, or if the authorities refuse, or prove unable, to provide effective protection.'[1]

Where an applicant's country has denied her protection, such denial may confirm or strengthen the applicant's fear of persecution and may indeed be an element of persecution.[2] Commentators have consistently supported this approach to the failure of State protection:

> 'Behaviour tolerated by the government in such a way as to leave the victims virtually unprotected by the agencies of the state constitutes persecution for the purposes of refugee determination.'[3]

> 'Persecution includes failure, voluntary or involuntary, on the part of the state authorities to prevent or suppress violence.'[4]

In cases where the persecutor is not directly related to the government, the representative should consider whether the government was unwilling or unable to protect the applicant. It is the responsibility of the representative to establish the following:

(1) whether the applicant sought and was denied protection by the government;
(2) whether governing institutions and/or government agents were aware of the harm to the applicant and did nothing to protect her or were unable to;
(3) whether the applicant has reasons to believe that it was or would be futile to seek the protection of the government (eg if the government has denied protection to similarly situated women, or if the government has systematically failed to apply existing laws).

Representatives should be aware that although there is seemingly a theoretical consensus on this issue, whether persecution by non-State agents should result in protection under the Refugee Convention is in reality a contentious issue. This issue has been widely discussed in the **UK**, most recently by the House of Lords in *Horvath*.[5]

The issue of whether persecution by non-State agents can constitute a failure of State protection within the meaning of the Refugee Convention has been the subject of an important case at the Court of Appeal. *Adan, Subaskaran and Aitseguer*[6] concerned three applicants from Somalia, Sri Lanka and Algeria who claimed that they would be persecuted by non-State agents if returned to the country of origin. Each had passed through a 'safe third country' before seeking asylum in the UK, and the Secretary of State wanted to return them to these safe third countries for substantive consideration of their claims. Each argued that the

---

1 UNHCR 1979, para 65.
2 UNHCR 1991.
3 Grahl-Madsen 1966, p 191.
4 Goodwin-Gill 1982, p 291.
5 *Horvath v SSHD* [2000] 3 WLR 379 (HL).
6 *R v SSHD ex parte Adan, Subaskaran and Aitseguer* [1999] INLR 1362, Imm AR 521 (CA).

refugee jurisprudence of those countries was such that their applications for asylum would not properly be dealt with there because France and Germany did not recognise persecution by non-State agents as qualifying under the Refugee Convention. The Court of Appeal accepted that in the UK, unlike in France and Germany, persecution by non-State agents is recognised for the purposes of the Convention where the State is unwilling or unable to provide protection against it, and indeed whether or not there exist competent or effective governmental or State authorities in the country in question.

Representatives should be aware that these issues have recently been canvassed again in *Horvath*[1] which considered whether the failure of the State to protect itself exacerbated the seriousness of the harm suffered or feared:

> 'It is our view that the line between discrimination and persecution may be crossed when the state becomes involved (as in *Gashi*) or when the state does not provide a "sufficiency of protection" for its citizens against the most blatant forms of discrimination by sections of the populace.'

According to the decision in *Horvath* at the Court of Appeal,[2] acts by private citizens when combined with State inability to protect, may constitute 'persecution'. But it is the failure of the State to provide protection which in the view of the Court of Appeal converted the discriminatory acts into persecution (that is an objective test) rather than looking at the issue from the perspective of the allegedly persecuted (the subjective test). Perhaps the most problematic aspect of this decision, however, is Lord Stuart-Smith's minority ruling that where there are formal mechanisms in place to protect against non-State agents there is an assumption of protection:

> 'No State can guarantee the safety of its citizens. And to say that the protection must be effective suggests it must succeed in preventing attacks, which is something that cannot be achieved ... there must be in force in the country in question a criminal law which makes the violent attacks by the persecutors punishable by sentences commensurate with the gravity of the crimes. The victims as a class must not be exempt from the protection of the law. There must be a reasonable willingness by the law enforcement agencies, that is to say the police and courts to detect, prosecute and punish offenders.'

The issue of persecution by non-State agents was considered at length by the House of Lords which considered the test for determining whether there is sufficient protection against persecution in the person's country of origin.[3] Is it sufficient, to meet the standard required by the Refugee Convention, that there is in that country a system of criminal law which makes violent attacks by the persecutors punishable and a reasonable willingness to enforce that law on the part of the law enforcement agencies? In his leading judgment, Lord Hope emphasised the principle of surrogacy, and highlighted that the general purpose of the Refugee Convention is to enable a person who no longer has the benefit of protection against persecution in his own country to turn for protection to the international community. However, Lord Hope then went on to limit the

---

1   *Horvath v SSHD* [2000] 3 WLR 379 (HL).
2   *Horvath v SSHD* [2000] INLR 15 (CA).
3   *Horvath v SSHD* [2000] 3 WLR 379 (HL).

obligation for providing surrogate protection through reference to an inability on the part of States to provide complete protection:

> 'The primary duty to provide protection lies with the home state. It is its duty to establish and operate a system of protection against persecution of its own nationals. If that system is lacking the protection of the international community is available as a substitute. But the application of the surrogacy principle rests upon the assumption that, just as the substitute cannot achieve complete protection against isolated and random attacks, so also complete protection against such attacks is not to be expected of the home state. The standard to be applied is therefore not that which would eliminate all risk and would thus amount to a guarantee of protection in the home state.'

However, the judgment by Lord Clyde supports the existing approach to persecution by non-State agents insofar as a toleration of persecution is viewed as constructive persecution:

> 'The responsibility to protect the citizen which is abrogated in a case of active state persecution is still relevant in assessing what may be seen as constructive state persecution, where the ill-treatment by other citizens is encouraged or tolerated by the state without direct participation on its own part. Here the concept of encouragement or toleration on the one hand may be seen as expressing the same thing as the failure of the state to provide adequate protection. A toleration which amounts to a constructive persecution by the state and the failure of the state to provide adequate protection may be two sides of the same coin. It may be permissible to use the language of a failure of protection against the abuse as equivalent to an encouragement or toleration of the abuse or to an acquiescence in it.'

In the light of this judgment, careful analysis is required as to whether the State has encouraged or tolerated the persecution of its citizens in cases of harm inflicted by non-State agents.

3.4.4 War and effective State collapse

> 'A gender-related claim cannot be rejected simply because the claimant comes from a country where women face generalised oppression and violence.'[1]

Women are frequently subjected to various forms of serious harm during civil wars and other internal or generalised armed conflicts where the State has, to all practical purposes, collapsed. The 'privatisation' of sexual violence is particularly apparent in these contexts where it continues to be viewed as a 'normal' by-product of war. This problem is acknowledged by the UNHCR which accepts that women who are attacked by military personnel may find difficulty in showing that they are victims of persecution rather than random violence:

> 'Even victims of rape by military forces face difficulties in obtaining refugee status when the adjudicators of their claim view such attacks as a normal part of warfare.'[2]

The UNHCR Handbook (1979) at para 98 gives specific examples of circumstances in which an applicant may be unable to gain the protection of her State. These can include a state of war, civil war or other grave disturbance, which prevents the country of nationality from extending protection or makes such

---

1   CIRB 1996, section C.
2   UNHCR 1991, p 36.

protection ineffective. Representatives should be aware that some countries are also attempting to negate their international obligations in this respect.[1]

In **Canada**, the CIRB has published *Guidelines on Civilian Non-Combatants Fearing Persecution in Civil War Situations*.[2] The guidelines address the particular difficulties which are raised in claims made by civilian non-combatants fearing return to situations of civil war. A major difficulty in analysing these claims is whether or not a linkage exists between the persecution feared and one or more of the Refugee Convention grounds. The CIRB has determined in many cases that civilian non-combatants fearing return to situations of civil war are included within the definition of a Convention refugee:

> 'There is nothing in the definition of a Convention refugee which excludes its application to claimants fearing return to situations of civil war. Conversely, those fearing return to situations of civil war ought not to be deemed Convention refugees by that fact alone.'

This approach can be seen in case-law. For example, in the case of a young woman from Somalia, the CRDD held that she faced a serious risk of persecution by reason of her membership of the particular social groups of the Asharaf clan and young women without male relatives, and she would be unable to avail herself of the protection of any authority, either civil or *de facto* in Somalia.[3]

The matter of Convention-based persecution and civil wars has been the subject of determinations by **Australian** courts. For example, it has been found that '. . . it is not enough that there be a fear of being involved in incidental violence as a result of civil war or communal disturbances'.[4] In that case, the Tribunal found that the examples of harm experienced were not specifically related to the applicant's Madiban identity 'but were the result of the misfortune of being in a war-torn city and country where government had broken down and there was little protection for civilians'. However, in other cases, the Tribunal has found that being female, without the protection of male kin, does put the appellant differentially at risk of persecution. For example, the Tribunal concluded that a young woman with no family in Somalia was a refugee within the meaning of the Refugee Convention because she was differentially at risk as a result of her clan membership and gender.[5]

---

1   Eg in an Act (Council of the European Union Joint Position defined by the Council on the basis of Article K3 of the Treaty on European Union on the *Harmonised Application of the Definition of the term 'Refugee' in Article 1 of the Geneva Convention of 28 July 1951 Relating to the Status of Refugees*) adopted by the Member States of the European Union pursuant to Title VI of the Treaty setting out their Joint Position as at 4 March 1996 on the meaning of the term 'refugee', victims of generalised armed conflict are seen to fall outside the meaning of the Refugee Convention; section 6 of the Act deals specifically with civil war and other internal or generalised armed conflicts: 'Reference to a civil war or internal or generalised armed conflict and the dangers which it entails is not in itself sufficient to warrant the grant of refugee status. Fear of persecution must in all cases be based on one of the grounds in Article 1A and be individual in nature . . . in principle, use of armed forces does not constitute persecution where it is in accordance with international rules of war and internationally recognised practice'.
2   March 1996. Available on-line at http://www.cisr.gc.ca/legal/guidline/civilian/index e.stm
3   CRDD U98–01741 27 April 1999.
4   Federal Court (unreported) 28 July 1997.
5   RRT V97/07494 2 October 1997.

In the **UK**, asylum seekers from countries where there is generalised violence have typically been granted Exceptional Leave to Remain (ELR) and have not been recognised as Convention refugees:

'There is no government in Somalia, therefore it follows that there is no government persecution . . . in those circumstances, the appellant's claim must fail.'[1]

However, in this case the appellant, a citizen of Somalia, appealed against the decision to grant her ELR, and the IAT, in upholding her appeal, held that the conclusion of the adjudicator was flawed:

'It does not follow that because there is no government, or effective government, in a country riven by civil war like Somalia, an individual with identifiable tribal or factional loyalties cannot claim refugee status within the Convention.'

In *Adan*,[2] the House of Lords also considered the case of a Somali national. The House held that killing and torture incidental to a clan and sub-clan based civil war did not give rise to a well-founded fear of being persecuted within the meaning of Article 1A(2) of the Refugee Convention where the asylum-seeker was at no greater risk of such ill-treatment by reason of his clan or sub-clan membership than others at risk in the war; a 'differential impact' had to be shown.

Whether gender puts an individual female applicant from a situation of generalised violence at differential risk has been addressed by the Tribunal in several recent cases of women from Sri Lanka. In each case, it is evident that the success, or otherwise, of these arguments will continue to be closely tied to developments regarding whether women constitute a particular social group within the meaning of the Refugee Convention because they are at particular risk *because of* their gender (see below). In *Thangarajah*,[3] it was argued that the applicant had a well-founded fear of being persecuted (in the form of rape or sexual violence) on account of her membership of a particular social group, namely a woman Tamil from Jaffna. It was argued that Tamil women from Jaffna have been raped by members of the Sri Lankan army, and that because it still continues despite efforts made by the Sri Lankan authorities to put a stop to it, Tamil women from Jaffna constitute a group defined by an innate and unchangeable characteristic. The Tribunal found that there was no evidence of any concerted action on the part of the Sri Lanka army to rape or sexually assault Tamil women from Jaffna, nor was there any evidence that there is any concerted action on the part of the Sri Lankan government or authorities to rape or sexually assault Tamil women from Jaffna: 'Furthermore, all the evidence shows that the Sri Lankan authorities are, and have been, taking action to put a stop to such sexual activities by army personnel, although, unfortunately, such actions have not always been successful'.

Muralitharali[4] similarly addressed the narrow issue of whether the appellant had established a well-founded fear of persecution in Sri Lanka by virtue of a reason set out in the Refugee Convention, either as a result of her perceived political

---

1   Appeal No TH/5074/92 (unreported) 1994.
2   *SSHD v Adan* [1998] INLR 325, [1998] Imm AR 338 (HL).
3   *Thangarajah v SSHD* (unreported) 7 August 1998 (16414) (IAT).
4   *Muralitharali v SSHD* (unreported) 1 January 1999 (B20813) (IAT).

opinion, or as a member of a particular social group, that is to say a Tamil woman. It was submitted by the representative that the appellant had been the subject of a gender-based differential impact as a Tamil woman and, relying upon the judgment of Lord Hoffmann in *Shah and Islam*,[1] pointed to the need to consider discrimination as a factor contributing to her experience of persecution. This was not upheld by the Tribunal.

3.4.5   Must State protection be sought?

> 'When considering whether it is objectively unreasonable for the claimant not to have sought the protection of the State, the decision-maker should consider, among other relevant factors, the social, cultural, religious and economic context in which the claimant finds herself.'[2]

In the context of gender-related persecution, a further problem is raised by Hathaway: there is no obvious failure of State protection 'where a government has not been given an opportunity to respond to a form of harm in circumstances where protection might reasonably have been forthcoming'.[3] But when can one reasonably expect a person to turn to the authorities?

> 'There is a sufficient state connection if violence has been committed by others and theoretically speaking it is conceivable that the authorities could give effective protection, but the woman concerned cannot reasonably be expected to turn to the authorities, because she would run the risk of having to endure further violence or harassment, or because she can have reasonable doubts as to whether she will be given protection.'[4]

Both Spijkerboer (1994) and Castel (1992) argue that a woman cannot be expected to alert the authorities if this would put her life in danger. This position is supported by Justice la Forest in the much cited Canadian case of *Ward*:[5]

> 'It would seem to defeat the purpose of international protection if a claimant were required to risk his or her life seeking ineffective protection of a State, merely to demonstrate that ineffectiveness.'

In cases such as these, however, where there is not an obvious failure of State protection, the burden of proof is on the applicant. Given that refugee law applies only where national protection is unavailable, representatives must establish whether there were remedies which were meaningful, accessible and effective in the country of origin. In the **UK**, the problems for women of gaining meaningful State protection have sometimes been acknowledged. For example, a woman from Iran feared that if she were to return to Iran her life and liberty would be in danger, either from the authorities directly, or through her husband who had been violent towards her, and who under Islamic law has permission to kill her for being an unfaithful wife. The Home Office representative argued that if she had suffered at the hands of her husband she would have reported this to the

---

1   *Islam v SSHD; R v IAT ex parte Shah* [1999] INLR 144, Imm AR 283 (HL).
2   CIRB 1996, section C2. See also ADIMA 1996, para 4.14.
3   Hathaway 1990, p 130.
4   Spijkerboer 1994, p 24.
5   *Canada (Attorney General) v Ward* [1993] 2 SCR 689. This case was cited with approval by the Court of Appeal in *Horvath v SSHD* [2000] INLR 15 (CA).

authorities and obtained their protection as well as a divorce, but this was rejected by the adjudicator:

> 'The appellant did not go to the authorities in Iran for herself or her daughter to complain about her husband's violence because her husband had threatened that he would kill her if she did.'[1]

In a similar appeal case, the adjudicator recognised the futility of any approaches that the appellant might make to the Algerian authorities in protecting her from *mut'a* (temporary pleasure marriage):

> 'Certainly, as far as women in Algeria are concerned, in my view they are not a top priority as far as the government is concerned and I am not surprised that the appellant did not think it was worth her while to approach the authorities to seek protection.'[2]

3.4.6 Is there an Internal Flight Alternative (IFA)?

> 'The fear of being persecuted need not always extend to the whole of the territory of the refugee's country of nationality. Thus in ethnic clashes or in cases of grave disturbances involving civil war conditions, persecution of a specific ethnic or national group may occur in only one part of the country. In such situations, a person will not be excluded from refugee status merely because [she] could have sought refuge in another part of the same country, if under all the circumstances it would not have been reasonable to expect [her] to do so.'[3]

The principle that international protection becomes appropriate where national protection is unavailable also means that, in order to be eligible for refugee status, an applicant must demonstrate there is no reasonable internal flight alternative to leaving the country. The underlying assumption of the Refugee Convention is that sufficient national protection is inconsistent with status as an internationally recognised refugee. Refugee law exists in order to interpose the protection of the international community in situations where resort to national protection is not possible.

> 'A person cannot be said to be at risk of persecution if she can access effective protection in some part of her state of origin. Because refugee law is intended to meet the needs of only those who have no alternative to seeking international protection, primary recourse should always be to one's own state.'[4]

As a result, in assessing whether a refugee claimant's fear of persecution is well-founded, many countries take into account whether the claimant can avail him or herself of a safe place in the country of origin. This concept, sometimes known under the name of the internal flight alternative and sometimes under the name of relocation, has not, however, always been applied on a principled basis.

The issue of whether or not there is an internal flight alternative is one which is becoming increasingly important in the general context of efforts to limit overall recognition rates. In many jurisdictions around the world, 'internal flight' or

1   Appeal No HX/83732/95 (unreported) 5 December 1996.
2   Appeal No HX/66670/96 (unreported) 22 October 1996.
3   UNHCR 1979, para 91.
4   Hathaway 1991, p 133.

'internal relocation' rules are increasingly relied upon to deny refugee status to persons at risk of persecution for a Refugeee Convention reason in part, but not all, of their country of origin. In this, as in so many areas of refugee law and policy, the viability of a universal commitment to protection is challenged by divergence in State practice. Indeed, the UNHCR has expressed concern at the way in which the notion of internal flight is increasingly being used to reject asylum seekers.[1]

Because so much of the analysis of the refugee definition takes as its focus the twin issues of persecution and Refugee Convention reason, there is a tendency to overlook the fact that the fundamental concept on which the Refugee Convention is based is the notion of protection. It is in this context that *The Michigan Guidelines on the Internal Protection Alternative* (April 1999), a collective study of the relevant norms and State practice, have been produced.[2] The guidelines were initiated and drafted by James Hathaway and convened by the Programme in Refugee and Asylum Law, The University of Michigan Law School. The guidelines conclude that there is no justification in international law to refuse recognition of refugee status on the basis of a purely retrospective assessment of conditions at the time of an asylum seeker's departure from the home State. The duty of protection under the Refugee Convention is explicitly premised on a prospective evaluation of risk. Because this prospective analysis of internal protection occurs at a point in time when the asylum seeker has already left his or her home State, a present possibility of meaningful protection inside the home State exists only if the asylum seeker can be returned to the internal region adjudged to satisfy the 'internal protection alternative' criteria. A refugee claim should not be denied on internal protection grounds unless the putative asylum State is in fact able safely and practically to return the asylum seeker to the site of internal protection. Legally relevant internal protection should ordinarily be provided by the national government of the State of origin, whether directly or by lawful delegation to a regional or local government. In keeping with the basic commitment of the Refugee Convention to respond to the fundamental breakdown of State protection by establishing surrogate State protection through an interstate treaty, return on internal protection grounds to a region controlled by a non-State entity should be contemplated only where there is compelling evidence of that entity's ability to deliver durable protection. The guidelines also express a preference for the term 'internal protection alternative' over the term internal relocation/flight alternative. Internal protection emphasises that the central core of the inquiry is protection from persecution. The 'internal

---

1   See *An Overview of Protection Issues in Western Europe: Legislative Trends and Positions Taken by UNHCR* (UNHCR 1995b), pp 30–32. Surveys of the recent (and not always reconcilable) international jurisprudence are to be found in G de Moffarts, *Refugee Status and the 'Internal Flight Alternative', Refugee and Asylum Law: Assessing the Scope for Judicial Protection* (International Association of Refugee Law Judges, Second Conference, Nijmegen, 9–11 January 1997) (Nederlands Centrum Buitenlanders, 1997) 123; Hugo Storey, 'The Internal Flight Alternative Test: The Jurisprudence Re-Examined' (1998) 10 IJRL 499; ELENA Paper on the Application of the Concept of Internal Flight Alternative (October 1998); Refworld CD-Rom 7th edn (January 1998); UNHCR Position Paper, Relocation Internally as a Reasonable Alternative to Seeking Asylum – (The So-Called 'Internal Flight Alternative' or 'Relocation Principle') (February 1999).

2   See Appendix 9.

protection alternative' label itself emphasises that the issue is not one of flight or relocation, but of protection. In **New Zealand**, the Michigan guidelines were very comprehensively analysed in the case of a male applicant from India.[1]

In the **UK**, it has been held that where an asylum seeker has a well-founded fear of persecution in one part of their country of origin or habitual residence, but it is *reasonable* to expect them to locate to another part of that country, then they will not be entitled to refugee status.[2] This principle of reasonableness becomes critical when the applicant alleges that the State will not protect against so-called 'private' actions. In such situations, the representative must explore the extent to which the government can or does offer protection or redress, and the extent to which the harm extends nationally. Representatives must carefully examine the circumstances giving rise to the harm or risk of harm, as well as the extent to which government protection would be available in other parts of the country. Representatives should ask first, whether there is protection from non-State agents in other parts of the country, and secondly, even if there is, whether it is 'unduly harsh' to expect a woman to relocate there (see Box 3.3). The implications of gender in determining the reasonableness of an IFA must be recognised. For example, financial, logistical, social, cultural and other barriers may significantly affect a woman's ability to travel to another area of the country, and stay there without facing hardship, insecurity or the right to be with her family.[3] There may, however, be evidential problems in establishing this.

Box 3.3

The claimant and her teenage daughter were Tamils. Documentary evidence indicates that thousands of Tamils have been arrested in Sri Lanka and that torture and ill-treatment in army and police custody are wide-spread. There are reports of extrajudicial executions and rape by members of the security forces. In addition, the Liberation Tigers of Tamil Eelam (LTTE) continue to conscript teenage children. Jaffna would not be safe for a woman alone and her children. The claimant did not have an internal flight alternative. She did not speak Sinhala and had no family or friends in Colombo. She had been in Canada since the mid-1990s. It would be unreasonable to ask her, a young woman without her husband, to seek protection in Colombo, or any other place in Sri Lanka, with two minor children. The Refugee Division also commented on issues of support; and cordon and search, arrest and checkpoint circumstances.[4]

---

1   Refugee Appeal No 71684/99 29 October 1999.
2   See *Robinson v SSHD and IAT* [1997] Imm AR 568 (CA).
3   *Robinson v SSHD and IAT* [1997] Imm AR 568 (CA).
4   CRDD M97–06183 1 June 1999.

3.5 ESTABLISHING THE REFUGEE CONVENTION GROUND

'Serious harm', even where there is a sufficient link with the State, must also have a persecution ground if it is to form the basis for a successful asylum claim. Some of the most difficult issues in current jurisprudence arise over whether a gender-related asylum claim involves persecution 'on account of' one of the five enumerated grounds which are norms of non-discrimination:

> 'The risk faced by the refugee claimant must have some nexus to her race, religion, nationality, political opinion or membership of a particular social group. The critical question is whether but for her civil or political status she could reasonably be said to be at risk of serious intentional harm. If the risk that motivates her flight to safety is not causally related to civil or political status, the requirements of the Convention refugee definition are not met.'[1]

With the exception of 'membership of a particular social group', the enumerated persecution grounds within the Refugee Convention are relatively clear and claims to refugee status by women can often be framed within them. It has been increasingly recognised, however, that in many cases refugee women face barriers to protection which centre around the issue of ground, even though their claims of a well-founded fear of persecution are comparable to those of members of the delineated groups. For example, it is evident from existing determinations both in the UK and elsewhere, that sexual violence frequently obscures the relationship between persecution and Refugee Convention grounds. Survivors of sexual violence perpetrated in prison camps by officials, by the military or paramilitary forces often find it difficult to establish that their victimisation was linked to their religion, race, nationality, political opinion or membership of a particular social group, rather than a random expression of individual sexual violence.

In this context, feminist scholars and advocates have criticised the Refugee Convention, as well as the asylum law of individual countries, for the failure to recognise gender as a category on which a well-founded fear of persecution may be based, and several authors have called for the addition of gender as a prohibited ground of persecution, arguing that persecution may be inflicted because of the applicant's gender. These critiques suggest, for example, that the persecution of women as women exists where there is persecution for violation of societal norms requiring them to live with male relatives or persecution for refusal to conform to norms severely restricting their rights and activities.[2] Although this argument is a powerful one, it is not the principal position adopted in this book. Although there are cases where gender is the only reason for the infliction of serious harm (eg in some cases involving female genital mutilation) there is a tendency to misinterpret the causal relationship between gender and persecution. The idea of women being persecuted as women is not the same as

---

1   Hathaway 1991, p 136.
2   Cipriani 1993; Kelly 1994.

women being persecuted because they are women.[1] Often women are not persecuted because they are women but, as Spijkerboer (1994) suggests, because they refuse to be 'proper' women. This is a political issue and was examined at length in the previous chapter.

There has been increasing criticism of the failure of representatives and decision-makers to incorporate the gender-based persecution claims of women into one of the existing enumerated grounds. Political opinion and social group in particular need to be properly interpreted to encompass gender-related persecution claims, but in practice these grounds have been construed in a way which frequently serves to exclude the experiences of women as asylum seekers. In this context, the approach to the issue of persecution ground in this book follows that of the Canadian gender guidelines which encourage decision-makers to let gender inform their assessment under race, religion, nationality, or political opinion. As a last resort, 'women' (or some sub-category thereof) might qualify as a 'particular social group':[2]

> 'Although gender is not specifically enumerated as one of the grounds for establishing Convention refugee status, the definition of Convention refugee may properly be interpreted as providing protection for women who demonstrate a well-founded fear of gender-related persecution by reason of any, or a combination of, the enumerated grounds.'[3]

The grounds of political opinion and religion can, in many cases, better accommodate the experiences of women fleeing gender-based persecution:

> 'Most of the gender-specific claims involving fear of persecution for transgressing religious or social norms may be determined on grounds of religion or political opinion. Such women may be seen by the governing authorities or private citizens as having made a religious or political statement in transgressing those norms of their society, even though UNHCR Conclusion No. 39 ... contemplates the use of "particular social group" as an appropriate ground.'[4]

It is critical to the asylum applications of refugee women that those who are acting as their representatives challenge the normative interpretation of the grounds enumerated within the Refugee Convention. This will also require that detailed information about the social, political and legal position of women in their country of origin is available to the representative. Representatives should also be aware of the possible use of the ECHR and Human Rights Act 1998 where establishing the persecution ground is problematic.[5]

> 'It should be noted that these guidelines do not advocate gender as an additional ground in Refugee Convention definition. However, it should be accepted that gender can influence or dictate the type of persecution or harm suffered and the reasons for this treatment.'[6]

---

1   Macklin 1995.
2   See also Macklin 1995.
3   CIRB 1996, A.I.
4   CIRB 1996, A.III.
5   See Appendix 5.
6   ADIMA 1996, para 2.15.

3.5.1 Race

'Race . . . has to be understood in its widest sense to include all kinds of ethnic groups that are referred to as "races" in common usage . . . [R]acial discrimination . . . represents an important element in determining the existence of persecution.'[1]

Whilst race is clearly not specific to women, persecution of women for reasons of race frequently takes a gender-specific form, and both the Canadian and Australian guidelines note that race and gender may operate in tandem to explain why a claimant fears persecution:

'There may be cases where a woman claims a fear of persecution because of her race and her gender. For example, a woman from a minority race in her country may be persecuted not only for her race, but also for her gender.'[2]

'In general racism knows no gender, however persecution may be expressed in different ways against men and women. For example the persecutor may choose to destroy the ethnic identity and/or prosperity of a racial group by killing, maiming or incarcerating the men whilst the women may be viewed as propagating the ethnic identity and persecuted in a different way, such as through sexual violence.'[3]

This is reflected in Canadian case-law. For example, there have been several cases involving Somali women who are Midgans and whose husbands have died.[4] The CRDD has found that race and gender intersect in these cases to explain the extent of the discriminatory treatment to which they are subjected. Women may be targeted not simply because of their own race but also because they are perceived as propagating a racial group or ethnic identity through their reproductive role. This may also affect the form which persecution on the grounds of race takes, for example, sexual violence or control of reproduction. The association of sexual violence with persecution for reasons of race has been noted elsewhere:

'[She] has suffered discrimination and harassment by reason of her Kurdish ethnic origin since her childhood . . . The rape of the appellant is linked inextricably to her political activities . . . and also therefore inextricably linked to her Kurdish ethnic origin . . . [she] had and has a genuine fear of persecution for a Convention reason at the hands of the Turkish authorities . . . the maltreatment and sexual abuse were acts of persecution by the state.'[5]

3.5.2 Nationality

'The term "nationality" is not to be understood only as "citizenship". It also refers to membership of an ethnic or linguistic group and may occasionally overlap with the term "race". Persecution for reasons of nationality may consist of adverse attitudes and measures directed against a national (ethnic, linguistic) minority and in certain circumstances the fact of belonging to such a minority may in itself give rise to a well-founded fear of persecution.'[6]

---

1   UNHCR 1979, para 68.
2   CIRB 1996, A.II.
3   ADIMA 1996, para 4.29.
4   CRDD A98–0007325 January 1999; CRDD A98–00950 11 May 1999.
5   Appeal No HX/73695/95 (unreported) 17 May 1996.
6   UNHCR 1979, para 74.

The UNHCR Handbook (1979) also notes that 'it may not always be easy to distinguish between persecution for reasons of nationality and persecution for reasons of political opinion when a conflict between national groups is combined with political movements, particularly where a political movement is identified with a specific "nationality"'[1] and that 'although in most cases persecution for reason of nationality is feared by persons belonging to a national minority, there have been many cases in various continents where a person belonging to a majority group may fear persecution by a dominant minority'.[2] Although persecution on the grounds of nationality (as with race) is clearly not specific to women, in many instances the nature of the persecution takes a gender-specific form, most commonly that of sexual violence including rape directed particularly, although not exclusively, against women and girls. This has been recognised in an appeal case where refugee status was granted to a Bosnian woman seeking asylum in the UK:

> 'I note and accept that rape and sexual abuse of women has taken place throughout the war in the former Yugoslavia and that as a woman the appellant is at risk of such abuse ... I accept that she is at particular risk by reason of her ethnic origin and her political opposition to the authorities, probably from a non-Serb man or men, once a political opposition is apparent.'[3]

As Macklin (1995) suggests, a gender-related claim of fear of persecution may also be linked to reasons of nationality in situations where a law causes a woman to lose her nationality (ie citizenship) because of marriage to a foreign national. Whilst some nationality laws are therefore discriminatory, fear of persecution must arise not from the fact of losing nationality itself but rather the consequences which may be suffered as a result. This point is also made in the Australian guidelines:

> 'Rather than the loss of citizenship itself, [representatives] should enquire into what harm results from this loss. For example, whether it leads to loss of right of residence or loss of other privileges or benefits.'[4]

3.5.3 Religion

It is acknowledged in the UNHCR Handbook (1979) at para 71 that persecution for reasons of religion may assume various forms:

- prohibition of membership of a religious community;
- prohibition of worship in public or private;
- prohibition of religious instruction;
- serious measures of discrimination imposed on persons because they practice their religion or belong to a particular religious community.

Whilst the asylum claims of refugee women on the grounds of religion are in many cases relatively straightforward, it should be recognised that in addition to the forms indicated in the UNHCR Handbook (1979), the religious practices of many countries have significant implications for gender relations, and in

---

1   UNHCR 1979, para 75.
2   UNHCR 1979, para 76.
3   Appeal No HX/75012/94 (unreported) 24 March 1995.
4   ADIMA 1996, para 4.31.

consequence for the persecutory harm suffered or feared by the applicant. It is impossible, however, to generalise about the implications of any specific religion for women per se because much will depend upon the political context in which particular religious tenets are interpreted by the State. For example, Islam, as a religious philosophy, is interpreted through laws, regulations and social norms governing behaviour which differ significantly between countries such as Afghanistan, Algeria, Iran, Pakistan, the Sudan and Turkey. Thus the role ascribed to women in certain societies may be attributable to the requirements of the State or official religion:

> 'The failure of women to conform to this role or model of behaviour may then be perceived by the authorities or other agents of persecution as the failure to practise or to hold certain religious beliefs and as such an attempt to corrupt the society or even as a threat to the religion's continued power. This may be the case even though the woman actually holds the official religious faith but it is not evidenced by her outward behaviour.'[1]

> 'The political nature of oppression of women in the context of religious laws and ritualisation should be recognised. Where tenets of the governing religion in a given country require certain kinds of behaviour exclusively from women, contrary behaviour may be perceived by the authorities as evidence of an unacceptable political opinion that threatens the basic structure from which their political power flows.'[2]

The asylum applications of some refugee women therefore clearly reflect more generalised oppression of women through social mores which have been developed as an interpretation of certain religious principles by both the State and society:

> 'A woman who, in a theocracy for example, chooses not to subscribe to or follow the precepts of a State religion may be at risk of persecution for reasons of religion. In the context of the Convention refugee definition, the notion of religion may encompass, among other freedoms, the freedom to hold a belief system of one's choice or not to hold a particular belief system and the freedom to practice a religion of one's choice or not to practice a prescribed religion. In certain States, the religion assigns certain roles to women; if a woman does not fulfil her assigned role and is punished for that, she may have a well-founded fear of persecution for reasons of religion.'[3]

A woman may face harm for her particular religious beliefs or practices, including her refusal to hold particular beliefs, to practise a prescribed religion or to conform her behaviour in accordance with the teachings of a prescribed religion (see Box 3.4).

---

1   ADIMA 1996, para 4.30.
2   CIRB 1996, A.II.
3   CIRB 1996, A.II.

Box 3.4

Mrs S is a 32-year-old woman from Pakistan who sought asylum in the UK because she no longer believed in Islam. She feared persecution if she were forced to return to Pakistan because she had challenged the fundamentalist laws of Pakistan by trying to divorce her husband who, with his family, had subjected her to a terrifying ordeal of abuse, violence and imprisonment. Having escaped from him and come to the UK she become involved in a relationship with a man who then initiated a campaign of harassment when she ended the relationship. He subsequently contacted her husband and her father informing them of her 'adultery', 'western lifestyle' and 'blasphemous beliefs'. In the eyes of her community, Mrs S is deemed to have blasphemed by rejecting Islam. As a woman she has doubly transgressed by refusing to submit to the will of her husband and family. The case of Mrs S was initially refused by the Home Office but was allowed on appeal on grounds of religious persecution.

In another case, an Indian woman who had converted to Islam feared retribution from her family and was granted full refugee status on the grounds that her persecution was because of her religious beliefs. Her fear of reprisals were exacerbated because of both her caste and gender, as was suggested by one of the expert reports used to support her case:

> 'It is extremely unusual for a woman from such a caste to convert to Islam, and such a conversion, especially by a woman, would almost certainly lead to that person's exclusion from the society of their caste fellows and their own family ...'[1]

There is a considerable degree of overlap between the religion and political opinion grounds in many cases which involve social mores. This reflects, in considerable part, conditions in the country of origin:

> 'Given the theocratic nature of the current regime in Iran, the appellant's opposition, both to the patriarchal society comprising her extended Arab family and to the male domination of women in Iranian society at large, is conveniently addressed under both the "religion" and "political opinion" grounds ... We are satisfied on the evidence that a very substantial element of the appellant's case, falls within the "religion" and "political opinion" categories of the Convention.'[2]

As a result, a substantial component of the analysis relating to religion and gendered social mores is confined to the subsequent section, partly to avoid repetition but also because political opinion is the most accepted, and possibly also the most flexible, ground enumerated within the Refugee Convention. This is not to imply, however, that one ground has greater validity than another or that a claim for asylum cannot be based on two grounds simultaneously. Where religious tenets require certain kinds of behaviour from a woman, contrary

---

1   Appeal No TH/61272/94 (unreported) 7 February 1996.
2   New Zealand Refugee Status Appeals Authority Appeal No 2039/93 12 February 1996.

behaviour may be perceived as evidence of an unacceptable religious opinion regardless of what a woman herself actually believes.

3.5.4 Actual or imputed political opinion

'Political opinion', actual or imputed, is probably the least disputed of all the grounds included in the Refugee Convention definition, not least because it implies some direct relationship to the State. What constitutes political opinion as a ground for persecution is outlined in the UNHCR Handbook (1979):[1]

> 'Holding political opinions different from those of the Government is not in itself a ground for claiming refugee status, and an applicant must show that [she] has a fear of persecution for holding such opinions. This presupposes that the applicant holds opinions not tolerated by the authorities, which are critical of their policies or methods. It also presupposes that such opinions have come to the notice of the authorities or are attributed by them to the applicant.'[2]

Persecution for reasons of political opinion implies, therefore, that an applicant holds an opinion that either has been expressed or has come to the attention of the authorities. However, the UNHCR Handbook (1979) accepts that there may be situations in which the applicant has not given any expression of her opinions:

> 'An applicant claiming fear or persecution because of political opinion need not show that the authorities of [her] country of origin knew of [her] opinions before [she] left the country. [She] may have concealed [her] political opinion and never have suffered any discrimination or persecution. However, the mere fact of refusing to avail [herself] of the protection of [her] Government, or a refusal to return, may disclose the applicant's true state of mind and give rise to a fear of persecution. In such circumstances the test of well-founded fear would be based on an assessment of the consequences that an applicant having certain political dispositions would have to face if [she] returned.'[3]

Such an interpretation is also found in Macdonald and Blake which accepts that 'a person who has not previously expressed [her] political dislike of the regime may be exposed by the very fact of flight and claiming asylum'.[4] This aspect of actual or imputed political opinion may be particularly relevant for women fleeing gender-based social mores and discrimination, and also where generalised oppression has rendered the expression of political opinion particularly difficult for women.

Given the overwhelming emphasis and legitimacy placed by the jurisdiction of most States on political opinion as the grounds for persecutory treatment, those representing refugee women need to argue claims on this basis wherever possible. However, the archetypal image of a political refugee as someone who is fleeing persecution for their direct involvement in political activity does not always correspond with the reality of many women's experiences. The predominant interpretation of persecution on the grounds of political opinion exemplifies the problem of a definition which has typically been seen in terms of male

---

1   UNHCR 1979, paras 80–86 inclusive.
2   UNHCR 1979, para 80.
3   UNHCR 1979, para 83.
4   Macdonald and Blake 1995, p 394.

experience and this is reflected, for example, in the questions asked at asylum interviews and in asylum questionnaires. Women are less likely than their male counterparts to be involved in high profile political activity and are more often involved in so-called 'low level' political activities which reflect dominant gender roles. Women may themselves not describe their activities as 'political'. They are also frequently attributed with political opinions and subjected to persecution because of the activities of their male relatives. The implications of such an interpretation for female refugees form the basis of the analysis in this section, not least because women's asylum claims frequently concern declarations of fear on account of a political opinion which relates directly to gender:

> 'In some societies, overt demonstration of political opinion by women may not be possible as women are not allowed to formally participate in political life ... Furthermore, the fact that a woman may challenge particular social conventions about the manner in which women should behave may be considered political by the authorities and may attract persecutory treatment on this basis.'[1]

Framing women's asylum claims as related to actual or imputed political opinion avoids the practical and political problems often associated with 'membership of a particular social group', and more accurately reflects the socio-political context of women's experiences which was discussed in Chapter 2. Proper interpretation of the Refugee Convention requires recognition of the conflict over what is 'public' and what is 'private':

> 'Whether or not the state may infringe on the religious or political views citizens hold is a deeply political issue. Therefore questions of whether or not a woman is free to choose to wear a veil or not, to be circumcised, to exercise the human right to have an education, to be free from male violence are about the demarcation of the "public" and "private" sphere. Conflicts concerning the demarcation of privacy are conflicts of a most essentially political nature, and should be considered as such in evaluating a claim to refugee status.'[2]

Whilst political opinion appears to suggest traditional 'public' political activity, a broad interpretation of the ground is possible and may include, for example, opposition to social mores and institutionalised discrimination against women.

> 'Where the persecution of women is concerned, it should be recognised that an imputed Convention ground is an important aspect to consider.'[3]

To make a claim of persecution on the basis of political opinion, a woman has to demonstrate a relationship between her political opinion and her fear of persecution. In evaluating whether a woman's fear of persecution is 'on account of political opinion', it will be argued here that where she is not directly involved in political activity in the conventional sense, a claim for refugee status requires that political opinion be properly understood to include an opinion regarding the treatment or status of women within her country, culture or social, religious or ethnic group.[4] It should also be recognised that women are often aligned with the views of their male relatives. This interpretation is consistent with the UNHCR

---

1   ADIMA 1996, para 4.25.
2   Spijkerboer 1994, p 46.
3   ADIMA 1996, para 4.23.
4   Kelly 1994.

Handbook (1979) at para 80, which holds that persecution on account of political opinion includes persecution because the authorities attribute an opinion to the applicant and, as such, does not require prior political activity. It is also compatible with case-law in the US, specifically *Hernandez-Ortiz*[1] and *Bolanos-Hernandez*[2] which has concluded that the determination of what is 'political' need not focus solely on the actions of the applicant.[3] This interpretation of the definition suggests that political opinion encompasses actions of the government as well, particularly whether the government restricts a person's privilege to hold a certain opinion.

The experiences of women must be located in the political context in which they occur. Women may not directly claim, in either oral or written statements, that persecution in their home country was due to political opinion although the existing regime may in fact impute them with holding such an opinion.

3.5.5 Membership of a particular social group

The UNHCR Handbook includes a definition of social group which is notable for its breadth and simplicity: 'a "particular social group" normally comprises persons of similar background, habits or social status'.[4] Whilst noting that mere membership of a particular social group will not normally be enough to substantiate a claim to refugee status, the UNHCR Handbook does accept that 'there may, however, be special circumstances where mere membership can be a sufficient ground to fear persecution'.[5] Given that the intentions of the drafters of the Refugee Convention remain opaque, it is perhaps not surprising that the interpretation of 'membership of a particular social group' should have provided the focus of extensive debate as to its meaning. What is clear, however, is a general consensus that any attempt at a definition should be open-ended so that it can include different groups suffering persecution:[6]

> 'A broad interpretation of the term social group is ... the only reasonable interpretation.'[7]

> 'The intention of the framers of the Convention was ... in order to provide a "safety net" for asylum-seekers who, fleeing persecution, should qualify for refugee status but fail to fall neatly into one of the enumerated categories.'[8]

Hathaway (1991) proposes three alternative classes for social group membership which are closely reflected in the Supreme Court of Canada decision in *Ward*.[9] The most important point to note is that the court named gender, along with linguistic background and sexual orientation, as an example of a particular social group in the first category. Meanwhile, as is noted by Macdonald and Blake

---

1 *Hernandez-Ortiz v INS* 777 F.2d 509 (9th Cir) (1985).
2 *Bolanos-Hernandez v INS* 767 F.2d 1277 (9th Cir) (1984).
3 Mulligan 1990.
4 UNHCR 1979, para 77.
5 UNHCR 1979, para 79.
6 Grahl-Madsen 1966; Goodwin-Gill 1983; Hathaway 1991.
7 Helton 1983, p 59.
8 Neal 1988, p 229.
9 *Canada (Attorney General) v Ward* [1993] 2 SCR 689.

(1998) at p 394, the definition of social group in the US case of *Acosta*[1] has been widely cited:

> 'We interpret the phrase to mean persecution that is directed toward an individual who is a member of a group of persons all of whom share a common immutable characteristic. The shared characteristic might be an innate one such as sex, colour, or kinship ties, or in some circumstances it might be a shared characteristic that defines the group such as former military leadership or land ownership ... whatever the common characteristic that defines the group, it must be one that the members of the group cannot change because it is fundamental to their individual identities or conscience. Only when this is the case does the mere fact of group membership become something comparable to the other four grounds for persecution.'

In other jurisdictions, therefore, the concept of social group has been carefully considered, but it has been fully canvassed before the English courts only more recently in *Savchenkov*[2] and *Shah and Islam*.[3]

In *Savchenkov*,[4] the court was referred to the approach of Hathaway and the decision in *Ward*.[5] The most important aspect of the case is that Treasury counsel advanced the view that social group could be defined as follows:

(1) membership of a group defined by some innate or unchangeable characteristic of its members analogous to race, religion, nationality or political opinion, for example, their sex, linguistic background, tribe, family or class;
(2) membership of a cohesive, homogenous group whose members are in a close voluntary association for reasons which are fundamental to their rights;[6]
(3) former membership of the group covered in (2).

However, the court also concluded that a social group for Refugee Convention purposes must be identifiable by something other than the risk of persecution and cannot be defined solely by common victimisation:

> 'The concept of a "particular social group" must have been intended to apply to social groups which exist independently of the persecution. Otherwise the limited scope of the Convention would be defeated: there would be a social group, and so a right to asylum, whenever a number of persons fear persecution for a reason common to them.'

One of the implications of this ruling, therefore, is that the shared experience of women who have suffered violence is not sufficient to make them a social group unless the fact of their violation will, in the future, make them a target of persecution.

That women constitute a particular social group within the meaning of the Refugee Convention definition has been the pervasive position in literature

---

1   *Acosta v INS* [1985] Int Dec 2986 (BIA).
2   *SSHD v Savchenkov* [1996] Imm AR 28 (CA).
3   *Islam v SSHD; R v IAT ex parte Shah* [1999] INLR 144, Imm AR 283 (HL).
4   *SSHD v Savchenkov* [1996] Imm AR 28 (CA).
5   *Canada (Attorney General) v Ward* [1993] 2 SCR 689.
6   It should be noted that the requirement for 'cohesiveness' was disapproved by the House of Lords in *Islam v SSHD; R v IAT ex parte Shah* [1999] INLR 144, Imm AR 283 (HL).

addressing gender-related persecution and the problem of establishing the persecution ground.[1] It is also the position taken by Hathaway:

> 'Gender is properly within the ambit of the social group category ... [g]ender-based groups are clear examples of social subsets defined by an innate and immutable characteristic.'[2]

He offers the example of single women living in a Muslim country without the protection of a male relative who suffer persecution as a result, pointing out that in this case group members cannot control gender or the absence of male relatives, and that choice of marital status is a fundamental human right that no one should be required to relinquish. The argument is that women constitute a social group both because they share certain 'immutable' characteristics and because they are frequently treated differently from men: '[t]o a greater extent than most social groups, women are an easily identifiable "group" ... possessing a combination of biologically and socially attributed characteristics'.[3] This position suggests that 'more liberal interpretation', 'innovative use' and 'development' of the concept of social group membership would meet the protection needs of women seeking asylum.

The use of the particular social group basis of the refugee definition to extend protection to women who face persecution for having transgressed religious or social mores finds strong support in the pronouncements of the UNHCR and governmental bodies and the administrative decisions of several countries. During the 1980s, the UNHCR adopted a series of Executive Committee Conclusions aimed at affording more meaningful protection to women fleeing persecution in their home countries,[4] and its *Guidelines on the Protection of Refugee Women* (1991) encourage States to address the claims of women who face violence as severe as death for violating social mores under the particular social group category. Meanwhile, as early as 1984, the European Parliament adopted a resolution calling upon States to accord refugee status to women within the particular social group category in certain circumstances, a position reflected in the policies of the Dutch Refugee Council.[5] The CIRB has also affirmed gender-related social group classification in cases involving Lebanese, Turkish Muslim and Sri Lankan Tamil women reflecting a recognition of gender-based social groups in its own guidelines:

> 'Gender is an innate characteristic and, therefore, women may form a particular social group within the Convention refugee definition.'[6]

The argument for framing the asylum claims of women within a 'particular social group' as the persecution ground is a powerful one and has proved to be a relatively acceptable approach in some jurisdictions. Yet there are both political and strategic concerns associated with arguing for women as a social group which

---

1   See, eg, Neal 1988; Greatbach 1989; Stairs and Pope 1990; Castel 1992; Goldberg 1993; Fullerton 1993; Kelly 1993, 1994; Binion 1995.
2   Hathaway 1991, p 591.
3   Stairs and Pope 1990, p 167.
4   See Appendix 1.
5   Schilders 1988.
6   CIRB 1996, A.III.

should be recognised. The first of these relates to the size of the social group itself, although this argument has no basis in fact or reason:

> 'The fact that the particular social group consists of large numbers of the female population in the country concerned is irrelevant – race, religion, nationality and political opinion are also characteristics that are shared by large numbers of people.'[1]

Recognising that some 'women' constitute a 'particular social group' does not lead inexorably to the consequence that all women are automatically entitled to refugee status. The applicant will still be required to establish that the fear of persecution is well-founded, that the nature of the harm inflicted or anticipated rises to the level of serious harm, and that there is a failure of State protection. Nonetheless, the reality is that the perceived size of the prospective social group is important in a context where there is an overall trend towards trying to reduce the number of asylum seekers and limit recognition rates.

More importantly, arguing that 'women' per se constitute a 'particular social group' is unlikely to be widely accepted, not simply because of the issue of numbers but because, in reality, 'women' are not a cohesive group. Even within individual countries, women fall into their own sub-groups, economically, socially and culturally. Whilst there are undoubtedly cases where gender alone is the basis for persecutory treatment, more often the persecution is not applied equally to all women. Neal offers the example of a woman who is forced to flee because she has in some way violated oppressive laws and regulations imposed by the government and fears persecution, possibly even in the form of execution, as a result. Whilst these rules are specific to women 'not every woman who comes from an oppressive society will qualify [for refugee status]',[2] partly because women have different experiences of these rules but also because the relationship between the persecution and the ground will vary dependent upon the circumstances of the individual woman. Despite the arguments in favour of recognising women as a social group, therefore, the very assumption that women have common experiences which can be explained by reference to their gender alone can itself undermine the argument.

Examining more rigorously the relationship between the nature of persecutory measures against women and the potential grounds of the application shows that, in many cases, such claims can be framed within more conventional and accepted grounds if gender relations, which by implication involve issues of power, are reconceptualised. Going beyond the public/private dichotomy, it could be argued that women who refuse to comply with, or transgress social mores, for example by choosing to remain single, are not being persecuted because they are women but because they are actively opposing a political/ religious norm.[3] Returning to the example cited by Hathaway (1991) of 'single women living in a Muslim country without the protection of a male relative' as constituting a particular social group within the meaning of the definition, it could be argued that such women are actually being persecuted because they are expressing a political or religious opinion. This case highlights the importance of

1   CIRB 1996, A.III.
2   Neal 1988, p 245.
3   This approach to the political identity of women is examined in detail in Chapter 2, above.

examining and framing each claim on the basis of the individual woman's experience. If women have chosen to live without a male relative and are then persecuted because of this decision, the ground should be political opinion (or at the very least imputed political opinion). The level of proactivity on the part of the applicant then becomes critical. By subsuming the claims of all women into the social group category, proactivity may be lost. In many cases, the asylum claims of women argued on a social group basis are more likely to fail than the claims of men, in part because the relationship between persecution and ground is incorrectly conceptualised. As is suggested in the Australian guidelines,[1] 'the important principle to consider is whether the persecution suffered or feared is for reasons of membership of a particular social group'. Framing the appellant's claim with race, nationality, religion or political opinion (actual or imputed) as the grounds for the persecution not only more accurately reflects women's specific experiences in many cases, but also enables the representative to argue that the claim fits comfortably within the Refugee Convention and that she should be granted full refugee status. Strategically, it is also the favoured approach given the Home Office position on the issue of social group:

> 'The UK Government interprets paragraph (k) of EXCOM 39 as indicating no obligation to grant asylum on the basis of women being a social group ... gender is taken into account in the assessment of individual asylum claims where this is relevant. However, casework experience suggests that in practice few, if any, asylum applications made in the UK by women turn solely on the question of gender-based persecution.'[2]

Nonetheless, recent case-law, most notably *Shah and Islam*,[3] has changed this position. Syeda Shah was born in Pakistan but lived in the UK between 1968 and 1972. When she was 17 she returned to Pakistan and married. She had six children. Throughout the marriage her husband beat her up regularly and finally, in 1992, she returned to the UK, leaving her children with members of the extended family in Pakistan. She was granted leave to enter for six months as a visitor. On arrival in the UK she discovered that she was pregnant and her seventh child was born in this country in December 1992. In June 1994 (having been served in the meantime with notice of illegal entry), she applied for asylum on the basis that if she were to return to Pakistan she would be accused of adultery and exposed to the operation of the *sharia* law statutes which prescribe stoning to death as punishment. Her application for asylum was refused by the Home Office and her case heard by an adjudicator in July 1995. Her fear of persecution by her husband was held to be well-founded, aggravated, as it now was, by the fear that he would treat her seventh child as illegitimate and rely on that to brand her as an adulteress and bring or support criminal proceedings against her. However, the adjudicator dismissed her appeal on the basis that Mrs Shah came within no accepted definition of a particular social group within the meaning of the Refugee Convention. Having been refused leave to appeal by the IAT, she obtained leave to apply for judicial review to challenge that refusal. In October 1996, Mr Justice Sedley, in quashing the determination of the IAT, implicitly accepted that where gender-based discrimination is enforced through law, either

---

1   ADIMA 1996, para 4.33.
2   *International Journal of Refugee Law* (Special Issue) Autumn 1997, p 71.
3   *Islam v SSHD; R v IAT ex parte Shah* [1999] INLR 144, [1999] Imm AR 283 (HL).

in the form of a law or policy which is inherently discriminatory or as a law or policy for which the penalty for non-compliance is disproportionately severe, then State responsibility, and hence persecution, can be said to exist. He also held that whilst the final outcome would depend on the factual findings, the facts so far gathered suggested that Mrs Shah was capable of bringing herself within the definition of membership of a particular social group. The Secretary of State appealed against this decision.

The case of Shahana Islam was similar to that of Syeda Shah in some respects. Mrs Islam was born in Pakistan where she trained as a teacher. Whilst she was at college she was supporter of the PPP. She married her husband in 1976 and only afterwards discovered that she was his second living wife. Although she was shocked, the marriage was maintained and she subsequently had two children. Throughout the marriage Mrs Islam was subjected to abuse and physical violence by her husband. Then, in 1990, a fight broke out in her school between young people who supported the PPP and others who supported the MQM. She intervened and incurred the hostility of the MQM faction who subsequently harassed her and made accusations of infidelity against her. These were made, inter alia, to her husband who, in consequence, beat her more violently. Her injuries were serious enough to require hospital treatment. She left her husband and went to the house of her brother who is paralysed and could not protect her. Night visits were made to his home by unknown men threatening him and carrying guns. In October 1991, following a short stay in an Army Club, Mrs Islam and her children came to the UK. She was granted leave to enter as a visitor for six months and applied for asylum five days later. Mrs Islam believed that if she returned she would be abused and probably killed. She could not seek assistance from the authorities because in Pakistani society women are either not believed or are treated with contempt by police. Mrs Islam was refused asylum by the Home Office and appealed. Her fear of persecution was held to be well-founded but her appeal was dismissed by the IAT on the basis that she had established no Refugee Convention ground for the persecution. Mrs Islam appealed against this decision.

The cases of *Shah and Islam*[1] were heard together by the Court of Appeal in 1997. After lengthy deliberations, the Court concluded that neither woman could be protected as Refugee Convention refugees but recommended that they be granted exceptional leave to remain given that the facts of the case, and the existence of a well-founded fear of persecution should they be returned, were not in dispute. The Court of Appeal accepted that both women had a well-founded fear that in the event of their being forced to return to Pakistan they would suffer persecution. This would take the form of physical and emotional abuse by their husbands which the local Islamic law would not only condone but would aggravate. Under the criminal processes of *sharia* law, the punishment for sexual immorality is severe and may lead to death by stoning. In reaching its decision, the Court of Appeal gave consideration to both domestic and international

---

1   *R v IAT and SSHD ex parte Shah* [1998] 1 WLR 74, [1998] INLR 97 (CA).

authority, specifically *Trujullo*[1] in the United States and *Ward*[2] in Canada. The three possible sub-categories which were accepted as coming within the category of a particular social group were subsequently qualified in *Chan*.[3] The court also referred to the Australian case of *A*[4] in the High Court which dealt with refugees from China's enforced sterilisation or abortion policy. The domestic authority which was considered was principally the cases of *Savchenkov*[5] and *Quijano*.[6] The Court of Appeal referred to the 'Savchenkov principles' which were advanced by the Secretary of State without dissent. These principles are that:

(1) the Refugee Convention does not entitle a person to asylum whenever he fears persecution if returned to his own country but rather must establish that the fear of persecution is related to one of the grounds enumerated in Article 1A(2) of the Refugee Convention;

 (2) to give the phrase 'membership of a particular social group' too broad an interpretation would conflict with this objective;

(3) whilst the other 'Refugee Convention reasons' (race, religion, nationality and political opinion) reflect a civil or political status, 'membership of a particular social group' should be interpreted *eiusdem generis*; and

(4) the concept of a 'particular social group' must have been intended to apply to social groups which exist independently of persecution.

Otherwise, the limited scope of the Refugee Convention would be defeated. There would be a social group, and so a right to asylum, whenever a number of persons fear persecution for a reason common to them.

In the cases of both *Shah and Islam*,[7] the adjudicators at the first-level appeal stage had concluded that the social group of which it was claimed they were members did not exist independently of the persecution feared. In *Shah*,[8] the special adjudicator had concluded that 'it is no more possible for a woman who has suffered domestic violence to bring herself within the meaning of social group in the Refugee Convention than it is for anyone who has been divorced to say that she/he is a member of a social group for the purposes of [the] Convention or,

---

1   *Sanchez Trujullo v INS* [1986] 801 F.2d 1571. This case dealt with a claim to refugee status by El Salvadorans who had been non-combatants in the war in their own country and feared persecution on that account if they were repatriated.

2   *Ward v Attorney General* [1993] 2 SCR 689. This case dealt with an asylum claim by a resident of Northern Ireland who had joined a paramilitary terrorist group (the INLA) and had been sentenced to death for a breach of the group's orders.

3   *Chan v Canada* [1996] 28 DLR 213. This case concerned an applicant fleeing from China's policy of forced sterilisation and the consequences for those with more than one child. The three possible sub-categories identified by Judge la Forest were '(1) groups defined by an innate and unchangeable characteristic; (2) groups whose members voluntarily associate for reasons so fundamental to their human dignity that they should not be forced to forsake the association and (3) groups associated by a former voluntary status, unalterable due to its historical permanence.' In *Chan*, Judge la Forest felt obliged to qualify his second category by saying ' . . . a refugee alleging membership in a particular group does not have to be in voluntary association with other persons similar to him – or herself. Such a claimant is in no manner required to voluntarily associate, ally, or consort with kindred persons'.

4   *A v Australia (MIEA)* [1998] INLR 1 (High Court of Australia).

5   *SSHD v Savchenkov* [1996] Imm AR 28 (CA).

6   *Quijano v SSHD* [1997] Imm AR 227 (CA).

7   *Islam v SSHD; R v IAT ex parte Shah* [1999] INLR 144, Imm AR 283 (HL).

8   *R v IAT and SSHD ex parte Shah* [1997] Imm AR 145 (IAT).

indeed, for anyone who has a criminal record to be able to say similarly'. In Islam, the IAT has concluded that Pakistani women subjected to violence within the family were not a social group within the Refugee Convention: 'That they are simply women does not make them a social group: the only characteristic identified is that they are subject to violence within marriage, the only common features, beyond their sex, is the persecution to which they are alleged to be subject within marriage, that is the persecution itself'. The Court of Appeal similarly accepted the Secretary of State's argument that the social group has to exist independently of the persecution feared. Waite LJ concluded that the features relied upon in this case could not be shown to exist independently of the persecution feared: 'The heads of persecution relied on are extreme violence at the hands of a husband or his associated, legal disabilities and discrimination, the harshness of *sharia* law and the absence of protection by the authorities. Take all those away, and the stigma and the isolation necessarily depart with them. They are not independent attributes of a particular social group.' Mrs Shah and Mrs Islam subsequently sought and were granted leave to appeal to the House of Lords. The principal issue before the House of Lords was the meaning and application of the words 'membership of a particular social group'. In a split decision, the House of Lords concluded that women in Pakistan did constitute a particular social group within the meaning of the Refugee Convention. This position was held particularly strongly by Lord Hoffmann who argued that there was an important relationship between the discriminatory treatment feared by the two appellants, and their inability to access the protection of the State. Pakistani women are discriminated against and as a group they are unprotected by the State. Indeed, the State tolerates and sanctions the discrimination. The House of Lords held that, in line with the *Savchenkov* principles, this group, whose unifying characteristics included gender, suspicion of adultery and lack of protection, existed independently of the persecution.

Following the House of Lords decision in *Shah and Islam*,[1] the Asylum Directorate's Instructions to decision-makers on the definition of particular social groups within the meaning of the Refugee Convention were revised.[2] The impact on asylum claims made by women is not yet clear. Much will be dependent upon the future development of appropriate case-law which responds to the needs of gender-defined social groups. Whilst it is important that political opinion is considered where appropriate, an approach to refugee determination which unjustifiably favours the political opinion ground to the exclusion of the social group ground will tend to reinforce the male gender bias complained of by female asylum seekers, and inhibit the development of refugee jurisprudence which properly recognises and accommodates gender issues within the legitimate bounds of the Refugee Convention. There may be some cases, for example those involving FGM, where gender is the most critical aspect of the applicant's case. For these cases, the existence of case-law recognising that women or particular sub-sets of women can constitute a particular social group within the meaning of the Refugee Convention is a welcome development. However, actual or imputed political opinion remains the most appropriate ground for the majority of claims involving women as asylum seekers.

---

1   *Islam v SSHD; R v IAT ex parte Shah* [1999] INLR 44, [1999] Imm AR 283 (HL).
2   See Appendix 10.

Chapter 4

WOMEN'S POLITICAL PARTICIPATION AND RESISTANCE

4.1 WOMEN AND POLITICS

The concept of 'politics' is critical to any analysis of the determination process. This is reflected in the tendency to refer to the concept of 'political asylum' despite the existence of the other enumerated grounds. However, the dominant interpretation of 'politics' as being concerned principally or wholly with the public sphere is problematic because it fails to take into account the context in which women's participation and resistance takes place. Women are as vulnerable to political violence as their male counterparts even though their political participation often takes place at a so-called 'low level'. In some cases, they are even more likely to be persecuted. However, women's political participation continues to be marginalised within existing policy and practice and the challenge which is posed to the authority of the State by various forms of gendered resistance is underestimated. Women's experiences are effectively depoliticised. This can be illustrated by the now infamous case of *Campos-Guardado*[1] in the US in which the court considered the claim of a woman whose family members had been politically active in El Salvador. Armed attackers came to her home, bound the applicant and other female family members and forced them to watch while the attackers murdered male family members. The attackers then raped the applicant and the other female family members while one attacker chanted political slogans. In what might appear to be an extreme assessment of the evidence, the court affirmed the Immigration Board's determination that the applicant had not established that the attackers were motivated by a political opinion they imputed to the victim. This interpretation of the Refugee Convention has been explicitly criticised in the INS guidelines:

> 'Reasonable minds could differ over this record. The court might reasonably have concluded that the chanting of political slogans during the rape indicated not merely that the attackers were politically motivated, but more specifically that they believed the appellant to have contrary political views and that they punished her because of it.'[2]

By contrast, the Third Circuit in *Fatin*[3] held that there is 'little doubt that feminism qualifies as a political opinion within the meaning of the relevant statutes'. The political opinion of the applicant in that case did not, however, provide a basis for refugee status; although she had shown that she generally possessed political beliefs about the role of women in society which collided with those prevailing in Iran, the appellant had not shown that she would risk severe

---

1   *Campos-Guardado v INS* [1987] 809 F.2d 285 (5th Cir).
2   INS 1995, IIIA.
3   *Fatin v INS* [1993] 12 F.3d 1233 (3rd Cir).

enough punishment simply for holding such views. However, the case makes it clear that an applicant who can demonstrate a well-founded fear of persecution on account of her beliefs about the role and status of women in society could be eligible for refugee status on account of actual or imputed political opinion.

The tendency to depoliticise and 'personalise' the experiences of women as asylum seekers is particularly evident where the serious harm suffered or feared takes the form of sexual violence. The occurrence of sexual violence in refugee producing situations has been well documented and would appear to be a major factor in forced migration, although the true scale of sexual violence against refugee women is unknown because numerous incidents are never reported.[1] Sexual violence, including rape, occurs in a variety of different situations. It may be explicitly politically motivated (eg as a method of interrogation or as part of a process of 'ethnic cleansing') or can occur in situations of generalised violence such as civil war. Women who are on their own may be particularly vulnerable to this kind of abuse, as are women detained on political grounds, either because of their own activities, or because of the activities of absent husbands or other family members. However, representatives should be aware that the appearance of sexual violence in an asylum claim has specific implications for the way in which the relationship between women and the State is conceptualised, and therefore the decision as to whether a failure of State protection can be said to have occurred. Even where women are sexually abused by agents of the State, the sexual nature of the offence may serve to incorrectly personalise it in the eyes of the decision-maker.

The concept of politics includes those forms of participation and resistance in which women are more likely to be involved. The term should also be understood to include an opinion regarding the treatment or status of women within their country, culture or social, religious or ethnic group. Where the persecution of women is concerned, a political opinion may be imputed to her, regardless of what she herself actually believes. This may result from her actions or failure to act or may stem from the fact that the views of women are often aligned with those of their male relatives and/or associates. The interpretation of political opinion to include an opinion which is imputed is consistent with the UNHCR Handbook[2] which holds that persecution on account of political opinion includes persecution because the authorities attribute an opinion to the applicant and, as such, does not require prior political activity. This wider interpretation of the definition suggests that political opinion encompasses actions of the government as well, particularly whether the government restricts a person's privilege to hold a certain opinion. This has been accepted in the **UK** in *Asante*[3] and *Danian*.[4] It is also consistent with the approach of Hathaway (1991) who points out that the broad characterisation of political opinion is an important means of maintaining the Refugee Convention's vitality in circumstances where the basis for oppression may not be readily ascertainable.

---

1   Spijkerboer 1994; UNHCR 1995a.
2   UNHCR 1979 at para 80.
3   *Asante v SSHD* [1991] Imm AR 78 (IAT).
4   *Danian v SSHD* [1999] INLR 533 (IAT).

In order to understand properly the experiences of women as asylum seekers, representatives must ensure that those experiences are located in the political context in which they occur. Women may not directly claim, in either oral or written statements, that persecution in their home country was due to political opinion although the existing regime may in fact impute them with holding such an opinion. It is important not to underestimate the political dimension in these cases, although women may not regard themselves as making a political statement, but merely a statement of their discontent.

4.1.1 Direct involvement in formal political activity

Women are generally assumed to participate in politics less frequently, less forcefully, and less readily than men. Where women's political participation is acknowledged, it is commonly held to be less sophisticated and, in many cases, less 'authentically' political. The male-oriented portrayal of women's relation to politics has served to exaggerate gender differences in political participation. Many women from a variety of different countries *do* participate in politics as conventionally defined. This includes, but is not limited to, the following:

– political parties or organisations;
– resistance groups;
– revolutionary struggles and State militaries;
– trade unions;
– women's/feminist organisations;
– grassroots and/or community organisations.

Women's participation in conventional politics is nonetheless limited by the masculinist nature of many political organisations and movements. Women around the world are often prevented from fully participating in formal political organisations by a number of factors including their domestic obligations, local customs, poverty and a lack of education, as well as structural reasons associated with the organisations themselves. This is reflected in the tendency for women to participate less than men in formal politics the higher up the echelons of power you look. For example, one woman seeking asylum in the UK commented that 'it is more difficult and more humiliating for women to participate because of their narrow minds . . . the authorities and the police. They try to put women aside in politics. But when I was released I continued my political activities in a clandestine way and tried to keep it a secret'.[1] Another woman who is currently awaiting a decision on her asylum claim following persecution on the basis of a political opinion imputed to her in the former Zaire, described how one of the soldiers who arrested her for her involvement in a student demonstration had said, '. . . you women should behave and not follow men . . .'.

There are two important consequences of this process of political marginalisation. First, the risks of participation may be even greater for women than their male counterparts, and secondly, women find ways of exercising informal political influence when politics is less institutionalised and may prefer, even in institutionalised political systems, to participate in ad hoc or protest politics.

---

1   Comments made by a Kurdish woman from Turkey during an interview with the author.

(1)   The risks of participation may be even greater for women than for their male counterparts

Whilst women are frequently engaged in so-called 'low level' political activity, they may actually be at greater risk of persecution. Women who are politically active are punished not only because they oppose the regime in some way, but because they challenge dominant gender ideologies by being politically active at all; in other words the challenge by politically active women to the ideological separation of public and private can exacerbate the persecutory treatment. Politically active women, therefore, run the risk of 'double punishment'. They are punished not only because they oppose the regime in some way, but because they shirk the traditional role of women by being politically active at all: 'in the case of political activists, women are not only assaulted on the basis of their political opinion, but also because, as women, they should not participate in the political arena'.[1] Agger (1992) and Pettman (1996) similarly argue that women who invade the symbolic 'male territory' of politics appear unruly and out of (men's) control and therefore threaten the gendered boundaries of a system that is already under threat in other ways. They are punished both as threatening political opponents and as 'dangerous' women. As such, they are vulnerable to 'body policing' and violence which aims to 'put them back in their place'.[2] In addition, women who are politically active may be particularly vulnerable to violence because of the nature of their activities and knowledge. So-called 'low-level' political activists may have access to information and/or political knowledge that others do not have. However, because their profile is less public there are fewer risks for the State in terms of adverse publicity.

(2)   Women find ways of exercising informal political influence when politics is less institutionalised and may prefer, even in institutionalised political systems, to participate in ad hoc or even protest politics

As is noted in the Canadian gender guidelines, in a society where women are 'assigned' a subordinate status and the authority exercised by men over women results in a general oppression of women, their political protest and activism do not always manifest themselves in the same way as those of men. The significance of these forms of political participation and resistance should not be underestimated.

4.1.2   Gendered forms of political resistance

'The political activities that women are involved in are, in many instances, not as "public" as making speeches, attending demonstrations and writing publications. Women may provide food, clothing, medical care, hide people, pass messages from one political activist to another and so on. All of these activities may be essential for the ongoing existence of the political organisation, and the knowledge women gain through these activities puts them in danger and at risk. However, these activities are

---

1   Spijkerboer 1994, p 25. Referring specifically to Cyprus, Iran, and Northern Ireland, Ridd 1986 suggests that during periods of conflict men, with power at their disposal, sense a danger in losing control over women and take steps to strenuously enforce the conceptual divide between public and private domains.

2   Agger 1992; Dutch Refugee Council 1994; Spijkerboer 1994; Pettman 1996.

not viewed as having sufficient public profile to attract attention from the authorities to put them at risk.'[1]

Although many women who claim refugee status are directly involved in formal political activity, it remains the case that, in general terms, women are less likely than men to participate publicly. Feminism has shed new light on the relationship between women and politics both by pointing to the structural features of political life which have tended to exclude women from positions of power, and by recovering from oblivion a hidden history of women's involvement in political action. In addition, it has challenged the continuing analytical separation of the public world of politics and employment from the private sphere of family and interpersonal relations. Even where women do not appear to step out of their domestic orientation in times of political conflict, they often exert political power, sometimes in covert, sometimes in symbolic, forms. Women who have had little or no involvement in formal political institutions take up all sorts of practical and innovative ways to exert pressure on the political scene in many different contexts. These forms of political participation by women often grow out of and subvert their gender roles as providers and nurturers, and are increasingly well documented in a number of studies which also suggest that because women are seen as political innocents they are able to use this immunity to take initiatives and responsibilities of a covert political nature.

The role played by Latin American women in supporting and opposing military regimes has been particularly well documented.[2] Waylen (1996b), for example, describes the collective survival strategies of predominantly poor, working-class women acting in their roles as mothers and household providers as their class and gender identities interacted. Although the women involved did not initially see their activities as 'political', as 'politics' was something men did in the institutional public sphere, changes occurred both in the ways they saw their activities and in the ways they were seen from outside. Once defined as subversive by the regime, women too began to see their activities as 'political'; soup kitchens became a visible political protest because their existence demonstrated the existence of hunger and unemployment and craft workshops produced embroideries which depicted scenes from everyday life and often bore oppositional messages. One of the most powerful symbolic and subversive acts carried out by women protesting at the disappearance of their relatives has been the take-over of public space for their protests through the use of spaces and places not normally seen as part of their domain. This point has often been made particularly strongly with reference to the Madres de Plaza de Mayo of Argentina (mothers of the Plaza de Mayo), who marched around the plaza demanding the return of their children and other relatives who had 'disappeared' following the seizure of power by the military in 1976. A similar point is made by Nzomo (1997) with reference to the democratisation process in Kenya and the actions of

---

1   Legal Aid Commission of NSW, Submission 588.
2   See, eg, Caldeira 1990; Feijoo and Gogna 1990; Jelin (ed) 1990; Waylen 1992, 1996b; Fisher 1993; Radcliffe 1993; and Blondet 1995.

---

mothers and relatives who went on hunger strike to demand the release of their sons who were political prisoners.[1]

The central issue in cases involving this type of political participation is the way in which the concept of 'political' is interpreted. Although the UNHCR Handbook (1979) does not give any clear definition of what is meant by the term, there is considerable evidence that decisions on whether a refugee claimant falls within the political opinion ground have frequently been based, in the past, on the male experience of more overt political activity and that private sphere activities, which are most commonly associated with women seeking asylum, are viewed as inherently apolitical. As is noted by the Dutch Refugee Council (1994), women who offer political resistance by carrying out 'odd jobs' often do not label their actions as political resistance, and asylum-granting countries may not judge these activities by their political merits, underestimating the political dimensions of these acts.

In this context, Spijkerboer (1994) argues that whilst one can say that refugee law is gendered on the basis that the very notion of a refugee is thought of as a 'public' phenomenon, it is not necessarily gendered. There are no such things as inherently political or apolitical activities. Activities commonly associated with women and occurring in the private sphere are not therefore inherently any less political than those taking place in the public sphere; indeed in some contexts these activities may become inherently political and women may be targeted as a result. It is very important that representatives recognise that these activities constitute political opinion and political resistance: they are no less valid than other forms which are dominated by men.

4.1.3 The politics of the veil

One of the clearest examples of the way in which political participation and resistance is gendered can be seen in the politics of dress codes, and specifically, the veil. The dominant image of women's experiences during the process of Islamisation in much of the existing literature has been almost overwhelmingly negative. In this vision, 'Middle Eastern women' are conceptualised as passive, universally oppressed and bound to a static and powerless tradition. However, women's opposition to the imposition of dress codes during the process of Islamisation must be seen in the context of the political symbolism of the veil historically. In order to understand the experiences of women in Islamic Middle Eastern societies, and consequently the basis of their claims for asylum in the UK, it is important to examine the historical development of various discourses around gender and Islam and the socio-economic and historical conditions in which these discourses are grounded. In other words, rather than simply adopting a stereotyped understanding of Islam, it is important to understand the *context* in which various religious texts are interpreted, and how historical, political and economic factors, as well as cultural, ideological and socio-psychological dimensions have together contributed to the revival of patriarchal Islamist fervour in certain countries. It is particularly important to understand

---

1   A similar role was played by women during the anti-apartheid struggle in South Africa and the miners' strike in the UK in 1984.

the ways in which the objectives of nation-building, national identity, strategies of socio-economic development and modernisation have historically been inter- woven with *mas'ale-ye zan* or the 'woman question'. Throughout history, gender identity has been a particular focus of political contestation with Europe and has been closely tied to colonial opposition.[1] As a result of this history of struggle around it, between Islamists and secularists, between advocates of veiling and its opponents, the veil has been encoded with considerable political meaning. It represents not just an issue about social reform but rather entire agendas and constructions of reform, State power, popular morality and religious values.

The particular difficulties facing women from countries such as Iran, Afghan- istan, Pakistan and the Sudan who are seeking asylum in the UK therefore stem not from the fact that Islam is inherently oppressive to women and inimical to women's human rights but rather from the fact that different regimes use their specific stand on 'the woman question' as a way of signalling their political agenda. In order to understand the experiences of women from countries such as these we need therefore to come to terms with the rise of the Islamic movements as a political phenomenon, rather than as a religious revival, as a conscious political rejection of the West and the political models associated with it.

Box 4.1 'The woman question' in Iran

Colonial discourses associated with the late nineteenth century sug- gested (and continue to suggest) that Islam is innately and immutably oppressive to women. The veil in particular was seen to epitomise that oppression. Veiling, to *Western* eyes, the most visible marker of differ- ence and of the inferiority of Islamic societies, became (and remains) the symbol of both the oppression of women and the backwardness of Islam. As a result, changing customs regarding women and changing their dress, abolishing the veil in particular, were seen by some as key to bringing about desired general social transformation and 'modernis- ation'. However, for others the veil became a marker of cultural, political and religious difference and identity in the context of European pen- etration and perceived 'Westernisation'. With the publication of Qassim Amin's *Tahrir al-mar'a* (The Liberation of Woman) in 1899 and the ensuing debate which it provoked, the veil came to symbolise not the inferiority of the culture and the need to cast aside its customs in favour of those of the West, but, on the contrary, the dignity and validity of all native customs, and in particular those customs coming under fiercest attack, the customs relating to women, and the need to tenaciously affirm them as a means of resistance to Western domination. Nationalist discourse should therefore be seen as part of the opposition to colonialism. Dress codes (specifically the veil in its various forms) have been an important symbol of anti-Westernisation.

---

1   The significance of the veil can be seen most recently in the way in which it has been politicised in other contexts, eg Turkey (women who wear the veil cannot hold public office), France (wearing of headscarves prohibited in schools) and Afghanistan.

The imposition of dress codes, and specifically the veil, therefore signifies a battle between women and the State over the control of the individual's body and personal space. However, the State policy on the veil and the forceful method of its imposition has been opposed by sections of Iranian society from the start. Many women who have been forced into segregation and *hejab* have therefore used every opportunity to defy it, for example, by showing strings of hair or leaving traces of makeup on their faces. In the process the stakes have become even higher. This has also provided a mechanism with which to 'get at' women who politically oppose the Islamic regime in more conventional ways. Women's opposition to the dress codes has not been without considerable personal cost and violation of their individual human rights. Many women who have opposed the regime have been forced to leave their jobs, families and country rather than submit to political repression and sacrifice their beliefs. The very act of seeking asylum represents a political statement against the regime, and is symbolic of women's refusal to conform. In this context, it is vitally important that representatives recognise that a woman who opposes institutionalised discrimination against women or expresses views of independence from the social or cultural norms of society may sustain or fear harm because of her actual political opinion or a political opinion that has been or will be imputed to her. She is perceived within the established political/social structure as expressing politically antagonistic views through her actions or failure to act. If a woman resists gendered oppression, her resistance is political.

4.1.4 Association/family membership

A woman may suffer harm on the basis of an imputed (attributed) political opinion as a result of the perception that her political views are aligned with those of dominant family or community members. Violence against those who oppose regimes is not confined to the public sphere because politics and political resistance are not exclusive to the public sphere. Political violence by the State aims to disable opposition or resistance by so intimidating a population as to forcibly 'depoliticise' it. Bringing violence into the 'private' sphere of the home and family appears to be a particularly effective means of achieving this aim. As a result, even where women do not participate in formal politics, a woman nonetheless may have a political identity which is defined by her relationship to the men in her family and by her role as mother and wife. As Macklin (1995) notes, women's identities, beliefs and status are frequently subsumed under their male kin and it seems reasonable to infer from this that a woman's kinship associations with men could precipitate her persecution on the basis of an imputed political opinion regardless of what she herself believes. In many contexts, there is an assumption that women defer to men on all significant issues and that their political views are aligned with those of the dominant (usually male) members of the family. This is reflected in the fact that many women asylum seekers are persecuted or face persecution because of the status, activities or views of their spouses, parents, children and siblings or other family members:

'After my husband came here [to the UK] the police came to my house looking for my husband and to ask me where he was and in order to find out where he was they harassed me and my children. Once they came and beat us and took away our passports . . . He was a wanted person . . . the police were after him. Because of my connection to him it was unbearable and I came here in order to escape the persecution . . . I know that if we were living in Istanbul, my husband would have disappeared and the family would have faced harassment. In Turkey I was beaten and kicked in front of the children. It was a real humiliation.'[1]

'I also had some problems when my husband was not at home. The gendarme, he said bad words to us. Once he put a gun on my child's head to threaten me . . . to push me to say where my husband was . . . They captured my husband. He was arrested and they tortured him terribly. The police captured me and the children. I was pregnant and they beat me up.'[2]

Such cases often involve violence, arbitrary imprisonment or other forms of abuse of women who are not themselves accused of holding any antagonistic views or political convictions. The harm to these women is often a means of intimidating, coercing or harming the family members who hold dissenting political views or who engage in political activities which are disapproved of by the persecutor. In other cases, women are harmed in order to pressure them into revealing information concerning the whereabouts or the political activities of their family members.

The persecution of women in their homes has powerful symbolic motives. It is often intended to demonstrate that the State does not recognise 'boundaries' between the public and private spheres, and that nowhere (and nothing) is sacred. As Spijkerboer suggests, 'when female relatives of male political activists are tortured, they are not only persecuted because of the activities of their kin, but also to take from these men their "possession"'.[3] This harm often takes the form of sexual violence. There are clear parallels between family torture, where women are tortured or raped in front of their children or husbands, and the way in which rape has been used as an instrument of war, as a means to terrorise the (male) enemy and brutalise the whole community through a violation of its 'property'. The sexual torture of women is often intended *for* men. Being forced to witness the rape and torture of female prisoners attacks their masculine role with the result that men suffer precisely because of their inability to protect.

The failure to recognise this relationship between the public and private spheres in political life can undermine the protection currently available to women who flee persecution. Although a woman's fear of persecution can clearly be derived from the terror campaign waged by government forces against an opposition, and reflects a well-documented strategy affecting countless women, such women are often refused refugee status in the UK because their case is not seen to fall within the recognised criteria. Decision-makers have often failed to recognise the significance of familial relationships in shaping women's experiences of persecution (see Box 4.2). Some women who suffer or fear persecution as a result of association or family membership may be either unable or *unwilling* to talk about the political activities of others for fears about confidentiality and concerns that the information they reveal may in some way be used to harm other family

---

1   Comments made by a Kurdish woman from Turkey during an interview with the author.
2   Comments made by a woman from the former Zaire during an interview with the author.
3   Spijkerboer 1994, p 25.

members, many of whom remain in the country of origin. This is discussed in more detail in Chapter 10.

Box 4.2

A Nigerian woman whose father was general secretary of a trade union attached to a large oil company claimed asylum in the UK fearing that she would be persecuted. After a strike at the plant, her father was arrested and the whole family put under house arrest. She was sexually assaulted by the soldiers guarding her. A family friend arranged for a forged passport because he was concerned that her name would give rise to suspicion at the airport when she left the country. When she arrived at Heathrow, immigration officials noticed that she had counterfeit documents and questioned her at length. She was detained and her application for asylum subsequently refused. At appeal, the adjudicator accepted that she was who she claimed to be, that is one of the children of a leading figure in the trade union movement who had been arrested and detained, and commented: 'to this extent I find the witness to be credible. I believe that she was present when her father was arrested, and that she, and other members of her family, were then subject to a form of house arrest'. However the appeal was dismissed on the grounds that the adjudicator could see no reason why the authorities in Nigeria should be particularly interested in her: 'Notwithstanding her father's position, the appellant herself has never been active in politics, and she has never been arrested ... I acknowledge that there have been instances in the past where those who have been wanted have been held. However, that could not be the case here because the appellant's father was already in custody.'[1]

4.1.5 The gendered politics of war

The experiences of women during periods of war and civil unrest are highly varied and representatives should ensure that they are aware of the full details of the basis of the claim when making an application for asylum.[2] It is particularly important that representatives are aware of the political significance of gender during war and the fact that the role of women in the biological and social reproduction of group identity places them in a position of particular vulnerability. This vulnerability and the political significance of gender during periods of war and civil unrest is currently rarely recognised in the asylum determination process.

Contrary to dominant assumptions about women as victims, women participate directly in war. Women may engage in forms of gendered resistance as a result of which they become the targets of persecution. In addition to direct participation

---

1   Appeal No TH/66818/96 (unreported) 29 July 1996.
2   It is essential to examine the context and facts of the individual case to establish whether a war, civil war or general conflict in fact exists or is relevant to the particular case.

as fighters, women often play diverse and vital supportive roles. Women may act as go-betweens and carriers of food and firearms, and generally provide a system of intelligence, to which there are considerable risks attached. Just as significantly, many women who flee from situations of civil war and seek asylum in the UK have not simply been 'caught in the crossfire' as is typically assumed, but rather have been targeted *because they were perceived as being 'on the wrong side'*. Many women are targeted for persecution because of their race, nationality, clan membership or association. In addition, women are targeted because *as women* they have a particular symbolic status. One obvious consequence of the symbolism of gender identities during armed conflict is the use of sexual violence as a weapon of war.

The use of rape and sexual violence in war has a long history and is probably as old as war itself. Yet many women who have experienced sexual violence within the framework of ethnic, religious or political conflicts are not recognised as Refugee Convention refugees, because sexual violence is not seen as related to the conflict in the context of which it occurred. At best it is viewed as a general but 'private' crime, unrelated to the political background. In such situations, decision-makers may sometimes decide that there is persecution, but no Refugee Convention ground. In addition, there is seen to be no requisite State connection. Thus, in times of war, direct State responsibility may be obscured by perceptions that sexual violence is inherently 'private' in its motivation despite the fact that 'official failure to condemn or punish rape gives it an overt political sanction, which allows rape and other forms of torture and ill-treatment to become tools of military strategy'.[1] Rape by hostile militia is viewed not as persecution but as the common fate of women caught in a war zone.[2]

By contrast, a gendered analysis of war reveals that the prosecution of mass, legitimised, psychotic violence depends upon a particular way of constructing and maintaining gender identities. Seen from this perspective, it becomes clear that the violence associated with war is not 'generalised' at all, but rather that women are specifically targeted for violence because of the symbolism of gender roles. The violation of women's bodies acts as a symbol of the violation of the country (or equally a given political, ethnic or national group). In order to gain a deeper understanding of the processes and impact of rape in war, the analysis has to expand out from an exclusive focus on women's experiences of sexual violence towards an awareness of its *symbolism* and *political significance*. During war, women's bodies become highly symbolic and the physical territory for a broader political struggle in which sexual violence including rape is used as a military strategy to humiliate and demoralise an opponent; women's bodies become the battleground for 'paybacks', they symbolise the dominance of one group over another. The notion of women's bodies as 'envelopes' to carry the message from the conquering group of men to the conquered may explain why so many women are raped in front of their husbands and (male) relatives in such publicly symbolic places as their doorsteps or yards.

The use of rape in war is just one manifestation of the gendered process of war which not only legitimates violence by the State (and other parties) but

---

1   Vickers 1993, p 21.
2   Macklin 1995.

exaggerates pre-existing myths about gender and sexuality, one of which is the belief that men have an uncontrollable sex-drive: 'from these fundamental assumptions grows the "keep-the-boys-happy" mentality that explains at least some of what happens to women in war'.[1] In this context, rape is used (or tolerated) as a *means of troop mollification* and as a 'just reward' for war-weary troops. War may also be viewed as an initiation into manhood, and the masculinity of those who choose not to partake is questioned. In this sense, it fosters exaggerated notions of male sexuality and virility.[2] However, it is important to recognise that sexual violence and rape is an actual *weapon* or a *strategy* of war itself, rather than just an expression or consequence.[3] Thompkins (1995) argues that the primary goal of the typical rapist is not achieving sexual satisfaction, but rather fulfilling a need to exercise control over a woman and thereby dominate her. In the context of armed conflict or civil war, the rape of women is also about gaining control over other men and the group (national, ethnic, political) of which they are a part. The representation of women as mothers of the nation locates and constrains women in particular ways not least because other men's/nations'/States' women become targets for 'legitimate' violence. It is only in recent years that the international human rights system has recognised the use of rape and sexual violence as a weapon of war (see Box 4.3).

Box 4.3

The Four Geneva Conventions and their two Additional Protocols contain provisions aimed at preventing rape and sexual violence in armed conflict. However it is only in recent years that important steps have been taken to end the impunity of assailants. Rape is now recognised in the statutes of the International Criminal Tribunal on the former Yugoslavia as a crime against humanity. The Security Council established the International Criminal Tribunal for the Former Yugoslavia (ICTY) in 1993 to prosecute war crimes committed during the Yugoslav conflict and the International Criminal Tribunal for Rwanda (ICTR) in 1994 to prosecute war crimes during the Rwandan civil war. For the first time in history, rape during wartime was explicitly stated to be a crime against humanity.

4.2 SERIOUS HARM

Women who are politically active experience many of the forms of violence and harm associated with the asylum claims of their male counterparts. In many societies, however, the penalties for political participation and resistance are even more severe for women than for men because of cultural and social norms that preclude women's involvement. For example, women who are imprisoned by the

---

1   Thompkins 1995, p 871.
2   Niarchos 1995.
3   Bennett et al 1995.

authorities run the risk of 'double punishment'. They are punished not only because they oppose the regime in some way, but also because they shirk the traditional role of women by being politically active at all. Women are not only persecuted on the basis of their political opinion, but also because, as women, they should not participate in the political arena.[1] As a result, they are often 'put back in their place' by prison guards or military men.[2] The persecuting authorities may therefore deal doubly hard with women who are politically active.

Women who are persecuted as a result of their political opinions, or a political opinion which has been imputed to them, may be subjected to similar forms of harm to those experienced by their male counterparts, many of which are commonly held to constitute serious harm within the meaning of persecution. In addition, however, women may be subjected to gender-specific forms of harm, often involving sexual violence including rape. Political violence, including State violence, is often sexualised, and women who are persecuted for political reasons are frequently subjected to sexual violence (along with other forms of torture) with specific sanction from, or the tacit approval of, the authorities (see Box 4.4). For this reason, sexual violence will form the basis of the analysis in this section, although representatives should not assume that rape and sexual violence is inevitable.[3] Whilst the reasons or grounds leading to the use of sexual violence including rape are clearly critical in the context of an asylum claim, and are discussed below, what is of concern in this section is sexual violence including rape as a gender-specific form of persecution.

Box 4.4

Mrs S is a Ugandan citizen. Her father was a member of the UPC and her grandfather was one of the founder members of the party. UPC meetings also used to be held in her husband's building and he used to entertain party members whenever they came to a conference. As a result of the political activities of her male family members, Mrs S was herself arrested. She was taken to the local barracks where she was tortured and raped. She was kept in a cell with three or four other women and each of them was tortured and raped in front of the others. They would be urinated on and made to drink the urine, and when Mrs S refused to do this, she was pushed against a piece of broken glass and her leg injured to the extent that she could not walk.[4]

1 Spijkerboer 1994.
2 Dutch Refugee Council 1994.
3 Chapter 10 provides detailed information on the procedural and evidential issues that can arise in claims involving sexual violence.
4 Appeal No HX/70880/96 (unreported) 10 February 1997. The appellant's appeal was refused but the adjudicator made a recommendation that ELR be granted given the horrific nature of her experiences.

The use of sexual violence to punish politically active women has a more potent and symbolic purpose than is typically assumed because rape and sexual violence are utilised as part of the political process, as strategies of power and domination:

> 'When aggression and sexuality are intertwined, it is especially difficult to maintain a psychological defence, particularly to defend yourself against the sense of shame at being an accomplice to the forbidden deed: this can threaten the innermost, most central part of your identity. The widespread use of sexual assault against political prisoners can, therefore, be seen as an effective strategy if the aim is to break down a political opponent's personal identity – and thereby also her *political* identity' (emphasis in original).[1]

Reflecting this, Agger (1989) classifies sexual violence as psychological rather than physical torture in that it is designed to break down and shatter the victim's psychological defence mechanisms by emphasising existing or potential conflicts between women's identities as mothers and their identities as political activists. This conflict can be seen in particular kinds of torture and mutilation. For example, Hollander (1996) at p 69 cites the case of a mutilated body of a dead pregnant woman, whose foetus had been slashed out of the abdomen and stuck in her mouth: 'this particular method of terror is a brutal symbolic representation of the intersection between psychological and political processes. It reflects both the unconscious male dread and hatred of the fertile omnipotent mother who, it is feared, consumes rather than feeds the baby, as well as the conscious sadistic rage aimed at woman who, through her political opposition and her capacity to bring forth from the womb more rebels, is seen as a challenge to male authoritarian power.' Hollander (1996) also emphasises the psychological impact of State terror and comments on the paucity of sources on the psychological meaning of the political repression of women. She argues that, with some (limited) exceptions, more attention is paid to the personal consequences of sexual violence for individual women than it is to developing a theory which explains how political repression interacts with the determinants of patriarchal culture and the extent to which State terror functions to reinforce and/or challenge the existing gendered arrangements of society. Sexual violence against women in detention must, therefore, be seen as a reflection of, and connected to, sexual-political power structures *outside* the prison and in particular with historically transmitted definitions of 'the shameful' and 'the unclean'. Pettman similarly suggests that 'local and national cultures of honour and shame, social valuing of women's virginity and notions of sexually "experienced" women as soiled goods link into the effects and intentions of the torturers'.[2]

Although sexual violence should be one of the least controversial examples of 'serious harm' in the context of a definition of persecution, the interpretation of sexual violence against women has often differed substantially from the interpretation of other forms of serious harm, including sexual violence,

---

1   Agger 1992, p 8.
2   Pettman 1996, p 102.

experienced by men.[1] Increased recognition of the political use of sexual violence has, however, begun to have some impact on case-law. **Canadian** tribunals have explicitly found that threats of rape and rape itself 'are degrading and constitute quite clearly an attack on the moral integrity of the person and, hence, persecution of the most vile sort'. In *Smith*,[2] the CRDD, referring to the UDHR and the Convention on Consent to Marriage, also arrived at the conclusion that the forced marriage of a 15-year-old Zimbabwean girl to a polygamous man, followed by years of physical and sexual brutality, amounted to persecution.[3] The intersection of race and gender in cases of sexual violence has also been recognised in a more recent case involving two ethnic Hungarians who were targeted by the police.[4] That targeting included the rape of the female claimant by two men. The CRDD found that, even cumulatively, the treatment that the male claimant had faced because of his ethnicity amounted only to discrimination, not persecution. The rape of the female claimant amounted to persecution on the basis of her gender and her membership in a particular social group, victims of violence against women in Romania. There were safe places that the claimants could relocate in Romania. However, the female claimant was suffering from post-traumatic stress syndrome and was 'severely impaired' and in a state of constant dread. Because of her vulnerability, as verified in a medical report, and because she would receive no support as a rape victim, it would be unduly harsh and unreasonable to expect her to seek an internal flight alternative. The female claimant was a Convention refugee. Considering the female claimant's condition and the close family bond between the claimants, it would be unduly harsh and unreasonable for the male claimant to return alone to Romania. He too was a Convention refugee.

In the **US**, serious physical harm has consistently been held to constitute persecution. Rape and other forms of sexual violence can clearly fall within this rule. For example in *Lazo-Majano*,[5] in which a Salvadoran woman was raped and brutalised by an army sergeant who denounced her as subversive, it was ruled that the applicant had been 'persecuted' within the terms of the Refugee Convention. The court found that the appellant's story and evidence were uncontroverted and established a well-founded fear of persecution. The issue, according to the court, was whether the petitioner was persecuted by a government agent because of her political beliefs or whether the persecution was based on a personal relationship between them. The court found that 'political opinion' means the political opinion of the victim as perceived by the persecutor. Because the persecutor regarded the appellant as a subversive, he persecuted her. Therefore, the appellant suffered persecution for her political opinion. The decision of the BIA denying her asylum was overturned.

In the **UK**, sexual violence has generally been recognised as serious harm but has still been insufficient to find a claim for refugee status under the Refugee

---

1   Chapter 3 provides an overview of the physical, social, intellectual and psychological consequences for women associated with rape and sexual violence, and the interpretation of such harm in case-law.
2   *Smith v Canada (MEI)* 19 February 1993.
3   The issue of marriage-related harm is discussed in detail in Chapters 5 and 6 below.
4   *Sooriyakumaran v MCI* (FCTD, No IMM-4099–97), 1 October 1998.
5   *Lazo-Majano v INS* [1987] 813 F.2d 1432, 1439 (9th Cir).

Convention. For example, in the case of a Kenyan woman who was arrested and detained and tortured twice by the authorities because of her involvement with the Safina party, the letter from the Home Office refusing her claim states that 'rape is a criminal matter and as such not the basis of a claim to asylum under the 1951 United Nations Convention'. Sexual violence as a violation of fundamental human rights has been recognised in several appeal cases. In the case of a Kurdish woman from Turkey who had been gang-raped by Turkish police, the special adjudicator upheld her right to asylum in the UK noting that 'the maltreatment and sexual abuse [she suffered] were acts of persecution'.[1] A Kenyan woman, who was detained and repeatedly raped by police officers because of her alleged political opposition, has been recognised as a Convention refugee.[2]

The circumstances in each of these cases were such that both the failure of State protection and the grounds of the persecution were clear. Even where the grounds of the persecution are not accepted, there appears to be growing recognition among adjudicators of the implications of the sexual violence for the appellant, which may lead to a recommendation that ELR be granted. For example, in dismissing the appeal of a woman from Ghana, raped and tortured because of the political activities of her father and husband, the adjudicator made the following comments:

> 'I believe it would be quite wrong to return the appellant if she were medically unfit. That includes her psychological well-being. Rape is an appalling abuse leaving its mark for many years and which, if not dealt with by expert counselling at an early stage can leave emotional scars so deeply embedded that call for the most compassionate treatment. I thus recommend no steps be taken to remove the appellant until her medical condition permits and that her overall circumstances be given the most compassionate consideration.'[3]

Rape and sexual violence are a breach of Article 3 of the ECHR. This is particularly significant in view of the incorporation of the ECHR into domestic jurisdiction in October 2000:

> '. . . while being held in detention the applicant was raped by a person whose identity has still to be determined. Rape of a detainee by an official of the State must be considered an especially grave and abhorrent form of ill-treatment given the ease with which the offender can exploit the vulnerability and weakened resistance of his victim. Furthermore, rape leaves deep psychological scars on the victim which do not respond to the passage of time as quickly as other forms of physical and mental violence. The applicant also experienced the acute physical pain of forced penetration, which must have left her feeling debased and violated both physically and emotionally . . . the [European] Court [of Human Rights] is satisfied that the accumulation of acts of physical and mental violence inflicted on the applicant and

---

1   Appeal No HX/73695/95 (unreported) 17 May 1996.
2   Appeal No HX/70880/96 (unreported) 10 February 1997. Whilst the determination of the adjudicator does not explicitly refer to the rape as persecution, implicit within the decision is a recognition that sexual violence including rape constitutes a violation of fundamental human rights.
3   Appeal No HX/73663/94 (unreported) 27 October 1995.

the especially cruel act of rape to which she was subjected amounted to torture in breach of Article 3 of the Convention [ECHR].'[1]

4.3 THE FAILURE OF STATE PROTECTION

Chapter 3 provides a framework for assessing whether there has been a failure of State protection in cases involving women as asylum seekers. According to this framework, a failure of State protection exists if serious harm has been inflicted by the State or by associated organisations or groups; or if serious harm has been committed by others and the authorities are *unwilling* to give effective protection; or if serious harm has been committed by others and the authorities are *unable* to give effective protection. Representatives should remember that where State protection exists it must be meaningful, accessible, effective, sufficient and available to a woman regardless of her culture and position. In addition, however, representatives should be aware of further difficulties which may arise in these cases which are specific to women. On the one hand, sexual violence experienced by women is often considered to be irrelevant within the normative framework of asylum determination. Sexual violence is viewed as something inherently private, and it is this conceptualisation that is reproduced in refugee law. In addition, laws implemented by the State and/or punishment for their violation may be legitimated.

(1) Sexual violence experienced by women is often considered to be irrelevant within the normative framework of asylum determination: sexual violence is viewed as something inherently private, and it is this conceptualisation that is reproduced in refugee law

Women are sexually assaulted by agents of the State in a variety of circumstances. Women detained for political reasons may be sexually abused or raped (along with other forms of torture) with specific sanction by, or the tacit approval of, the authorities. Women may be raped by government or opposition militia as part of a campaign to terrorise the local populace, punish politically active males by proxy or 'reward' victorious combatants. Whilst there is increasing acknowledgement in many jurisdictions that sexual violence constitutes serious harm within the meaning of persecution, the problem in cases of sexual violence including rape frequently lies in the State connection requirement. Applications involving sexual violence are dealt with in a bewildering way. In the **US**, the cases of *Campos-Guardado*[2] and *Lazo-Majano*[3] have both been widely cited as examples in which rape was interpreted by the judge as not being political but 'personal'.[4] In *Campos-Guardado*,[5] the court concluded that the persecutor's motives for raping her were different from the political motivation behind the torture and execution of her male family members which she was forced to

---

1   *Aydin v Turkey* (1997) 25 EHRR 251.
2   *Campos-Guardado v INS* [1987] 809 F.2d 285 (5th Cir).
3   *Lazo-Majano v INS* [1987] 813 F.2d 1432, 1434 (9th Cir).
4   Castel 1992.
5   *Campos-Guardado v INS* [1987] 809 F.2d 285 (5th Cir).

witness. In the case of *Klawitter*,[1] where the applicant feared the unwanted sexual advances of a colonel in the Polish secret police, the court agreed with the position of the Board that there was no motive behind his behaviour towards her aside from personal ones:

> 'However distasteful his apparent treatment of the respondent may have been, such harm or threats arising from a personal dispute of this nature, even one taking place with an individual of a high governmental position, is not a ground for asylum ... Although the petitioner's testimony recounts an unfortunate situation, harm or threats of harm based solely on sexual attraction do not constitute persecution.'

Noting that this line of reasoning seems to be specific to acts of sexual abuse, Spijkerboer (1994) criticises the implicit view of sexual violence in asylum-related situations as derailed sexuality and not as torture, and suggests that it presupposes a very particular conception of male sexuality. Male sexuality is seen as an innate, independent and quasi-biological drive which seeks satisfaction and can suddenly overwhelm a man. As a result, it is viewed as 'private' even when it is committed during an interrogation, and dismissed as the aberrant act of an individual which is to be expected, rather than as behaviour condoned or encouraged by the government.[2] This can be seen, for example, in the Australian case of a Kurdish woman from Turkey who was detained at Istanbul airport, beaten until unconscious and raped by two soldiers.[3] The Tribunal accepted that she had been raped but was unable to find a relationship between the act of violence and the lack or failure of State protection.

Under the ECHR, the 'authorities are strictly liable for the conduct of their subordinates, they are under a duty to impose their will on subordinates and cannot shelter behind their inability to ensure that it is respected'.[4] In this context, it is critical that representatives argue that the failure of State protection of women has occurred in cases of sexual violence perpetrated by the State or an agent of the State. This position is supported by the UNHCR's *Guidelines on the Protection of Refugee Women* (1991) and Macdonald and Blake (1995):

> 'Sexual violence against women is a form of persecution when it is used with the consent or acquiescence of those acting in an official capacity to intimidate or punish.'[5]

> 'The security forces of the country do not cease to be agents of official persecution because it is not the policy of central government to persecute the victims in question.'[6]

In addition to the issues which arise where sexual violence is at the hands of the authorities or individuals connected to them, there are a variety of other scenarios where sufficient State connection can be said to exist. This includes cases where sexual violence has been committed by non-State agents and where the authorities are unwilling to give protection, either because they support the

---

1   *Klawitter v INS* [1992] 970 F.2d 149 (6th Cir).
2   Kelly 1993.
3   RRT V95/05221 29 May 1997.
4   *Ireland v UK* (1978) 2 EHRR 25.
5   UNHCR 1991, p 40.
6   Macdonald and Blake 1995, pp 390–391.

actions of the individuals concerned, because they tolerate them or because they have other priorities.[1] This position is supported in the UNHCR's *Sexual Violence Against Refugees: Guidelines on Prevention and Response* and in international case-law:

> 'The Government on whose territory the sexual attack has occurred is responsible for taking diligent remedial measures, including conducting a thorough investigation into the crime, identifying and prosecuting those responsible, and protecting the victims from reprisals.'[2]

> 'Current international law establishes that sexual abuse committed by members of the security forces, whether as a result of deliberate practice promoted by the State or as a result of failure by the State to prevent the occurrence of this crime, constitutes a violation of the victims' human rights, especially the right to physical and mental integrity.'[3]

(2) Laws implemented by the State and/or punishment for their violation may be legitimated

A woman's claim to Convention refugee status cannot be based solely on the fact that she is subject to a national law or policy to which she objects. The applicant will need to establish either that the policy or law is inherently persecutory, that the policy or law is used as a means of persecution for one of the enumerated reasons, that the policy or law, although having legitimate goals, is administered through persecutory means, or that the penalty for non-compliance is disproportionately severe.[4] In this context, the existence of particular laws or social polices or the manner in which they are implemented may themselves constitute or involve a failure of State protection. This may be particularly evident where dress and/or behaviour codes are violated. There is a tendency among decision-makers to legitimise the laws of other States and thereby justify a failure to grant protection. In these cases, decision-makers should be reminded that the international legal obligations of the State to avoid discriminating against women are found in international treaty and customary law including Article 3 of the ICCPR, Article 3 of the ICESCR and Article 2 of the UDHR.

4.4 REFUGEE CONVENTION GROUNDS

There is a tendency within the decision-making process to depoliticise the experiences of women seeking asylum and a failure to recognise the gendered forms that political participation and resistance may assume in different geographical contexts. It has been suggested that this is because the archetypal image of a political refugee, as someone who is fleeing persecution resulting from their direct involvement in political activity, does not always correspond with the

1 Spijkerboer 1994.
2 UNHCR 1995, p 53. The issue of violence, including sexual violence, perpetrated against women by non-State agents is discussed in detail in the following chapter and throughout this book.
3 *Raquel Marti de Mejia v Peru*, Case 10.970, Report No 5/96, Inter-American Commission on Human Rights, 1 March 1996.
4 Goodwin-Gill 1983; Hathaway 1991.

reality of women's experiences. In many cases where women have expressed or been imputed with a political opinion, it has been argued by advocates and practitioners themselves that women have been persecuted not because of their political opinion but because of their membership of a particular social group. As a result, case-law is disparate and, in some cases, confused.

4.4.1 Direct involvement in formal political activity

The representation and characterisation of women's experiences where women have either been directly involved in formal political activity or have used gendered forms of political resistance to exert themselves on the political scene, varies enormously depending upon the country of origin and the facts of the individual case. As with many asylum claims based on politics, including those made by men, the success or otherwise of the application is often dependent upon credibility and evidential issues.[1]

There are several other issues which arise in the claims of women of which representatives should be particularly aware. The first of these reflects a more general point made throughout this book – that the assumptions which are commonly made are that women are not and cannot be politically active. As the brother of a politically active Ugandan woman commented, 'the Home Office seem to have a low opinion about women's political activity back in the original country but at least 50 per cent of the strong campaigners and voters are women'. This is reflected in case-law. For example, in the case of a Kenyan woman who had been arrested and taken by three policemen to a police station where she was detained and questioned as to what she thought of President's Moi's government and tribal clashes in the area where she lived, the Home Office had initially rejected her asylum application on the basis that she was not a member of a political party and held no political views.[2] In a separate case involving a Kenyan woman who was an active member of the Democratic Party of Kenya, the Home Office, in refusing her protection under the Refugee Convention, argued that it was 'implausible' that she would have attended a political rally.[3]

Moreover, where women's participation in political activity has been accepted by the Home Office, it is frequently argued that, because this participation has been at a so-called 'low-level', their fears of persecution are unfounded. These activities are not viewed as having sufficient public profile to attract attention from the authorities and put them at risk. This can be seen in the case of a Ghanaian woman who had supported the PNP. After her father was elected local chairman of the PNP, she was taken by soldiers to the army barracks and raped and was subsequently detained on two separate occasions. In refusing her application for asylum, the Home Office had argued that even if her account of events was true (which it did not believe them to be) the Secretary of State did not believe that she was engaged in activities which would bring her to the adverse attention of the authorities. At her appeal hearing the adjudicator described her political participation as being 'very low level. She had attended meetings and rallies. She had sewn flags and clothes for supporters'. He subsequently

1   This issue is discussed at length in Chapter 10.
2   Appeal No HX/75299/95 (unreported) 23 March 1996 (overturned on appeal).
3   Appeal No HX/82029/95 (unreported) 27 June 1997 (overturned on appeal).

dismissed her appeal on the basis that 'even if . . . a low level of activity is relevant, any interest the authorities might have had . . . was in the appellant's father and not her'.[1] In a similar case, a woman from Sierra Leone was refused asylum because her involvement with the All-People's Congress (APC) was at a minor level and unlikely to cause her to suffer persecution in Sierra Leone.[2] In the case of a Kenyan woman arrested and detained twice by the authorities and raped because of her involvement with the opposition Safina party, the Home Office refused her case arguing that 'by your own admission, you only attended four rallies and your political activity was limited to making T-shirts for Safina'.[3]

These problems may be exacerbated by the inability of some women to give information about, and evidence of, their political allegiances. For example, in the case of an Iranian woman who was repeatedly detained and beaten, the letter from the Home Office in which her asylum claim was refused states that 'you have never been a member of any political party or organisation, and your involvement with [Monarchist group] was limited to administrative duties . . . you were only able to demonstrate a very basic understanding of the organisation for which you alleged to have provided administrative support'.[4] This decision was eventually overturned by an adjudicator who concluded: 'I find that the appellant was involved in political activity in Iran. I accept that this was at a relatively low level. I do, however, consider that this level of activity, coupled with her husband's death in custody, coupled with her absence from Iran for an extended period, would lead to her being of interest to the authorities if she were returned.' The depoliticisation of women's experiences of persecution is particularly evident in cases involving sexual violence.

4.4.2 Gendered forms of political resistance

Claims based on gendered forms of political resistance often experience many similar problems to those where women have been involved in so-called 'low-level' political activities. However, in the **US**, women who have been engaged in gendered forms of political resistance and opposition have been recognised as refugees within the meaning of the Refugee Convention on the basis of their political opinions or one that has been imputed to them. Jurisprudence on this issue includes a number of cases of women from Afghanistan whose involvement in family planning activities contravenes the political agenda of the Taliban regime.[5] For example, one case concerned an Afghan woman who became involved in women's health programmes under the Najibullah People's Democratic Party government and subsequently joined the PDP Women's Association because it was defending women's rights. She attended meetings and demonstrations, did literacy work, and worked to educate Afghani women about women's rights, birth control, education and work outside the home.[6] She was granted asylum on the basis of a well-founded fear of

---

1   Appeal No HX/73663/94 (unreported) 27 October 1995, emphasis added.
2   Appeal No HX/70343/95 (unreported) 19 June 1995.
3   Refusal letter dated April 1996 obtained through the Refugee Legal Centre.
4   Appeal No HX/75299/95 (unreported) 23 March 1996.
5   The politics of reproductive rights are discussed in more detail in Chapter 7 of this book.
6   Available on-line through the Centre for Gender and Refugee Studies at http://www.uchastings.edu/cgrs/summaries/summaries.html

persecution on account of political opinion due to membership of the women's association. Another woman who was trained as a pharmacist and worked in Pakistan was forced to leave her employment due to threats from Islamic extremists resulting from her views on birth control and abortion. In granting her asylum the BIA accepted that she had a well-founded fear of persecution on account of political opinion.

4.4.3 The politics of the veil

Political opinion includes women's opposition to extreme, institutionalised forms of oppression. A woman who opposes institutionalised discrimination against women, or expresses views of independence from the social or cultural dominance of men in her society may be found to have been persecuted or to fear persecution because of her actual political opinion, or a political opinion that has been or will be imputed to her. In this instance, a woman is not being punished solely because she is a woman, since those women who wear the veil are not punished, but because her actions are not accepted. In other words, she is punished because she refuses to be a 'proper' woman.[1] She is perceived, within the established political/social structure, as expressing politically antagonistic views through her actions or failure to act. If a woman resists gendered oppression, her resistance should be regarded as political activity. According to Macklin, 'identifying women's resistance to gender subordination as political opinion . . . [is] . . . profoundly feminist, if indeed one believes that the personal is political and that patriarchy is a system constituted primarily through power relations and not biology'.[2]

There is a growing acceptance on the part of decision-makers in different jurisdictions that women's resistance may take the form of opposition to gender social mores and attitudes, and that their opposition to State-imposed dress codes is politically, as opposed to personally, motivated. In **Canada**, the gender guidelines explicitly promote the recognition of resistance to societal mores, such as female genital mutilation and dress codes, as political opinion. This position is reflected in existing jurisprudence. For example, the Canadian Immigration Appeal Board concluded that the unwillingness of an Iranian woman to wear the chador and attend Islamic functions constituted political opinion. In a subsequent case, it was decided that the claimant's opposition to the government's enforcement of the dress laws, 'could possibly result in her being persecuted because of political opinion should she be returned to Iran'. The clearest ruling however is in *Namitabar*:[3]

> 'I consider that in the case at bar the female applicant has demonstrated that her fear of persecution is connected to her political opinion. In a country where the oppression of women is institutionalised any independent point of view or act opposed to the imposition of a clothing code will be seen as a manifestation of opposition to the established theocratic regime.'

---

1   Spijkerboer 1994.
2   Macklin 1995, p 260.
3   *Namitabar v MEI* [1994] F.2c 42 (TD).

Case-law on this issue in the **US** follows the decision in *Fatin*[1] which held that Iranian women who refuse to conform to repressive gender-specific regulations constitute a particular social group within the meaning of the Refugee Convention. However, the political nature of this opposition is also recognised. For example, one case concerned a woman from Iran who organised a women's group in the late 1970s.[2] The group began publishing an underground newsletter urging women's participation in the movement to oust the Shah. The newsletter emerged from secret publication after the Shah fell from office, and began also calling for unionisation and improved working conditions for women. By mid-1979, the situation for women in Iran began to worsen. A dress code was established requiring women to wear the *hejab*. The applicant organised a march and rally in opposition to the new rules in a major Iranian city. She was attacked, beaten and cursed while speaking at the rally. Because the Islamic fundamentalists had not yet consolidated their hold on power, she was not arrested. The group intensified its opposition, but had to resume clandestine publication of the newsletter after the government cracked down on newspapers. By mid-1981 she was in hiding to avoid arrest. The newsletter continued to oppose the regime, including the Iran–Iraq War. In mid-1982 the government authorities came to her home with an arrest warrant. She was not there but still in hiding. Two women from her group were executed, others fled the country. She stayed in hiding and then fled with her husband. She was granted asylum in May 1993 on the basis of well-founded fear of persecution on account of political opinion.

It should be noted that, in many cases, refugee status has been granted to women who had left Iran as children or young adults and who have never actually been subject to persecution and/or discriminatory treatment in Iran but do not want to conform with gender-specific rules and regulations or wear the veil. The basis of these claims has been a well-founded fear of future persecution on account of actual and imputed political opinion of gender equity (see Box 4.5).

Box 4.5

This case concerns a young Iranian woman who had been in the US since she came in 1983 at the age of three. In 1992, her parents applied for, and were denied, suspension of deportation. She became very frightened about being returned to Iran. Her fears intensified the more she learned about Iran, and eventually she attempted suicide in 1995. If returned she feared she would be alienated from Iranian society and unable to conform her behaviour to what would be expected of her. The BIA accepted that she feared persecution for her political opinion. The BIA held that the restrictions and discrimination against those viewed as 'westoxicants' amount to persecution. The applicant had never worn a veil and would refuse to wear one. Requiring her to change her dress and demeanour would destroy her self-esteem and confidence. The

---

1   *Fatin v INS*, 12 F.3d 1233 (3rd Cir. 1993).
2   Available on-line through the Centre for Gender and Refugee Studies at http://www.uchastings.edu/cgrs/summaries/summaries.html

cumulative stress of dealing with being returned to Iran might cause her to again attempt suicide. She was granted asylum in August 1998 on the basis of a well-founded fear of persecution on account of political opinion in favour of women's rights; on account of membership of a particular social group of persons raised in the West and viewed by the Iranian regime as 'westoxicants' because they know little of Iranian culture, cannot speak or read Farsi, and are non-practising Muslims; and on account of religion, as she is a non-practising Muslim.[1]

The most significant case in the **UK** in which a violation of social mores was interpreted as constituting political opinion is that of *Fathi and Ahmady*.[2] The Iranian applicant was arrested for wearing make-up and for failing to cover her hair properly. She was detained, taken to court and in place of receiving 50 lashes was fined. She was forced to leave her employment at a primary school due to her incorrect dress and she was unable to find alternative employment. It was argued on appeal that the appellant's behaviour was seen by the regime as opposition to it, a political act, and that the adjudicator was wrong to conclude otherwise. The IAT accepted that, in Iran, there is no clear and defined boundary to political opinion. In allowing the appeal, the IAT made a number of comments which are extremely significant in the context of the preceding discussion and which reinforce the argument that refugee women's experiences must be interpreted within the social and political context in which persecution has occurred. It is also, strategically, an important line of reasoning given the problems associated with the recognition of gender-defined social groups in the UK which were discussed in Chapter 3:

> 'A woman who is westernised must we think have considerable difficulty in concealing it. If she reveals it in our view it is perceived in Iran to be the expression of a political opinion contrary to the state. It is not merely transgression of Islamic mores, it is transgression of an Islamic mora as interpreted by this particular regime and the two are indistinguishable. We are not going so far as to say that every woman can say that she will not abide by the dress laws and by so doing bring herself within the Convention, it depends on the circumstances, but in this case ... the perception will be that she is making a political statement and therefore the persecution will be for a Convention reason on that basis.'[3]

4.4.4 Association/family membership

The decision-making authorities in various jurisdictions have generally failed to acknowledge that many women are imputed with a political opinion as a result of the activities and/or beliefs of their (usually) male family members. This can be seen in the **US** in the *Matter of E-L*,[4] which concerns a woman from El Salvador who lived with her husband and her parents until he was forcibly recruited into the armed forces. She was subsequently gang-raped by guerrillas looking for him (see Box 4.6).

---

1   Available on-line through the Centre for Gender and Refugee Studies at http://www.uchastings.edu/cgrs/summaries/summaries.html
2   *Fathi and Ahmady v SSHD* (unreported) 1 December 1996 (14264) (IAT).
3   *Fathi and Ahmady v SSHD* (unreported) 1 December 1996 (14264) (IAT).
4   Immigration Court, Seattle, WA, March 1, 1996. Available on line at http://www.uchastings.edu/cgrs/law/ij/137.html

Although it is generally recognised in **Canada** that women may be imputed with the political opinions of male family members, case-law on this issue is inconsistent. For example, in one case the claimant alleged a fear of persecution in Lithuania because of her ethnic identity as a Russian and her relationship with her husband, a well-known senior Russian military officer.[1] The CIRB found that whilst it would be difficult to conclude that Russian nationals in general have a well-founded fear of persecution in Lithuania, the claimant's case was exceptional because of her husband's prominent military role and her own status as a well-known supporter of Russian culture. Because of the claimant's age and gender, which made her more physically vulnerable, a threat of a minor assault by a gang of youths had potentially far more serious consequences than it would for a young man. The claimant had a well-founded fear of persecution because of her prominence and that of her husband and because of her age and gender. However, in another case concerning a Nigerian woman whose father, a political activist, was arrested in the mid-1990s and has not been seen since, the CRDD took a very different approach.[2] Following the disappearance of her father, the applicant went to live with her uncle, who was also politically active, but in the late 1990s the uncle was arrested and the claimant, who was 16 years old at the time, was raped by three policemen. The CRDD held that she did not have a well-founded fear of persecution on the basis of her political opinion of membership in a particular social group. She was not politically active, had never been charged with an offence or arrested and was not being sought by the authorities. Moreover, efforts were underway in Nigeria to restore democratic civilian rule. However, the CRDD did recognise that the claimant's mistreatments and the rape, together with the arrest and mistreatment of her family members, were severe and appalling and constituted compelling reasons why she should not be returned to Nigeria.

Box 4.6   Matter of E-L

This case concerned a woman from El Salvador who lived with her husband and her parents until he was forcibly recruited into the armed forces. She was subsequently gang-raped by guerrillas looking for him. He deserted the armed forces three months later. When guerrillas came to her looking for him, the applicant truthfully told them she did not know about his whereabouts. They tied up her parents and put something over her mouth, making her unconscious, and then gang-raped her. After the rape, the applicant left her home town to protect her parents, and met a man who took her into his family home for two years. Throughout those years, the applicant did not correspond with her parents in fear that she would be tracked down by the armed forces. The woman eventually went to the US but continued to suffer from physical and emotional trauma due to the rape. The court found her testimony to be consistent and credible but concluded that it was not possible to say that the soldiers were looking for her husband. They did not say anything as to the fact that she was raped because her husband was in the Salvadoran army, nor the

---

1   CRDD A98–00425 2 September 1998.
2   CRDD T98–06364 6 May 1999.

> fact that they believed she supported the Salvadoran army. The court
> held that the harm that she suffered was not 'on account of' a political
> opinion imputed to her by the armed men: 'Her rape seemed to be an
> isolated incident which is not related to any political opinion'.

In **Australia,** the Refugee Review Tribunal accepted that a Tamil woman from
Sri Lanka, whose Sinhalese spouse was from a high profile UNP family and who
was raped by the LTTE, was persecuted because of a political opinion which had
been imputed to her:[1]

> 'I accept that the applicant was raped and harassed by the LTTE. The rape clearly
> amounts to persecution. This occurred because the applicant was a Tamil woman
> married to a Sinhalese whose family had a high profile in the local area as UNP
> supporters. Because of her husband's profile and the refusal of the applicant and her
> husband to help the LTTE, the applicant was seen as a traitor to the Tamil race. I
> accept that the applicant was raped because of her race and her political opinion (that
> is, her lack of support for the LTTE and her imputed support for the UNP). Thus,
> the abuse and harassment occurred for Convention reasons.'

It should be noted that her claim of sexual abuse was not divulged to the
interviewing officer nor was it mentioned in any written material provided to the
Department or the Tribunal before the hearing.[2]

In **Germany**, a similar approach has been taken in cases involving family
membership or association. This can be seen in the case of an Iranian woman
who joined her husband in Germany in 1986.[3] Her husband was a member of an
opposition movement in Iran and was arrested and tortured. He was granted
asylum. The applicant was not politically active in Iran but she was interrogated
by the authorities on several occasions in connection with her husband's
activities. She was initially refused asylum, but was recognised as a Convention
refugee on appeal. The court ruled that, although in Iran spouses will not always
be persecuted together because of the activities of one of them, political
opponents will be actively sought, and persecution of family members is likely to
occur, if they engage in spreading their opinions to persons who are not (yet)
political opponents to the government. The husband of the applicant fell into
that category and the applicant thus had to fear persecution. Another similar case
also involved an Iranian woman who fled to Germany with her grandson.[4] All of
her seven children were then living in exile. Two of her daughters were already in
Germany where one had been granted asylum. The applicant claimed that she
had been ill-treated during interrogations about the whereabouts of her children
and her son-in-law who were in hiding. The court ruled that persecution of the
family for political crimes or actions of its members is an objective post-flight
reason for persecution entitling as such to asylum. The court was convinced that
persecution of kin was being exercised in Iran. As a dependant of recognised

---

1   RRT V96/05479 29 January 1997.
2   The reticence of many women to discuss their experiences of sexual violence during the
     interview, and the implications in establishing the basis of the asylum claim, are discussed in
     more detail in Chapter 10.
3   BayVG Ansbach AN K 88.35474 23 November 1989.
4   OVG NRW 16 A 10001/88 3 May 1988.

political refugees, the appellant would be with likelihood subjected to political persecution. Persecution of kin is independent of the refugee's own behaviour and, therefore, is not a subjective or self-serving post-flight rationale. It is an objective reason which can be compared to the persecution of members of a specific social group. The threat of political persecution is based on the persecution others suffer.

In the **UK**, the approach has been somewhat different because of the emphasis on whether 'a family' constitutes a particular social group within the meaning of the Refugee Convention. For example in *de Mello and de Araujo*,[1] Laws J reasoned (*obiter*) that family members could form a particular social group and 'if then they are persecuted because of their connection with [the father], it is, as a matter of ordinary language and logic, for reasons of their membership of the family, the group, that they are persecuted'. However, there has been some recognition that a political opinion may be imputed to a woman because of her relationship with male family members:

> 'The appellant shares her husband's political opinions and there is a reasonable possibility that if she were returned to Ethiopia she might be persecuted because of her association with her husband's activities. I have therefore concluded that the appellant does have a well-founded fear of persecution for a Convention reason.'

In *Findik*,[2] the IAT commented on submissions by the Home Office that the rape and torture suffered by the appellant had nothing to do with her husband's political activities and views:

> 'We have to say that this suggestion is not an attractive argument, and that the whole story is really linked to the husband's activities. In her evidence before us, the second appellant specifically said that she was questioned about her husband and that the authorities were concerned to find out about him. We reject [the Home Office's] submission and find as a fact that the detentions, tortures and rape arose as a result of her husband's political activities.'

In addition, family or kin associations have been recognised as defining a particular social group in *Quijano*.[3]

4.4.5 The gendered politics of war

The case-law from various jurisdictions on whether women who are sexually abused during periods of war and civil unrest can be recognised as refugees within the meaning of the Refugee Convention is similarly inconsistent. Much of the current case-law on this issue concerns applicants from Somalia and Sri Lanka.

In **Canada**, the courts have found that women are differentially at risk during periods of civil unrest by virtue of their gender. This can be seen in the case of a female Somali member of the Hawiye clan in Mogadishu who was accused, along with her brother, of aiding the United Somali Congress (USC), a Hawiye opposition group, by soldiers of the Somali President Mohammed Said Barre.[4]

---

1   *R v IAT ex parte de Mello and de Araujo* [1997] Imm AR 43 (HC).
2   *Findik* (17029) 12 May 1998 (IAT).
3   *Quijano v SSHD* [1987] Imm AR 227 (CA).
4   Canada [1991] CRRD No 606 24 December 1991.

They were detained for seven days until the family paid a substantial bribe. Civil war then broke out in late 1990, and the Hawiye tribe was targeted as USC sympathisers. The applicant escaped to Canada. After her flight, her sister was raped and killed in Mogadishu by members of the warring factions. Her brothers had fled and her father was deceased. It was ruled that a female Hawiye clan member without male protection is differentially at risk of serious harm in Somalia and has a well-founded fear of persecution based on membership in her social group. There is a difference between a well-founded fear based on Refugee Convention criteria and a well-founded fear of harm facing citizens in a civil war where all are equally at risk. The applicant's case shows the difference because, without male protection, she is unequally at risk. The Somali government cannot protect her. No one actually appears to control Mogadishu and the city is in a state of anarchy. The Board determined that the applicant was a Convention refugee.

In **Australia**, the determining authorities accepted that women are at risk of being sexually assaulted by soldiers in Sri Lanka but that the applicant was not differentially at risk and could not therefore claim to fear persecution for a Refugee Convention reason.[1]

In the **UK**, the IAT reached a similar conclusion in *Thangarajah*[2] where it was argued that the applicant had a well-founded fear of being persecuted (in the form of rape or sexual violence) on account of her membership of a particular social group, namely a woman Tamil from Jaffna. It was argued that Tamil women from Jaffna have been raped by members of the Sri Lankan army and army personnel have not been punished in respect of it and, despite efforts made by the Sri Lankan authorities to put a stop to it, it still continues. As such, Tamil women from Jaffna constitute a group defined by an innate and unchangeable characteristic. However, the IAT found that there was no evidence of any concerted action on the part of the Sri Lankan army to rape or sexually assault Tamil women from Jaffna, nor was there any evidence that there is any concerted action on the part of the Sri Lankan government or authorities to rape or sexually assault Tamil women from Jaffna. Furthermore, all the evidence showed that the Sri Lankan authorities were, and had been, taking action to put a stop to such sexual activities by army personnel, although, unfortunately, such actions had not always been successful.

> 'It is not the purpose of the Convention to protect women against rape or sexual assault, because that is an internal matter for the Governments of the countries in which these women live, but would come within the Convention if such activities were tolerated by the Government, or if the Government were unable or unwilling to put a stop to it. However, in Sri Lanka, as the evidence indicates, the Sri Lankan government is taking steps and has been taking steps, to put an end to such activities by the Sri Lankan Armed Forces.'

---

1   RRT V98/09334 13 April 1999.
2   *Thangarajah v SSHD* (unreported) 7 August 1998 (16414) (IAT).

Chapter 5

GENDERED SOCIAL MORES AND THE CONCEPT OF 'HONOUR'

5.1 GENDER, SEXUALITY AND THE CONCEPT OF 'HONOUR'

> 'Gender-based persecution is sometimes more subtle than other forms. It can take the form of restrictions on the way a woman behaves or it can involve forcing her to act in a certain way.'[1]

There has been increasing concern among advocates and practitioners about the way in which the asylum claims of women who experience gendered social norms and mores are interpreted within international refugee law. In many contexts, women are subjected to discriminatory treatment and social mores which are enforced through law or through the imposition of cultural or religious norms which restrict their opportunities and rights. Women have to keep certain rules for dressing and they are not allowed to receive certain kinds of education, or to practice certain professions, they are forced to marry the man selected for them by their family, or they are denied important civil and political rights.

Gendered social mores and discrimination are seen in, but are not limited to:

– **Legislated Discrimination,** for example Pakistan's *Hudood* laws or restrictions on women's movements and/or activities in Afghanistan

– **Dress Codes**

– **Employment or Education Restrictions**

– **Behavioural Restrictions,** for example, not going out in public without a male 'protector'

– **Marriage Related Harm** including the consequences of remaining single, separating, divorce and widowhood.

This chapter examines the consequences of gendered discrimination for women and the ways in which asylum claims made on this basis are best approached. It is suggested that, in order to respond appropriately to such claims, representatives need to understand the political significance of gender and of women's sexuality. This is reflected in the importance of the concept of 'honour' in many of the countries from which women flee. Whilst this has been associated in many cases with the process of Islamisation, it is by no means limited to these contexts.

The theoretical overview in Chapter 2 provides some insights into the politicisation of gender identity in the context of nationalism and ideological

---

1   ADIMA 1996, para 4.10.

struggles over national identity. Many anti-colonial nationalist projects aim to recover or reinvent 'tradition' in order to develop a new nationalist consciousness. Within this process, national difference is often constructed in cultural terms against the West, and because this difference is often located in the private sphere, in family and sex roles, women have been constructed as the bearers of an authentic/authenticated culture. This process can also be seen in the fact that issues which might typically be associated with the 'private' sphere have become politicised. For example, polygamy and choice in marriage were similarly treated not only as 'social issues' on which (male) politicians and thinkers had different views, but as varying signifiers of religious, social or political progress, or of the stability and well-being of the 'nation' or 'people'. In the context of nationalism, gender and sexuality therefore become powerful indicators of political and social identity. As De Groot suggests, 'to debate forms of marriage or the merits and demerits of the segregation, education or disenfranchisement of women was not just to address discreet political topics but to construct an overarching *topos* of power and difference for the whole debate. The fact that such matters were taken up by radicals *and* conservatives, by religious specialists *and* secularists, by autocrats as well as democrats shows their importance as topics, but equally the centrality of gender in the very articulation of projects of reform, nationalism, State power and social change ... Thus, at the core of discussions on State, nation, or public good lay profoundly and powerfully gendered and sexualised notions of the polity itself'.[1]

The politics of gender and sexuality is reflected in the concept of 'honour' which has become strongly associated with women's sexual behaviour in many contexts. Within this concept, any actual or perceived violation of what are deemed to be 'appropriate' gender relations are viewed as defiling the honour of the woman and, in turn, the honour of the nation itself. Protecting the honour of the woman, and in turn the honour of the nation, therefore gains political significance, and will be enforced either directly through the State, as seen in legislated discrimination and laws regulating women's behaviour, or through a woman's family and community (see Box 5.1). The latter becomes particularly important in many contexts because it is practically and ideologically impossible for the State to be directly in control of women's sexuality and relations with men.

Box 5.1

Mrs M came to the UK from Pakistan for medical treatment during her second pregnancy. Whilst she was here her husband claimed that her first child was not his son and that because she had given birth to a girl she had brought shame upon him and his family. Mrs M became convinced that he would murder her if she returned to Pakistan after he wrote a letter to the authorities in the UK requesting that they send her back and suggesting she should be arrested at the Pakistani airport and punished by stoning to death under the law, before her feet touched the purity of the soil in Pakistan. In refusing her claim for asylum on the basis

---

1   De Groot 1993, p 263.

> that it did not fall within the Refugee Convention, the adjudicator accepted that the appellant would suffer ostracism if not punishment on her return to Pakistan by reason of the vindictive action taken by her husband in the context of society where the appellant would be regarded as having transgressed the norms associated with wives in particular and women in general in Pakistan.[1]

The consequences for women of the gendered social mores and the concept of honour vary enormously within and between different countries. In some contexts, women are punished by the State for violating laws regulating their behaviour. For example, the material presented in the previous chapter illustrated the ways in which gender identity has become a focus for political contestation through the imposition of, and resistance to, the veil. In addition, however, there is also an argument which holds that, in certain cases, persecution is not a punishment that the woman endures for having violated the norm, but rather the imposition of the law or norm in and of itself. This has been recognised in case-law:

> '[The appellant's] clothing, manner of dress and behaviour were also the subject of close scrutiny to ensure that she acted within the confines of the new Islamic dress and behaviour code imposed by the Khomeini regime. The relentless pressure and harassment eventually took their toll and the situation became unbearable ... The appellant felt as if she was being tortured to death.'[2]

Critical to the formulation of these claims is the fact that the applicant must establish that the government is the source of the persecutory measure or that the government is unwilling or unable to protect her from persecution. When the treatment is through discriminatory statutes or laws which may be gender-neutral but are applied in a manner which target women and which are enforced by the government, State involvement is clear.[3] However, when the discriminatory practice is not applied by the government, but through cultural norms which discriminate against women, such as those which prevent them from studying or holding certain professions, the applicant must demonstrate both the existence of the norms and the failure or inability of the government to protect her from their imposition.

The issue of the failure of State protection is often one which is critical in asylum cases involving social mores and discrimination because, as was suggested above, it is often members of the family and community who ensure that the State's approach is enforced. Although a woman who is perceived to have brought shame upon her family, community and nation may have very real fears that she will be punished by the State if forced to return, more commonly she will fear persecution from her family and/or community. This fear is reflected in the term 'honour killing' which refers to the practice in a number of Middle Eastern and South Asian countries in which male members of the family are duty-bound to kill a female family member whom they think has brought dishonour and shame

---

1   Appeal No HX/75169/94 (unreported) 2 October 1996.
2   New Zealand Refugee Status Appeals Authority, Appeal No 2039/93 12 February 1996.
3   Kelly 1994.

to their family. The male members of the family believe they can only regain their honour and that of the family and/or community by murdering the woman for her alleged sexual transgressions. Moreover, there is evidence that in some countries, for example Pakistan, notions of what defiles honour have continually widened beyond defiance of sexual norms to include other forms of perceived deviation from social norms by women. These include the desire of women to choose a marriage partner and to seek divorce. Women victims of rape have also been seen to defile their male relatives' honour. Where women have been sexually active or abused, they may face harsh punishment because it is a condition of marriage that a woman be a virgin. The hymen, in this context, is both a physical and a social sign that both guarantees virginity and gives the woman a stamp of respectability and virtue. The inability to fulfil this condition seriously jeopard-ises her honour and that of her family and in a wide variety of different countries girls and young women may be forced to undergo virginity control examin-ations.[1] Where she is found not to be a virgin, or if she fails to bleed on her wedding night, the family may disown the woman or she may be killed by her father or brother to save face. This is despite the difficulties of defining virginity physiologically and conveniently ignores the fact that between 40 and 80 per cent of women do not bleed during their first intercourse. Alternatively, her family may insist that she undergo treatment to 'reconstruct' her hymen so that the loss of her virginity before marriage is not known to her husband.[2] The courts, however, have typically been dismissive of such violations of women's rights (see Box 5.2).

Box 5.2

Ms A is a Jordanian woman who claimed asylum in the US fearing that she would be killed by the male members of her family because of her alleged sexual transgressions. Ms A lost her virginity prior to marriage, left Jordan without her family's permission and married against her family's wishes. She learnt through letters from her sister that her father had declared that the shame she has brought on the family can only be removed by 'blood'. He made her brothers swear to kill her at any place and time they find her, and he has also demanded that all her male relatives kill her. Ms A was refused asylum on the basis that she did not have a well-founded fear of persecution. Although it was accepted that honour killings do occur in Jordan, the judge stated that these are violent episodes in specific families and not a pattern or practice against Jordanian women in general. The judge held that her fear of becoming a victim of an honour killing was a 'personal problem' that 'without more, cannot be the basis of an asylum claim'. This decision was upheld by the BIA on 20 August 1999, which similarly ruled that Ms A's fear of being the victim of an honour killing was the unfortunate consequence of a

---

1   See, eg, Decker 1998 on the increased prevalence of virginity control examinations in Turkey.
2   For further information on the social construction of the hymen, see Bekker et al 1996.

'personal family dispute'. On 20 January 2000 an appeal was lodged against this decision.[1]

Although such practices may not be officially sanctioned by the State, the authorities may be unable or unwilling to stop them. Similarly, women who are divorced or separated, whether or not by agreement, may be subjected to a whole range of discriminatory measures which can amount to 'serious harm' (see Box 5.3).

Box 5.3

Ms S arrived in the UK from Fiji in 1988 to join her husband, but the marriage broke down after she was abused and ill-treated by both her husband and in-laws. In 1989, the police told her that the Home Office had refused her application to remain here and that she was liable for deportation because her marriage had broken down within the first 12 months (the 'one year rule'). An application for asylum was made on the basis that she would experience violence and even possible death from her father and brothers, and ostracism/ harassment from the wider Hindu community if she returned to Fiji following the breakdown of her marriage. Ms S twice attempted to commit suicide rather than return. She was eventually granted ELR.[2]

5.2 SERIOUS HARM

It is important to note that the serious harm experienced or feared by women in cases involving social mores and the concept of honour is extremely varied and overlaps and intersects with all the other forms of harm which are examined in this book. In an effort to simplify the analysis, the serious harm women may face in these circumstances can be divided into three categories: State punishment; gendered discrimination; and social mores and 'crimes of honour'.

5.2.1 State punishment

As is noted in the Australian guidelines, 'the status of women in some societies may be restricted and dictated by legal, social or religious mores'. The restrictions will vary from mere inconvenience to oppression. In addition, a broad range of penalties may be imposed for disobeying restrictions placed on women.[3] Neal (1988) cites Iranian law that makes women's failure to wear the *hejab* a criminal act punishable by 74 lashes as an example of this. A further illustration of State punishment which discriminates against women is that

---

1   For a legal update see http://www.uchastings.edu/cgrs/campaigns/honor/honor.htm
2   Case-study provided by Southall Black Sisters. Representatives should note that in the subsequent period there have been policy changes with regard to both the 'one year rule' and the domestic violence concession.
3   ADIMA 1996, para 4.9.

enshrined in the *Hudood* Ordinance (1979) in Pakistan. The provisions of the Ordinance deal with a variety of offences, including the security of property, by prescribing such punishments as amputating the fingers and hands of the accused, as well as the number of public lashings appropriate for a particular crime. In addition, the Ordinance is fixated on moral and sexual offences, and it is the part relating to *zina* (extra-marital sex) and *zina-bil-jabr* (rape) which has had the most significant implications for women. Under these provisions, men and women accused of *zina* are to be meted equally stringent sentences, namely death by stoning or 100 lashes. Self-confession or the testimony of four Muslim males of known moral repute is sufficient for establishing the guilt of the suspects. However, by applying the same set of principles to cases of *zina-bil-jabr*, the Ordinance effectively blurred the distinction between rape and adultery. Failing a confession by the rapist, the presence of four morally upright Muslim men at the scene of the crime is necessary to establish guilt. A married woman who is raped can consequently stand accused of adultery and be punished accordingly (see Box 5.4).

Box 5.4

Ms M is a citizen of Pakistan who came to the UK as a visitor and subsequently married. However, the marriage was not a happy one and she petitioned for divorce. Unable to obtain leave to remain in the UK, Ms M applied for asylum on the basis that she could not go back to Pakistan because she had married someone from a different caste. Her brother would not tolerate that because in their family marriages were always arranged. The Secretary of State refused her claim on the grounds that she was not at risk of persecution for a Refugee Convention reason. The alleged threats from members of her own family could not be regarded as coming from agents of persecution for the purpose of the Refugee Convention. She had failed to show that the authorities in Pakistan were unable or unwilling to offer effective protection. Ms M appealed against this decision. It was argued that the appellant's behaviour transgressed the norms of Islamic society and would be regarded as an expression of a political opinion. The Tribunal dismissed the appeal stating that 'the appellant would not face reaction from her family or indeed the courts because of her political opinions but because of her failure to comply with the laws and social norms of the country. This does not amount to the expression of a political opinion as envisaged by the Convention'. However, following the decision in *Shah and Islam*[1] Ms M was granted leave to remain.[2]

There are many examples where women are punished for transgressing social mores or for finding themselves in circumstances deemed socially and culturally unacceptable. The severity of the punishment may be disproportionately severe

---

1   *Islam v SSHD; R v IAT ex parte Shah* [1999] INLR 144, Imm AR 283 (HL).
2   *Mirza v SSHD* (unreported) 30 January 1998 (16977) (IAT).

and may violate recognised international human rights principles. In these cases, such punishment will constitute 'serious harm' within the meaning of persecution.

In the **US**, the Third Circuit in *Fatin*[1] considered whether an Iranian woman faced with having to wear the traditional Islamic veil and to comply with other harsh rules imposed on women in Iran risked 'persecution' as the Board has defined it. The applicant asserted that the routine penalty for women who break the moral code in Iran is '74 lashes, one year's imprisonment, and in many cases brutal rapes and death'. These, the court stated, would constitute persecution. The court went on to note that 'the concept of persecution is broad enough to include governmental measures that compel an individual to engage in conduct that is not physically painful or harmful but is abhorrent to that individual's deepest beliefs'. Having to renounce religious beliefs or to desecrate an object of religious importance might, for example, be persecution if the victim held strong religious beliefs. In the **UK**, the courts have recognised the excessive nature of State punishment in cases involving the transgression of gendered social mores and laws regulating women's behaviour in *Gilani*:[2]

> 'We accept the penalties which can be imposed for transgressing against the "social mores" of dress and behaviour can amount to persecution and indeed in Iran may amount to persecution.'

5.2.2 Gendered discrimination

Women may be subjected to discriminatory treatment which is enforced through law or through the imposition of social or religious norms which restrict their opportunities and rights. Social mores and discrimination can in themselves constitute 'serious harm' within the meaning of persecution. However, although the legal obligation to eliminate all forms of discrimination against women is a fundamental tenet of international human rights law, the level of discrimination sufficient to rise to the level of 'serious harm' is not a point on which States readily agree. The UNHCR Handbook (1979) specifically addresses the issue of discrimination in the context of the definition of 'persecution'. If measures of discrimination lead to consequences of a substantially prejudicial nature for the person concerned then 'serious harm' can be said to have occurred:

> 'Where measures of discrimination are, in themselves, not of a serious character, they may nevertheless give rise to a reasonable fear of persecution if they produce, in the mind of the person concerned, a feeling of apprehension and insecurity as regards [her] future existence. Whether or not such measures of discrimination in themselves amount to persecution must be determined in the light of all the circumstances. A claim to fear of persecution will of course be stronger where a person has been the victim of a number of discriminatory measures of this type and where there is thus a cumulative element involved.'[3]

The UNHCR Handbook (1979) cites the examples of serious restrictions on the right to earn a livelihood, the right to practise his or her chosen religion and his or

---

1   *Fatin v INS* [1993] 12 F.3d 1233 (3rd Cir).
2   *Gilani v SSHD* (unreported) 3 June 1987 (5216) (IAT).
3   UNHCR 1979, paras 54–55.

her access to normally available educational facilities as examples of discrimination rising to the level of persecution.

The UNHCR's *Guidelines on the Protection of Refugee Women* (1991) do not clarify this issue any further insofar as they do not distinguish persecution from 'mere' discrimination. Other authors are very much clearer and locate discrimination within Hathaway's framework, which was discussed in Chapter 3. For example, in addition to the punishment inflicted for failing to abide by social mores, a policy compelling women to wear the veil violates her 'first order' freedom of religion or conscience. The premise is that if the law discriminates by selectively abrogating fundamental human rights of designated groups, the law itself persecutes. In principle, it should not matter that it would be relatively 'easy' for the claimant to obey the law, and thus avoid prosecution, by wearing a veil, if in doing so she must forsake a protected freedom.[1] More often, however, the wearing of the veil constitutes only one element in a plethora of rules, policies and customs circumscribing the lives of women from particular countries. Therefore, in a claim based on discriminatory treatment and/or social mores, the decision-maker must evaluate all the circumstances, including the type of right or freedom denied, the manner in which the right is denied, the seriousness of the harm to the applicant, and any non-persecutory justification for the discriminatory treatment. Any harm to a right lower than level 1 or 2 may be persecutory if the harm is systematic or cumulative and seriously affects the integrity of the applicant.[2]

The assessment of whether gendered discrimination constitutes 'serious harm' within the meaning of persecution varies enormously both within and between different refugee receiving countries, and to a certain extent reflects the general approach to discrimination within the jurisdictions. In **Canada**, for example, the CRDD concluded that a Muslim woman from the Lebanon who had joined her Christian boyfriend in Canada and who feared that her father might kill her to preserve the family honour was not a refugee within the meaning of the Refugee Convention.[3] Although it was accepted that, as an unmarried woman with children, she would be shunned by her family and treated as a prostitute, it was not accepted that her life was in danger, and the CRDD determined that any discrimination she might face would not amount to persecution. However, the CRDD took a different approach in the case of a woman from Saudi Arabia who had an illicit affair with a Jordanian whom she subsequently married, and who feared that she would be stoned to death.[4] The Refugee Division accepted that women are subject to severe legislated discrimination in Saudi Arabia and that this would be exacerbated by the fact that she was of Malaysian extraction and substantial prejudice based on ethnic or national origin also exists. The applicant had subsequently been abandoned by her husband, and women in Saudi society are dependent on their husbands for accessing even limited rights, such as the right to movement. The CRDD determined that, taken individually, none of the three factors justified the claim. Taken together, they did. In several cases, the CRDD has also held that depriving a woman of custody of her children on the

---

1   Macklin 1995.
2   Hathaway 1991.
3   CRDD V98-02496 19 April 1999.
4   CRDD T98–01731 5 February 1999.

sole basis of her gender is a fundamental violation of her basic human r
constitutes discrimination which was serious enough to amount to persecution
(see Box 5.5).[1]

Box 5.5[2]

A recent Canadian case concerned a 34-year-old Iranian woman who claimed that her rights and responsibilities as a mother were violated after the death of her husband. The Refugee Division found that, under Iranian law, the principal claimant would have lost the custody of her children for a significant part of their childhood had they remained in Iran and would have lost the ability to influence guardianship decisions in respect of the children. This constituted discrimination which was serious enough to amount to persecution. Depriving a woman of custody on the sole basis of her gender is a fundamental violation of her basic human rights. The principal claimant had a well-founded fear of persecution on the ground of membership of a particular social group: widowed mothers in Iran. The Refugee Division also found that the minor claimants had established their claims as members of a particular social group: children of widowed mothers in Iran.[3]

In **New Zealand**, gendered discrimination has been explicitly acknowledged in several important cases:

> 'The Authority should ... consciously strive both to recognise and to give proper weight to the impact of discriminatory measures on women.'[4]

> 'Discrimination can affect gender-based groups to different degrees ... various acts of discrimination, in their cumulative effect, can deny human dignity in key ways and should properly be recognised as persecution for the purposes of the Convention.'[5]

In the **UK**, case-law relating to discrimination as 'serious harm' is clearer in cases which are not gender-specific. For example, in *Chiver*[6] the IAT ruled that discrimination could constitute 'serious harm' where the respondent, a Romanian, had suffered serious discrimination in being barred from employment and State benefits because of his political opinions:

> 'We agree with the adjudicator that persecution ... will be shown if the appellant establishes a reasonable likelihood that he will be unable to obtain employment.'

---

1   See, eg, CRDD V97–01419 9 August 1999; CRDD V96–02102 28 May 1999.
2   CRDD V97–01419 9 August 1999.
3   There have been recent changes in Iranian custody law. Representatives should ensure that their information on the situation is up to date. See Chapter 10 for further information on how to achieve this.
4   New Zealand Refugee Status Appeals Authority, Appeal No 1039/93 13 February 1995.
5   New Zealand Refugee Status Appeals Authority, Appeal No 2039/93 12 February 1996.
6   *Chiver v SSHD* (unreported) 24 March 1994 (10758) (IAT).

In *Gashi and Nikshiqi*,[1] the IAT referred to Hathaway's human rights framework, which was discussed in Chapter 3, and accepted that human rights violations below level 1 can also constitute 'serious harm' within the meaning of 'persecution':

> 'We do not think that when the Convention was drafted it was intended to include the right to be free of arbitrary deprivation of property or to be protected against unemployment (Professor Hathaway's fourth category) . . . However there seems to be no dispute that it includes not only the first category but the second category as well and some aspects of the third category.'

By contrast, in cases of gender-specific discrimination, there has sometimes been a failure on the part of adjudicators to recognise general human rights as women's rights. For example, in *Islam*,[2] the IAT stated that 'we do not think that the purpose of the Convention is to award refugee status because of disapproval of social mores or conventions in non-western societies'. However, in *Fathi and Ahmady*,[3] there was recognition that gender-specific treatment of women in the Iranian context amounts to serious harm:

> 'The next question then is whether the treatment amounts to persecution. I think that the cumulative effect of her being arrested because of her failure to observe the dress laws, the fact that she has been dismissed from her employment for the same reason and that she has been harassed on occasions by security forces might well amount to persecution.'[4]

5.2.3   Social mores and 'crimes of honour'

As has already been indicated in this chapter, the consequences for women of failure or refusal to comply with social norms and mores regarding their behaviour can vary enormously. The examples presented in this section are therefore only illustrative and are not definitive.

At one extreme, a woman may fear that she will be subjected to threats on her life if she is forced to return to her country of origin (see Box 5.6). Honour killings are prevalent in a number of countries including, for example, Jordan, where they have been recognised as a gross human rights violation that is inadequately dealt with by the Jordanian government. According to the 1998 US State Department Report on Human Rights Practices, more than 20 'honour killings' were reported in Jordan that year. The Report points out, however, that most honour killings go unreported and the actual number is believed to be four times as high. The only form of protection offered by the Jordanian government for women who fear becoming victims of honour crimes is their own imprisonment and, in 1998,

---

1   *Gashi and Nikshiqi v SSHD* (unreported) 22 July 1996 (13695) (IAT).
2   *Islam and Others v SSHD* (unreported) 2 October 1996 (13956) (IAT). This case was subsequently heard in both the Court of Appeal and House of Lords where it was determined that Mrs Islam was a refugee within the meaning of the Refugee Convention. See *Islam v SSHD; R v IAT ex parte Shah* [1999] INLR 144, Imm AR 283 (HL).
3   *Fathi and Ahmady v SSHD* (unreported) 1 December 1996 (14264) (IAT).
4   *Fathi and Ahmady v SSHD* (unreported) 1 December 1996 (14264) (IAT). This comment was made by the initial adjudicator who had refused her appeal on the grounds that the persecution suffered was not for a Refugee Convention reason.

there were up to 50 women involuntarily detained in this form of 'protective custody'. Article 340 of the Jordanian Penal Code provides that men accused of honour killings are not prosecuted for murder but instead for 'crimes of honour', which carry lenient sentences, averaging between three months to one year (the penalty for murder under the Jordanian Penal Code, by comparison, is death). Recently, there was a governmental proposal to abolish Article 340. Despite being supported by a worldwide campaign, the proposal was defeated in Parliament in November 1999. Members of Parliament stated that abolishing Article 340 would amount to 'legislating obscenity' and that the efforts in support of the proposal 'are attempts by the West to infiltrate Jordanian society and demoralise women'.

Box 5.6[1]

In this case, the applicant was an unmarried Assyrian Christian woman from Iraq who arrived in Australia as a prospective bride under a proposed marriage arranged by her father. Shortly after meeting her fiancé, she decided not to proceed with the marriage. However, he insisted that the marriage go ahead and that they separate after two months so saving his honour. When she refused this proposition, his three brothers in Iraq attacked her father, following which he suffered a heart attack. The applicant feared that if she were to return to Iraq she would be at risk both from her fiancé's family and her own father for refusing to proceed with the marriage. Her father had already threatened to kill her and had told members of her family that she was already dead. In addition, her fiancé's brothers in Iraq had spread an untrue story that she was sexually assaulted by her fiancé, and that her father was even more angry with her as she had disgraced the family by being dishonoured.

Even where a woman does not fear threats on her life, she is often forced to submit to measures to retain or re-establish her honour. The harm experienced or feared in these cases will often be marriage-related including forced marriage, which may often involve children and is a form of abuse that is often not recognised. In many cases of women who refuse to agree to such arrangements, it will be the punishment inflicted as a refusal to abide by discriminatory social mores, rather than the marriage itself, which will rise to the level of 'serious harm':

> 'Many societies practice arranged marriage and this in itself may not be a persecutory act. However, the consequences of defying the wishes of one's family when viewed against the background of the State's failure to protect a person should be carefully considered.'[2]

The repercussions for women of divorcing their husbands or entering into mixed marriages may be equally devastating. In countries such as Algeria, women face

---

1   RRT Reference: V96/04752 11 September 1996.
2   ADIMA 1996, para 4.10.

mut'a, or 'temporary pleasure marriage', in which a man may marry a woman for just three hours before passing her to male friends or relatives for their enjoyment. There have been a number of reports about single women being abducted, raped and even killed after entering into temporary pleasure marriages. In Iran this practice is known as *siqa* and is condoned and lawful.[1]

There are many situations where harm inflicted, either as a result of marriage or because of a refusal to conform to prescribed norms of behaviour, constitutes cruel, inhuman or degrading treatment. In addition, however, there are Articles within the ICCPR which indicate that there are certain rights around the institution of marriage which may be utilised in some cases to argue that the marriage itself deprives a woman of her fundamental rights and freedoms. Article 16 of the Convention on the Elimination of All Forms of Discrimination against Women (CEDAW) also explicitly details the content of women's equal rights within the family, regarding entry into marriage, choice of spouse and rights within marriage. This Article also prohibits child marriages.

5.3 THE FAILURE OF STATE PROTECTION

In addition to establishing a well-founded fear of 'serious harm', a woman must also show that the State has failed to protect her, or would fail to do so. There is a failure of State protection if 'serious harm' has been inflicted by the authorities or by associated organisations or groups, or where the harm has been committed by others and the authorities are *unwilling* to give effective protection, or where harm has been committed by others and the authorities are *unable* to give effective protection.

In asylum claims involving social mores and the concept of honour, representatives should be aware that, in addition to those instances where the State is directly responsible for the harm that individual women face or fear, for example through discriminatory legislation, women often fear harm from non-State agents against which the State has failed to provide effective protection (see Box 5.7).

Box 5.7

On 6 April 1999, 27-year-old Samia Sarwar was gunned down in her attorneys' office in Lahore by a hit man retained by her family. Her mother, father, and paternal uncle were all accomplices to her murder. She was killed because she was seeking a divorce from her estranged husband – an action her family deemed 'dishonourable' and, hence, warranting death. Ms Sarwar's transgression, in the eyes of her family, was seeking a divorce; other women are attacked, by or at the instigation of family members, for choosing their spouses. In addition, countless women suffer from battery, rape, burning, acid attacks, and mutilation.

---

1   For further information see Afkhami and Friedl (eds) 1994.

Estimates of the percentage of women who experience spousal abuse alone range from 70 to upwards of 90 per cent. If there is anything more disturbing than the prevalence of these crimes, it is the impunity with which they are committed. Samia Sarwar's case is an example not only of the violence experienced by Pakistani women but also of the lack of governmental will to do anything about it.[1]

In some cases, the State actually institutionalises social mores and the concept of honour and, therefore, can be held directly responsible for the harm experienced or feared by women asylum seekers. This can be seen, for example, in Pakistan's *Hudood* Ordinances and the measures imposed on women in Afghanistan by the Taliban. Although the *Hudood* Ordinances affect all citizens of Pakistan, they are applied to women with particularly disastrous effects. Women are discriminated against by law. They find it extremely difficult to prove rape and may face criminal prosecution if they fail to do so. One component of these laws requires that a woman alleging rape corroborate her complaint with the testimony of four male witnesses. Failure to prove that sexual contact occurred without consent leaves the complainant vulnerable to criminal prosecution for adultery or fornication. Moreover, the existence of these laws provides a framework within which women are subjected to other forms of abuse. Women who behave in ways which their husbands or fathers dislike, or who seek to divorce and re-marry, or who choose to marry against the will of their parents, or who happen to be related to a man wanted by the authorities may get wrongly accused of *Hudood* offences as a means of intimidating their relatives, and risk criminal prosecution under the *Hudood* laws, often with no basis in fact. In these cases, it will be necessary for representatives to argue that the law or policy is either inherently persecutory or has a 'legitimate' aim but is effected through discriminatory measures.

This approach to a failure of State protection is also relevant in cases from countries such as Iran, where those who contravene the dress code are subject to punishment which may range from a verbal reprimand, to a fine, to 74 strokes of the lash, to a prison sentence of up to one year. Women are regularly harassed and arrested or detained under legal pretexts for wearing make-up or being improperly veiled. In addition, sexual segregation means that any form of friendship or association between the sexes outside the marriage contract is punishable by flogging, imprisonment, forced marriage or stoning to death. The wide range of measures imposed on women by the authorities in Iran is illustrative of the State's direct involvement in persecuting women through the institutionalisation of social norms and mores regarding their behaviour:

> 'Iranian women suffer one of the most discriminatory set of laws in the world. They are denied many basic opportunities and access to many positions in the religious, political, judiciary and military arenas. An assortment of supervisory social regulations regarding women's behaviour in public areas has been designed to restrict women's participation in public life and further isolate and restrict their lives to the private domain of their homes. They are denied many basic rights and at the same time they are punished, both inside and outside the law, more severely than their male counterparts. The discriminatory laws regarding women's rights cover a

---

1   Human Rights Watch 1999.

wide range of areas in marriage, divorce, child custody, and inheritance, as well as anti-women labour laws and social policies. These have had the devastating results of economic deprivation and social isolation of women and their children.'[1]

In *Fathi-Rad*,[2] the courts in **Canada** had to deal with the issue of whether the Islamic dress code is a policy of general application applied to all citizens of Iran.[3] In its decision, it is clear that the court regarded the law as persecutory against women. In the alternative, the court concluded that the punishment for minor infractions of the Islamic dress code was disproportionate to the objective of the law, and therefore constituted persecution:

> 'The Islamic dress code is a law applicable only to women in Iran. It dictates the manner in which Iranian women must dress to comply with the beliefs of the theocratic governing regime and prescribes any punishment for any violation of the law. A law which specifically targets the manner in which women dress may not properly be characterised as a law of general application which applies to all citizens.'

In these cases, the State connection is therefore usually clear. However, decision-makers may attempt to dismiss the claim on the basis that it is morally or culturally inappropriate for the authorities in the determining country to pass judgment on the legitimacy or otherwise of State legislation in other countries.[4]

In many asylum claims made by women involving gendered social mores and the concept of honour, the failure of State protection arises not from the fact that its agents are directly implicated in the harm experienced or feared, but rather because the State has failed to provide effective protection against the harm to which a woman fears she will be subjected to by members of her family or community. Often the State's own attitude to particular issues, for example the institution of marriage and women's sexuality, provides an important context in which this harm is experienced or feared. In many cases, however, the harm suffered or feared is not directly at the hands of the State but family and community members. In such cases, the State often fails to provide effective protection for women (see Box 5.8).

Box 5.8[5]

A recent Canadian case concerned a woman from Bangladesh who was continually mistreated by her in-laws after her spouse was forced to flee. They had never accepted their son's marriage to her. Her mother-in-law humiliated her and made her perform degrading work for several years. The applicant left and moved in with her parents, who attempted to force

---

1　Iranian Human Rights Working Group's statement on the occasion of the UN's Fourth World Conference on Women, 5 September 1995. Available on-line at http://www.gpg.com/MERC/org/ihrwg/women95.html
2　*Fathi-Rad v SSC* (unreported) 13 April 1994.
3　It should be noted that there are some dress codes which apply to men, eg, the wearing of short-sleeved T-shirts or those with 'Western' images or logos may be prohibited. However, it is rare that such restrictions are formally legislated.
4　This issue is discussed in more detail in Chapter 3.
5　CRDD M98-05727 4 May 1999.

her to divorce and remarry, but she refused. They also pressured her in various ways since the local community frowned upon a young woman living alone with her child. She repeatedly said that she was afraid her child would be taken away from her. According to the documentary evidence, the social context in Bangladesh made the situation of most women in the country precarious and vulnerable. The family context often lent itself to certain forms of oppression towards which the authorities in power appeared indifferent. The CRDD accepted that there had been a failure of State protection and granted Convention refugee status.

As is evident from the framework which was presented in Chapter 3, State responsibility includes those instances where social mores dictate gender-related abuse as an acceptable practice and where there are no effective means of legal recourse to prevent, investigate or punish such acts. Where the State fails to provide sufficient protection, it does not matter whether this derives from collusion, indifference or impotence. It amounts to official acquiescence. The State is liable for human rights violations by private individuals where it refuses or is unable to provide effective protection or redress. State inaction includes, but is not limited to, official legislation (eg marital rape exemptions in law), lack of police response to pleas for assistance and/or a reluctance, refusal or failure to investigate, prosecute or punish individuals. Where a State facilitates, accommo-dates, tolerates, justifies or excuses denials of women's rights, there is a failure of State protection.

The concept of a failure of State protection includes those instances where social mores dictate gender-related abuse as an acceptable practice and where there are no viable means of legal recourse to prevent, investigate or punish such acts. In this sense, as long as the State fails adequately to protect the claimant, it does not matter whether inaction derived from collusion, indifference or genuine impotence (see Box 5.9).

Box 5.9[1]

The applicant, a woman from Pakistan, was beaten and threatened with death by her brother-in-law when she refused to marry, and was harassed and sexually assaulted by the police when she attempted to file a complaint. She subsequently went to stay with her family in the US. When she returned to Pakistan for a family wedding she discovered that her family had arranged her marriage to an older widower. She refused the marriage and was beaten and her life threatened. The CRDD accepted that violence against women is widespread in Pakistan and that the police and the courts rarely become involved. She was granted asylum.

---

1   CRDD M97-06821 14 July 1998.

International jurisprudence on the failure of State protection in cases involving gendered social mores and the impact on women of the concept of honour is extremely varied and in significant part reflects the general approach taken in the various jurisdictions to persecution by non-State agents which was discussed at length in Chapter 3. As was noted, decision-makers in **Canada** have generally recognised State liability for private actions. In the **US**, the INS Manual (1980) states that a person is a refugee for purposes of asylum eligibility if 'he or she has a well-founded fear of persecution (as a result of one of the five factors in the definition) because he or she is not adequately protected by his or her government'. Case-law in the US, most notably *McMullen*[1] and *Matter of Villalta*,[2] establishes that the persecutor can be either the government or a non-government entity that the government is unable or unwilling to control.

In the **UK**, the Home Office has typically failed to recognise women who have been persecuted for transgressing social mores regarding their behaviour as Refugee Convention refugees (see Box 5.10).

Box 5.10[3]

Ms B is from the Rajput community, which originates from Rajasthan, India. The Rajput are known for their highly restrictive, traditional beliefs on the role of women in society, marriage and divorce. The practice of *sati* originates in Rajasthan and many accept it as part of their cultural heritage. After Ms B came to the UK, her marriage to a British citizen who mentally abused her broke down, and she was thrown out of the matrimonial home. Her family said that they would rather she kill herself in the UK than return to India. Ms B was fearful that she would be ostracised and vulnerable to violence, persecution and even death should she be deported. Although Ms B is not a widow, she would be encouraged to kill herself because she is a divorced woman. Suicide in this case would be seen as a substitute for *sati* and regarded as a sacrifice which will help to restore the honour of the family. Her application for asylum has been refused and she is now waiting for the appeal to be heard. Her refusal letter stated that 'the Secretary of State ... does not consider that the remit of the Refugee Convention extends to people who fear personal difficulties due to their marital status ... the expectation is that persecution normally relates to action by the authorities of a country'.[4]

---

1   *McMullen v INS* [1982] 658 F.2d 1312, 1315 n.2 (9th Cir).
2   *Matter of Villalta* [1990] Int Dec No 3126 (BIA).
3   Case study provided by Southall Black Sisters.
4   Representatives should be aware of the existence of the domestic violence concession and apply its provisions wherever possible. Violence within the family as the basis of an asylum claim is discussed in detail in Chapter 6.

In some cases, however, decision-makers have recognised that women asylum seekers have not been able to access State protection. In one case where an Algerian woman was told that she must marry the local Emir of the GIA in the form of a *mut'a* or temporary pleasure marriage, the adjudicator recognised that the Algerian State had failed to protect her against this arrangement, and even though it was not directly implicated, upheld her appeal and granted full status:

> 'I am satisfied of the authorities' inability to guarantee the safety even of VIPs, not to talk about ordinary citizens. Certainly, as far as women in Algeria are concerned, in my view they are not a top priority as far as the government is concerned and I am not surprised that the appellant did not think it was worth her while to approach the authorities to seek protection. I am satisfied that she was unlikely to receive effective protection from the authorities against the GIA groups who were threatening her safety.'[1]

Perhaps the most important decision is that taken recently in *Shah and Islam*[2] which was discussed at length in Chapter 3. Although this case principally addresses the issue of whether women (or a sub-group thereof) constitute a particular social group within the meaning of the Convention, it also raises the issue of State responsibility in cases of gender-related persecution and may have important implications for women seeking asylum from harm associated with social mores and the concept of honour. Lord Hoffmann concluded that the failure of the State to protect women from violence by members of their family and community means that the harm they experience or fear rises to the level of persecution within the meaning of the Convention:

> 'Domestic violence . . . is regrettably by no means unknown in the United Kingdom. It would not however be regarded as persecution within the meaning of the Convention. This is because the victims of violence would be entitled to the protection of the State . . . What makes it persecution in Pakistan is the fact that . . . the State was unable or unwilling to offer her any protection.'

5.4 REFUGEE CONVENTION GROUNDS

As with many of the issues which are addressed in this book, the most relevant Refugee Convention ground to which the actual or feared persecution can be linked in cases involving social mores, marriage-related harm and/or actual or perceived breaches of 'honour' will be dependent upon the particular circumstances of the claim, and in particular whether the persecutory treatment is the harm itself (as, eg, in dowry death and *sati*), the persecutory consequences of refusal to submit to such treatment (as, eg, in refusing to accept forced marriage or *mut'a*), or the consequences for a woman of events which may be beyond her control (such as divorce or accusations of adultery). It is increasingly evident, however, that in many of these cases a political opinion may be imputed to the woman concerned. The most appropriate basis for the claim should be

---

1   Appeal No HX/66670/96 (unreported) 22 October 1996.
2   *Islam v SSHD; R v IAT ex parte Shah* [1999] INLR 144 (HL).

established at an early stage through careful consultation and research on conditions for women in the applicant's country of origin.

5.4.1 Religion

There is often an overlap between religious and political persecution, and the distinction between religion and politics is frequently a difficult one to make. Religion may be used to justify particular attitudes towards women, including the concept of honour. In particular, representatives should be aware of the *political nature* of gender in the context of religious laws. Where religious tenets require certain kinds of behaviour from a woman, contrary behaviour may be perceived as evidence of an unacceptable political opinion regardless of what a woman herself actually believes. In cases involving an actual or perceived violation of social mores, it could be argued that the ground for the persecution was either a religious or a political opinion which has been attributed to the applicant. Arguing for either or both grounds are valid approaches in representing such claims.

5.4.2 Political opinion

Challenges to social mores and norms, differing as they do from conventional forms of political contestation, have typically been considered 'personally motivated' and have not been categorised as political. As a result, women persecuted for such transgressions have typically had difficulties bringing themselves within the protection of refugee law. It was argued in the previous chapter that political opinion should include women's opposition to extreme, institutionalised forms of oppression. A woman who opposes legislated discrimination against women or expresses views of independence from the social or cultural dominance of men in her society may be found to have been persecuted or to fear persecution because of her actual political opinion or a political opinion that has been or will be imputed to her. She is perceived within the established political/social structure as expressing politically antagonistic views through her actions or failure to act. If a woman resists gendered oppression, her resistance should be regarded as political activity. According to Macklin, 'identifying women's resistance to gender subordination as political opinion ... [is] ... profoundly feminist, if indeed one believes that the personal is political and that patriarchy is a system constituted primarily through power relations and not biology'.[1] The fact that a woman may challenge particular social conventions about the manner in which women should behave may be considered political by the authorities and may attract persecutory treatment on this basis. The strength of this approach is particularly clear in the case of women's refusal to wear the veil. Clearly, in this instance, women are not being punished solely because they are women, since those women who wear the veil are not punished, but because their actions are not accepted. In other words, they are punished because they refuse to be 'proper' women.[2]

---

1   Macklin 1995, p 260.
2   Spijkerboer 1994.

In addition, there are cases where women do not directly or intentionally challenge institutionalised norms of behaviour but are nonetheless imputed (ie attributed) with a political opinion as a consequence of their experiences. This can be seen, for example, in the characterisation of a raped woman as adulterous, in the social ostracism of an unmarried, separated, divorced, widowed or lesbian woman, and in the politicisation of (unintentional) violations of dress codes (see Box 5.11).

Box 5.11

Ms A is from Kabul in Afghanistan. She arrived in the UK with her husband and three sons and had been subjected to physical and sexual abuse throughout her marriage. In 1994, Ms A finally managed to escape the matrimonial home. Her husband abducted their youngest son and Ms A presently lives in the UK with her two other sons. If her application for asylum is refused, she will eventually be sent back to Afghanistan where, in addition to the brutality women have been subjected to throughout the war, the establishment of the Taliban regime in Kabul has led to the drastic reduction of women's rights. As a 'westernised', divorced woman, Ms A would be perceived as being non-Islamic and disobedient. She will be ostracised by the community for having brought dishonour upon her family and will be subject to persecution both from her immediate community and from the Taliban regime. She is already marked as having been politically active in defiance of her husband and this will further mark her out as having transgressed the boundaries women are supposed to operate within. She fears that her husband may arrange to have her killed and will be able to escape criminal prosecution through his considerable wealth, influence and political connections.

The issue then is not one of refugee law per se, but of how women's experiences are interpreted by representatives and decision-makers:

> 'If a woman refuses to oblige with a social practice she finds oppressive, be it a dress code or a denial of education, then that is a political issue. The demarcation of public and private spheres at stake here is a political issue of great importance.'[1]

Conceptualising political opinion in a way which goes beyond the public/private dichotomy pervasive in the normative structures of international refugee law reflects the agency of those represented. It is also the basis of more appropriate and improved decision-making. This position is reinforced by UK jurisprudence, most notably in the case of *Fathi and Ahmady*.[2] However, a woman who is gravely discriminated against without ever offering resistance, for example if she has been divorced by her husband or accused of adultery, may find it difficult to substantiate her plea of being persecuted on one of the other grounds enumerated in the Refugee Convention, and the social group strategy may be the

---

1   Spijkerboer 1994, p 66.
2   *Fathi and Ahmady v SSHD* (unreported) 1 December 1996 (14264) (IAT).

preferred, and possibly only, option. Much will depend upon the details of the particular case and the religious and political context in which the discrimination took place.

5.4.3 Social group

The academic and legal debate around whether women constitute a particular social group within the meaning of the Refugee Convention has frequently centred around the issue of gendered discrimination, social mores and so-called 'crimes of honour'. As was indicated in Chapter 3, the Canadian gender guidelines address the social group category by acknowledging that there is increasing international support for the application of the particular social group ground to the claims of women who allege a fear of persecution by reasons of their gender. The guidelines divide women refugee claimants into four broad categories, although they acknowledge that these categories are not mutually exclusive or exhaustive.[1] Two of these categories are particularly relevant to the experiences of women fleeing gendered social mores and harm related to the concept of honour:

> 'Women who fear persecution resulting from certain circumstances of *severe discrimination on grounds of gender* or *acts of violence* either by public authorities or at the hands of private citizens from whose actions the state is unwilling or unable to adequately protect the concerned persons' (emphasis in original).

> 'Women who fear persecution as the consequence of failing to conform to, or for transgressing, certain gender-discriminating religious or customary laws and practices in their country of origin.'

As the guidelines suggest, claims of the second of these two categories may be determined on grounds of religious or political opinion but also on grounds of membership in a 'particular social group' because

> '[s]uch laws and practices, by singling out women and placing them in a more vulnerable position than men, may create conditions for the existence of a *gender-defined social group*. The religious precepts, social traditions or cultural norms which women may be accused of violating can range from choosing their own spouses instead of accepting an arranged marriage, to matters such as the wearing of make-up, the visibility or length of hair, or the type of clothing a woman chooses to wear' (emphasis in original).[2]

Even before the guidelines were issued, the **Canadian** Refugee Board had on several occasions found women refugee claimants to have a well-founded fear of persecution by reason of membership of a particular social group, including the following: a claimant and her two daughters were deemed to have a well-founded fear of persecution on the basis of their membership of a particular social group, 'consisting of women and girls who do not conform to Islamic fundamentalist norms';[3] a Somali claimant who was found to be a refugee on the basis of her

---

1   CIRB (1996b), section A.I.
2   CIRB (1996b), section A.I.
3   CRDD T89–06969, T89–06970, T89–06971 17 July 1990.

membership of a particular social group, 'young women without male protection';[1] a woman who was a divorced woman living under the jurisdiction of *sharia* law had a well-founded fear of persecution by reason of her membership in a particular social group of 'women';[2] and a woman was found to be a member of a particular social group composed of women who belong to a 'women's organisation objecting to the treatment of women in Iran'.[3] Additional case-law also supports this approach in cases involving arranged marriage (see Box 5.12).

Box 5.12[4]

This case concerned a woman from Albania who refused to marry the man to whom she was betrothed at the age of 10. Her family tried to break off the engagement but he made several violent attempts to abduct her. Her father was brutally beaten by him, assisted by two members of the secret police, with whom his financial support for the ruling socialist party gave him leverage. The documentary evidence indicated that the kidnapping of young girls and women is not uncommon in Albania and that the police are implicated in these kidnappings. The Kanun of Lak requires that a woman marry the man to whom she is engaged. If the engagement is broken, the groom's family can take revenge on the family of the intended bride. State protection was not available to her. The CRDD ruled that she had a well-founded fear of persecution as a member of a particular social group, 'women who fear persecution as the consequence for failing to conform to, or for transgressing gender-discriminating religious or customary laws and practices in their country of origin'.

In the **US** there have been a large number of cases involving Iranian women who have been divorced and who fear that, if they return to Iran, they will be subjected to abuse and disdain, and treated as prostitutes. In many of these cases, it has been recognised that women face persecution on both religious and political grounds. However, it has also been accepted that divorced Iranian women constitute a particular social group within the meaning of the Refugee Convention,[5] and that women who have not married may be persecuted as members of a particular social group.[6] There have also been a number of cases involving women from Afghanistan. However, the approach adopted in these cases has been more varied. For example, a woman who was widowed whilst living in Afghanistan and who fled with her children to the US claimed asylum on the basis that if she and her daughters were forced to return, the Taliban would strip them of their basic human rights. The Taliban prohibit women from

---

1   CRDD U91–04008 24 December 1991.
2   CRDD T93–05935/36 31 December 1993.
3   CRDD T89–02248 3 April 1990.
4   CRDD T97–06758 18 February 1999.
5   See, eg, Case Summaries 6 and 49 available on-line at http://www.uchastings.edu/cgrs/summaries/summaries.html
6   See, eg, Case Summary 7 ibid.

attending schools, working, leaving their homes unless they are in the company of a male relative, and receiving care from most medical facilities. Women must cover themselves from head to toe when they are in public. If a woman breaks any of these rules, she is subject to punishment, including beatings, arrest and even death. It was argued that she had a well-founded fear of future persecution on account of her membership in the particular social group of women with no male family members who have female children. However, her claim was refused because she had never been politically active in Kabul, and that her fear of reprisals for non-compliance with the Taliban restrictions on women was based upon uncertainty and the unknown rather than upon any specific events or circumstances. Moreover, it was determined that her fear was based simply upon 'dislike of the religious and political system dictated by the Taliban'.[1]

In the **UK**, case-law on whether women fleeing gendered social mores are members of a particular social group within the Refugee Convention has been largely negative. However, the recent decision in *Shah and Islam*[2] which was discussed at length in Chapter 3, may have implications for the way in which such cases are determined in the future. Although cases of marriage-related harm often involve women who are effectively made refugees *sur place* through separation or divorce which has occurred whilst they have resided in the UK, the IAT decided, in *Sarfraz*,[3] that the applicant had brought fears upon herself that she would be accused of adultery if returned to Pakistan. In this case it was argued that the appellant was a member of a particular social group of women from that society who have been (or will be) rejected by their husbands on the grounds of adultery. The case of *Danaei*[4] is also interesting because although the appeal was lost, it was accepted that the appellant, who was male, would be persecuted by the Iranian authorities because he had been involved in an adulterous relationship.

---

1   Case Summary 129 available on-line at http://www.uchastings.edu/cgrs/summaries/
     summaries.html
2   *Islam v SSHD; R v IAT ex parte Shah* [1999] INLR 144, Imm AR 283 (HL).
3   *Sarfraz v SSHD* (unreported) 6 February 1998 (16179) (IAT).
4   *Ex parte Danaei* [1998] Imm AR 84, INLR 124 (CA).

Chapter 6

VIOLENCE WITHIN THE FAMILY

6.1 DEFINITIONS OF VIOLENCE WITHIN THE FAMILY

The problem of violence against women within the family, commonly referred to as 'domestic' violence, is enormous and multifaceted. Violence within the family is a broader term than either domestic or intimate violence. For example, it also refers to the abuse inflicted by fathers on their daughters. This violence includes physical, sexual and psychological abuse inside and outside the home, and is deeply intertwined with prejudices viewing women as inferior, as the property of their male relatives and requiring women to be obedient and sacrifice their needs to serve men. In some contexts, it takes a specific form, for example, so-called 'honour killing', dowry-death or bride-burning and the custom of *sati*. All of these are manifestations of the prevalence of violence against women by family members and reflect varying levels of tolerance of such violence by the State.

In many areas of the world, violence within the family is receiving only belated attention from academics and feminists and, until very recently, has been largely ignored officially. In this context, it is perhaps not surprising that these forms of violence and persecution continue to be viewed with considerable scepticism by many within the determination process. Just as the police have been reluctant to intrude into the 'private' sphere of the home, so too the international human rights regime has proved itself reluctant to intrude into the 'private' sphere of domestic law and its enforcement. Until very recently, there has been no discussion about whether women fleeing violence within the family can claim refugee protection, and case-law has almost invariably gone against women in these circumstances. However, in recent years there has been increased emphasis on the ways in which violence within the family can form the basis of a claim for asylum or may interrelate with other forms of persecution to explain the harm which women fear. This is particularly apparent in cases involving gendered social mores and the concept of honour where members of a woman's family and/or community are commonly responsible for punishing women who fail or refuse to conform, and can be seen in the recent case of *Shah and Islam*.[1] This issue is discussed at length in Chapter 5. In addition, familial violence may be seen in claims based upon reproductive rights (Chapter 7), sexual orientation (Chapter 8) and female genital mutilation (Chapter 9). In each of these, violence within the family may form an important part of a woman's fear of returning to her home country, even though it may not be the central or primary basis of the claim.

Violence within the family is a widespread and often gender-specific form of abuse. However, despite growing acknowledgement of its existence, its conceptualisation within the asylum determination process remains highly problematic.

---

1   *Islam v SSHD; R v IAT ex parte Shah* [1999] INLR 144, Imm AR 283 (HL).

Representatives should be aware of three main problems facing claims made on this basis as they relate to the elements of the Refugee Convention definition of a refugee. The first and perhaps most significant of these is the role of the public/private dichotomy in undermining the seriousness of the harm. Although violence within the family is now recognised as a human rights concern (eg in the Declaration on the Elimination of Violence against Women) it nonetheless remains on the margin. As Copelon (1994) suggests, violence within the family is still considered different, less severe, and less deserving of international condemnation and sanction than officially sanctioned violence. This results primarily from the fact that it tends not to be viewed as violence at all. It is seen as 'personal', 'private' or a 'family matter', its goals and consequences are obscured, and its use justified as chastisement or discipline. The fact that it takes place in the 'private' sphere of the home, behind closed doors, is critical in understanding this conceptualisation. These effects are not limited to claims made by women asylum seekers but also affect those made by men who have experienced and/or fear violence within the family. This can be seen in the recent Canadian case of a man from Mexico who was a victim of abuse at the hands of his mother and suffered from neglect and her practice of 'witchcraft'. In refusing his asylum claim the Refugee Division found that the claimant was the victim of domestic neglect rather than violent abuse.[1]

The second problem facing asylum claims involving violence within the family stems from the failure to appropriately and accurately conceptualise the relationship between the harm feared and the relevant Refugee Convention ground. This is reflected in a tendency among advocates and practitioners to confuse the key issues and elements of the Refugee Convention definition in cases of gender-related persecution. For example, the case of *Shah and Islam* was formulated as a 'domestic violence' case and addressed as such by the courts.[2] However, whilst both women had been subjected to violence within the family, the main aspect of their persecution was the fear that they would be accused of adultery and punished accordingly by the Pakistani State and/or their husbands. Although it was argued that the violence they experienced within the family was the basis of a potential social group membership, in fact it was relevant to their claims only to the extent that it 'proved': (a) their fears that the husbands in each case would have made such accusations to the State were well-founded; and (b) that the husbands would have taken matters into their own hands, had the State not punished them. Inadequate and/or inappropriate conceptualisation of the relationship between the harm feared and the reasons why such harm is feared can lead to problems in establishing a Refugee Convention basis for the claim.

The final concern in cases involving violence within the family is a more general one which is discussed elsewhere in this book, namely the very pervasiveness and universal nature of violence against women. As Goldberg (1995) suggests, violence against women within their homes is not limited to the countries of the so-called 'developing world' but also exists in the countries in which women seek asylum. As a result, the issue of whether or not violence within the family can form the basis of a claim for asylum remains contentious and widely debated.

---

1   CRDD V97–03500 31 May 1999.
2   *Islam v SSHD; R v IAT ex parte Shah* [1999] INLR 144, Imm AR 283 (HL).

However, the critical issue which representatives need to address in such cases is the failure of the State in the countries from which women flee to provide effective protection. Whilst measures to protect women from violence within the family are patchy in many countries, there is usually a conscious effort on the part of the State to provide an effective remedy where this is sought. However, even in States where mechanisms for protection exist, the particular circumstances of the individual woman may mean that she is unable to access that protection which is available. This can be seen in the recent **Canadian** case of a woman from Portugal who was subjected to chronic physical abuse by her husband and who was recognised as a refugee within the meaning of the Refugee Convention.[1] The Refugee Division concluded that there are serious gaps and inadequacies in the protection currently available to abused women in Portugal. The onus of filing a report is on the victim and the police try to discourage women from making a complaint. In the claimant's case, as she was black, police indifference may have been exacerbated by racism. Given the claimant's visible minority status, in combination with her status as an abused woman, State protection was not available.

6.2 SERIOUS HARM

Violence within the family can take many different forms, but commonly involves some form of psychological and/or physical brutality and can include, but is not limited to, beating with hands or objects, biting, spitting, punching, kicking, slashing, stabbing, strangling, scalding, burning, attempted drowning and food deprivation. Sexual abuse, including rape, is likewise a common concomitant of violence within the family and takes many different forms. As in other contexts, sexual abuse including rape, which may do less physical damage than beatings, is often experienced by women as the gravest violation. In addition to these forms of abuse, women may be subjected to forms of violence which are more subtle than physical violation but equally as damaging. Women may be confined to the home so that they become isolated from friends, family and others, their lives and those of their family may be threatened and they may be made to fear for the loss of their children. These forms of psychological and emotional abuse suggest the need for a definition of 'violence' which includes both the use of force and its *threat* as both compelling and constraining women to behave or not to behave in particular ways. Kelly (1993), Copelon (1994b), and Romany (1994) argue that there is, effectively, nothing to differentiate the position of a man who is locked in a torture cell and a woman who is repeatedly abused within the confines of her own home. The same processes which are used to break the will of political prisoners are used by domestic aggressors to render women, despite their apparent freedom to leave, captive. Moreover, the very fact that such violence involves a breach of trust should not be underestimated. As Copelon suggests, 'the shock of being beaten by a partner as opposed to a jailer can be [even] more numbing and world-destroying'.[2]

---

1   CRDD T98–02359 31 March 1999.
2   Copelon 1994b, p 138.

It is important to counter explicitly the tendency to trivialise violence within the family. The process of battering, whether physical or psychological or both, often produces anxiety, depression, debility and dread as well as the same intense symptoms which comprise the post-traumatic stress disorders experienced by victims of official violence as well as by victims of rape. Analytically, violence within the family, as with any other form of violence, should be considered as a violation of fundamental human rights within the Universal Declaration of Human Rights. This point is made particularly strongly by Copelon who makes the comparison with other recognised methods of torture, and concludes that 'when stripped of privatisation, sexism and sentimentalism [violence within the family] is no less grave than other forms of inhumane and subordinating official violence, which have been prohibited by treaty and customary law and recognised by the international community as *ius cogens*, or peremptory norms that bind universally and can never be violated'.[1] The nature and the degree of the harm perpetrated in the course of such violence constitute a serious, if not egregious, violation of women's human rights. Moreover, even if the acts are considered to be neither torture nor gross human rights violations, forms of violence within the family at a minimum constitute serious abuse of a woman's human rights and as such rise to the level of serious harm within the meaning of persecution.

In many cases involving violence within the family, the focus of the decision-maker is usually on whether the harm experienced or feared relates to a Refugee Convention ground. The issue of whether the harm itself rises to the level of serious harm within the meaning of persecution is often not explicitly addressed. In **Australia** this issue was, however, raised in a case involving a woman from the Philippines whose claim related entirely to long-term experience of domestic violence.[2] In determining whether the harm amounted to persecution, the Tribunal noted that the applicant had been subjected to continued physical violence and to cruel, inhuman and degrading treatment for a period of approximately 27 years. The Tribunal found that such treatment violated her fundamental human rights as set out in Articles 3 and 5 of the United Nations Universal Declaration of Human Rights.[3] As is stated by Hathaway (1991), these are recognised by the international community as being core human rights which all States are bound to respect.[4] They are basic and inalienable and no derogation whatsoever is permitted. Failure to recognise these rights is appropriately considered to be tantamount to persecution.[5] In this case, the applicant's core human rights had been violated by an individual, her husband, for a sustained period of time.

---

1   Copelon 1994b, p 114.
2   RRT N93/00656 3 August 1994.
3   Article 3 states that 'everyone has the right to life, liberty and security of person'; and Article 5 states that 'No one shall be subjected to torture, or to cruel, inhuman or degrading treatment or punishment'.
4   See Hathaway's framework for the analysis of asylum claims as outlined in Chapter 3.
5   Hathaway 1991, pp 108–109.

This case can be contrasted by the approach which was taken by the IAT in the **UK** case of *Ranjbar*,[1] which concerned a young Iranian woman who had been severely beaten by her father. In allowing her appeal against the Home Office, the adjudicator determined that the harm fell into the category of inhuman or degrading treatment. However, the Secretary of State appealed against this decision. The grounds of appeal against this decision, which were accepted by the IAT, included not only that this type of violence is not condoned by the authorities and that gender is too broad a category to be recognised as a 'particular social group', but also that the harm inflicted was not serious enough to rise to the level of persecution:

> 'The degree of hostility and repression . . . the respondent has suffered does not, in our view, amount to persecution . . . We confine ourselves to the conclusion that the degree of ill-treatment the respondent claims to have suffered, solely within the small family, is not persecution within the meaning of the Convention.'

This case highlights some of the problems associated with claims for asylum made by women involving violence within the family. It should be noted, however, that there is very limited current case-law in the UK on this issue, partly as a consequence of the introduction of the concession outside the immigration rules for victims of domestic violence in 1999.

6.3   THE FAILURE OF STATE PROTECTION

It is clearly important that representatives establish that violence within the family constitutes 'serious harm'. However, this will not be sufficient to constitute persecution. Acts of serious harm, no matter how severe they may be, cannot be based solely on personal dispute.[2] The failure of the State to protect against the perpetration of such violence must also be shown and this has proved highly problematic in cases involving violence within the family. Women fleeing violence within the family do not fit the popular conception of a refugee because of the source and location of the persecution.[3] Such violence generally occurs in the home and by definition the assailant has a personal relationship with the potential claimant and is not an anonymous representative of the State. As a result, the State connection required in the definition of a refugee may be difficult to see since the State never actively commits and seldom overtly condones this type of violence against women. This problem is exacerbated by the fact that there is little documentary evidence concerning the particular treatment of women in this area and, in many countries, statistics regarding violence within the family are not available.

Although the harm in these cases is not inflicted by the authorities, or by associated organisations or groups, the State in the country of origin is frequently *unwilling or unable* to offer *effective* protection to women, either because it supports the actions of the individuals concerned, because it tolerates them or because it has other priorities. This is despite the international obligations of the

---

1   *SSHD v Ranjbar* (unreported) 28 June 1994 (IAT).
2   Goldberg 1993.
3   Stairs and Pope 1990.

State in treaty and customary law which include specific obligations to protect women's rights. In such cases, the failure of State protection may take one of several forms.

(1) The existence of official legislation which condones violence within the family

Perhaps the most obvious example of State complicity in violence against women within the family can be seen in legislation which condones such violence. For example, in some systems a 'defence of honour' recognised by law or custom allows a husband's jealousy or rage over the real or imagined offences by his wife to excuse even homicide. This is not limited to the Islamic world with which 'crimes of honour' are most commonly associated. For example, the pervasiveness of violence against women in Brazil has been analysed by Romany (1993) who points out that, in a two-year period, at least 400 women were murdered by their husbands or lovers in one State alone. In the face of this pervasive violence, the Brazilian criminal justice system sanctions defences which either reduce the punishment for such violence or absolve perpetrators altogether. This defence, available only to men, licenses not only 'impulsive', but deliberate vengeance. So too does the marital rape exemption which is still the law in most countries.[1]

(2) A refusal to investigate or prosecute individual cases and/or a reluctance to convict or punish

States are internationally responsible not only for legislating against violence within the family but for making this legislation effective through judicial, police and other organs of State power. However, there are many examples of such violence where, despite the existence of such legislation, in reality there is no effective State protection available to women. This is particularly evident in the case of 'dowry death', which is another manifestation of violence within the family most commonly occurring in India and some adjoining countries such as Pakistan and Bangladesh.[2] The practice of dowry transcends religion, caste and language and is in no way tied to Hinduism, Islam or any other religion. Dowry is simply what is given to the groom and his family at the time of marriage. It is a transfer of wealth from the bride's family to the groom's family which takes the form of payment in kind or cash or both. 'Dowry death', which is also known as 'bride burning', often happens when a wife and her family cannot meet the demands of her husband and/or his family for additional money or property, or when a husband wishes to gain an additional dowry by remarrying. Although the practice of giving and taking of dowries varies in different communities, it has

---

1   It is worth noting that the marital rape exemption was only removed from UK law in 1993. To this day, section 261 of the California Penal Code defines 'rape' as a crime committed against someone '*not* the spouse of the perpetrator'.

2   Another very clear example of this can be seen in legislation to prevent the practice of female genital mutilation (FGM). Formal legislation prohibiting FGM, or more specifically, infibulation exists in the Sudan and in Kenya whilst official declarations against the practice have been made in Burkina Faso and Senegal (Minority Rights Group, 1993). Moreover, FGM is explicitly prohibited in CEDAW, the UN Declaration on the Elimination of Violence Against Women and in the UN Platform for Action to which many of the countries in which FGM takes place are signatories. The reality of the situation, however, is that such laws are rarely applied and that perpetrators act with virtual impunity.

become an increasingly common excuse for the harassment of daughters-in-law. The husband and his family begin physically and psychologically abusing the bride, and the abuse, if it does not drive the wife to suicide, often ends in her death by burning, with the husband claiming that the wife caught fire while cooking on a kerosene stove. More than 5,000 dowry deaths occur every year, and that number has been rising particularly rapidly over the past 10 or 15 years. Dowry and 'dowry deaths' continue despite the fact that dowry transactions have been illegal in India since the Dowry Prohibition Act 1961. As a result of pressure by women's organisations, subsequent amendments to the Act in 1984 and again in 1996 have strengthened the laws against dowry and dowry harassment. However, in spite of some landmark rulings by the Indian Supreme Court, the government, police and conservative ruling classes have made little effort to implement these changes in criminal law. As a result, husbands act with virtual impunity and there is no effective protection for women who are subject to violence within the family.[1]

Even where the State does not directly condone violence within the family, and indeed even where it legislates against it, the reality is that in many States women subjected to violence within the family still cannot obtain effective protection from the police or other law enforcement officials. The situation in Pakistan is illustrative of this problem. The recent report by Human Rights Watch (1999) examines in detail the State response to violence against women including gender bias in the criminal justice system and the role of the police including delayed and mishandled processing of complaints, harassment and abuse of victims and inadequate and improper investigations (see Box 6.1).

Box 6.1

Women in Pakistan face staggeringly high rates of rape, sexual assault, and domestic violence while their attackers largely go unpunished owing to rampant incompetence, corruption, and biases against women throughout the criminal justice system. Victims of violence within the family have virtually no access to judicial protection and redress. Violence within the family is virtually never investigated or prosecuted. Such violence is routinely dismissed by law enforcement authorities as a private dispute and women who attempt to register a police complaint of spousal or familial physical abuse are invariably turned away. Worse, they are regularly advised and sometimes pressured by the police to reconcile with their abusive spouses or relatives. In fact, Pakistani law fails to criminalise a common and serious form of domestic violence: marital rape. Even complaints regarding acts of violence that fall within the ambit of the criminal law, such as assault or attempted murder, are routinely ignored or downplayed by the police as a result of biased attitudes, ignorance and lack of training with respect to the scope of the law.

---

1   Mertus 1995.

A further recently documented example is that of China.[1] Although new laws have raised the issue of violence against women within the family, the legal system remains severely inadequate in addressing this problem.

Representatives should be aware that in the light of *Horvath*[2] it may be argued by decision-makers that it is not possible for States to prevent all crime and that imperfections in the legal mechanisms for protection are to be expected.

(3) A lack of police response to pleas for assistance

A further example which demonstrates the failure of effective State protection in cases of violence within the family, and one that is closely related to the points made above, relates to the attitudes of the State's officials towards such violence. This violence is, typically, not considered a concern of the State, and even when it is, law enforcement officials are often unwilling to get involved.[3] In addition, therefore, to the obvious restrictions placed on women by the violence of their male family members, police routinely fail to respond to calls for help or do not arrest abusive male partners and relatives, displaying dismissive attitudes towards 'family disputes' and women complainants.[4] Moreover, because prosecutors allow women abused within the family much more discretion in deciding whether to prosecute than they do with other violent crimes, women may be more vulnerable to ongoing threats from their attackers. When a woman has sought, to no avail, police or court protection, or where such efforts would be futile because no protection is available to her, the State may be held responsible for, if not complicitous in, those acts.[5]

A failure of State protection must be properly interpreted to include not only actions directly committed by States, but also States' systematic failure to prosecute acts committed by private actors. Understanding how the State can be seen to condone activities within the home both justifies and lays the basis for the establishment of State connection to persecution that takes the form of violence within the family. Where a State facilitates conditions, accommodates, tolerates, justifies, or excuses private denials of women's rights, the State will bear responsibility. The State will be responsible not directly for the private acts but for its own lack of diligence to prevent, control, correct, or discipline such private acts through its own executive, legislative or judicial organs.[6] Developments at the international level strengthen the argument of female asylum claimants that the State is sufficiently implicated in the harm done to them to constitute persecution within the parameters of the refugee definition. Most notable among these is the UN Declaration on the Elimination of Violence Against Women (1993), which refers explicitly to violence against women occurring in public and private life, and which delineates the obligations of States to develop enforceable

---

1   See China Rights Forum (1995) *Caught between Tradition and the State: Violations of the Human Rights of Chinese Women*.
2   *Horvath v SSHD* (unreported) 6 July 2000 (HL).
3   Tickner 1992; Seith 1997.
4   Hirschmann 1996.
5   Goldberg 1993.
6   Cook 1994.

laws and appropriate sanctions to prevent violence against women from occurring and to punish those acts to the full extent of the law, whether perpetrated by the State or by private individuals.

Despite this, the approach within the case-law of the various jurisdictions towards the failure of State protection in cases of violence within the family is highly varied. In **Canada**, it is generally recognised that *effective* State protection often does not exist for women who are subject to violence within the family despite the existence of legislation which theoretically protects them. This position reflects long-standing decisions in both *Rajudeen*[1] and *Surujpal*.[2] Since then both of these cases, as well as paragraph 65 of the UNHCR Handbook (1979) have been specifically approved by the Supreme Court of Canada in *Ward*[3] which ruled unequivocally that 'State complicity in persecution is not a pre-requisite to a valid refugee claim'. The general approach can be seen in the case of a woman from Jamaica who feared persecution at the hands of her abusive estranged husband.[4] The Refugee Division accepted that State protection was not provided to the claimant when she reported her husband's serious threats to the police. Despite the passage of legislation aimed at domestic violence, spousal abuse is not taken seriously in Jamaica. Moreover, the claimant was both poor and uneducated and therefore would not be able to to enforce her rights under the Domestic Violence Act 1995. Another recent Canadian case concerned a woman from the Philippines who had experienced a history of violent physical abuse by her husband and feared he would kill her if she returned.[5] She had made at least three attempts to gain police protection but her husband was never detained or charged. In considering the claim, the Refugee Division referred to the gender guidelines. The documentary evidence indicated that violence against women, particularly domestic violence, is a serious problem in the Philippines, that domestic violence is considered a personal rather than a criminal matter and that cases of domestic violence are rarely prosecuted. State protection would not be available to the claimant. Since the claimant's husband had links with the police, he would be able to find her anywhere in the Philippines. It would not be reasonable to expect her to live in hiding in her own country. She did not have an internal flight alternative. In this case, refugee status was granted. Refugee status was similarly granted in another recent case of a woman from Honduras.[6] The CRDD accepted that remedies and protection for women who are victims of domestic violence in Honduras are almost non-existent, despite the existence of a law against domestic violence. However, this general approach has not been consistent. For example, a woman from South Korea whose husband was an alcoholic and verbally and physically abused her whenever he was drunk was refused asylum on the basis that the authorities in South Korea had brought two laws into effect which had the objective of eliminating domestic violence.[7]

---

1   *Rajudeen v MEI* [1984] 55 NR 129.
2   *Surujpal v MEI* [1985] 60 NR 73.
3   *Canada (Attorney General) v Ward* [1983] 2 SCR 689.
4   CRDD T98–05518 3 December 1998.
5   CRDD M96–06372 16 April 1999.
6   CRDD M98–09327 25 August 1999.
7   CRDD U98–01321 12 July 1999.

The courts in **Australia** have recognised that there is often a lack of *effective* State protection in cases involving violence against women within the family; protection often exists in principle but not in reality. This can be seen in a case involving a woman from Tonga.[1] In granting asylum, the Tribunal noted that there are considerable social pressures on victims, particularly wives, not to report such abuse, or even to speak publicly about it, and that wives who seek to escape domestic violence are open to blame for desertion. It has similarly been accepted that there is a lack of effective State protection for women who are subjected to violence within the family in Colombia[2] and in the Philippines.[3]

The role of the State in 'setting the scene' for violence against women within the family has been recognised in a recent determination from **New Zealand** in the case of an Iranian woman who was persecuted by her male family members:

> 'Because the religious and political imperatives that operate at state level are intended to operate and in fact operate at the domestic or family level as well, we see no distinction on these facts between persecution by the state and persecution by male family members.'[4]

In the **UK**, by contrast, asylum claims involving violence within the family are routinely dismissed as 'frivolous' and the failure of the State to protect women against violence within the family disputed.[5] For example, in *Ranjbar*,[6] the Secretary of State appealed against the decision of an adjudicator to allow the appeal of an Iranian woman who had been beaten by her father. In the grounds of the appeal it was argued that the applicant could look to the Iranian State for protection against maltreatment and that the authorities do not condone such violence. The IAT upheld the appeal:

> 'There is no acceptable evidence in our view that the authorities in Iran would not accord protection to those severely ill treated within a family. No doubt the standards which would be applied by the authorities in Iran would differ from those in some other countries: no doubt the status of women and children will be differently regarded. The Convention however is not designed to give relief to all those who live under a less liberal social order than that in some Western countries.'

The recent case of *Shah and Islam*,[7] which was discussed at length in Chapter 3 and has been referred to elsewhere in this book, clearly raises the issue of State responsibility in cases of gender-related persecution. The applicant, a citizen from Pakistan, was a battered wife who had been forced to flee to the UK but who on arrival discovered that she was pregnant. She was afraid to return because she believed that she would be accused of adultery and exposed to the operation of the *sharia* law statutes that prescribe stoning to death as punishment.

---

1   RRT Reference V96/04080 5 August 1996.

2   RRT Reference V97/06529 17 March 1998.

3   RRT Reference N93/00656 3 August 1994; RRT Reference N99/26779 14 April 1999.

4   Refugee Appeal No 71427/99 (16 August 2000) available on-line at http://www.refugee.org.nz

5   It is essential that representations are made in cases involving violence within the family. There are many cases where such violence in the country of origin has resulted in the applicant being granted leave to remain but these cases are not widely known because they do not reach the courts.

6   *SSHD v Ranjbar* (unreported) 28 June 1994 (11105) (IAT).

7   *Islam v SSHD; R v IAT ex parte Shah* [1999] INLR 144, Imm AR 283 (HL).

Conclusions may also be drawn from the judgment regarding the responsibility of States to protect women from violence within the family.[1]

6.4 REFUGEE CONVENTION GROUNDS

Establishing the failure of State protection in cases involving violence within the family has proved problematic because such violence is conceived of as 'private', a situation that is exacerbated by its occurrence in the geographically and ideologically 'private' sphere of the home. Equally as significant in such cases, however, has been finding a categorical basis for the persecution. In this context there are two possible ways to characterise the group in claims based upon violence within the family. Despite the problems inherent with the concept of particular social groups which have been discussed elsewhere in this book, this is the most common approach in cases involving violence within the family. It can be argued that 'women' or a sub-group thereof are members of a particular social group. As Goldberg (1993) suggests, this social group must be seen in a social context where women are considered or treated as inferior to men, as property of men and as subject to male domination without regard to their own will. It could be argued that the State's failure to protect a woman who experiences violence within the family is simply by virtue of the fact of her gender. It is due only to her gender that another individual is allowed to beat her or threaten her on an ongoing basis and it is only due to her gender that she is denied protection, either through lack of recourse or through failure or refusal to enforce existing laws that could protect her against such conduct. There are, however, problems with the social group approach when it is constructed along the lines of 'women from country x who are subject to wife abuse'; first it necessitates a requirement of past persecution which is not a prerequisite for being recognised as a Refugee Convention refugee; and secondly, defining a group by reference to the common experience of a particular form of persecution is tautological. Some of these difficulties are discussed below. In this context, representatives should consider arguing that women are persecuted as a result of actual or imputed political opinion.

6.4.1 Political opinion

This approach to cases of women asylum seekers who have experienced or fear violence within the family has been most successful in the **US**. As early as 1987, the Ninth Circuit held that a woman's resistance to violent domination by her male partner can be an expression of political opinion.[2] This has been followed in a number of cases of violence within the family. For example, in the *Matter of A and Z*,[3] the US Immigration Court recognised that a Jordanian woman who had

---

1   It should be noted that many of the difficulties in cases involving violence within the family stem from an absence of documentary and other supporting evidence, especially with regard to the sufficiency or otherwise of State protection. This problem is discussed in more detail in Chapter 10.

2   *Lazo-Majano v INS* [1987] 813 F.2d 1432 (9th Cir).

3   *Matter of A and Z* A72–190-893, A72–793-219 (20 December 1994) reported in Interpreter Releases 72, 521 (17 April 1995) and in the *New York Times* (National) (27 May 1995) A1.

been abused by her husband over decades, had been persecuted because of her political opinions. The respondent's husband punished her with verbal and physical abuse, social isolation, house arrest, separation from her family, and travel restrictions. He also made her economically dependent on him. The Court found that there was no legal protection available to the respondent. Jordanian law allows men to control their wives, by controlling where she lives and whether she can travel. The Court recognised that the respondent had been abused specifically because of her belief and her expression of her individual autonomy, which did not accord with the belief of her husband or Jordanian society generally relating to women. This decision was followed by a similar ruling in the *Matter of M-K* which concerned a Sierra Leonian woman who testified about her attempts to assert her individual autonomy and her refusal to act in a subservient manner as is expected of women in Sierra Leone's male-dominated society (see Box 6.2).

Box 6.2

The applicant, a woman from Sierra Leone, objected to the way in which her husband expected her to behave. Her husband said that she was 'mouthy' and verbally and physically abused her on a number of occasions. On three occasions after being severely beaten, she went to the police. They said there was nothing they could do because it was a domestic matter and told her to return home. After she had a second child she was subjected to female genital mutilation. Her husband then told her he was going to get a second wife. She objected and told her husband she would leave if he did so. He continued to beat her, including during her pregnancies. After bearing him two children, because of the repeated beatings she refused to bear him more children. This further angered her husband, the beatings got worse and she left him. She travelled to the US and initiated divorce proceedings. Her husband has threatened to kill her if she returns to Sierra Leone. The US Immigration Court ruled that the appellant had been persecuted by being punished with physical spousal abuse. It was accepted that physical spousal abuse is common in Sierra Leone society and that women are believed to deserve any abuse they are given. She was granted asylum because of her past attempts to assert her individual autonomy, resulting in physical spousal abuse, and because of her fear of future harm given her husband's threats to kill her. This can be classified as either: 'persecution on account of political opinion' for her resistance to mandated female subservience and complaints about physical spousal abuse; or 'persecution on account of membership in the social group that consists of women who have been punished with physical spousal abuse for attempting to assert their individual autonomy'.

However, this approach has been less successful more recently, particularly following the decision in the *Matter of R-A*[1] when the BIA determined there was

---

1   *Matter of R-A* Int Dec 3403 (BIA 1999). See Box 6.3.

no evidence that Ms Alvarado's husband persecuted her for any political opinion that she had, or that he thought she had. Similarly, in the *Matter of Kuna*, it was not accepted that a woman from Democratic Republic of Congo who was subjected to domestic violence by her husband, a military officer during the regime of former President Mobuto, had been persecuted for a Refugee Convention reason:

> 'It appears to this Court that the Respondent was harmed simply because her husband was a despicable person. While this Court does not want to belittle the tragedy of domestic violence in any way, the Respondent has simply not shown that the violence against her is related to anything more than evil in the heart of her husband.'

The conclusion to be drawn from this is that violence within the family continues to be seen largely as a private matter and therefore not political. It should be noted, however, that in the case of *Kuna*, an Immigration Judge found, on 8 August 2000, that certain acts of violence within the family constituted torture under the Convention Against Torture (CAT) and thereby rendered the respondent eligible for withholding of removal. Additionally, in finding that Congolese 'police [were] aware of the chronic instances of domestic abuse, and despite their legal responsibility to intervene, fail[ed] to act in a preventative or protective manner', the Judge determined that Congolese authorities gave 'the respondent's husband an implicit license to torture her with impunity'. Thus, 'the respondent is exactly the type of individual the Torture Convention was designed to protect'.

6.4.2 Social group

Asylum claims involving violence within the family have often been at the centre of both the academic and legal debate about the construction of particular social groups within the meaning of the Refugee Convention. The problem in these cases has frequently revolved around the need to define the social group without reference to the harm that has been experienced or feared. As was indicated in Chapter 3, the courts in all jurisdictions have held that the concept of a 'particular social group' must have been intended to apply to social groups which exist independently of the persecution. Otherwise, the limited scope of the Refugee Convention would be defeated: there would be a social group, and so a right to asylum, whenever a number of persons feared persecution for a reason common to them. However, in some jurisdictions, it has been accepted that women's particular vulnerability may stem from the fact that their gender undermines their access to protection against violence within the family.

The courts in **Canada** have held that a sub-group of women can be identified with reference to the fact of their exposure of vulnerability for physical, cultural or other reasons, to violence, including domestic violence, in an environment that denies them protection. These women face violence amounting to persecution because of their particular vulnerability as women in society and because they are so unprotected. This approach is reflected in the recent case of a woman from Jamaica who feared persecution at the hands of her abusive estranged husband and was determined to be a Convention refugee because she was a member of a particular social group – abused women in Jamaica who are unable to avail themselves of the strict provisions of the law – which on the face of it might appear to provide some measure of protection.[1] The CRDD also accepted that her delay in making an asylum claim was explained by her initial lack of awareness of the fact that she could make a claim on the ground of domestic abuse. In recent years, women fearing violence within the family from a variety of countries including Iran,[2] Albania[3] and Peru[4] have been recognised as members of particular social groups within the meaning of the Refugee Convention and granted asylum on that basis. This approach can also be seen in recent cases involving children who are victims of parental abuse. In one case, it was argued that the claimants, aged 19 and 15, feared persecution as members of a particular social group, children of an abusive father.[5] Both boys were verbally and physically abused by their father because the eldest did not agree with the father's political views and resisted the father's attempts to have him join a radical Islamic organisation. As the level of violence was escalating, their mother made arrangements to take them out of the country. The CRDD concluded that abused children are in the same position as abused women and that, in many ways, such children may be even more vulnerable. The claimants faced more than a mere possibility of persecution as a result of their social group: abused children without access to State protection.

The social group approach to claims involving violence within the family has also been successful in the **US**. For example, it was determined that a woman from Guatemala who was beaten, kept captive, denied medical care, stalked and threatened with death by her husband, was persecuted on account of her membership in the particular social group of women who are or have been affiliated with men who believe it is their right to dominate 'their women' by force or violence. However, this approach to cases involving violence within the family is currently being comprehensively re-examined in the *Matter of R-A* (see Box 6.3).[6] In January 2000, briefs were submitted to the Attorney-General arguing that she should reverse the US Immigration Court's decision.[7] Although this case has yet to be decided finally, it is clear that it has potentially disastrous consequences for women seeking asylum in the US on the basis of harm suffered or feared within the family. This can be seen in the recent case of a woman from Mexico subject to domestic violence who was granted asylum as a member of the particular social group of 'victims of domestic violence'. This was reversed by the BIA on 17 June 1999, just after the Board's decision in the *Matter of R-A*.

1   CRDD T98–05518 3 December 1998.
2   CRDD T98–07559 9 June 1999.
3   CRDD A97–00808 21 October 1998.
4   CRDD V97–00708 11 August 1998.
5   CRDD V97–00156 23 July 1998.
6   *Matter of R-A* Int Dec 3403 (BIA 1999).
7   See http//www.uchastings.edu/cgrs/campaigns/alvarado/alvarardo.htm#update for current position.

Box 6.3[1]

The *Matter of R-A* concerns a woman from Guatemala, who for nearly ten years was subjected to brutal violence at the hands of her husband, including rape, beatings, manipulation and taunting. He dislocated her jaw and nearly cut off her hands with a machete. Even though many assaults took place in public, she was never offered protection or assistance. When she tried to obtain a divorce, the court would not permit the divorce without the consent of her husband. She tried on several occasions to leave her husband, but each time he forced her to return. The abuse took place in the context of a country where domestic violence is pervasive, where patriarchal attitudes are entrenched, and where there is a broad culture of impunity. The police and the courts tend to see domestic violence as a family affair, and women seeking help are encouraged to keep the problem to themselves. She was granted asylum by an immigration judge who held that she faced persecution on account of her membership in the social group of Guatemalan women who are intimately involved with a male companion who believes that women are to live under male domination. Deciding that she also faced persecution due to her resistance to her husband's violence, the judge granted asylum on political opinion grounds as well. The INS appealed against the decision and it was subsequently reversed by the BIA in June 1999, by a divided 10–5 vote. In its reversal, the Board did not contest that the appellant was persecuted or faces future persecution. Instead, the majority of Board members rejected the immigration judge's ruling that she was targeted for abuse because of her membership in a social group. The decision prompted a vigorous dissent, with five members of the Board pointing out that the majority's 'differentiation between the supposedly more private forms of persecution, typically suffered by women, and the more public forms of persecution, typically suffered by men, is exactly the type of outdated and improper distinction that the [INS's Gender] Guidelines were intended to overcome.'

In the **UK** there are only a limited number of cases which specifically address whether women fearing violence within the family are members of a particular social group within the meaning of the Refugee Convention. This is largely a reflection of the fact that such cases are routinely dismissed as manifestly unfounded and therefore do not reach the appellate authorities. In addition, many cases are granted exceptional leave. In those cases which do reach the IAA, the general approach has tended to reflect the decision of the IAT in *Ranjbar*[2] in which the Tribunal overruled the reasoning of the adjudicator that the respondent was a member of a particular social group, 'namely those who are subject to physical attack as a result of being the female child of a person who expresses his institutionalised attitude to women in the form of physical attacks

---

1   *Matter of R-A* Int Dec 3403 (BIA 1999).
2   *SSHD v Ranjbar* (unreported) 28 June 1994 (IAT).

which fall within the category of inhuman or degrading treatment'. A similar position was also taken by the IAT in *Islam*:[1]

> 'We do not consider that Pakistani women subject to violence within the family are a social group within the Convention. That they are simply women does not make them a particular social group: the only common characteristic identified is that they are subject to violence within marriage: the only common feature, beyond their sex, is the persecution to which they are alleged to be subject within marriage – that is the persecution itself.'

This decision followed logically from the ruling in *Savchenkov*[2] that the social group must exist independently of the persecution. To describe a social group of 'women who are battered' does not explain why such harm occurred. It simply notes that there are characteristics which are common to a number of individuals. However, the decision in the House of Lords in *Shah and Islam*[3] to recognise that women can be granted asylum on the basis of their membership of a particular social group should be utilised, where appropriate, by representatives to ensure protection for women fleeing violence within the family.

6.5   SOURCES OF INFORMATION AND SUPPORT

British Colombia Institute against Family Violence

http://www.bcifv.org

Established in 1989 as a private, non-profit organisation, the Institute works to increase public awareness and understanding of family violence through education and dissemination of information. It provides continuing education for professionals, conducts research, and develops and distributes resources to community organisations. The website provides an on-line library catalogue and access to other web resources.

Centre for the Prevention of Sexual and Domestic Violence

http://www.cpsdv.org

The Centre for the Prevention of Sexual and Domestic Violence is a non-profit organisation based in Washington and describes itself as an inter-religious educational resource addressing issues of sexual and domestic violence. Its goal is to engage religious leaders in the task of ending abuse and to serve as a bridge between religious and secular communities. The emphasis is on education and prevention.

---

1   *Islam and Others v SSHD* (unreported) 2 October 1996 (13956) (IAT). This decision was subsequently reconsidered by the House of Lords in *Islam v SSHD; R v IAT ex parte Shah* [1999] INLR 144, Imm AR 283 (HL), although the social group which was accepted did not relate specifically to the appellants' experiences of violence within the family.
2   *SSHD v Savchenkov* [1996] Imm AR 28 (CA).
3   *Islam v SSHD; R v IAT ex parte Shah* [1999] INLR 144, Imm AR 283 (HL).

Domestic Violence and Incest Resource Centre (DVIRC)

http://www.vicnet.net.au/~dvirc

The Centre is based in Australia and was established in 1986 as a State-wide resource for information on domestic violence and child sexual assault. It provides resources and education to professionals and to those who have experienced domestic violence or sexual assault. The website provides access to a range of resources, including pamphlets, booklets for those who have experienced abuse or violence, manuals and other publications. There are links to other websites with information on domestic violence and child sexual abuse. DVIRC also produces a quarterly newsletter which contains legal updates, lists of current support groups for survivors in Victoria, articles on current issues and lists of new resources and books. The Centre has a specialist reference library focusing on domestic violence, incest and child sexual abuse.

Chapter 7

REPRODUCTIVE RIGHTS INCLUDING FORCED STERILISATION AND ABORTION

7.1 THE CONCEPT OF REPRODUCTIVE RIGHTS

The UN Platform for Action (1995), at para 95, defines reproductive health as 'a state of complete physical, mental and social well-being and not merely the absence of disease or infirmity, in all matters relating to the reproductive system and to its functions and processes'.[1] Reproductive rights embrace certain human rights that are already recognised in domestic law, international human rights instruments and other consensus documents. These definitions recognise that States have positive obligations to promote reproductive and sexual health and that reproductive and sexual health covers a broad range of rights. These rights rest on the recognition of the basic right of all couples and individuals to decide freely and responsibly the number, spacing and timing of their children and to have the information and means to do so, and the right to attain the highest standard of sexual and reproductive health. It also includes their right to make decisions concerning reproduction free of discrimination, coercion and violence.

Within asylum case-law and analysis, violations of reproductive rights have typically focused on the experiences of women (and men) in the People's Republic of China as a result of the 'one-child policy'. Whilst this chapter inevitability refers to this case-law at some length, representatives should be aware that reproductive rights violations are not limited to this context. It should be noted, for example, that the concept of reproductive rights often closely relates to other issues which are discussed in detail elsewhere in this book, including marriage-related harm, violence within the family and female genital mutilation. The concept of reproductive rights includes the right to *not* have children as well as the right to have children (see Box 7.1). It also relates to the use of rape and sexual violence because this form of harm undermines women's ability to assert their reproductive rights.

Box 7.1

The applicant, a Nigerian woman, arrived in the UK in 1997 when she was granted leave to remain as a visitor for six months. Although she already has seven children her husband, who remains in Nigeria, wanted her to have more. He refused to allow her to use contraception and refused to permit her to have any termination. He would not let her separate from him and said she had no right to say what she wanted. She fears that if she returns to Nigeria she would not receive any protection

---

1   See Appendix 8.

> from the State against forced sex, enforced pregnancies, lack of sexual freedom and general mistreatment at the hands of her husband. A decision is pending.

The inter-relationship between these different forms of harm can be seen in a **Canadian** case involving a woman from India who was subjected to violence, sexual assault, and intimidation because she had daughters rather than sons.[1] She was forced to participate in sorcery and various rituals. She was confined to her room as punishment for contradicting the sorcerer's predictions and becoming pregnant with female children. Her husband tried to coerce her into having an abortion during her third pregnancy. Her father-in-law complained about the size of her dowry and spoke of bride burning. She was isolated by her husband and his family and was unable to tell anyone of the abuse. In granting asylum, the CRDD found that State protection was not available to the claimant and that there was nowhere in India where she could live in safety without coming to the attention of her husband and in-laws.

The struggle of women for reproductive rights has been at the heart of feminist campaigns. The right of women to chose whether they have children, as well as how many to have and when, has been seen by many feminists as the basic 'touchstone' of feminist politics. Most of the discussions on women's reproductive rights, however, until the last decade at least, have been concentrated on the effects of the existence or absence of these rights on women as individuals. There were discussions, for instance, on how these rights affect women's health, how they affect their working lives and opportunities for upward mobility; and how they affect their family life. More recently, however, the focus has shifted towards examining the role of reproduction in broader political struggles including those over national identity. Often the pressures on women to have or not to have children relate not to them as individuals, workers, and/or wives, but as members of specific national collectivities. According to different national projects, under specific historical circumstances, some or all women of childbearing age groups have been called on, sometimes bribed, and sometimes even forced, to have more, or fewer children.

There are three main approaches associated with population control policies, each of which affect women differently.

(1) Measures to get women to have more children
The 'people as power' discourse sees maintaining and enlarging the population of the national collectivity as vital for the national interest. The future of 'the nation' may be seen to depend on its continuous growth and women may be called upon to have more children. The need for people, often primarily for men, can be for a variety of nationalist purposes, civil and military. Examples of countries where there have been measures to get women to have more children include France, Germany, Israel, Lebanon, Cyprus, the former Yugoslavia and Palestine.[2]

---

1   CRDD C97–00534, 13 January 1999.
2   A variety of different strategies have been adopted in different countries and contexts. These include, eg, financial payments and tax incentives.

(2) Eugenicism

The eugenist discourse aims at improving the 'quality of the national stock' by encouraging those who are 'suitable' in terms of origin and class to have more children and discouraging others from doing so. This discourse has resulted in programmes of forced sterilisation, for example in Germany, Sweden and Singapore. There has also been alleged forced sterilisation of gypsies in Eastern Europe.[1]

(3) Malthusianism

This discourse sees the reduction of the number of children as the way to prevent future national disaster. Population control policies are primarily aimed at reducing the rate of growth overall and women are often the target populations for such policies. For example, in Brazil up to 45 per cent of women who undertake Caesarean operations end up being sterilised and such stories are common elsewhere. In India, during the 'emergency period' in the 1970s, sterilisation policies were primarily aimed at men. However, the country which has gone furthest is probably China.[2]

The effects on women of the policies which are pursued in any particular context will be largely dependent upon the way in which the issue of reproduction relates to a broader political agenda. This reflects the theoretical analysis presented in Chapter 2. For example, nationalist projects which focus on genealogy and origin as the major organising principles of the nationalist collectivity would tend to be more exclusionary than other nationalist projects. Only by being born into a certain collectivity could one be a full member in it. Control of marriage, procreation and, therefore, sexuality would thus tend to be high on the nationalist agenda. When constructions of 'race' are added to the notion of a common genetic pool, fear of miscegenation becomes central to the nationalist discourse. In its extremity this includes the 'one-drop rule' which dictates that even if 'one drop of blood' of members of the 'inferior' race is present, it could 'contaminate' or 'pollute' that of the superior race. The central importance of women's reproductive roles in ethnic and national discourses becomes apparent when one considers that, given the central role that the myth (or reality) of 'common origin' plays in the construction of most ethnic and national collectivities, one usually joins the collectivity by being born into it. In some cases, especially when nationalist and racist ideologies are very closely interwoven, this might be the only way to join the collectivity, as those who are not born into it are excluded. It is not incidental, therefore, that those who are preoccupied with the 'purity' of the race would also be preoccupied with the sexual relationships between members of different collectivities.

As was suggested in Chapter 2, a variety of cultural, legal and political discourses are used in constructing the boundaries of nations. Women's position in, and obligations to, their ethnic or national collectivities, as well as in and to the States

---

1   Freedman and Issacs 1993.
2   Representatives should ensure that they are familiar with the current situation in China as policies vary considerably between regions and over time. There are many sources of additional information. See, eg, *China: One-Child Policy Update* which has recently been produced by the Research Directorate of the CIRB (June 1999) available on-line at http://www.irb.gc.ca

they reside in and/or are citizens of, also affect and can sometimes override their reproductive rights. The policy responses of governments that are attempting to speed up, slow down, or reverse the declining birth rates in their countries have elicited a great deal of interest among those concerned with potential human rights violations. Some countries have deliberately restricted access to contraception and abortion in order to raise the birth rate, which constitutes a clear violation of people's right to family planning and hits hardest those who cannot obtain private services. Other governments have introduced economic incentives or special privileges to promote childbearing among particular sub-populations. For example, Singapore's policy of selecting women with higher education for pro-natalist incentives has triggered charges of ethical violations because similar benefits are not available for women with less schooling. Among anti-natalists, China's policy is clearly the most restrictive with its top-down, multi-layered and multi-faceted scheme for rewarding one-child families, penalising most couples with more children, and imposing fertility targets at the State, district, community, workplace and household levels. Justified on the grounds that personal freedoms must be subordinated to collective needs if the population's long-term welfare is to be assured in the face of limited economic and natural resources, China's policy has stimulated international debate on ethical grounds. It has also elicited considerable domestic resistance from rural couples who refuse to abide by its provisions. Anti-natalist programmes combining intensive persuasion, widespread family planning services, and in some cases, small-scale incentive schemes are also found in countries such as Indonesia, Thailand, Sri Lanka, Bangladesh, the Republic of Korea, Columbia, Mexico, Tunisia and India, among others. These, too, have raised some charges of violations of the rights of individuals who are persuaded, tricked or coerced into accepting contraception or sterilisation by family planning promoters in the absence of truly informed consent.

As with other issues discussed in this book, a woman's claim to protection under the Refugee Convention cannot be based solely on the fact that she is subject to a national law or policy to which she objects. The concept of reproductive rights is illustrative of a potential tension between the protection of individual freedoms and the common good. The role of governments, ideally, is to balance the sometimes contradictory demands of individual freedom and social entitlement as abstractly defined. The dilemma of how to reconcile these rights in a socio-political context of customary beliefs and practices is confronted head-on in the design and implementation of population policies. In this context, decision-makers may argue that violations of women's human rights by the State are 'legitimate'. However, representatives should emphasise that, whilst a policy or law may have 'legitimate' goals, it is often administered through persecutory means and/or the penalty for non-compliance with the law or policy may be disproportionately severe. Where women's reproductive rights are violated not by the State but by members of her family or community, the failure of the State to provide effective protection must be demonstrated.

7.2 SERIOUS HARM

Women's reproductive rights are well established under international law. International human rights treaties adopted and widely ratified by nations around the world have contributed to the development of reproductive rights. Various human rights treaties articulate some of the broader categories of reproductive rights as women's rights such as the right to health, and the right to reproductive self-determination and decision-making. A right to reproductive freedom was first implied in the Universal Declaration of Human Rights, which was adopted by the United Nations General Assembly in 1948. The right to health, including the right to family planning, was refined in subsequent human rights treaties adopted by the international community. The International Covenant on Economic, Social and Cultural Rights was the first human rights treaty to require States to recognise a right to health and to take steps to achieve the realisation of that right for the benefit of families. A woman's right to health and family planning is also specifically addressed in the Convention on the Elimination of All Forms of Discrimination against Women. The Convention on the Rights of the Child further reiterates the right to reproductive freedom. In addition, the International Covenant on Civil and Political Rights states that men and women of marriageable age have the right to marry and found a family. Reproductive rights and their centrality to achieving equal rights for women has also been recognised in subsequent United Nations' conferences such as the 1994 International Conference on Population and Development and the 1995 Fourth World Conference on Women.

Decision-makers in **Canada** have considered refugee claimants from China alleging fear of persecution in the form of sterilisation dozens of times in the last five years alone. As early as 1989, the Refugee Board accepted the testimony of a refugee claimant alleging sterilisation as a form of persecution.[1] *Cheung*[2] provides a clear and forceful judicial statement concerning the practice of forced sterilisation of women amounting to persecution within the meaning of the Refugee Convention. The court in *Cheung* found that forced or strongly coerced sterilisation in the context of China's one child policy constitutes persecution because it violates Articles 3 and 5 of the Universal Declaration of Human Rights. This practice subjects women to cruel, inhuman and degrading treatment and is a serious and totally unacceptable violation of her security of person. Furthermore, and in light of the court's characterisation of forced sterilisation as an 'intrusive' and 'brutal' practice, it was held that coerced sterilisation of women could be considered as persecution within the meaning of the Convention refugee definition, regardless of whether it is sanctioned by law. The court in *Cheung* also addressed the issue of cultural relativity and the argument that such polices and infringements of women's human rights are 'legitimate':[3]

> 'If the punishment or treatment under a law of general application is so Draconian as to be completely disproportionate to the objective of the law, it may be viewed as persecutory. This is so regardless of whether the intent of the punishment or

---

1   See *H (W.1) (Re)* [1989] CRDD No 15 (No V89–00501).
2   *Cheung v Canada (MEI)* [1993] 2 FC 314 (FCA).
3   For further discussion of the issue of the legitimacy of State policies, see **7.3**.

treatment is persecution. Cloaking persecution with a veneer of legality does not render it not persecutory. Brutality in furtherance of a legitimate end is still brutality ... There are few practices that could be more intrusive and more brutal than forced sterilisation ... There is a point at which cruel treatment becomes persecution regardless of whether it is sanctioned by law; the forced sterilisation of women is so intrusive as to go beyond that point.'

In a similar case, *Chan*,[1] a majority in the Supreme Court of Canada assumed, without deciding, that *Cheung* was correct:

'Basic human rights transcend subjective and parochial perspectives and extend beyond national boundaries. Recourse can be had to the municipal law of the admitting nation, nevertheless, because that law may well animate a consideration of whether the alleged conduct fundamentally violates human rights. Forced sterilisation constitutes a gross infringement of the security of the person and readily qualifies as the type of fundamental violation of basic human rights that constitutes persecution. Notwithstanding the technique, forced sterilisation is in essence an inhuman, degrading and irreversible treatment.'

The CIRB dismissed the appeal on credibility grounds, however, concluding, interestingly, that physically coercive penalties for breach of the policy were applied principally against women (the appellant in that case was male). In a strong minority judgment, La Forest J also addressed the issue of the boundary between legitimate and illegitimate policy.

In the **Australian** case of *A*,[2] which was discussed in Chapter 3, the respondent did not dispute that forced sterilisation would amount to persecution and this concession was accepted by the court. By contrast, but also implicitly referring to the legitimacy of State policies in the area of population control, the **New Zealand** Refugee Status Appeals Authority in *Re ZWD* held that whilst compulsory abortion and sterilisation may in certain circumstances constitute torture or inhuman or degrading treatment, this is not the case where it is sanctioned by society as a result of a pressing social need.

In the **UK**, Ann Widdecombe, MP, made the following policy statement which resulted in an internal memo which deals specifically with this issue being issued to immigration officers by the Asylum Policy Unit:

'I stress that ... I utterly accept that forcible abortion, sterilisation, genital mutilation and allied practices would almost always constitute torture. In fact, they would probably always constitute torture ... We would regard enforced abortion as torture, as we would enforced mutilation or sterilisation.'[3]

In addition to the direct violations of women's physical integrity associated with population control policies, children born outside of these policies may be the subject of a range of discriminatory measures which cumulatively can amount to serious harm within the meaning of persecution. For example, children may be prohibited access to normally available health or educational facilities.

---

1   *Chan v Canada (MEI)* [1995] 3 SCR; (1995)128 DLR (4th) 213.
2   *A v Australia (MIEA)* (High Court of Australia) [1998] INLR 1.
3   See Asylum Policy Unit Internal Memo ATP 13/96 and House of Lords considerations of Lords amendments 15 July 1996, Hansard cols 822–825. See also Baroness Blatch, House of Lords reports 20 June 1996, Hansard cols 476–477. These statements can also be found in *The Asylum and Immigration Act 1996: A compilation of ministerial statements made on behalf of the government during the Bill's passage through Parliament* (ILPA 1996).

7.3 THE FAILURE OF STATE PROTECTION

Reproductive rights violations often, although not always, constitute an example of gender-based discrimination enforced through the law. As was outlined in Chapter 3, a woman's claim to Convention refugee status cannot be based solely on the fact that she is subject to a national law or policy to which she objects.[1] However, where such policies are discriminatory this may constitute a failure of State protection within the meaning of the Refugee Convention. An example of a discriminatory policy with a 'legitimate' end pursued through persecutory means is the one child policy in the People's Republic of China. While the goal of population control might be defensible, forced sterilisation and abortions are each persecutory means of achieving the objective.

Reproductive rights in the context of population control policies raise critical issues around the legitimacy or otherwise of State policy in this area. This issue has been addressed at length by the courts in other jurisdictions when determining whether forced sterilisation and abortion are persecutory. In the **Canadian** case of *Cheung*,[2] the approach to this issue was that, where a punishment or treatment under a law of general application is so Draconian as to be completely disproportionate to the objective of the law, it may be viewed as persecutory. This is so, regardless of whether the intent of the punishment or treatment is persecution: 'Brutality in furtherance of a legitimate end is still brutality . . .' The CIRB in *Chan*[3] noted that the implementation of China's one child policy, through sterilisation by local officials, can constitute a well-founded fear of persecution. The alleged persecution does not have to emanate from the State itself to trigger a Refugee Convention obligation. Serious human rights violations may well issue from non-State actors or from subordinate State authorities if the State is incapable or unwilling to protect its nationals from abuse. Determination of the precise degree of involvement by the Chinese government was neither necessary nor possible from the evidentiary record.

> 'When the means employed place broadly protected and well understood basic human rights under international law such as the security of the person in jeopardy, the boundary between acceptable means of achieving a legitimate policy and persecution is crossed.'

Serious human rights violations may well issue from non-State actors if the State is incapable or is unwilling to protect its nationals from abuse:

> 'The evidence does not lead to the conclusion that the central government of China is unable to protect its citizens from the excesses of the local authorities. Rather, it indicates a central government which, by its passivity, is either tolerating or abetting the enforcement of the population control policy by a means which it officially disavows . . . It is evident, then, that the Chinese government, if nothing else, creates a climate in which incentives for mistreatment are ripe.'[4]

By contrast, the New Zealand Refugee Status Appeals Authority in *Re ZWD*[5] held that whilst compulsory abortion and sterilisation may, in certain

---

1 CIRB 1996.
2 *Cheung v Canada (MEI)* [1993] 2 FC 314 (FCA).
3 *Chan v Canada (MEI)* [1995] 3 SCR; (1995)128 DLR (4th) 213.
4 *Chan v Canada (MEI)* [1995] 3 SCR; (1995)128 DLR (4th) 213.
5 Refugee Appeal No 3/91 (New Zealand Refugee Appeal Board).

circumstances constitute torture or inhuman or degrading treatment, this is not the case where it is sanctioned by society as a result of a pressing social need.

In much of the international case-law addressing Chinese family planning policy, the issue of whether there has been a failure of State protection has not been expressly addressed, largely because it is implicitly accepted that the Chinese government is responsible for the conduct of its own officials. In *Matter of Chang*,[1] however, the **US** BIA accepted the assertions of the Chinese government that it uses economic incentives and birth control measures, but forbids coercive techniques. However, Amnesty International (1995) has reported that it has been unable to find any instance of sanctions taken against officials who perpetrated human rights violations in the course of enforcing the policy. The implementation of China's family planning laws by means of forced abortion and sterilisation is, therefore, a clear example of a policy which may have legitimate ends being implemented by persecutory means with the acquiescence of the governing authorities.

This issue was addressed in a recent Tribunal case in the **UK**:[2]

> 'We are prepared to accept that forcible abortion or forcible sterilisation is a grave violation of human rights. There is no evidence, in our view, that the policy of the Chinese government is that their one child policy is to be enforced in that manner. We agree that there is evidence that in some areas local officials resort to excessive and unauthorised methods of enforcing the policy. We do not know but given the somewhat questionable record of China in the realm of human rights, we are prepared to accept that whatever they may wish to do they do not succeed in curbing these excesses and are unlikely to punish any official for being guilty of it. In the area therefore in which it is carried out we would accept that there is no protection.'

Representatives will also need to address the issue of whether there is an internal flight alternative. The difficulties faced by migrant women in China have been highlighted by Amnesty International and the CIRB.[3] In particular, such women are at particular risk of sexual violence, and the *hukou* system of household registration means that they are easily identifiable, and without appropriate documentation may be forced to take low-paid jobs and unable to avail themselves of social and medical benefits. Regular checks make the long-term position of such women insecure in the extreme.

7.4   REFUGEE CONVENTION GROUNDS

Much of the international jurisprudence on violations of reproductive rights has centred on Chinese one child policy. Within this, legal debate has focused on whether women fearing violations of their reproductive rights can be protected as members of a particular social group within the meaning of the Refugee Convention. This focus has inevitably detracted from other scenarios where women's reproductive rights are violated. In addition, the emphasis on social group has depoliticised the analysis even where women have used reproductive

---

1   *Matter of Chang* Int Dec 3107 (BIA 1989) (Abstract at (1990) 2 IJRL 288).
2   *Hua v SSHD* (unreported) 21 April 1999 (IAT).
3   *Women in China – imprisoned and abused for dissent* (Amnesty International, 1995); *Women in China* (CIRB, October 1993).

rights as a focus of political opposition and resistance. As in all cases, however, the most appropriate ground will depend on the particular circumstances of the individual applicant and the context from which she is fleeing.

7.4.1 Social group

In the **Canadian** case of *Cheung*,[1] the Federal Court of Appeal held that 'women in China who have more than one child and are faced with forced sterilisation' constitute a particular social group, on the basis that they 'share a similar social status and hold a similar interest which is not held by their government . . . All of the people coming within this group are united or identified by a purpose which is so fundamental to their human dignity that they should not be required to alter it on the basis that interference with a woman's reproductive liberty is a basic right ranking high in our scale of values'. This finding was accepted by the minority in the Supreme Court of Canada in the case of *Chan*,[2] applying the *Ward*[3] categories, and holding that the key issue is whether an appellant was voluntarily associated with a particular status for reasons so fundamental to (her) human dignity that (she) should not be forced to forsake that association. This is reflected in other more recent cases including that of a woman with three children who had an IUD forcibly inserted.[4] The CRDD found that the claimant had a well-founded fear of persecution by reason of imputed political opinion, her demonstrated determination to exercise reproductive choice in defiance of China's one child policy. It was also found that she was a member of a particular social group, namely 'women in China who fear forced sterilisation because they have violated the Chinese birth control policy by having more than one child'. The CRDD found that there was wide variance in the degree and manner in which the one child policy was being applied. However, it would have been unreasonable to expect the claimant to stand up to the authorities, in the hope that any penalty imposed might have stopped short of forced sterilisation.

The social group argument has been less successful in other jurisdictions. In the **Australian** case of *A*[5] the majority held that the characteristics defining a social group could not be a common fear of persecution as this would negate the purpose of linking the refugee definition to civil or political status. The existence of a social group depended in most, if not all, cases on the external perceptions of the group, and that the actions of the persecutors could serve to identify or even create a social group. In the case of couples who had infringed the Chinese family regulations, however, it was held that there was no *social* attribute or characteristic linking couples who wished to have more than one child contrary to the one child policy:

> 'There is simply a disparate collection of couples throughout China who want to have more than one child contrary to the one child policy. Some may wish to have a child as soon as possible; some in the near future; and others in the distant future. There is no social attribute linking the couples, nothing external that would allow

1   *Cheung v Canada (MEI)* [1993] 2 FC 314 (FCA).
2   *Chan v Canada (MEI)* [1995] 3 SCR; (1995)128 DLR (4th) 213.
3   *Canada (Attorney General) v Ward* [1993] 2 SCR 689.
4   CRDD V95–02063, 22 April 1997.
5   *A v Australia (MIEA)* [1998] INLR 1 (High Court of Australia).

them to be perceived as a particular social group for Convention purposes. To classify such couples as "a particular social group" is to create an artificial construct that bears no resemblance to a social group as that term is ordinarily understood. Indeed it is hard to see how such couples are even a group for demographic purposes.'

It was noted, however, that such persons could come to be perceived as a particular social group if, for example, they had joined with others and publicly demonstrated against the government's policies and had thereby gained sufficient notoriety. In these circumstances the political opinion ground would also apply. This decision is reflected in recent cases involving Chinese nationals.[1]

In *Re ZWD*,[2] the social group argument was rejected by the **New Zealand** Refugee Status Appeals Authority. The Authority criticised the tendency in some jurisdictions to impose a requirement of voluntary association (an internally defining factor), holding that this approach failed to recognise the importance of the perceptions of the persecutor and the wider community in defining a social group. Nevertheless, it held that the social group category should not be viewed as an all-embracing safety net, and that there had to be some causative link between the persecution feared and the applicant's civil or political status. The authority examined whether the group was definable by a shared characteristic fundamental to the identity of its members. In that case, the appeal failed on the basis that a coherent formulation of the group was not possible. Again, this has been the general approach in cases involving both Chinese and Fujian nationals.[3]

7.4.2 Political opinion

An alternative approach to reproductive rights violations takes into account the political context of population policies. There may be cases where the grounds for the persecution are those of actual or imputed political opinion as opposed to social group. For example, if the sterilisation or abortion is seen as effectively constituting punishment for refusal to abide by government policies or if other penalties were imposed which constituted discrimination rising to the level of persecution, then the grounds for the claim could be argued as actual or imputed political opinion. Forced sterilisation and abortion constitute a fundamental violation of women's human rights as recognised in international law, and in the case of China's one child policy, the State is directly implicated. The law or policy, although having legitimate goals, is administered through persecutory means. In this context, it could be argued that where a woman is subjected to forced abortion or sterilisation or where she is punished through discriminatory measures which rise to the level of 'serious harm', the State is effectively imputing a political opinion to her because it brands her as an opponent of the regime and punishes her on this basis. Arguing imputed political opinion as the grounds for

---

1   See, eg, RRT Reference V98/09505 10 March 1999 and RRT Reference V99/09862 19 May 1999.

2   Refugee Appeal No 3/91 (New Zealand Refugee Review Board).

3   See, eg, Refugee Appeal No 794/92 *Re WWH* 12 April 1995; Refugee Appeal No 2258/94 *Re NSG & YH* 21 November 1996; Refugee Appeal No 70919/98 12 November 1998.

persecution may, in some cases, therefore, be an appropriate strategy and avoids some of the problems associated with the particular social group approach, especially given that the social group must exist independently from the persecution itself.

> 'Opposition to the Chinese family planning policy, as manifested in a refusal to be sterilised or have an abortion, is essentially political in nature, regardless of whether the individual concerned expressly articulates it as such. A refusal to be sterilised represents a fundamental challenge to the power asserted by the Chinese state to intervene in matters which are internationally recognised as falling within the private sphere . . . In essence, by refusing to abide by the one child policy, a woman is defying the Chinese government's authority to violate basic and fundamental personal rights.'[1]

The planned parenthood policy has always been viewed by the Chinese authorities as a political issue. A measure of the ideological importance of the policy is the enshrinement of the duty to practise family planning in Article 49 of the Chinese constitution. A breach of the regulations is seen as a political crime. Those who assist women to oppose the policy are imprisoned on counter-revolutionary charges and the entire history of the policy demonstrates its ideological and political significance. The use of political propaganda and 'ideological education' to ensure compliance also underscores the political nature of the policy.

This is perhaps clearest in the **US** where following the Board's ruling in *Matter of Chang*,[2] the Attorney-General promulgated a new regulation, binding on the Immigration and Naturalization Service, Immigration Judges and the Board of Immigration Appeals, ordering that past or threatened forced abortion or sterilisation provides a basis for asylum or withholding of deportation as persecution due to political opinion. This protection was to be extended to *all* foreign nationals who are victims of coercive population policies, not only to Chinese nationals. That forced sterilisation of an individual who has infringed the Chinese family planning regulations amounts to persecution on account of political opinion was accepted in the case of *Guo Chun Di v Carroll*.[3] In this case, involving a Chinese man and his wife, the court was asked to determine whether the Immigration and Naturalization Act 1980 sanctions asylum to an alien who fled his country to avoid arrest, imprisonment and involuntary sterilisation because he and his wife oppose and refuse to obey their country's policy of coercive population control through involuntary sterilisation and abortion. It was held that the appellant's opposition to coercive population control constituted a political opinion, that he had a particularised well-founded fear of persecution based on this political opinion and that he had established statutory eligibility for asylum. The court stated that political opinion encompasses an individual's views regarding procreation. The right to make procreative decisions is analogous to other fundamental human rights. Expression of one's views on this issue, in opposition to a government's official policy on population control and

---

1   Tennant 1998, p 15.
2   *Matter of Chang* Int Dec 3107 (BIA 1989) (Abstract at (1990) 2 IJRL 288).
3   *Guo Chun Di v Carroll* US Virginian District Court 842 F. Supp. 858 (unreported January 14 1994).

family planning, especially those involving coercive sterilisation and abortion, are political. An individual's expression of his view in opposition to a country's coercive population control measures may constitute a political opinion. To establish eligibility for asylum based on a well-founded fear of persecution, the appellant must have expressed an 'overt manifestation of a political opinion' by showing that: (a) there is a significant relationship between him and the persecutor; and (b) he has engaged in sufficiently conscious and deliberate decisions or acts which attribute to him certain political opinions. In this case, the appellant established a threshold well-founded fear of particularised persecution, even if the policy of coercive population control is not viewed as inherently persecutory. His opposition to the policy had led to a situation where the government directly persecuted him and his family as a result of his opposition to the policy. The court concluded that ' . . . it is beyond dispute that the expression of one's views regarding issues relating to the right to procreate is political . . . the petitioner's opposition to the PRC's population control policies constitutes a political opinion . . .'. This approach was also accepted more recently in the *Matter of C-V-C,*[1] in which the Board indicated that an alien whose spouse was forced to undergo forced sterilisation could establish past persecution on account of political opinion and qualifies as a refugee within the meaning of the Refugee Convention:

> 'The right to privacy, the right to have a family, the right to bodily integrity, and the right to unfettered reproductive choice are fundamental individual rights recognised domestically and internationally. We view those rights as fundamental rights and that the election to exercise them should be respected and not trampled constitutes a political opinion . . . Neither sterilisation nor abortion in and of itself constitutes persecution per se . . . However as a consequence of opposition to those practices either procedure may constitute persecution. In being forced to comply with the very violation of fundamental human rights which one opposes on political, religious, or other grounds constitutes a type of punishment for a characteristic which the persecutor, in this case the Chinese government, wishes to quash or overcome.'

In **New Zealand** there has been some acknowledgement of the political nature of resistance to family planning programmes.[2] In one case the applicant directly assisted women to avoid abortions as a result of which she and her family were beaten and threatened. She was detained and convicted of being anti-government and undermining the Family Planning Association. She was sentenced to two years' imprisonment and re-education, publicly humiliated for her crime, and released after one year upon payment of a bribe. Both the appellant and her husband were fired from their jobs and expelled from the Communist Party. She was granted asylum on the basis of a political opinion that had been imputed to her.

In the **UK**, this approach has been more successful than arguments involving the construction of particular social groups. This can be seen, for example, in the case of *Shuo Jin Chen*, which was not appealed by the Home Office.[3]

---

1   Int Dec 3319 (BIA 1997).
2   Refugee Appeal No 71131/98 17 December 1998.
3   *Chen v SSHD* (unreported) 29 October 1997 (CC/55095/97) (IAT).

'In the case of this Appellant, the manner in which local officials intended to implement the law in question was a direct threat to the Appellant's physical integrity and family life. Her response, namely her refusal to undergo abortion or sterilisation, was intended to protect her physical integrity but it was also a political act. It was a political act because of the nature of what the officials were expecting the Appellant to undergo and because the officials themselves were purporting to act in the exercise of their public duties. In stating this I do not mean to suggest that any failure to comply with the direction of a public official is a political act but in this appeal the public officials were seeking to interfere with the Appellant's physical integrity in a most invasive manner.'

That resistance to the one child policy could, in some circumstances, amount to an expression of political opinion was also accepted in the case of *Hao Cai Cheng*:[1]

'... it is my view that giving birth to a child contrary to the one-child policy, in the circumstances of this case, does not place this appellant in fear of persecution by reason of his political opinion. He is in fear of persecution by reason of the fact that a family planning official was killed by him when that official came to collect the fine for the breach of the policy.'

Similarly, in *Huang and Lang*[2] the adjudicator found both appellants to have a fear of persecution because of their perceived political opinion as a result of their breach of the one child policy.

There are also some cases from countries other than China which illustrate the way in which struggles around reproductive rights represent a form of political resistance by women. Perhaps the clearest example of this from recent **UK** case-law is *Ouanes*.[3] In November 1996, the IAT held that the appellant had a well-founded fear of persecution for a Refugee Convention reason if returned to Algeria. She had trained as a midwife and was employed by the Ministry of Health and one of her duties was to advise about contraception. She was threatened by Islamic fundamentalists opposed to the use of contraception. The IAT concluded that she was a refugee within the meaning of the Refugee Convention:

'We are unanimously of the opinion that the [respondent] is a member of a group namely government employed midwife. One of her duties is to advise on contraception. She is opposed by the fundamentalists. It is clear from the reports we have read and the background material that we have studied that she is at risk and the authorities are unable to provide protection for her. She personally has suffered in that she had received threats and her nephew has been shot at. In our view, it is not reasonable to expect her to act as a midwife and not provide advice on contraception. She is further at risk because she does not wear the veil.'

The Home Office challenged this decision which was subsequently upheld by the Court of Appeal.[4] However, the Court did not consider whether she was persecuted on the basis of her political opinion or one which was imputed to her.

---

1   *Cheng v SSHD* (unreported) 29 July 1999 (G00101) (IAT).
2   *Huang and Lang v SSHD* (unreported) 15 June 1999 (TH/23675/94 and HX/85806/98) (IAT).
3   *R v SSHD ex parte Ouanes* [1998] INLR 230 (CA).
4   *R v SSHD ex parte Ouanes* [1998] INLR 230 (CA).

7.5 SOURCES OF INFORMATION AND SUPPORT

Centre for Reproductive Law and Policy (CRLP)

http://www.crlp.org

The CRLP is a non-profit legal and policy advocacy organisation dedicated to promoting women's reproductive rights. The Centre has information on reproductive rights worldwide. It also has a list of publications and press releases and on reproductive rights in the refugee context. CRLP's domestic and international programs engage in litigation, policy analysis, legal research, and public education seeking to achieve women's equality in society and ensure that all women have access to appropriate and freely chosen reproductive health services. CRLP works to broaden the use of a rights-based approach to reproductive health, and to recast the discussion of women's reproductive rights in terms of human rights. It lobbies at international, regional and national levels about the manner in which reproductive rights fit within the human rights framework, monitors laws and policies that affect reproductive rights and health and undertakes independent fact-finding missions in different countries in collaboration with national-level organisations.

Global Reproductive Health Forum

http://www.hsph.harvard.edu/organizations/healthnet

This site provides extensive information on research on reproductive rights, discussion forums and a search engine.

International Planned Parenthood Federation (IPPF)

http://www.ippf.org

The IPPF is the largest voluntary organisation in the field of sexual and reproductive health including family planning and is represented in over 180 countries worldwide. It has produced a Charter on Sexual and Reproductive Rights. The website has resources, links, country profiles and a search engine.

Ipas

http://www.ipas.org/

Ipas works globally to improve women's lives through a focus on reproductive health. Its work is based on the principle that every woman has a right to the highest attainable standard of health, to safe reproductive choices, and to high quality health care. Its website has a Reproductive Health Gateway which provides a one-stop search facility of over two dozen reproductive health sites.

Chapter 8

SEXUAL ORIENTATION

8.1 SEXUAL ORIENTATION AS THE BASIS OF AN ASYLUM CLAIM

'In every region of the globe, lesbians experience severe and in some cases life-threatening persecution based on their status as lesbians, including sexual and physical violence, forced psychiatric treatment, and denial of employment, housing, education, health care, and basic social services.'[1]

Violence and discrimination against lesbians pervade the cultural and legal norms of countries around the world. According to Amnesty International (1997a), formal laws which criminalise both male and female same-sex relationships exist in a large number of countries. These include Afghanistan, Algeria, Angola, Bahrain, Bangladesh, Cape Verde, Cuba, Ethiopia, Iran, Kuwait, Morocco, Mozambique, Namibia, Pakistan, Somalia, the Sudan and Zaire. In countries where *sharia* laws apply, punishment for lesbianism can include execution by stoning or cleaving in two, amputation of hands or feet and lashing.

Human rights violations targeting gay men and lesbians include, *but are not limited to*:

- extrajudicial executions and disappearances;
- arbitrary killings by armed opposition groups;
- torture and ill-treatment;
- rape and sexual abuse;
- forced 'medical treatment' to change sexual orientation;
- laws criminalising same-sex relationships;
- detention;
- the death penalty;
- abuses based on real or perceived HIV status.

As Minter (1996) suggests, however, lesbians often experience different forms of persecution than those characteristically targeted at gay men (see Box 8.1). Representatives should note, for example, that social and cultural norms regarding appropriate gender roles and behaviour may mean that, even where there are larger groups of persecuted women, lesbians are specifically targeted by the State:

'In 1984 in Lima a violent raid was carried out in the capital where about seventy-five lesbian women were beaten up and ill-treated by the police. Prostitutes get a very rough time in jail. But the treatment of lesbians was even worse. Lesbians were

---

1   Minter 1996, p 3.

beaten up because, however degrading prostitution can be, it is still regarded as normal behaviour, whereas lesbianism is seen as too threatening to the status quo.'[1]

In addition, women may be forced to marry or to conform with gendered norms and social mores regarding their behaviour which are inappropriate in view of their sexual orientation.[2] This is reflected in comments made by a woman from the former Yugoslavia:

'If I go back … my father will try to force me to marry. I cannot marry. In this situation I would be forced to flee, and in [my country] no one would protect me. If I told my father that I am a lesbian, my father could subject me to the worst of punishments – perhaps even execution – and no one would protect me.'[3]

Representatives whose clients may have claims for asylum based wholly, or in part, upon their sexual orientation should ensure that they are aware of the forms of abuse suffered by lesbians in different countries. They should also be aware of the shortage of information which currently exists in this area.

Box 8.1

A case currently pending in the UK concerns a couple from a Baltic State involved in a same-sex relationship. The couple had met in a Baltic State where same-sex relationships are socially unacceptable. They lived together but were evicted by their landlady when she discovered that they were having a relationship. They were subsequently harassed by others who learnt that they were having a relationship, and began to receive telephone calls from men who offered them money to appear in pornographic films. The women were too frightened to report the calls to the police. In Autumn 1996 they were abducted in the street after attending a lesbian disco together and taken by men claiming to be the police to a house where they were forced to drink vodka, which was probably spiked, and raped. The women were forced to have sex together and were photographed and filmed. They were dumped near where they had been abducted. Shortly afterwards the couple were stopped by one of the men who had abducted them. They were forced into a car and abducted a second time. Once again they were drugged and forced to have sex whilst being filmed. They were repeatedly raped. One woman cannot speak about what happened to her and her partner. Both women were physically and mentally ill after the attacks and one of them attempted to kill herself. The couple moved to other addresses in the city where they lived but did not feel safe and fled to the UK where an in-country application for asylum was made.

---

1   Testimony of an anonymous Peruvian witness cited in Amnesty International 1997a, p 23.
2   Representatives are referred to the information in Chapter 5 which deals specifically with gendered social mores and the concept of honour. Many of the issues which are addressed there may be relevant in cases involving persecution on the basis of sexual orientation.
3   Testimony of a woman asylum seeker during an interview with the author.

In recent years, a growing number of countries have granted refugee status to gay and lesbian asylum seekers. These include Australia, Canada, Denmark, Finland, Germany, Ireland, the Netherlands, New Zealand, Norway, the UK and the US. This includes some very high profile cases, for example, that of Flavio Alves, a media celebrity and very active gay-rights campaigner in Brazil, who sought and was granted asylum in the US. There is now a body of case-law, particularly from Canada and the US, addressing sexual orientation as the basis of an asylum claim and some case-law in the UK which focuses principally on the issue of whether homosexuals constitute a particular social group within the meaning of the Refugee Convention.[1] However, asylum claims based on sexual orientation remain relatively rare, with less than 200 having been identified by the International Gay and Lesbian Human Rights Commission (IGLHRC). Information provided by the IGLHRC also suggests that lesbian asylum seekers are at a disadvantage even *vis-à-vis* gay men: 'access to asylum is an all but unreachable goal for the vast majority of lesbians who need protection'.[2] Lesbians account for only a fraction of all cases worldwide, for example, there are only five known cases in the US in which lesbians have received asylum on the basis of their sexual orientation, and at least two in which claims made on this basis have been denied.

There are several reasons for the low numbers of asylum claims based on sexual orientation made by women. Many of these are procedural including clients' unfamiliarity with their eligibility to apply, reluctance to disclose their fears based on their sexual orientation to a solicitor, advocates' difficulties in eliciting from clients such relevant information or, once discovered, the difficulties in evaluating or developing asylum claims.[3] Applicants claiming asylum on this basis are reluctant to disclose information about experiences relating to their sexual orientation and this problem is exacerbated by existing procedural and evidential concerns which are discussed in Chapter 10. The effects of age, as it intersects with gender and sexual orientation, should also be taken into account. Minors may be particularly fearful of 'coming out' to an advocate let alone an immigration officer, given their developmental stage and the stigma attached to same-sex relationships. Claims based on sexual orientation therefore raise specific issues for the process of finding out about women's experiences:

> 'Past and continuing homophobia has resulted in a failure to ensure adequate protection of people fleeing persecution on the basis of sexual orientation. The same prejudices that contribute to the persecution play a role in the denial of protection to refugees.'

It is clear from this limited analysis that those representing the asylum claims of refugee women must be sensitive to issues of sexual orientation, as well as gender,

---

1   See below. There have also been a number of cases in Canada and the US involving transsexuals and/or those who have undergone gender realignment therapy. Whilst these cases should not be confused with those based on sexual orientation, the existing case-law tends to confuse and/or conflate the two, and therefore may be of some relevance.
2   Minter 1996, p 3.
3   See Appendix 11.

because they often provide the first point of contact with the legal system for lesbians seeking to determine whether or not they qualify for political asylum. It is particularly critical that representatives make every effort to obtain information relating to their client's case, and that they challenge decision-makers to recognise the validity of claims for asylum based upon sexual orientation.

There are also a series of evidential and substantive problems associated with the way in which claims based on sexual orientation are determined, including particular problems in obtaining information about the situation of lesbians in specific countries and documentary evidence of the persecution which they may have experienced or fear. This problem has been noted by the courts in **New Zealand** in the case of a woman asylum seeker from Malaysia fearing the effects of *sharia* laws as used against lesbians.[1] In some cases, decision-makers may not believe that the applicant is gay or lesbian at all. This may be particularly evident where the applicant has not 'come out' and will particularly affect women who, because of social mores and stigma, may have married and had children.

8.2 SERIOUS HARM

'Every day, in countries throughout the world, the fundamental human rights of lesbians, gay men, bisexuals, transgendered people and people with HIV and AIDS are violated. These abuses include: murder; incarceration; forced psychiatric "treatment"; torture; arbitrary arrest and detention; denials of freedom of association, press and movement; denial of the right to seek refuge/asylum; immigration restrictions; forced marriage; the revocation of parental rights; and numerous other forms of discrimination.'[2]

As was noted above, human rights violations targeting gay men and lesbians include, but are not limited to, extrajudicial executions and disappearances, arbitrary killings, torture and ill-treatment and rape and sexual abuse. The use of forced 'medical treatment' to change sexual orientation has also been examined by Goodman (1995) who draws parallels with the treatment of homosexuals by the Nazis and argues cogently that forced 'medical' intervention should be recognised as persecution within the meaning of the Refugee Convention. However, he also notes that, due to a void in precedential guidance and a legal grant of discretion, immigration judges and asylum officers may well consider the claimed injuries too insubstantial to constitute serious harm. In some recent cases, for example, the courts in the **US** have held that forced 'medical' treatment designed to alter sexual orientation did not rise to the level of persecution. In *Chau*,[3] a gay man sought refuge from the Chinese government's version of forced 'medical' intervention. The judge specifically noted that the issue of whether sexual orientation is a social group was not in question. However, he concluded that China's forced psychiatric procedures, including 'electroshock therapy' and re-education camps, though classifiable under 'discrimination of various kinds', fell short of persecution. *In Re Pitcherskaia*[4] concerned a lesbian

---

1   Refugee Appeal No 2151/94 13 November 1997.
2   International Gay and Lesbian Human Rights Commission 1999, see **8.4.2**.
3   *In Re Chau*, No A-71039582 (Immigration Judge 14 June 1993).
4   *In Re Pitcherskaia*, No A-72143932 (Immigration Judge 13 June 1994).

applicant who claimed a fear of institutionalisation in Russian psychiatric hospitals and of compulsory 'medical' procedures, including the administration of mind-altering drugs. She had been repeatedly arrested, subjected to involuntary psychiatric treatment, expelled from medical college, kidnapped and assaulted because she was a lesbian and had a high visibility role in gay activism in Russia, as a result of which she was repeatedly harassed by the Russian Mafia and charged with 'hooliganism' by the police. She was refused asylum in the US on the basis that Russia's involuntary institutionalisation and forced shock treatment of lesbian women was not sufficiently serious to constitute serious harm within the meaning of persecution.

In this context, representatives should be aware that, in many situations, lesbians are subjected to a whole series of discriminatory treatments, including in the areas of employment, housing, and access to health care.[1] It has also been the focus of some case-law in relation specifically to claims based on sexual orientation, although the approach adopted has often varied according to the individual facts of the case. For example, in **Canada**, discrimination against gay men has generally been found not to be sufficiently severe to constitute persecution within the meaning of the Refugee Convention. This is particularly evident where there are formal laws against such discrimination. This can be seen, for example, in the case of a male applicant from Brazil who had a history of being discriminated against in employment because of his sexual orientation, although he was rarely unemployed.[2] He complained to the police but was not taken seriously and, in fact, was beaten up by a police officer. The Refugee Division concluded that the discrimination and harassment suffered by the claimant did not amount, either individually or cumulatively, to persecution. The documentary evidence indicated that the practice of homosexuality between consenting adults is lawful and tolerated in Brazil and that State protection and recourse are available from discrimination on the basis of sexual orientation. Seventy-four Brazilian cities have laws protecting homosexuals from discrimination on the basis of sexual orientation. While gay men in general may experience harassment and discrimination and rare incidents of violence, they are not subject to serious harm amounting to persecution. Similarly, in the recent case of a gay man from Poland, the Canadian CRDD found that, while there is some discrimination and even some violence against gay men, it is not widespread, systematic or systemic and does not amount to persecution.[3] By contrast, however, in an earlier case also involving a Polish homosexual, the applicant was granted asylum.[4] The applicant suffered several serious beatings over the years. One of his lovers committed suicide as a result of family and social ostracism and another friend was fatally stabbed. The Refugee Division ruled that cumulatively his treatment amounted to persecution, and took into account the fact that in order to access State protection, homosexuals must 'come out'.

1   Whether discrimination can constitute serious harm within the meaning of persecution is addressed at length in Chapter 5.
2   CRDD A98–01128 13 May 1999.
3   CRDD A98–00522 10 August 1999. See also CRDD T98–04881 7 January 1999 involving applicants from Uruguay who were found to have faced discrimination and not persecution.
4   CRDD A98-01243 24 June 1998.

The applicant adamantly refused to do so because there is still a strong stigma attached to same-sex relationships in Poland, reinforced by the condemnation of the Roman Catholic Church.

There are fewer cases involving lesbian applicants. This reflects lesbian invisibility generally. However, in one recent case, asylum was granted to a Russian woman who was subjected to various forms of discrimination.[1] According to the documentary evidence which was accepted by the CRDD, lesbians in Russia have in the past been forcibly incarcerated in psychiatric institutions and subjected to chemical and shock therapy, and a strong social stigma is still attached to same-sex relationships. Victims of sexual assault are not well protected by the militia, and the claimant's sexual orientation and ethnicity increased her vulnerability to rape and physical assault by marginalising her economically and socially. Taking into account the claimant's sexual orientation, her ethnic identity and her identity as a woman, the **Canadian** authorities determined that there was a reasonable chance of her being persecuted if she returned to Russia.

Representatives should be aware that whilst discrimination against lesbians frequently exists, in many cases the abuses are not very public. One of the most significant problems faced by lesbians is the constraint on freedom of expression. For example, lesbian mothers fear that if they become too open about their sexuality, they will lose custody of their children.[2] Working lesbians fear getting fired, and it is not uncommon for women who publicly reveal their lesbianism to lose their employment, ostensibly for other reasons. In this context, serious harm is often related to gendered social mores, particularly around the institution of marriage.[3] This can be seen in the case of a Malaysian woman who applied for asylum in **New Zealand** (see Box 8.2). This example is illustrative of the intersection of a variety of issues and concerns affecting women asylum seekers in cases based on sexual orientation.

8.3 THE FAILURE OF STATE PROTECTION

In a number of countries, same-sex relationships are prohibited through State legislation. In Iran, for example, lesbians and gay men are viewed as criminals and/or deviants, labelled as *ham jens baz* and are forced to deny their feelings and live undercover out of fear of execution by the government. The official punishments include 100 lashes for the first conviction and death for the third. In Afghanistan, Orthodox Islamic scholars believe homosexuals must be punished by having a wall felled on them or being flung from a hilltop. In March 1998, Taliban Islamic authorities in Heart province bulldozed a wall onto two convicted homosexuals, killing them.[4]

---

1   CRDD A98–00268 29 July 1998.
2   This was reflected in UK family case-law until relatively recently.
3   This issue is addressed at length in Chapter 5.
4   Amnesty International 1999.

Box 8.2[1]

This case concerned a lesbian from Malaysia for whom a marriage was arranged by her parents. Although she objected, she was subjected to intense family pressure and it was made clear that cancelling the wedding would bring an enormous disgrace upon the family. The marriage went ahead but she tried to avoid having sexual relations with her husband. Her mother became aware of this and took the view that there was something wrong with her and that she must have been 'charmed'. Her husband agreed with this and together they took measures to 'cure' her. She was required to follow a special diet, drink special potions and partake in other special rituals. When she was offered a good job her husband would allow her to accept it only on the condition that she returned to his home to be his 'full-time wife'. She refused and left for New Zealand. She subsequently applied for residence, but was forced to go back to Malaysia. After returning again to New Zealand she became involved in a lesbian relationship. She applied for asylum and when interviewed disclosed her lesbian relationship, her attitude to her family's efforts to force her to marry and remain with her husband, and her view of Malaysia as a repressive society. She feared that if she was forced to return to Malaysia she would not be able to live openly as a lesbian and would be rejected by her family. She further feared that she would be punished in terms of *sharia* law. Her application was refused and she appealed against the decision. The Refugee Appeals Authority accepted that lesbians are discriminated against in Malaysia, but concluded that there was no real chance that the appellant would be prosecuted under *sharia* law by reason of her lesbianism.

State legislation prohibiting same-sex relationships is not limited to Islamic countries. In 1998, the Home Affairs Minister in Zambia threatened to arrest the leaders of a newly formed movement of gays and lesbians should they try to register the association. Homosexuality is a felony which carries a minimum sentence of 14 years in Zambia and is regarded by the government as 'unAfrican'. Meanwhile, as recently as 1999, the Jamaican government reiterated its intention to stand firm against homosexuality. The Justice Minister dismissed calls from a gay rights group to abolish laws which make same-sex relationships illegal, arguing that the law is founded in moral imperative which has not changed. Same-sex relationships have become a contentious issue throughout much of the Caribbean recently and the UK government is urging some of its present and former colonies in the region to liberalise anti-gay laws.[2]

The determining authorities in most countries have generally been more willing to accept that there has been a failure of State protection where there remain State sanctions against same-sex relationships, although the case-law on this issue is varied. In one recent case in **Canada**, the applicant claimed that he had been

1   Refugee Appeal No 2151/94 13 November 1997.
2   LGIRTF Newsletter available on-line at http://www.lgirtf.org/newsletters

subjected to insults and physical assaults because of his sexual orientation and his nationality as a Jew and was denied State protection.[1] Same-sex relationships in the region of Moldova, where the claimant lived for most of his life, are a criminal offence and are punished with possible imprisonment. He was determined to be a Convention refugee. In another case involving a gay man from Iran,[2] the CRDD granted asylum even though there was evidence that very few gay men have in fact been tried, sentenced or executed. It was accepted that the possibility of abuse of power by the authorities to humiliate and abuse homosexuals existed. It was not reasonable to ask the claimant to be discreet in his homosexuality, as his sexual orientation was a basic human right. Considering country conditions in Iran, the arbitrariness with which authority is exercised in Iran, and the aversion to Western lifestyles (which the claimant, by virtue of his open homosexuality, would be perceived as exhibiting), there was more than mere possibility that the claimant would be persecuted if returned to Iran. By contrast, however, the Canadian authorities have held that there has been no failure of State protection in the case of a gay man from the Philippines because same-sex relationships are not illegal in the Philippines and the gay community is tolerated.[3] Similarly, the CRDD has found that gay men in Lebanon are not the victims of persecutory acts because, in practice, same-sex relationships are not generally prosecuted. There have been no reported cases of homosexuals arrested, imprisoned or put on trial for their sexual orientation since 1990.[4] This decision can be contrasted with that made by the CRDD only two months later involving a female-to-male transsexual from Lebanon.[5] In granting the applicant refugee status, the CRDD acknowledged that Lebanon is a highly traditional and patriarchal society where deviation from well-defined gender-roles is not tolerated. Homosexuals suffer persecution at the hands of the police, Syrian military authorities and the Hezbollah, and may also be the victims of 'crimes of honour' committed by their own family members.

As with many other gender-related asylum claims which are addressed in this book, claims based on sexual orientation often raise concerns about the extent to which the concept of human rights, including the right to determine one's own sexuality, are universal, and the attitude of States towards lesbians and gay men in all States and not simply those which are typically considered to be 'refugee-producing'. However, the important point which needs to be made by representatives to counter the argument that homosexuals are everywhere discriminated against, is that there are significant differences in the level and effectiveness of protection available in different contexts. The level and effectiveness of this protection must be taken into account when considering whether an individual should be recognised as a refugee within the meaning of the Refugee Convention. For example, in a recent **Canadian** case, a US citizen claimed that he would face systematic harassment and mistreatment amounting to persecution should he return.[6] The Refugee Division noted that while the track

---

1   CRDD A98–00492 14 April 1999.
2   CRDD V96–03502 29 May 1998.
3   CRDD T98–08222 17 June 1999.
4   CRDD A98–00298 19 November 1998.
5   CRDD T94–07963 25 January 1999.
6   CRDD T97–06740 7 October 1998.

record with respect to equal rights for homosexuals in the US has been mixed, some positive steps have been taken. The applicant was not recognised as a refugee within the meaning of the Refugee Convention.

8.4 REFUGEE CONVENTION GROUNDS

The debate about which Refugee Convention ground is most appropriate in cases based on sexual orientation has very much centred on whether sexual orientation is an innate and/or unchangeable characteristic and, correspondingly, whether gay men and lesbians are members of a particular social group. This is reflected in current case-law from both the UK and elsewhere. Representatives should be aware, however, that where gender identity has been politicised, women's inability or refusal to conform with gendered social norms relating to sexual orientation, particularly with regard to the institution of marriage, may mean that actual or imputed political opinion is a relevant ground to consider. In addition, religion and/or nationality may intersect to define the form that the harm takes and the availability or otherwise of State protection.

8.4.1 Social group

In **Canada**, there is an increasing body of case-law which accepts that homosexuals constitute a particular social group within the meaning of the Refugee Convention. A male applicant from China was recently found to have a well-founded fear of persecution by reason of his membership in a particular social group – homosexuals in China.[1] In another recent case, the CRDD found that female-to-male transsexuals in Lebanon are a social group within the meaning of the Refugee Convention.[2] Interestingly, the applicant's mother was also ruled to have a well-founded fear of persecution because of her membership in a particular social group (family) because she supported the claimant and refused to cleanse the family name by killing him.

In the **US**, an administrative decision in June 1994 designated sexual orientation as an eligible social group category under US asylum law.[3] This is reflected in a number of cases in the US where it is accepted that lesbians constitute a particular social group within the meaning of the Refugee Convention (see Box 8.3).

In the **UK**, the issue of whether gay men constitute a particular social group within the meaning of the Refugee Convention has been the subject of debate since the decision in *Binbasi*[4] which concerned a Turkish Cypriot who claimed a well-founded fear of persecution on the basis that, if he returned to Turkey, he would be persecuted as a practising homosexual. The Secretary of State refused the application on the grounds that homosexuals per se could not constitute a particular social group within the meaning of the Refugee Convention. It was

1   CRDD T98–04956 30 March 1999.
2   CRDD T94–07963 25 January 1999.
3   By Attorney-General Order No 1895-94, 19 June 1994, Attorney-General Janet Reno elevated to precedent the BIA decision in *In Re Toboso-Alfonso*, thereby classifying sexual orientation as a social group eligible for asylum status under US immigration law.
4   *R v SSHD ex parte Binbasi* [1989] Imm AR 595 (QBD).

argued that a true interpretation of the Refugee Convention would exclude homosexuals unless they were overt homosexuals because the Refugee Convention did not guarantee an individual the full range of freedoms in his home country that he might enjoy in the UK. The High Court saw no duty to adopt the UNHCR's broad interpretation of social group that would include homosexuals in general. The High Court reasoned that a group cannot be a social group if its only common characteristic is concealed.

Box 8.3[1]

A Kurdish woman from Iran went to the US as a student and subsequently became involved in a lesbian relationship. She had always been attracted to women as she grew up but had suppressed her feelings because of the harsh consequences awaiting lesbians in Iran. She feared that she would face torture and execution in Iran due to her sexual orientation. Under Iranian law, lesbians are punished with 100 lashes for their first offence, and execution for their third offence. She also feared mistreatment in Iran on account of her gender and feminist ideas. She would be stigmatised and harassed for remaining unmarried, and for rejecting the traditional lifestyle approved by the Islamic Republic. She would be unable to practise her chosen career and would face gender discrimination. She also feared religious persecution for her refusal to practise Islam. In May 1998, she was recognised as a Convention refugee and granted asylum. The courts accepted that she had a well-founded fear of persecution on account of membership of the particular social groups of lesbians and of women who refuse to comply with Iran's gender-specific laws and social norms; on account of political opinion supporting feminist views; and on account of religion, because she has rejected Islam.

Homosexuals have the common characteristic of sexual preference that, if revealed at all, is normally revealed only in private. The appeal in *Binbasi* was therefore dismissed. In *Golchin*,[2] similarly, the Tribunal held that homosexuals are not a social group. However, in *Vraciu*,[3] a differently constituted Tribunal considered that the way in which the IAT had reached its decision in *Golchin*, by equating 'social group' with a 'minority group' sharing historical and cultural characteristics transmitted by descent was wrong, and instead held that homosexuals are a 'particular social group' within the meaning of the Refugee Convention. The Tribunal was impressed by the approach taken by the US Board of Immigration Appeals in *Matter of Acosta*[4] which held that the rather general words 'membership of a particular social group' should be read in the

---

1   Case summary available on-line http://www.uchastings.edu/cgrs/summaries/summaries.html
2   *Golchin v SSHD* (unreported) 1991 (7623) (IAT).
3   *Vraciu v SSHD* (unreported) 21 November 1994 (11559) (IAT).
4   *Matter of Acosta*, citing *Kovac v INS* 407 F.2d 102, 107 (9th Cir) (1969).

same way as the other four, more specific, grounds of persecution for a Refugee Convention reason (race, religion, nationality and political opinion), all of which involve 'an immutable characteristic: a characteristic that either is beyond the power of an individual to change, or is so fundamental to individual identity or conscience that it ought not to be required to be changed'. The very next day, the IAT came to a different decision in *Jacques*,[1] when it held that *Golchin* was not wrongly decided and that homosexuals per se do not constitute a social group. In the period since these decisions there have been a number of cases involving homosexual men from a variety of countries including Iran,[2] Syria,[3] Romania[4] and Bulgaria.[5] For example, in *Tanase*,[6] the IAT granted asylum to a gay Romanian man who had been harassed and detained by both the police and private individuals as a result of his sexual orientation. Homosexual relationships in Romania are forbidden by law. In *Apostolov*,[7] which concerned a citizen of Bulgaria who had been arrested and detained for 'immoral behaviour', the Tribunal again looked at the issue of whether homosexuals constitute a 'particular social group' within the meaning of the Refugee Convention. Although the case failed on its facts, the Tribunal found that sexual orientation is an immutable characteristic, an innate and unchangeable characteristic and that homosexuals are, therefore, a social group per se as they fall within the first category referred to in *Savchenkov*.[8] In this context, representatives should be aware that the approach in the UK as to whether homosexuals constitute a particular social group within the meaning of the Refugee Convention has closely followed the wider debate and case-law developments regarding the construction of particular social groups more generally. In this context, the decision in *Shah and Islam*[9] may have important implications for the determination of cases based wholly or primarily on sexual orientation not least because the re-written Asylum Directorate Instructions for decision-makers note the relevance of this decision in such cases and advise decision-makers accordingly:

> 'In the light of the judgement we can no longer argue that homosexuals (or other persons defined by sexual orientation) are not capable of being a social group. Discrimination against homosexuals in a society *may be such as to single them out as a social group depending on the factual circumstances in the country concerned*' (emphasis in original).

Whilst this development is to be welcomed, representatives should continue to ensure that all possible Refugee Convention grounds are addressed when considering the asylum claims of lesbians and gay men including actual or imputed political opinion.

---

1   *Jacques v SSHD* (unreported) 22 November 1994 (11580) (IAT).
2   Appeal No HX/75394/95 (unreported) October 1995.
3   Appeal No HX/75712/94 (unreported) August 1995.
4   *Rezmives v SSHD* (unreported) 20 December 1996 (14388) (IAT); *Sealeunu v SSHD* (unreported) 20 June 1997 (CA); *Tanase v SSHD* (unreported) 27 January 1998 (16136) (IAT).
5   *Apostolov v SSHD* (unreported) 24 September 1998 (18547) (IAT).
6   *Tanase v SSHD* (unreported) 27 January 1998 (16136) (IAT).
7   *Apostolov v SSHD* (unreported) 24 September 1998 (18547) (IAT).
8   *SSHD v Savchenkov* [1996] Imm AR 29 (CA).
9   *Islam v SSHD; R v IAT ex parte Shah* [1999] INLR 144, Imm AR 283 (HL).

8.5 SOURCES OF INFORMATION AND SUPPORT

International Lesbian and Gay Association

http://www.ilga.org

ILGA's aim is to work for the equality of lesbians, gay men, bisexuals and transgendered people and their liberation from all forms of discrimination. It seeks to achieve this aim through the worldwide co-operation and mutual support of its members. The organisation focuses public and government attention on cases of discrimination against lesbians, gay men, bisexuals and transgendered people by supporting programs and protest actions, asserting diplomatic pressure, providing information and working with international organisations and the international media. The ILGA website provides information on discrimination against lesbians and gay men around the world.

Lesbian and Gay Immigration Rights Task Force

http://www.lgirtf.org

The Lesbian and Gay Immigration Rights Task Force is a non-profit organisation addressing the widespread discriminatory impact of immigration laws on the lives of lesbians and gay men and people with HIV through education, outreach, advocacy and the maintenance of a nation-wide resource and support network. The site contains various links to information about asylum claims in the US based on sexual orientation. It produces newsletters which give world news in brief outlining the legal, political and social situation in a number of countries worldwide. The organisation has also produced a Handbook for advocates and practitioners entitled *Preparing Sexual-Orientation Based Asylum Claim: A Handbook for Advocates and Asylum Seekers* which is available from the Heartland Alliance for Human Needs and Human Rights, 208 S. La Salle St., Suite 1818, Chicago, IL 60604 or on-line at http://www.lgirtf.org/html/order.html

International Gay and Lesbian Human Rights Commission (IGLHRC)

http://www.iglhrc.org/asylum/index.html

The IGLHRC's mission is to protect and advance the human rights of all people and communities subject to discrimination or abuse on the basis of sexual orientation, gender identity or HIV status. A US-based non-profit, non-governmental organisation (NGO), IGLHRC responds to such human rights violations around the world through documentation, advocacy, coalition building, public education, and technical assistance. It has an Asylum Project which supports claims for asylum made by those who fear persecution because of their sexual orientation, gender identity or HIV status and provides documentation of human rights abuses perpetrated against lesbians, gay men, bisexuals, the transgendered and people with HIV/AIDS to clients' lawyers, the media, persons considering an asylum claim and other interested parties. For more information contact asylum@iglhrc.org

The organisation has produced an important guide *Asylum Based on Sexual Orientation: A Resource Guide* to assist asylum seekers in the US, particularly those who have been persecuted on the basis of sexual orientation, gender identity or HIV status. The aim of this resource, which brings together court decisions, legal articles and referral information, is to help lawyers and their clients better prepare their cases. The 500-page *Asylum Guide* contains articles from nationally renowned lawyers and legal advocates detailing their work, court decisions and relevant legislation from all over the world, including Australia, Canada, Germany, Ireland, New Zealand, the UK and the US, as well as supporting documents from United Nations Commissions and the US Justice Department. The *Guide* is available from the IGLHRC, 1360 Mission Street, Suite 200, San Francisco, CA 94103.

Other resources available from IGLHRC include:

- country files containing documentation of persecution due to sexual orientation or HIV status;
- written decisions (US and foreign tribunals) from successful cases;
- authoritative declarations on the human rights status of sexual minorities in a particular country;
- advisory opinions from UNHCR;
- referral to an international network of lawyers who have represented asylum cases based on sexual orientation of HIV status;
- contacts with grassroots gay, lesbian and bisexual liberation organisations and/or AIDS non-governmental organisations in over 130 countries worldwide;
- Other IGLHRC publications available include: *The Rights of Lesbians and Gay Men in the Russian Federation* (1994); *Unspoken Rules: Sexual Orientation and Women's Human Rights* (1995); *No Human Being is Disposable: Social Cleansing, Human Rights and Sexual Orientation in Colombia* (1995); *Epidemic of Hate: Violation of Human Rights of Gay Men, Lesbians and Transvestites in Brazil* (forthcoming).

World Organisation Against Torture (WOAT)

The World Organisation Against Torture has looked at use of the Convention Against Torture (CAT) to protect victims of persecution on the basis of sexual orientation. The organisation has prepared an information pack on CAT protections and procedures which includes sample petitions, legal briefs and question-and-answer forms. The pack is available on-line at http://www.omct.org/woatusa

Queer Immigration

http://www.qrd.org/www/world/immigration/index.html

This site has links to gay/lesbian organisations, as well as links to asylum cases, legal rulings and current law.

Stonewall Immigration Group

http://www.stonewall.org.uk

Stonewall is a lobbying and advocacy group based in London. Stonewall works for change by influencing public opinion, and the opinions of parliament. The

group provides regular summaries of any determinations or judgments that may
be of assistance to group members and their advisers.

Chapter 9

FEMALE GENITAL MUTILATION (FGM)

9.1 THE PRACTICE OF FEMALE GENITAL MUTILATION (FGM)

Female Genital Mutilation (FGM) which is sometimes misleadingly referred to as female circumcision is the collective name given to traditional practices which involve the partial or total excision of the female genitals. The World Health Organisation (WHO) has defined FGM as all procedures involving partial or total removal of the external female genitalia or other injury to the female genital organs whether for cultural or other non-therapeutic reasons.[1] Female Genital Mutilation takes a variety of different forms (see Box 9.1). Occurring predominantly in rural areas, it is mostly carried out in unsanitary conditions using unclean sharp instruments such as razor blades, scissors, kitchen knives and pieces of glass. These are frequently used on several girls in succession causing infection and the transmission of viruses including HIV. Antiseptic techniques and anaesthesia are generally not used. The procedure is usually carried out by older women from the community and is generally performed between the ages of three and ten years although it may be carried out during infancy, adolescence, on marriage or during a first pregnancy.

9.1.1 Where is FGM practised?[2]

The availability of reliable figures on the prevalence of female circumcision has increased greatly in recent years. National data have now been collected in the Demographic and Health Survey (DHS) programme for six countries – the Central African Republic, Cote d'Ivoire, Egypt, Eritrea, Mali and the Sudan.[3] In these countries, from 4 per cent to 97 per cent of women of reproductive age have been circumcised. Estimates for other countries are generally based on local surveys or anecdotal information. The WHO estimates that over 130 million women and girls have undergone FGM and that every year around 2 million mutilated girls are added to this number. FGM in a variety of its forms is practised throughout the world. However, it is mostly in the Horn of Africa that the practice is deeply rooted in socio-cultural norms, affecting more than 20 African countries. The prevalence varies widely, from about 5 per cent in the Democratic Republic of Congo (former Zaire) and Uganda to 98 per cent in

---

1   WHO June 2000 Fact Sheet No 241.
2   Representatives are reminded of the need to undertake specific research, where necessary, on the prevalence of FGM in particular countries. For further information see, eg, Minority Rights Group (1992). The Amnesty International FGM Human Rights Information Pack (1998) which is available on-line at http://www.amnesty.org has information on FGM in Africa by country.
3   Amnesty International 1997b.

Somalia, as does the severity of the mutilations. According to a United Nations Children's Fund Report (1996) *The Progress of Nations*, Egypt, Ethiopia, Kenya, Nigeria, Somalia and the Sudan account for 75 per cent of all cases of FGM. It is estimated that 15 per cent of all circumcised women have undergone the most severe form of FGM, that is, infibulation. However, infibulation is reported to affect nearly all the female population of Somalia, Djibouti and the Sudan (except the non-Muslim population of southern Sudan), southern Egypt,[1] Ethiopia, Eritrea, northern Kenya, northern Nigeria and some parts of Mali. It also occurs in various forms in southern Algeria, Upper Volta, Ghana, the Gambia, Liberia, Cote d'Ivoire, Mozambique and Togo. Outside Africa, excision is also practised by some populations in Oman, South Yemen, Saudi Arabia, Iraq, Jordan and in the United Arab Emirates. Circumcision is practised by the Muslim populations of Indonesia and Malaysia and Bohra Muslims in India, Pakistan and East Africa.[2] There is evidence that it is being practised in those European countries with large settlements of communities from these countries. Even though FGM is practised mostly among Islamic countries, it is not an exclusively Islamic practice. FGM is a cross-cultural and cross-religious ritual.

Box 9.1

Type I: Circumcision or Clitoridectomy

–   removal of the prepuce ('hood') and/or the tip of the clitoris
–   known in Muslim countries as 'Sunna' (tradition)
–   this, the mildest type, affects only a small proportion of the millions of women who undergo FGM.

Type II: Excision

–   consists of the removal of the entire clitoris (both prepuce and glands) and with partial or total excision of the labia minora.

Type III: Infibulation

–   the most extreme form
–   in countries such as the Sudan, Somalia and Djibouti, 80–90 per cent of all FGM is infibulation
–   excision of part or all of the external genitalia and stitching/narrowing of the vaginal opening
–   consists of the removal of the clitoris, the adjacent labia (majora and minora), and the joining of the scraped sides of the vulva across the vagina, where they are secured with thorns or sewn with catgut or

---

1   According to research carried out by Badawi, over 80 per cent of Egyptian women have been subjected to FGM. The majority of these were never informed as to what they were being subjected to, let alone given the opportunity to give informed consent. See *The Epistemology of Female Sexual Castration in Cairo, Egypt* available on-line at http://nocirc.org/symposia/first/badawi.html
2   Minority Rights Group 1992; Toubia 1995a.

> thread. A small opening is kept to allow passage of urine and menstrual blood
> – in some cultures, her husband cuts the woman open on their wedding night with a double-edged dagger. She may be sewn up again if her husband leaves on a long trip.

The practice of FGM has now been made illegal in some countries where it had been widely practised. However, FGM continues to be prevalent in many of these countries, and there is even some evidence that its incidence is increasing rather than decreasing as a result of the process of modernisation.[1] The available data provide little evidence that the practice of FGM will decline substantially in the near future. The Central African Republic, where prevalence is moderate, is the only country in which steady decline seems to be occurring. However, it is important in this context to acknowledge that the practice of FGM is not intrinsic to such societies and is subject to change over time. FGM has also existed in the West where it can be traced back to the nineteenth century when it was carried out for psycho-sexual reasons. Victorian medicine presented women as susceptible to emotional disorders and mental diseases because of the nature of their reproductive organs. Their organs, and in particular the clitoris, had to be tempered. The medical theory was that, if exciting the clitoris caused insanity, its removal would cure the neurosis.[2] Ideas about the health benefits of FGM are not unique to Africa. In nineteenth-century England there were debates as to whether clitoridectomy could cure women of 'illnesses' such as hysteria and 'excessive' masturbation. Clitoridectomy continued to be practised for these reasons well into this century in the US.

9.1.2 Why is FGM practised?

Although its origins are unknown, FGM has been practised for 2,500 years in a wide variety of different countries.[3] It was practised in ancient Egypt and as recently as the 1940s and 1950s in England and the US to treat so-called 'female deviances' such as hysteria, lesbianism and masturbation. The different reasons given for FGM are bewildering, often conflicting, and often at odds with biological fact. Research into FGM has identified a complex web of inter-related reasons behind the practice. These include the following.

(1) Custom, tradition and ritual
Numerous ideas and myths exist regarding the clitoris and, in particular, the dangerous health implications which it can have for the health of any children which are borne to a woman who has not been genitally mutilated. There is frequent mention (eg in Mali, Kenya, Sudan, Nigeria) of the clitoris being

---

1   Rather than diminishing with modernisation, the practice of FGM is spreading. According to Mackie 1996, infibulation is not only nearly universal where practised, but is expanding its territory. It is spreading from Arabised northern Sudan further into indigenously populated areas of southern and western Sudan. For example, infibulation was unknown in Nyala in west Sudan 50 years ago, but it now saturates the area and is universal in Nyertete merely 20 years after introduction.
2   See J. Duffy (n/d) *Clitoridectomy: a nineteenth century answer to masturbation*, available on-line at http://www.fgmnetwork.org/intro/duffy.htm
3   Toubia 1995a.

believed to be an aggressive organ, threatening the male organ and even endangering the baby during delivery.

Meanwhile, in many regions the practice persists because the elderly women who perform it insist that it should be carried out as part of tradition. In some communities, circumcision is the traditional ritual that confers full social acceptability and integration into the community upon the females. For many women and young girls, circumcision satisfies a deep-seated need to 'belong' and ensures that they will not be ostracised. In some communities, female circumcision is a prerequisite for women to be accepted as members of their ethnic group. In this context, the practice is often sometimes explained in terms of initiation rites, of development into adulthood. However, excisions and infibulations are carried out at an increasingly young age. As is noted in the report of the Minority Rights Group (1992), in the absence of symbolism, with no feeling of 'stepping into a new life', and stripped of the rejoicing of the community, the psychological damage caused by the mutilation is likely to be more grave, and the physical pain harder to bear.

(2) Religion

Many people continue to believe that the practice of FGM is a religious one associated mainly with Islam. This is incorrect. FGM is primarily a social practice, not a religious one. Female genital mutilation predated Islam. It originated in Africa and remains today a mainly African cultural practice. Excision and infibulation are practised by Muslims, Catholics, Protestants, Copts, Animists and non-believers. FGM is widely practised in countries where the predominant religion is Christianity, for example Ethiopia and Kenya. It is rare or non-existent in many Muslim countries including Iran, Jordan, Lebanon, Syria and Turkey. It should be noted, however, that in those Muslim countries where it is practised, FGM has frequently been carried out in the genuine but erroneous belief that it was demanded by the Islamic faith, or perpetrated as a required Islamic custom. In particular, FGM is often justified by two controversial sayings of the Prophet Mohammed that seem to favour *sunna* circumcision. However, as has been suggested throughout this book, and in particular in Chapter 2, the use of Islam as a religion to justify the oppression of women in many contexts is a reflection of an ideological struggle which has often focused on gender identity and women's roles in society. Although circumcision has received less attention lately than dress codes, the ideological position that has been espoused by the Islamist movement is important to understand. It frames the argument on all of these issues in terms of cultural authenticity, arguing that their definition of authentic *Islamic* culture should supplant other practices which are considered to be pre-Islamic or non-Islamic.

(3) Hygiene and aesthetics

In many cultures, including European cultures, the female genitalia is held to be in some way unclean. Yet, in practice, FGM clearly has the opposite effect to that of promoting hygiene. FGM simply does not make women and young girls cleaner. To the contrary, FGM's post-operative health consequences such as urine retention and the accumulation of menstrual blood in the vagina, lead to discomfort, infection, and odours more offensive than those caused by normal hormonal secretions.

(4) Control of women's sexuality

The most convincing explanation for the continuing, and indeed in some areas, increasing use of FGM, is that it is a mechanism for controlling women's sexuality. FGM is an extreme example of efforts common to societies around the world to manipulate women's sexuality, ensure their subjugation and control their reproductive functions. Although it is often presented as tradition, custom or religion, the most common explanation given by participants is that infibulation is required for marriage and honour. Uncircumcised women are considered unsuitable for marriage in many cultures and are socially and economically ostracised for refusing to consent to the operation. FGM fosters virginity, first, because the physical barrier prevents rape, and secondly, because the physical barrier and the attenuation of sexual desire protect the supposedly oversexed and promiscuous woman from temptation. It is proof of virginity and secures fidelity by reduction of female desire and by reinfibulation upon the prolonged absence of the husband. This may also be tied up with ideas about women retaining a vestige of a male sex organ if they are not circumcised, and being more sexually aggressive (therefore unlikely to remain a virgin before marriage or faithful within marriage). FGM, and in particular the removal of the clitoris, leads to the attenuation of sexual desire and is therefore to protect the woman against her oversexed nature, saving her from temptation, suspicion and disgrace whilst preserving her chastity. These beliefs must be understood in the context of societies where female virginity is an absolute prerequisite for marriage, and where an extramarital relationship provokes the most severe penalties. So strong is the association of mutilation with premarital chastity that in many areas a non-excised girl (in Somalia, a non-infibulated girl) is ridiculed and often forced to leave her community, and regardless of her virginity will stand little or no chance of marriage. Female sexuality has been repressed in a variety of ways in all parts of the world throughout history and up to the present time. In this context, Mackie draws the comparison between FGM and Chinese footbinding:

> 'Both customs are nearly universal where practised; they are persistent and are practised even by those who oppose them. Both control sexual access to females and ensure female chastity and fidelity. Both are necessary for proper marriage and family honour. Both are believed to be sanctioned by tradition. Both are said to be ethnic markers, and distinct ethnic minorities may lack the practices. Both seem to have a past of contagious diffusion. Both are exaggerated over time and both increase with status. Both are supported and transmitted by women, are performed on girls about six to eight years old, and are generally not initiation rites. Both are believed to promote health and fertility. Both are defined as aesthetically pleasing compared with the natural alternative. Both are said to properly exaggerate the complementarity of the sexes, and both are claimed to make intercourse more pleasurable for the male.'[1]

When seen from this perspective, it is clear that FGM is political in its aim, insofar as it provides a mechanism for individuals in society to exert power over others.

Gruenbaum (1996) offers a political-economic analysis of FGM in central Sudan and suggests that those analysing its practice should ask 'who benefits?'

---

1   Mackie 1996, pp 999–1000.

rather than simply 'what function does it serve?' The former inquiry allows us to explore the different, even conflicting, interests among various groups within a society. Questions of patterns of adaptation and maladaptation are embedded in the political aspects and power relations of cultural patterns. Some cultural patterns, in this view, are good for some people but bad for others, harmful to the health of some but good for the power or wealth of others. A careful analysis of this sort might lead us to better understandings of whose interests are served by the preservation of, or challenges to, certain cultural patterns – understandings that in turn may suggest where to look for resistance to, or fostering of, change. Seen from this perspective, it is men who are the principal beneficiaries of a practice which jeopardises the physical and mental health of women. One argument is that men derive greater sexual pleasure from a woman whose vaginal opening has been surgically narrowed. However, a growing number of men from these communities are pointing out that the practice in fact causes great difficulties for them, making penetration harder and the sex act less mutually enjoyable. It is, in fact, the women who perpetuate the practice believing that this is the only way their daughters will achieve economic and social security. It is true, however, that the cult of virginity from which the practice derives its legitimacy makes it more possible for women to be controlled for the goal of maintaining family honour. By assuring verifiable virginity (the scar tissue barrier and reduced sensation are believed to make women less likely to engage in premarital sex), family prominence can more easily be achieved through appropriate marriages and the reproduction of large numbers of legitimate offspring.

Representatives are reminded that the particular circumstances of an asylum claim based on FGM must be taken into account when considering how such a claim might most appropriately be made. None of these reasons, together or separately, adequately explains why the central core of the custom has persisted, when many of the given reasons for it have either disappeared or are clearly given little or no credibility. There are a number of possible explanations, but there is probably no single explanation.[1] Representatives should also be aware that, because of the complexity of the factors behind FGM, and in particular the association with honour and custom, finding out about women's experiences may be particularly problematic. Those who interview women who have undergone FGM often do not ask the correct questions and may not be aware of the need for particular sensitivity. Representatives are advised to carefully consider some of the procedural and evidential issues that are discussed at length in Chapter 10.

9.2   FGM AS THE BASIS OF AN ASYLUM CLAIM

Historically, the issue of FGM has been largely avoided by practitioners and advocates because of its sensitive nature, and calls for its eradication by feminists

---

1   It has been increasingly suggested that a significant reason for the persistence of FGM is economic. The continuing existence of the procedure provides an irreplaceable source of revenue for the operators, mostly older women, who can bring to bear the influence of other older female relatives of the child to have it done.

and human rights activists, both in Africa and the West, have often provoked negative reactions. As Cisse (1997) points out, well-meaning articles have tended to emphasise the most shocking FGM practices and have consequently tended to portray African parents as barbaric child abusers and African societies as oppressors of women, without nuancing their analysis of FGM, perhaps for fear of providing any arguments that might legitimise the practice. Not surprisingly, this has often produced a defensive response. This critique, alongside a growing African activism,[1] has led to new ways of approaching the issue and to international awareness and recognition of FGM as a fundamental violation of women's and girls' human rights. As a result, a large number of UN bodies and conferences have specifically called on governments to adopt measures aimed at the elimination of this practice.

The emergence of FGM as a human rights concern is reflected in a recognition by the UNHCR that FGM can form the basis of a successful asylum claim:

'FGM, which causes severe pain as well as permanent physical harm, amounts to a violation of human rights, including the rights of the child, and can be regarded as persecution. The toleration of these acts by the authorities, or the unwillingness of the authorities to provide protection against them, amounts to official acquiescence. Therefore, a woman can be considered as a refugee if she or her daughter/daughters fear being compelled to undergo FGM against their will; or, she fears persecution for refusing to undergo or allow her daughters to undergo the practice.'[2]

'FGM has been acknowledged as a form of human rights abuse, and its threat or forcible imposition can amount to persecution. The authorities may be unable or unwilling to provide protection. Therefore a woman can be considered a refugee if she or her daughters fear being compelled to undergo FGM against their will ...'.[3]

In several jurisdictions, women have been recognised as refugees under the Refugee Convention on the grounds that they would be at risk of FGM if returned to their country. **Canada** was the first country in the world to grant asylum because of female genital mutilation in 1994. In *Farah*,[4] a woman fearing FGM was found to be subjected to persecution due to her membership in 'two particular social groups, namely women and minors'. Gender was determined to be an innate and unchangeable characteristic. In 1997, two families were granted asylum in **Sweden** on the grounds that the female members of these families would be in danger of genital mutilation if returned to their country of origin, Togo. Although the authorities did not recognise the families as refugees under the Refugee Convention, they did grant them residence permits on humanitarian grounds. The most significant recent cases, however, have been in the **US**. In *Kasinga*,[5] a 19-year-old woman, who fled from Togo to avoid FGM was granted asylum by the US Board of Immigration Appeals, the highest administrative tribunal in the US immigration system (see Box 9.2).

---

1 See, eg, Amna Hassan *Sudanese women's struggle to eliminate harmful traditional practices*, Executive Secretary of the Sudan National Committee on Harmful Traditional Practices (SNCTP) available on-line at http://www.fgm.org/SudanStruggle.html
2 Letter to the Refugee Legal Centre from UNHCR 1994.
3 Letter to the Refugee Legal Centre from UNHCR 21 February 1996.
4 *Farah v Canada (MEI)* (1994) 3 July.
5 *In Re Kasinga* Int Dec 3278 (BIA 1996).

Box 9.2

As a young girl, Fauziya Kasinga had escaped FGM due to her influential father's opposition to the practice. Upon his death, when Kasinga was 15, her aunt assumed control of the house according to tribal custom and arranged for Kasinga to marry. The husband selected by her aunt was 45 years old and had three other wives at the time of marriage. Under tribal custom, her aunt and her husband planned to force her to submit to FGM before the marriage was consummated. With the help of her older sister, Kasinga fled Togo for Ghana. However, she was afraid that her aunt and her husband would find her there and went to Germany, where she stayed for two months with a woman for whom she carried out domestic work. Whilst she was there she met a young Nigerian man who offered to sell the applicant his sister's British passport so that she could seek asylum in the US where she had an aunt, an uncle and a cousin. However, after claiming asylum on her arrival in the US, Kasinga was detained and held for more than a year. She testified that the Togolese police and the government of Togo were aware of FGM and would take no steps to protect her from the practice. Her aunt had reported her to the Togolese police. Upon return, she would be taken back to her husband by the police and forced to undergo FGM. However, an immigration judge initially rejected her asylum claim, saying, 'this alien is not credible'. His decision was eventually overturned and Kasinga was recognised as a refugee within the meaning of the Refugee Convention.

Most recently the case of a Ghanaian woman, Adelaide Abankwah, was well-publicised.[1] Her mother was 'Queen Mother' of her tribe, the highest position that a woman can hold. The tribal practice requires that the woman in line to be the Queen Mother must remain a virgin until she achieves that position. However, the applicant had a sexual relationship with a man from the same tribe. She feared that, when her mother died, her lack of virginity would be discovered upon her installation as Queen Mother, and subsequent arranged marriage, and that FGM would be performed as punishment or 'purification'. Rather than be subjected to FGM, she fled to live with friends in Accra. However, her presence was reported to her tribe, and she realised that it was not safe for her to remain in Ghana. She did not believe that either the police or anybody in her tribe would, or could, protect her from the tribal authorities. Like Kasinga, Abankwah was detained on arrival. She was refused asylum on the grounds that Ghana was taking steps against FGM, and FGM was not being practised in her region. The BIA subsequently rejected her appeal. She appealed to the Second Circuit Court of Appeals and on 9 July 1999 was granted asylum on the grounds that she feared being subjected to FGM if returned to Ghana.

It is important to note, however, that there are still only a tiny number of such cases and that the obstacles to securing protection for women fleeing FGM

---

1   *Abankwah v INS* 98–4304, reported in the *New York Times* (18 and 20 August 1999) and *Marie Claire* (May 1998).

remain considerable. These obstacles are related not only to the current approach towards the various elements of the Refugee Convention definition of a refugee, which are discussed below, but also broader debates and concerns about the purpose of asylum, which were discussed in detail in Chapter 2 and are often particularly evident in claims involving FGM. The first of these relates to concerns about cultural imperialism which, as has been suggested elsewhere in this book, have been used by some decision-makers to justify the failure to offer protection to women fleeing from harmful practices which are deemed to be 'cultural'. In these cases, the existence of other normative frameworks is used to undermine the principle of universal human rights. This is perhaps no more evident than in cases involving FGM as seen, for example, in France in 1991, when the excision debate flared up anew following a much-publicised trial of an *exciseuse* (the woman who performs the operation) and the parents of the *excisées* (the girls having undergone the operation). The trial and the polemic around it threw into sharp relief just how complex and riddled with double-think the issue of 'cultural difference' has become in these 'post-modern' times and just how incapable Western legal systems are of addressing the problem adequately.

In the **US** in particular, circular arguments about the relative merits of cultural relativism and the universalism of human rights discourse have been evident in some of the arguments made by decision-makers in asylum claims involving FGM. Aware that the case of *Kasinga*[1] might have implications beyond its facts, the INS pointed out to the BIA that over 80 million females have been subjected to FGM and further noted in its brief that there is 'no indication' that 'Congress considered application of [the asylum laws] to broad cultural practices of the type involved here'. The INS maintained that 'the Board's interpretation of this case must assure protection for those most at risk of the harms covered by the statute, *but it cannot simply grant asylum to all those who might be subjected to a practice deemed objectionable or a violation of a person's human rights*' (emphasis added). The INS instead offered a 'framework for analysis' that included a new 'shocks the conscience' test for persecution which would exclude from asylum eligibility those who fear that they will be subjected to FGM by those who 'believe that they are simply performing an important cultural rite that bonds the individual to society', and past victims of FGM if 'they consented' or 'at least acquiesced', as in the case of a woman who experienced FGM as 'a small child'. However, the BIA was reluctant to endorse a significant new framework for assessing asylum claims in the context of one single novel case and recognised that there was a broader aim behind the framework: 'Its suggestion candidly is aimed at addressing issues it sees arising in relation to claims that may be made by women from other "parts of the world where FGM is practised" and by those "who have been subjected to it in the past".'

In a number of other cases, similarly, arguments about the dangers of cultural relativism have been used by decision-makers to justify refusing refugee status to asylum seeking women fearing FGM and it is important that representatives are aware of these debates. However, the problem of reconciling cultural relativism and universal human rights is not as intractable as it is often presented. This is particularly evident when it is recognised that the debate itself is less about the

---

1   *In Re Kasinga* Int Dec 3278 (BIA 1996).

women themselves than about the appropriation of women as political symbols.[1] When seen from this perspective, it is possible to find a way of reconciling, in a non-ethnocentric fashion, the enforcement of international, universal human rights standards with the protection of cultural diversity. To argue that human rights are universal is not equivalent to saying that their understanding or interpretation is self-evident or immutable, or to denying the various cultural contexts in which human rights must be embedded. Rejecting cultural relativism does not preclude flexibility in the conceptualisation, interpretation and application of human rights within and between different cultures. Human rights are universal but not absolute (in the sense of pure, unalloyed, completely uniform) in their application to various cultures. Respect for international human rights law does not, therefore, require that every culture use an identical approach, but it does require that human rights be defined and protected in a manner consonant with international principles.

The most important reason, therefore, why FGM should be recognised as a violation of women's fundamental human rights is because it is linked to the philosophical core of all international human rights law: the universal protection of individual autonomy. One of the essential norms underlying international human rights instruments, signed by States in which FGM is practised, is the moral wrongness of coercing a human being without just *and* legal cause. FGM without a woman's consent is a human rights violation because it fails to respect the right to corporal non-interference. The operation constitutes an unnecessary physical alteration of the women's genitalia leading to severe health problems and physical disability. In the vast majority of cases of FGM, it is at least questionable whether real consent was possible or forthcoming. Usually, the operation is performed on babies or young children. Babies and young girls lack the emotional and psychological maturity to decide on an informed and free basis whether to undertake the operation. Their sexual, cultural and religious orientations and affiliations might well change as they mature. The right to reconsider one's life projects in these ways is a fundamental human right.

'Culture' and 'tradition' cannot, therefore, be used to defend human rights abuses including FGM because cultural values and cultural practice are as legitimately subject to criticism from a human rights perspective as any other structural aspect of a society. Even well-established and on-going cultural practices are subject to universal human rights limitations. This approach has been followed by the courts in the US in the *Matter of U-S*:[2]

> 'I recognise that in the evaluation of long standing cultural traditions that have existed for hundreds if not thousands of years, we are on a slippery slope in trying to, in effect, make determinations based on our standard of values. However concerns about offending those who, in the words of the INS, feel that "they are simply performing an important cultural rite that bonds the individual to society" cannot override statutory enactments and obligations.'

In this case, it was also noted by the judge that concern about the numbers of potential refugee claims which could be made on the basis of FGM was one of the

---

1   James 1994.
2   Immigration Court, Anchorage, AK Dec 19, 1996. Available on line at http:// www.uchastings.edu/cgrs/summaries/51–99/summary54.html

principal driving forces behind the existing approach. This concern was exacerbated by the fact that there are increasing concerns about male circumcision as a violation of human rights: 'It is probably only a matter of time before males accompanied by an exigent set of facts and buttressed by expert testimony, will make similar claims'. Whilst this debate is not one which is addressed explicitly in this book, representatives should be aware of the growing literature which examines the similarities between male circumcision and FGM. Both rituals include the removal of well-functioning parts of the genitalia and are quite unnecessary. Both rituals also serve to perpetuate customs that seek to regulate and keep control over the body and sexuality of the individual.[1] Whilst the international community has typically failed to view male circumcision as a human rights abuse, representatives should be aware that some of the legal arguments advanced in opposition to FGM may likewise be utilised against male circumcision.

9.3 SERIOUS HARM

Female genital mutilation is increasingly recognised as a form of systematic violence against women and girls and a denial of their fundamental rights. Its consequences for the physical, psychological and psycho-sexual health of women and girls are devastating, and, in many cases, life-threatening. However, representatives should be aware that there are two possible approaches to the issue of serious harm in relation to FGM:

(1) that the act itself constitutes 'serious harm';
(2) that the refusal by the woman to allow FGM to be performed, either for herself or on behalf of her children, has consequences which rise to the level of serious harm within the meaning of persecution.

The analysis in this section will address each of these in turn. Much will depend on the individual case, but it should be noted that each of these lines of argument has different implications for the presentation of the grounds for the asylum claim.

The first issue concerns the practice of FGM itself which constitutes serious harm within the meaning of the Refugee Convention. The health risks and complications associated with FGM depend upon the gravity of the mutilation, hygienic conditions, the skill and eyesight of the operator, and the struggles of the child. However, whether immediate or long term, they are grave. As Winter suggests, 'the removal of the clitoris and also frequently the labia, with or without infibulation ... represents a severe physical and psychological mutilation, constituting a direct attack on women's sexuality'.[2]

FGM raises numerous human rights issues, including reproductive and sexual rights, the protection from violence, women's rights, the right to health, the right

---

1   See, eg, the comprehensive analysis and thought-provoking discussion provided by Chessler 1997.
2   Winter 1994, p 941.

to freedom from cruel, inhuman and degrading treatment and children's rights. The immediate and short-term consequences of the procedures include severe pain, shock, haemorrhage, and chronic infection, tetanus or septicaemia, and not infrequently, death. It is impossible to estimate the number of deaths, since the nature of the operation requires that unsuccessful attempts be concealed from strangers and health authorities, and a very small proportion of cases of immediate complication reach hospital. Beyond the obvious initial pain of the operations, FGM has long-term physiological, sexual and psychological implications. These include post-traumatic stress disorders, severe scarring (both internal and external genitals), chronic urinary infection, chronic pelvic infections, incontinence, infertility, infant/mother mortality, fibroids, fistula, sexual dysfunction and an entire range of obstetric complications due to obstruction of the birth canal by scar tissue. The unsanitary environment under which FGM often takes place can result in infection of the wound and transmission of viruses such as hepatitis and HIV. The absence of menstruation which can be caused by FGM may lead a family to think that a girl is pregnant. She is therefore killed for the honour of the family.

The long-term implications of FGM for refugee women should always be emphasised by those representing female refugees for whom FGM forms part of the claim for asylum. This is critical to counteract any suggestion that because FGM has already happened, or happens only once in a woman's lifetime, there is no 'well-founded fear' of persecution should she be returned. It should be noted, for example, that an infibulated woman must be cut open to allow intercourse on the wedding night and is closed again afterwards to secure fidelity to the husband. Further complications during childbirth are unavoidable for infibulated women. In some cases, an infibulated mother must undergo another operation whereby she is 'opened' to ensure the safe birthing of her child. Labour is often prolonged and may result in foetal asphyxia with the risk of neonatal brain damage and death.[1] In such cases, it is common to re-infibulate the woman after delivery. The pain and other sufferings that may result from FGM can, therefore, affect the victim's whole life. Some forms of FGM may also be at least partly undone, with the result that a woman suffers less. If the woman is denied this possibility, this may amount to persecution. Women on whose bodies FGM has already been carried out do not per se fall outside the scope of the refugee definition. This has been recognised in case-law from the **US**.

There is a powerful argument that female genital mutilation is a violation of women's fundamental human rights at a non-derogable level. FGM as described by Bunch (1990) and others constitutes 'cruel, inhumane and degrading treatment', a level one human rights violation, as prohibited in Article 5 of the Universal Declaration of Human Rights and a number of international instruments concerned with the protection of women's human rights. FGM is recognised as a violation of women's fundamental human rights by the UN:

> '[FGM] should be construed as a definite form of violence against women which cannot be justified or overlooked on the grounds of tradition, culture or social conformity.'[2]

---

1   Toubia 1995a.
2   UN Special Rapporteur on Violence Against Women 1994, unpublished.

This position was recently reaffirmed,[1] and is supported by a wide range of governmental and non-governmental organisations. The Convention on the Rights of the Child, the Convention on the Elimination of All Forms of Discrimination Against Women, and the Beijing Platform for Action similarly explicitly recognise harmful traditional practices such as FGM as violations of human rights.[2]

This international approach to female genital mutilation as a violation of women's human rights is reflected in a growing body of case-law in asylum cases involving this form of harm. One aspect of the claim for asylum made by a Somali woman and her two children in **Canada** was the mother's fear that, if returned to Somalia, her daughter would have to face the danger of being subjected to the custom of FGM. The court ruled that forcing a minor female to undergo FGM would grossly infringe her rights as secured in international human rights instruments, and recognised that the State in Somalia does not protect minor females from suffering this treatment.[3] The Board held that FGM, as practised in Somalia, grossly infringes minor females' rights contained in Article 3 of the Universal Declaration of Human Rights. This treatment also violates the specific rights included in Articles 19, 24 and 37 of the Convention on the Rights of the Child.

In the **US**, the BIA found in the *Matter of Konate*[4] that the physical abuse associated with FGM constitutes serious harm within the meaning of per-secution. The issue of non-repeatable harm arose in *In Re Kasinga*.[5] The INS, while agreeing that FGM could constitute persecution, urged the Board to adopt a broad analytic framework addressing, among other concerns, how to treat claims by women who, unlike Kasinga, sought asylum based upon past FGM rather than a well-founded fear of mutilation. The Board declined to formulate general rules for FGM claims, granting Kasinga asylum on the facts of her individual case.

In **Australia**, the Refugee Review Tribunal has concluded that FGM consti-tutes serious harm within the meaning of the Refugee Convention. In a case involving a Yoruba woman from Nigeria, the Tribunal stated that:

'There is no doubt that female genital mutilation as practised by the Yoruba people of Nigeria is a harmful procedure ... The harm is not confined to the actual operation of cutting into the female genitalia. The procedure itself can result in death by bleeding or septicaemia. Harmful effects including pain, vaginal tract infections and difficulty giving birth continue during the woman's life. The complications arising from FGM in regard to giving birth are significant ...'.[6]

---

1   General Assembly Resolution 52 (A/Res/52/99, 9 February 1998).
2   See, eg, Report of the Committee on the Elimination of All Forms of Discrimination
    Against Women, General Recommendation No 14, UN GAOR, 45th Sess, Supp No 38,
    pp 80, 438, UN Doc A/45/38; The Beijing Declaration and The Platform for Action,
    Fourth World Conference on Women, Beijing, China 4–15 September 1995, UN Doc
    DPI/1776/Wom (1996) 112–113.
3   *Farah v Canada (MEI)* 3 July 1994.
4   *Konate v INS* 5/17/99 (9th Cir).
5   *In Re Kasinga* Int Dec 3278 (BIA 1996).
6   RRT Reference V97/06156 3 November 1997.

In the UK, Ann Widdecombe MP (then Home Office Minister) made a number of comments during the penultimate debate of the then Asylum and Immigration Bill, which accepted enforced FGM, as well as forced sterilisation and abortion, as probably always constituting torture.[1] As a result, the Asylum Policy Unit has given explicit instructions to immigration officers which recognise that female genital mutilation is a form of torture:

> 'Current guidance on the consideration of claims involving allegations of torture stresses that torture can take many forms. But caseworkers are reminded that acts of forcible abortion, forcible sterilisation or acts involving genital mutilation are likely always to constitute torture. Applications involving such claims must therefore be considered in line with current guidelines for the consideration of asylum claims involving allegations of torture. It follows therefore, that a claim cannot be certified under paragraph 5 of Schedule 2 to the 1993 Act, as inserted by Section 1 of the 1996 Act, for the purpose of engaging the accelerated appeal procedure, if the evidence establishes a reasonable likelihood that the applicant has been subjected to forcible abortion, sterilisation, genital mutilation, or any other act of torture in the country or territory to which it is proposed the applicant should be returned.'[2]

Following this statement, representatives may be more willing to argue for their clients on this basis, including ensuring that any female applicant who has experienced FGM is not subjected to accelerated procedures for determination of their claims.

Whilst there is no case-law specifically pertaining to FGM, there appears nonetheless to be some sensitivity to this issue among adjudicators especially in cases where the appellant has young female children. In the recent case of an Eritrean woman, for example, the adjudicator recognised the dangers facing the appellant's children if she were returned to Eritrea although the principal basis for the claim was her and her husband's involvement within the Eritrean Liberation Front:

> 'I also see that female genital mutilation, which is widely considered by international health experts as damaging to both physical and psychological health, is practised extensively on girls at an early age. The government, through the Ministry of Health and National Union of Eritrean Women, is actively discouraging this practice but it still exists. I am very conscious of the fact that the appellant has three young daughters.'[3]

The argument that female genital mutilation without a woman's consent constitutes cruel, inhuman and degrading treatment is so strong that even where the claim cannot be framed within the Refugee Convention, leave to remain should be allowed on compassionate and humanitarian grounds.

As was indicated at the beginning of this section, however, an alternative approach to the issue of FGM that may be relevant in some cases is that the refusal by the woman to allow FGM to be performed, either for herself or on

---

1   House of Commons considerations of Lords amendments 15 July 1996, Hansard cols 822–825. See also Baroness Blatch, House of Lords Reports 20 June 1996, Hansard cols 476–477. These statements can also be found in *The Asylum and Immigration Act 1996: A compilation of ministerial statements made on behalf of the government during the Bill's passage through Parliament* (ILPA, 1996).

2   Asylum Policy Unit Internal Memo APT 13/96.

3   Appeal No HX/76443/95 (unreported) 4 December 1996.

behalf of her children, has consequences which rise to the level of serious harm within the meaning of persecution. There may be strong societal pressures on a woman to undergo FGM, or to allow her children to be circumcised:

> 'To be different produces anxiety and mental conflict. An unexcised, non-infibulated girl is despised and made a target of ridicule, and no one in her community will marry her. Thus what is clearly understood to be her life's work, namely marriage and childbearing, is denied her. So, in tight-knit village societies where mutilation is the rule, it will be the exception who will suffer psychologically, unless she has another very strong identity to substitute for the community identity which she has lost.'[1]

Where social mores and norms dictate that women must be circumcised in order to access their social, cultural and economic rights, this may lead to discrimination which is sufficiently severe to constitute serious harm within the meaning of the Refugee Convention. In many cultures, considerable social pressure is brought to bear on families who resist conforming to the tradition of female circumcision. A girl who has not been circumcised may not be considered marriageable. Girls' desires to conform to peer norms may make them eager to undergo circumcision, since those who remain uncut may be teased and looked down on by their peers. Girls have very little choice. Given their age and their lack of education, they are dependent on their parents, and later their husband, for the basic necessities of life. Those who resist may be cut by force. If they remain uncircumcised and their families are therefore unable to arrange a marriage, they may be cast out without any means of subsistence.[2]

These arguments were recounted before the French Commission for Appeals of Refugees in a request for refugee status submitted by Ms Aminita Diop of Mali, who refused to be subjected to FGM.[3] It is important to note that Ms Diop's opposition to FGM was not viewed by her community as a reflection of her fear of death because a friend who underwent FGM three days before her had died. Rather, when Ms Diop refused to be subjected to FGM, her refusal was viewed as a threat to the survival of her community. The reaction to those opposing FGM can also include forced imposition of FGM and severe threats to life or freedom carried out by prospective spouses or other family members. As Cisse (1997) suggests, when an individual challenges societal norms by opposing FGM and his/her basic rights, as articulated in international instruments, are not or cannot be controlled by the *de jure* public authorities, international human rights principles are implicated. Representatives are referred to Chapter 5 where the issue of women's inability and/or refusal to comply with gendered social norms and mores regarding their behaviour – particularly where this concerns female sexuality and sexual behaviour – is addressed.

1   Minority Rights Group 1992, p 10.
2   Althaus 1997.
3   CCR 164078 18 August 1991. The Commission did not, however, grant her refugee status because she could not adequately document her claim.

9.4 THE FAILURE OF STATE PROTECTION

International standards underscore the obligations of States to respect and to ensure the protection and promotion of all human rights, including the right to non-discrimination, the right to physical and mental security and the right to health. A human rights perspective requires governments, local authorities and others in positions of power and influence to honour their obligations, established under international law, to prevent, investigate and punish violence against women. A human rights perspective also obliges the international community to assume its share of responsibility for the protection of the human rights of women and girls. The fact that FGM is a cultural tradition should not deter the international community from asserting that it violates universally recognised rights.

The subordinate position historically occupied by women and girls within the family, community and society has meant that abuses such as FGM have, to date, been mostly ignored, a marginalisation which has too often been reflected in the preoccupation of the international human rights movement. Nevertheless, a whole range of standards exist which present governments with a clear obligation to take appropriate and effective action (see Box 9.3).

Box 9.3

Article 5(a) of the Convention on the Elimination of Discrimination Against Women obliges State parties to take 'all appropriate measures to modify the social and cultural patterns of conduct of men and women, with a view to achieving the elimination of prejudices and customary and all other practices which are based on the idea of the inferiority or superiority of either of the sexes or on stereotyped roles for men and women'.

Article 24(3) of the Convention on the Rights of the Child states that: 'States parties shall take all effective and appropriate measures with a view to abolishing traditional practices prejudicial to the health of children'.

The Beijing Declaration and the Platform for Action, adopted by the Fourth World Conference on Women, call, inter alia, upon governments to enact and enforce legislation against the perpetrators of practices and acts of violence against women, such as female genital mutilation, female infanticide, prenatal sex selection and dowry-related violence, and to give vigorous support to the efforts of non-governmental and community organisations to eliminate such practices.

The United Nations[1] has recently emphasised the need for national legislation and/or measures prohibiting harmful traditional or customary practices as well as for their implementation, inter alia, through appropriate measures against those responsible.

---

1   General Assembly Resolution 52 A/Res/52/99, 9 February 1998.

Several governments in Africa and elsewhere have taken steps to eliminate the practice of FGM in their countries. These steps range from criminalising FGM to education and outreach programmes. A number of countries in Africa, including Burkina Faso, Central African Republic, Cote d'Ivoire, Ghana, Guinea, Senegal, Tanzania and Togo, have enacted laws criminalising FGM. The penalties range from a minimum of six months to a maximum of life in prison. Several countries also include monetary fines in the penalty. In Egypt, the Ministry of Health issued a decree declaring FGM unlawful. As of January 1999, there had been prosecutions in Burkina Faso, Egypt and Ghana. Significantly, however, and despite the fact that FGM is currently illegal in many countries in Africa and the Middle East, this has not reduced the number of girls that are mutilated every year. The governments of these countries have not established mechanisms for monitoring the spread and practice of FGM nor have laws been properly enforced. This fact is of critical importance in establishing whether State protection is available for women in these countries. In this context it is worth noting that, in his 1986 report, the Special Rapporteur on torture effectively attributes a quasi-public character to those enforcing broadly accepted customs such as FGM; the report notes that a State's failure to intervene in such instances, especially if they are not treated as criminal offences under the law, may be considered 'consent or acquiescence' (although he does not specifically classify FGM as torture).[1]

Representatives should also be aware, however, that the issue of whether there is an internal flight alternative for the applicant may be considered particularly relevant by decision-makers in cases concerning FGM, particularly for applicants from those countries where FGM is practised within only certain ethnic groups and where these groups are associated with certain geographic areas. For example, FGM is reportedly practised primarily in Nigeria's Christian south and in the north of Sudan which is primarily Muslim. An analysis of the applicability of internal flight alternative (IFA) in the African context should account for the fact that it would not be reasonable to expect certain individuals, particularly women, to move into areas dominated by other ethnic groups who speak different languages and may have drastically different customs.

With respect to determining the availability of an IFA, particular caution should be exercised when a small country is involved. The size of Ghana was taken into account by Canada's Federal Court Trial Division when it determined in a 1995 decision that the Ghana government had failed to demonstrate an intention to protect female citizens from excision and that there was no possibility of domestic flight in a small country.[2] The size of Togo was taken into account by the IS Board of Appeals (BIA) in *Kasinga*[3] to determine that the applicant for refugee status had a country-wide fear of persecution.

---

1   See *Report of the Special Rapporteur on Violence Against Women, Its Causes and Consequences* UN ESCOR, Commission on Human Rights, 53rd Session, 14 UN Doc. E/CN.4/1997/47 (1997).

2   *Annan v Canada (MCI)* (TD) [1995] 3 CF 25 (quashing the Immigration and Refugees Board's denial of refugee status and remitting for reconsideration).

3   Int Dec 3278 (BIA 1996).

If an individual fears persecution by entities (or agents) who cannot and will not be prosecuted by the State, the fear of future persecution is well founded. Thus, when analysing an asylum claim involving FGM, it is immaterial that the perpetrator of FGM is a private citizen and not an agent of the State. What is important, is that the government is unable or unwilling to control this individual. A situation in which the State is incapable of providing national protection against persecution by non-government agents clearly renders the individual unable to avail himself of the protection of his country of origin.

> 'Adjudicators should ... not view all perpetrators of FGM as private citizens in the Western sense, but should understand that in certain traditional societies, perpetrators of FGM have a quasi-public or de facto authority status or are perpetuating FGM with the consent of a quasi-public figure who may exert more influence than *de jure* authorities.'[1]

The failure of States to provide effective protection to women in asylum cases involving female genital mutilation is increasingly recognised in international case-law. In the **US**, the issue of FGM was first addressed in the context of a suspension of deportation proceedings for a woman from Sierra Leone.[2] It was accepted that the government was unable or unwilling to stop the practice of female genital mutilation which is mandated for non-Creole women by Sierra Leone society. Subsequently the applicant in the *Matter of Konate*[3] established that the authorities in Guinea are unwilling or unable to protect her from her husband. She presented evidence which indicated that her husband's conduct was sanctioned by the military, cultural tradition and customary laws of Guinea. The US State Department Country report on human rights practices in Guinea confirmed the applicant's claims of lack of legal redress for violence against women. In *Kasinga*,[4] the Board granted asylum to a woman who was fleeing FGM in Togo. The Board found that she had no meaningful legal protection. The practice of FGM was widespread in Togo and the government had not taken even minimal protective measures, such as condemnation of the practice or enactment of legislation against it. 'Acts of violence and abuse against women in Togo are tolerated by the police' and the government had a generally poor human rights record. The Board concluded that 'most African women can expect little government protection from FGM'.[5] In this context, the Board also held that there was no IFA available to her. Meanwhile, in the recent and highly publicised case of *Abankwah*,[6] decision-makers in the US also recognised that while Ghana has enacted a statute outlawing FGM, the practice continues to be widespread. The failure of the State to provide effective protection against FGM has also been recognised in a significant number of non-asylum cases involving both women and men from specific countries, particularly Nigeria, who have girl children born in the US. For example, in one case involving a 37-year-old married Nigerian man who had a poor immigration and criminal record, the

1   Cisse 1997, p 445.
2   *Matter of Oluloro* A72–147-491 23 March 1994 was reported in the *New York Times (Law)* 4 March 1994 B.12.
3   *Konate v INS* 5/17/99 (9th Cir).
4   *In Re Kasinga* Int Dec 3278 (BIA 1996).
5   Anker 1999.
6   *Abankwah v INS* 98–4304, reported in *New York Times* (18 and 20 August 1999) and *Marie Claire* (May 1998).

court accepted that while the Nigerian government has made certain efforts in recent years to minimise or stop the practice of FGM, it has not been very successful.[1] Referring to *Kasinga*[2] the court withdrew deportation proceedings.

In **Australia**, the Refugee Review Tribunal has recognised that the object of the Refugee Convention is to provide refuge for those groups who, having lost the *de jure* or *de facto* protection of their governments, are unwilling to return to the countries of their nationality (as in *A*[3]). In a recent case involving FGM,[4] it was held that the Nigerian government is powerless to assist those women who wish to avoid FGM. There is no agency or organisation to which they can turn to protect them from those who are intent on circumcising them. There is no redress that they can later take against those who harmed them. There is therefore no effective State protection from the harm feared.

Box 9.4

This case concerned an Ethiopian woman who belongs to a small, isolated ethnic group, the Harari. She was subjected to FGM as a child and feared that if she and her daughter were forced to return, her daughter would be subjected to FGM. Ninety per cent of Ethiopian women and close to 100 per cent of Harari girls are subjected to FGM. Ethiopian officials are aware of the prevalence of FGM in Ethiopia but have passed no law specifically outlawing the practice. The government outlaws 'harmful traditional practices' but does not enforce this provision to prevent FGM. The applicant believes that her relatives in Ethiopia will do whatever needed, including subjecting her daughter to FGM, in order to bring women 'in line' with their traditions. Furthermore, the applicant will return to Ethiopia as a single woman with a child of mixed heritage, and thus face an extreme level of scrutiny and will be ostracised by the Harari community. Although asylum was refused, the applicant and her daughter were allowed to remain in the US.

9.5 REFUGEE CONVENTION GROUNDS

An asylum claim involving FGM can be made on any of the enumerated grounds in the refugee definition. It is immaterial whether or not the perpetrator of FGM is of the same race, religion, nationality or social group. As is clear from the examples given below, much will depend upon the individual circumstances and background of the particular case.

9.5.1 Race/ethnicity

A woman applicant may have a well-founded fear of persecution for reasons of race. Such is the case where the practice of FGM is restricted to a particular

---

1   *Adewunmi Adeniji* (1998) 10 March, USA.
2   Int Dec 3278 (BIA 1996).
3   *A and Another v MIEA and Another* [1997] 142 ALR, Aust HC.
4   RRT Reference V97/06156 3 November 1997.

ethnic group such as the Mandinka group in Guinea-Bissau or the Bedouins in the Negev region of Israel. An applicant may have a well-founded fear of persecution for reasons of religion. This is the case for the Tchamba-Kunsuntu ethnic group, the Muslim minority in Togo who interpret the Quran to require FGM.

9.5.2 Religion

A person who is punished or fears punishment for failing to comply with FGM practices which are fundamentally abhorrent to that person's religious beliefs or that person's interpretation of Islam, has a valid asylum claim in a country like Togo, where Islam is invoked as the reason for imposing FGM. It is important to note that, within one country, different ethnic groups may interpret and apply principles of Islamic law differently and thus any notice taken by the adjudicator that interpreting the Quran to require FGM is unreasonable should not lead to a determination that the fear is not well-founded.

9.5.3 Nationality

A woman may have a well-founded fear of persecution for reasons of nationality. This is particularly the case in countries like Djibouti, Ethiopia and Somalia where FGM has been practised across ethnic groups.

9.5.4 Political opinion

An individual may have a well-founded fear of persecution for reasons of political opinion. Opposition to FGM constitutes a political opinion or it may be that a political opinion is attributed to the individual as a result of opposition to FGM. The attribution of a political opinion (eg belief in the equality of the sexes or feminism) to those who oppose FGM occurs in countries like Sierra Leone, where feminist and politically active women's groups oppose FGM. This approach has been followed in some cases in the **US**. For example, in the *Matter of M-K*,[1] it was accepted that a law or traditional belief that is forcibly imposed on women may constitute the basis of the claim (such as forced genital mutilation) or the claim may arise because an individual woman (or group of women) objects to a practice, resists the practice, and is then persecuted for doing so (such as resistance to mandated female subservience and being punished with physical abuse). In the *Matter of C-V-C*,[2] which was a case involving forced sterilisation, the BIA also referred to FGM in examining what could constitute a political opinion within the meaning of the Refugee Convention:

> 'The right to privacy, the right to have a family, the right to bodily integrity, and the right to unfettered reproductive choice are fundamental individual rights recognised domestically and internationally. We view those rights as fundamental rights and that the election to exercise them should be respected and not trampled constitutes a political opinion.'

---

1   *In Re M-K*, A72190893, A72793219 (Arlington, Va, Immigration Court Dec 20, 1995) 72 Interpreter Releases 1188 (1995).
2   Int Dec 3319 (BIA 1997).

Similarly, in the *Matter of Konate*,[1] the courts eventually accepted that opposition to the practice of FGM could form the basis of a valid claim for asylum on the grounds of actual or imputed political opinion (see Box 9.5).

Box 9.5

The *Matter of Konate* concerned a 32-year-old woman from Guinea who arrived in the US in March 1997 and in July 1997 claimed asylum. She is a member of the Malinke/Mandingo tribe and also a Muslim. She has three children including a 5-year-old daughter who has been threatened to be subjected to FGM against the wishes of the applicant. The applicant herself was subjected to FGM against her will at a young age. Her father died when she was very young leaving her a 'fartalen' and she lived with an uncle who severely beat her. Whilst she was still young she was forced to marry a sixty-year-old military officer who already had three wives. She was subsequently beaten, raped, drugged, forced to perform oral sex and threatened with death by her husband because of her opposition to forced polygamous marriage. On two occasions she unsuccessfully tried to escape and eventually sought help from a friend who helped her and her children obtain a false passport and flee to the US. The applicant believed that if she and her daughters were to return to Guinea her daughters would be subjected to FGM. She also feared that if she attempted to prevent the mutilation of her daughters, she would be an outcast in her community. It was found that she had suffered past persecution and has a well-founded fear of future persecution on account of her political opinion: 'The applicant has been abused and persecuted on account of her opposition to gender-specific Malinke culture societal norms. The applicant is opposed to forced polygamous marriage and female genital mutilation, both an integral and accepted part of Malinke culture. Furthermore, the applicant has refused to succumb to a life of subservience and mental and physical abuse. She has asserted this opinion several times by attempting to escape her abuser on three separate occasions and by refusing to have sexual relations with him and subjecting herself to severe beatings as a consequence.' Referring to *Lazo-Majano*, the court ruled that her flight stood for her political opinion that a woman has a right not to be dominated by a man. The applicant had also voiced her opposition to gender-specific cultural norms by refusing to allow her daughter to be subjected to FGM.

Australian case-law holds that persecution is more than simply a violation of human rights, the harm has to have a motivation (however twisted) to constitute persecution. A consideration of the evidence about the history and practice of FGM in Nigeria led the Refugee Review Tribunal (RRT) to conclude that there is a motivation for the infliction of this type of harm on women:

---

1   *Konate v INS* 5/17/99 (9th Cir).

'Harmful practices are inflicted on Yoruba women by Yoruba men in order that they – the men – are ensured virgin brides and faithful wives who are sexually undemanding and are best placed to give them large numbers of healthy children. The motivation is the enhancement of the position of men as the rulers of society and the arbiters of what is good and what is bad within the culture. It is the quality of unbridled female sexuality which is perceived to be dangerous to the established order of male superiority and which must be repressed or extirpated.'

The RRT concluded that the Yoruba practice of female circumcision 'is the infliction of serious harm with a view to the repression or extirpation of a quality in females which is perceived to be dangerous to the existing order of Yoruba society'. In a recent case involving a mother and her daughter from Ghana, the RRT was prepared to accept that the applicant's opposition to the practice of FGM was an expression of political opinion, reflecting both a gender-related human rights stand and an opposition to a religious/cultural practice.[1]

9.5.5 Social group

As was noted above, in 1994 **Canada** was the first country in the world to grant asylum because of FGM. In *Farah*,[2] a woman fearing FGM was found to be subject to persecution due to her membership of 'two particular social groups, namely women and minors'. Gender was determined to be an innate and unchangeable characteristic. The CRDD has subsequently determined that women fearing FGM from a number of other countries including Kenya[3] and the Ivory Coast[4] are refugees within the meaning of the Refugee Convention.

In the period since *Farah*, the issue of whether women are members of a particular social group in cases involving FGM has also been the subject of considerable debate in a number of other countries. In the **US**, the BIA found in the *Matter of Konate* that the applicant had been persecuted not only on account of her political opinion, but also because of her membership of a particular social group. She had been persecuted because she is a 'fartalen' Malinke woman who refuses to conform to gender-specific societal norms by refusing to submit to a polygamous marriage and refusing to accept her uncle's domination over her personal life. She had also refused to subject her daughter to FGM. The fact that the applicant is a 'fartalen' or 'without anyone to protect her rights' makes the reprisals and punishment she exposed herself to more imminent.

More recently in *Kasinga* (see Box 9.2),[5] the BIA, drawing on *Acosta*[6] concluded that the characteristics of being a 'young woman' and a 'member of the Tchamba-Kunsuntu Tribe' cannot be changed. The characteristic of having intact genitalia is one that is so fundamental to the individual identity of a young woman that she should not be required to change it. The BIA recognised that there was no legitimate reason for the practice of FGM to be carried out on the

---

1   RRT Reference N97/17540 27 January 1999.
2   *Farah v Canada (MEI)* (1994) 3 July.
3   CRDD U97–02965 27 October 1998.
4   CRDD V98–01328 20 May 1999.
5   *In Re Kasinga* Int Dec 3278 (BIA 1996).
6   *Acosta v INS* [1985] Int Dec 2986 (BIA).

applicant and that it is simply a mechanism for controlling women's sexuality. In this context, it was viewed as irrelevant that the persons performing or requiring the procedure may have believed it was beneficial to the victim. The BIA found that Kasinga had a well-founded fear of persecution on account of her membership of a particular social group, namely young women who are members of the Tchambe-Kunsuntu Tribe of Northern Togo who have not been subjected to FGM, as practised by that tribe, and who oppose the practice.

In **Australia**, the RRT similarly concluded that a Yoruba woman from Nigeria had a well-founded fear of persecution on account of both her political opinion and membership of a particular social group.[1] The RRT found that Yoruba people are a recognisable and cognisable group within Nigerian society and that it is also possible to distinguish Yoruba females as a particular social group without relying on a common fear of FGM as the uniting factor:

> 'Yoruba women are a group of Yoruba persons who share certain sex characteristics and other elements such as socio-economic status, which unite them and enable them to be set apart from Yoruba men. Women are united, and set apart from men, by the roles that they must play within Yoruba society and the options that are open to them.'

In France, the Refugee Appeal Commission has accepted that FGM may amount to persecution and those women wishing to avoid FGM can be considered as members of a 'particular social group'. This is reflected in *Diop*[2] where the applicant claimed refugee status after she left Mali because of mistreatment by her family for refusing to undergo FGM, although the Commission did not grant her refugee status because of failure adequately to document her claim.[3]

9.6 SOURCES OF INFORMATION AND SUPPORT

Amnesty International has a series of documents on efforts to prevent FGM http://www2.amnesty.se including a Human Rights Information Pack on Female Genital Mutilation (1998) which is available on-line at http://www. amnesty.org/ailib/intcam/femgen

Centre for Gender and Refugee Studies provides on-line case summaries of cases in the US involving FGM. The site also provides names and contact information for experts on this issue (based in the US) and other relevant documents and reading material. The site is at http://www.uchastings.edu/cgrs/summaries/summaries.html

Female Genital Mutilation Research Homepage contains a complete review of FGM, including US and international laws, films and other reference material, lists of anti-FGM groups, and many hyperlinks. Their site also has estimates of the numbers of mutilations in various countries. See http://www.hollyfeld.org/fgm/

---

1   RRT Reference V97/06156 3 November 1997.
2   CRR 164078 18 August 1991.
3   See also Kelson 1997.

FGM Education and Networking Project has information on British and Canadian legislation and a FGM and women's reproduction bibliography. Its website at http://fgmnetwork.org also contains general introductory material, articles of interest and links to educational, medical and legal resources. There is contact information for several FGM advocacy and discussion groups and the official statements of various international organisations.

Foundation for Women's Health, Research and Development (FOR-WARD) is the leading voluntary organisation in the UK working to eliminate FGM. The organisation offers a range of training fora on its activities in relation to FGM and has a list of publications available for purchase as well as details of other materials and links to other sites. FORWARD's website is at http://www.forward.dircon.co.uk or alternatively, FORWARD can be contacted at 40 Eastbourne Terrace, London W2 3QR Tel: 020 7725 2606.

International Planned Parenthood Federation (IPPF) at http://www.ippf.org/fgm published a bibliography of resources on FGM. For further information contact the IPPF Library, Regent's College, Inner Circle, Regent's Park, London NW1 4NS.

Raising Daughters Aware (RDA) is based in Oakland, California and provides free information and services for FGM affected women, their physicians, and other health care providers, social workers, counsellors and attorneys. The site, which is at http://www.fgm.org, contains useful background materials and links to other sites.

World Health Organisation (WHO) which is available on-line at http://www.who.int provides classification and definitions of FGM, information about WHO activities against FGM, an information package (WHO/FRH/WHD/96.26) and a bibliographic database which includes information about research carried out about FGM in a wide range of countries.

Chapter 10

PROCEDURAL AND EVIDENTIAL ISSUES

10.1 CURRENT PROCEDURES[1]

Procedures for refugee determination in the UK have undergone extensive and repeated change in recent years. They have also been the subject of considerable criticism by those concerned that both the information gathering process and the assessment of evidential issues fails adequately to take into account the difficulties experienced by many asylum seekers in putting forward information relevant to their application.[2]

Procedures for refugee determination are critical for those seeking asylum in the UK. However, whilst all applicants may experience serious difficulties, technical and psychological, in submitting their case,[3] there is increasing concern that these difficulties are exacerbated for women because the procedures themselves are modelled on the assumption that asylum seekers are *politically active men* who have been persecuted by the State as a result of those activities. The result is that if asylum procedures allow for the experiences of women at all, they tend to regard them as dependent wives, daughters and mothers. This is reflected in the fact that information on the human rights situation of women in countries of origin is all too often lacking, despite the fact that such information is necessary for the evaluation of any claim to asylum. In cases of gender-related persecution where limited information is available, the prospects for obtaining evidence relevant to the client's case are considerably jeopardised because the time allowed for the submission of further representations is restricted. Similarly, it may be impossible to obtain medical evidence or provide vulnerable individuals, including women who have been raped or sexually abused, with access to medical care and counselling. There is a particular need to take account of the fact that an applicant may be suffering from sexually related torture, abuse or other forms of gender-related persecution, yet under current procedures women may be interviewed immediately on arrival and this will not usually be by female staff or interpreters unless specifically requested. The interviewing officer may be unaware that the applicant may have experienced sexual violence and will therefore not know to ask questions regarding this. If the representative is aware of such details, he or she should endeavour to make them known in order that an appropriate line of questioning is pursued. In addition, the representative should

---

1   The information given in this chapter is not exhaustive and cannot hope to be in the context of continuing procedural changes. Representatives must ensure that they aware of any procedural changes which may affect the ability of their client to fully present the basis of an asylum claim, for example, through membership of organisations such as the Immigration Law Practitioners' Association (ILPA) and Refugee Legal Group (RLG).

2   See, eg, Asylum Rights Campaign 1996a, Justice, ILPA and ARC 1997, Refugee Legal Centre 1997 and ILPA 1999.

3   UNHCR 1979, para 190.

always give consideration to the possibility of submitting additional information or statements in support of the application.

The asylum determination process can be made more responsive to the experiences of women if representatives and others are aware of, and respond to, the procedural and evidential difficulties which they face.

10.2 DERIVATIVE STATUS OR INDEPENDENT CLAIM?

EXCOM Conclusion No 73 (XLIV) (1993) at para c 'calls upon states and UNHCR to ensure the equal access of women and men to refugee status determination'. It remains the case, however, that women who arrive as part of a family unit are sometimes not interviewed or are cursorily interviewed about their experiences, even when it is possible that they, rather than their husbands, have been the targets of persecution. Their male relatives may not raise the relevant issues because they are unaware of the details or ashamed to report them.[1]

> 'Women coming into the country with their spouses are often assumed to be dependants. The majority opt for that because of natural deference to their husband, not being accustomed to being addressed as an individual, and fear. They are not invited to a separate interview. Some are interviewed with their male relatives, brother, father, cousin. Very often the last person a woman can bear to tell her story to is her husband.'[2]

This is despite the fact that a woman's claim to refugee status may in some cases be as strong or stronger than that of her husband, as can be seen in *Fathi and Ahmady,*[3] where the appeal of a woman from Iran was allowed whilst that of her husband was refused.

The failure to identify whether a woman has a claim for asylum in her own right at the earliest possible stage can have serious implications for the way in which her application is assessed. If her experiences emerge only some time after the initial application or once the claim has been refused by the Home Office, she may be unable to make the case convincingly for being granted her own refugee status because the delay will undermine the credibility of her application. There is also increasing concern that if only the husband's experiences are considered during a family's request for asylum, this may have significant implications for her future. For example, there may be problems for a woman if she is entirely dependent on her husband for her status, especially if that status is ELR. If the family were to break up, a woman who has accompanied or joined her husband may find herself without any protection from forced return. She also risks expulsion if the application of her family member is denied or if he unilaterally decides to renounce his claim even though she may have a valid claim for protection in her own right.

---

1   UNHCR 1991, para 57.
2   Hinshelwood 1997.
3   *Fathi and Ahmady v SSHD* (unreported) 1 December 1996 (14264) (IAT).

'It is important to identify the person included in an application who has the strongest claims. An application written by, or an interview with, a male head of household may place little or no emphasis on a female family unit member's experience of persecution or discrimination, even though her experiences may carry the most weight. A woman who is included in the application as a member of a family unit should be given the opportunity of a separate interview so that she is able, with appropriate assurances of confidentiality, to outline her experiences.'[1]

It is essential that women are given equal access to the refugee determination process from their initial application. Where a woman arrives as part of a family unit, regardless of whether she is the principal applicant, she should be interviewed by the representative. Consideration should be given as to whether it is appropriate to submit a separate claim and/or a statement at that time. Accuracy is essential because of the possibility of discrepancies leading to adverse inferences on credibility. Any discrepancies must be explained. Different perceptions of the same event may appear inconsistent.[2]

'It should also be noted however that if gender-related claims are revealed separately from the rest of the family, representatives must treat the information provided with great care. This is particularly necessary if the woman has indicated that other members of the family are unaware of her experiences.'[3]

Representatives should be aware of professional duties of confidentiality and the potential for conflict of interests. Where a woman applies for asylum as a dependant, she should be informed *in private*, and in terms she understands, of her right to make an independent application for asylum at any stage, and should be advised to consult a legal representative before doing so.

10.3 FINDING OUT ABOUT WOMEN'S EXPERIENCES

It is generally acknowledged that women may face special problems in making their case to the authorities, particularly when they have had experiences which are difficult and painful to describe.[4] These problems are exacerbated by existing procedures which mean that many women are interviewed immediately upon their arrival in the UK (see Box 10.1). Changes to this policy which are currently being implemented mean that, although applicants will instead be issued with Statement of Evidence Forms (SEFs) to complete and return prior to any interview, an accelerated process remains. This process for the consideration of certain asylum claims by the Home Office lays the basis for differential treatment, not for individualised reasons, but depending on the nationality of the applicant or the port at which they arrived. Such procedures will continue to have a particularly serious impact on those who are traumatised or suffering the after-effects of persecution.

---

1   ADIMA 1996, para 3.10.
2   See also ILPA 1999.
3   ADIMA 1996, para 28.
4   See UNHCR 1991, para 58.

Box 10.1[1]

Ms D travelled to the UK with two other women and eight children. The women and a 19-year-old were interviewed substantively and were held for 14 hours before the entire party was placed in detention. Ms D received no advice and had no idea that the interview was her main opportunity to provide full details of her claim. She stated that 'during the interview I noticed that they didn't believe anything I was saying. I got the impression that they were dismissing anything I said. I felt they were contemptuous towards me'. Comments she made regarding the family's ill-treatment and discrimination by the authorities were not followed up. The group was held in detention for a further five days and so had no opportunity to make further representations. She said 'we had no chance ... the children were tired, they were crying. It was such a long way from the airport'. Her application was refused just 19 days later.

The Home Office has not acknowledged any particular problems which women may experience during the asylum process:

> 'The particular need for sensitivity in dealing with asylum applicants and the procedural and policy considerations involved in assessing the merits of asylum claims apply to both sexes. We have not yet identified a need to issue separate guidance on dealing with applications from female asylum seekers in the UK ... Our current approach to asylum claims from women is generally compatible with that set out in the US Guidelines.'[2]

By contrast, the guidelines which have been issued by the determining authorities in both the US (1995) and Australia (1996) make a number of procedural recommendations for the handling of gender-related claims. The aim of these recommendations is to create a 'customer-friendly' asylum interview environment, in which women claimants may freely discuss the elements and details of their claims. The interview room and surrounding environment should be conducive to open discussion. There must be sufficient time available and there should be no disturbances. Interviewers and decision-makers, as well as representatives, should be aware of, and take into account, specific difficulties which women may have, for example, their responsibilities as carers, distances to be travelled and issues of privacy.

There are a number of issues which need to be addressed during the interview process and which representatives should take into consideration during discussions with their female clients. The UNHCR has itself made a number of recommendations regarding the use of gender-sensitive techniques to obtain information from women during the status determination process.[3]

---

1   ARC 1996, pp 52–53.
2   Hinshelwood 1997, p 73.
3   See Appendix 12.

'Female applicants who are survivors of torture and trauma, in particular, require a supportive environment where they can be reassured of the confidentiality of the gender-sensitive claims they are making.'[1]

For women asylum seekers in particular, a non-confrontational interview is critical to allow for the full discussion of past experiences relating to their claim, yet the reality in many cases is an asylum interview which is harrowing for women, and in particular for those who have experienced sexual violence. There are a number of interrelated reasons why the interview process is particularly difficult for many women:

'Women refugee claimants who have suffered sexual violence may exhibit a pattern of symptoms referred to as Rape Trauma Syndrome, and may require extremely sensitive handling. Similarly, women who have been subjected to domestic violence may exhibit a pattern of symptoms referred to as Battered Wife Syndrome and may also be reluctant to testify.'[2]

For women who have been sexually abused there is the additional problem of conflicting interests. It is clear, and usually will be clear to the applicant, that it is important to tell the determining authorities about experiences of sexual violence. On the other hand, there are good reasons not to tell, which can range from the fact that it is very hard to do, to the fear that her experiences may become known to others and lead to her being ostracised from her family and/or community.[3] Women from societies where the preservation of virginity or marital dignity is the cultural norm may be very reluctant to disclose certain information relevant to their asylum claim or that of other members of their family:[4]

'Rape sometimes appears to be used as a form of torture because those responsible realise that their victims may be constrained from revealing what has occurred after their release from custody. The shame associated with rape can be a strong inducement to silence.'[5]

Women may also be stigmatised by the *assumption* that they have been sexually abused if, for example, they have been arrested, detained or involved in conflict. Whilst sexual violence is common in refugee-producing situations it is not inevitable. The stigma associated with sexual violence means that some women who have not been sexually abused, may be unable or unwilling to describe their experiences of persecution for fear that it will be assumed that they have been sexually abused.

If it becomes apparent that a woman needs additional support of any kind, for example, referral to a rape crisis centre or other specialist service, then the representative should offer to make such a referral.

---

1   ADIMA 1996, para 3.12.
2   CIRB 1996a, section D.
3   Spijkerboer 1994.
4   UNHCR 1991; CIRB 1996.
5   Amnesty International 1991, p 22.

10.3.1 Presence of family members

'Female victims of violence, discrimination and abuse often do not volunteer information about their experiences and may be reluctant to do so in the presence of family members.'[1]

Refugee women should be given the opportunity to be interviewed outside the hearing of other members of their family, especially male family members and children. Whilst the testimonial process is a highly stressful experience for anyone, woman applicants may communicate experiences of sexual abuse or other kinds of harm more freely when family members are not present. Sexual violence in particular may be viewed as a failure on the part of the woman to preserve her virginity or marital dignity. In this context, discussing her experience in front of family members may become a further source of isolation. Women should be asked *privately* whether they want to be interviewed outside the hearing of other members of their family, especially male family members and children. Whilst the giving of information is a highly stressful experience for anyone, women may only be able to communicate experiences of sexual abuse or other kinds of harm when family members are not present. Conflicts of interest can arise in some situations where information is revealed by one family member which may have implications for consideration of the case of another. Representatives should consider if there is a conflict or a potential breach of professional obligations and, if so, decline to act for any of the parties involved.

10.3.2 Interviewers and interpreters

Many women asylum seekers do not speak English and the interview will therefore need to be conducted through an interpreter, normally employed by the Home Office on a session basis. The use of interpreters has important implications for the ability and willingness of a woman to discuss her experiences.[2] According to the Home Office's own guidelines, the role of the interpreter is to be impartial and to bridge the linguistic gap between the two parties. The interpreter must interpret accurately, fully, distinctly and audibly using appropriate language and emphasis. Interpreters should not advise, or make judgements about, the applicant and her experiences. It is the duty of the interviewer to ensure that this role is fulfilled.

Women asylum seekers may be particularly reluctant to disclose their experiences to male interviewing officers and interpreters, including male representatives:

'In the vast majority of cases women who have suffered torture and/or trauma have suffered these abuses at the hands of men. Coupled with a fear and distrust of authorities, this fact is likely to seriously inhibit the capacity of a female applicant to divulge details of her experiences to a male interviewer.'[3]

---

1   ADIMA 1996, para 3.12.
2   See also ILPA 1999.
3   ADIMA 1996, para 3.13.

'The female victim of sexual torture obviously may be reluctant or find it very difficult to talk about it, particularly to a male interviewer.'[1]

It is also recognised in the guidelines from Canada, the US and Australia, that testimony on sensitive issues such as sexual abuse can be diluted when received through the filter of a interpreter. Some of these problems may be linguistic. For example, during the interview both the interviewer and the interpreter should be aware of the difficulties in interpreting particular words, such as 'rape' or 'assault', which may have different meanings or connotations in the applicant's language. In addition, however, it is not difficult to imagine the reluctance of a female applicant to testify about her experiences through a male (or even female) interpreter who is a member of her community:

> 'In particular, during interviews where an interpreter is used, a woman applicant may be reluctant to divulge information for fear that the interpreter may be an informer for the authorities in the country of origin or that they will divulge their story to others in the community. The applicant should be assured of the confidential nature of the interview process.'[2]

This problem, and its implications for the applicant's credibility, has yet to be recognised by decision-makers. In one case, the representative pointed out to the IAT that the appellant, being a Pathan woman, would have been frightened to explain her fears regarding sexual violence at the asylum interview, because both the counsellor and interpreter were male Muslims:

> 'We reject that contention as it appears to us that the appellant is an educated and sophisticated woman. She was not a rural agricultural worker from a remote village and we do not believe that had she anything to say she would not have done so simply because there were male Muslims present. Accordingly, in our view, our finding must reflect adversely on the credibility of the appellant.'[3]

Merely being female does not guarantee gender-sensitivity. Nonetheless, every effort should be made to ensure that female interpreters and interviewers are available where it appears that the presence of a man may prevent the claimant from presenting her case. Recent policy changes within the Home Office suggest that there is now some recognition of the need for same-sex interviewing officers and interpreters, and such requests will now be complied with 'as far as is operationally possible'. If it is not practical to provide an interviewer or interpreter of the same sex as the applicant, consideration will be given to deferring the interview.[4]

10.3.3   Asking the right questions

The information revealed during the course of an interview may reflect the ways in which questions are asked. Unless the right questions are asked, it is unlikely that a woman will be able to describe her experiences.[5] The questions which are

---

1   UNHCR 1991, para 60.
2   ADIMA 1996, para 3.13.
3   *Jamil v SSHD* (unreported) 25 June 1996 (13588) (IAT).
4   Letter from IND dated 27 March 2000.
5   ILPA 1999.

asked during the asylum interview are typically oriented at male asylum-seekers.[1] They tend to be about political activities narrowly defined rather than background activities in which women may be involved. They also tend to be specifically about 'torture', which female applicants may not equate with the types of harm that they fear, for example, sexual violence, female genital mutilation, and forced sterilisation or abortion. Female applicants are not routinely asked questions about gender-related persecution and even if it is mentioned by the applicant during interview, there may be no follow-up questions to ascertain details or the applicant's full experience.

For her claim to asylum to be properly considered, the asylum applicant must be allowed to state clearly what her fear of persecution consists of. There are a number of measures which can be adopted by representatives in response to some of the difficulties outlined above. For example, in order to establish the facts of the case and to ensure that the right questions are asked, representatives should familiarise themselves with the status and roles of women in the country from which a woman has fled. It is important, for example, that prior to the interview, research is conducted to establish basic information about women's status and roles in the country from which the applicant has fled. The information revealed during the course of the interview may also reflect the way in which questions are asked. Representatives should begin by explaining to the applicant why it is necessary to ask detailed questions about the basis of the claim. Non-confrontational, open and/or indirect questions should then be asked in order to establish a woman's reasons for fleeing. More direct follow-up questions should be asked to ascertain details of the woman's full experiences. Depending on what a woman says, the following types of questions may be of assistance:

–   Why did you leave your country?

–   Did you have any problems?

–   Were you treated badly?

–   Was anyone you know treated badly?

–   Why do you think this happened?

–   Who was responsible?

–   How did you feel?

–   What difficulties did these experiences cause you?

–   Did you complain to the authorities? If not, why not?

–   What would happen if you were to return to your country?

This is *not* a prescriptive or sequential list. Interviewers must consider other relevant follow-up questions. For example, at various stages it may be necessary to ask 'what else happened to you?'. Additional questions can be asked to obtain

---

1   Schilders 1988; Spijkerboer 1994.

information about whether gender-related harm has occurred. The types of questions to be asked might include the following:

– Are women treated differently than men?

– Were you, as a woman, treated badly?

To answer the first question, the woman may give relevant information about how women in her country are treated without necessarily speaking about herself, and yet may indirectly refer to herself. When asking the second question, it is essential to use the word 'bad'. This is understood by most cultures and is not confrontational. The statement by the asylum applicant that she has been 'badly treated' may be a euphemism for sexual violence and/or rape. Moreover, if the applicant is directly asked whether she has been raped her answer may be negative although she may have been subjected to other forms of sexual abuse. If there are indications that the applicant has experiences which are in some way related to her gender, it is essential for the success of the claim that more direct questions are asked to ascertain specific aspects of the woman's experience.

– What are the (possible) consequences of having experienced gender-specific harm, especially sexual violence including rape, for the refugee woman?

– Can it be said that the authorities and/or the community provided protection?

– What fear of persecution awaits a woman when she is forced to return to her country?

Wherever possible, representatives should assist their clients in the completion of any asylum questionnaire in order to ensure that all details relevant to the case are included in the form. Representatives should advise their clients prior to any Home Office interview and ensure that any relevant issues are brought to the attention of the Home Office. There are also additional problems which are specific to refugee women. The first of these reflects the point made above that, where a woman arrives with a spouse or male relative, and makes a separate claim, it is the man who will frequently complete the asylum questionnaire. As a result, details relevant to the woman's claim may be omitted. Moreover, women who have been involved in indirect political activity or to whom political opinion has been attributed may not include relevant information relating to their claim because of the nature of the questions asked on asylum questionnaires which reflect a male-orientated process of asylum determination. The questions asked in asylum questionnaires generally do not, in any way, allude to gender-related persecution and instead emphasise overt political activities, including the name of any political organisation with which the applicant has been involved and the nature of that involvement. Representatives and advisers should ensure that all details relevant to the client's application are submitted in the asylum question-naire, not least because revealing such details at a later date may undermine the credibility of the applicant. Additional information revealed at a later stage should be submitted in support of the application as quickly as possible.

10.3.4 Culturally sensitive communication

The failure to appreciate cross-cultural differences can jeopardise the quality of the information revealed by a female applicant and the way in which that information is then responded to by both the interviewer and the decision-maker:

> 'After the first interview we had a second interview at Gatwick. The man who did the interview was very rude. When I explained some things about my culture he just laughed. For example I was saying that my father and mother had only me and then he had another woman with whom he had a son. He had five children with her and my father had three wives altogether. He just started laughing. I asked him why. I explained that he should understand and shouldn't laugh. I was very frustrated and humiliated. I was not comfortable.'[1]

In the UK, the lack of culturally sensitive communication between the interviewing officer and the applicant is clearly a problem in some cases, despite protestations from the Home Office to the contrary:

> 'The particular need for sensitivity in dealing with asylum applicants is recognised and stressed in our training and guidance to staff involved in the asylum process. This focus ensures that all applications are handled sympathetically and that caseworkers appreciate cultural differences.'[2]

Where possible, representatives should challenge interviewing officers who do not communicate with their clients in a manner which is sensitive to cultural differences. In addition, however, they should also be aware of cultural sensitivities during their own interviews with refugee women. As the Australian gender guidelines (ADIMA 1996) at paras 3.22–3.26 indicate, this can most appropriately be demonstrated by attentive listening, including the following:

- reflective listening (ie paraphrasing what has been said by the applicant);
- not talking at the same time as the applicant;
- not making judgmental comments;
- maintaining composure if the applicant gets angry or upset;
- ensuring minimum interruptions and/or distractions;
- ensuring the interpreting is an accurate reflection of the applicant's testimony (eg relative length of translation, reaction from the applicant).

Discretion and tact are especially critical when dealing with deeply rooted traditions such as female genital mutilation. The UNHCR (1995a) has emphasised that interviewers should be conscious of possible reactions to trauma and familiar with culturally different patterns of behaviour and language.[3] Both interviewers and representatives should be aware that cultural and other differences and trauma play an important role in determining demeanour (ie how a woman presents herself physically) for example, whether she maintains eye contact, shifts her posture or hesitates when speaking. This is also noted in the Australian gender guidelines:

---

1 Testimony of a Somali refugee woman during an interview with the author.
2 *International Journal of Refugee Law* (Special Issue) Autumn 1997, p 73.
3 This issue, and its implications for assessing the credibility of the application, are discussed in more detail at **10.4.3**.

'The level of emotional distress exhibited by a female applicant during the recounting of her experiences should not automatically add more credibility to her claims than that of another who may be very calm and quiet when describing a similar event. A lack of emotion displayed at interview does not necessarily mean that the applicant is not distressed or deeply affected by what has happened. Cultural differences and trauma often play an important role in determining demeanour.'[1]

Body language can be interpreted in many different ways. It is important that interviewers avoid gestures that may be perceived as intimidating or culturally insensitive or inappropriate or inhibiting.

10.4 CREDIBILITY

Credibility is inextricably linked with the standard of proof and remains one of the most pervasive problems for almost all asylum applications made in the UK. Many refusals are on the basis that the asylum seeker's credibility has been weakened due to inconsistencies in the application.[2] Whilst this problem is not unique to female applicants, there is evidence that women may experience particular problems in maintaining their credibility. Procedural problems may undermine a claim, even where a woman has been persecuted because of her direct involvement in political activity, for example, where women are not given access to the determination process independently from their husbands or male relatives. In addition, credibility may be particularly problematic for claims where the experience of persecution is in some way related to a woman's gender status.

Many women, therefore, face additional problems in demonstrating that their claims are credible. A further example of this, which should be noted by representatives, is the particular difficulties which women may have in obtaining travel documents prior to their flight. Arriving in the UK without valid documentation or with forged papers has typically been viewed by decision-makers as undermining the credibility of the application and, indeed, is included in the immigration rules as a grounds on which a case may be certified for accelerated procedures and limited appeal rights. In *Adimi*,[3] however, it was recognised by the High Court that escapes from persecution have long been characterised by subterfuge and the use of false papers. The Court endorsed Article 31 of the Refugee Convention:

'The need for Article 31 has not diminished. Quite the contrary. Although under the Convention subscribing States must give sanctuary to any refugee who seeks asylum (subject only to refusal to a safe third country), they are by no means bound to facilitate his arrival. Rather they strive increasingly to prevent it. The combined effect of visa requirements and carrier's liability has made it well nigh impossible for refugees to travel to countries of refuge without false documents.'[4]

---

1   ADIMA 1996, para 29.
2   Refugee Council 1996.
3   *R v Uxbridge Magistrates Court ex parte Adimi and Others* [1999] Imm AR 560, INLR 490 (HC).
4   Comments made by Lord Justice Simon Brown.

The Court also questioned the value of prosecuting those who used false papers and suggested that this was in fact simply 'another weapon in the battle to deter refugees from ever seeking asylum in this country'. Any decision to prosecute should therefore be made only in the clearest of cases and where the offence itself appears manifestly unrelated to a genuine quest for asylum.

10.4.1 Inability to provide information

'Women from certain cultures where men do not share the details of their political, military or even social activities with their spouses, daughters or mothers may find themselves in a difficult situation when questioned about the experiences of their male relatives.'[1]

As has been recognised by UNHCR (1995a) at para 61, a woman is often interviewed primarily to corroborate the stories told by her husband or other male relatives. If she is unaware of the details of her husband's experiences (eg the number of her husband's military unit), the entire testimony may be discounted as lacking in credibility. Yet, in many cultures, husbands do not share many details about military or political activities with their wives. In two cases in the Federal Court of Canada, the issue of a woman's place within her society and her lack of knowledge about the activities of male family members was addressed. In *Roble*[2] and *Montenegro, Suleyama*,[3] it was accepted that in both Somalia and El Salvador, a woman's knowledge of her husband's occupation or political involvement may be based entirely on what he has been willing to tell her. An inability to provide information relevant to a claim should not, therefore, of itself undermine credibility. Gaps in a woman's knowledge should not be construed as lack of credibility.

10.4.2 Timing and circumstances of the application

Delay in applying for asylum is listed in the Immigration Rules as one of the circumstances when adverse inferences may be drawn on an applicant's credibility. Rule 341 of HC395 as amended (in particular by CM 3365) states that 'If the dependent has a claim in [her] own right, it should be made at the earliest opportunity. Any failure to do so will be taken into account and may damage credibility if no reasonable explanation for it is given'.

This approach makes no allowances for the fact that some people may not want, or be able to claim asylum on arrival because they are fearful or anxious about what will happen to them. Some may not know the correct procedure for applying for asylum, and may feel that it is safer to enter the UK in another category, for example, as a visitor, and/or have been advised to enter in this way. A woman's priority is to achieve safety for herself and/or family members. She may not claim asylum whilst she is able to achieve safety, however temporary or illusory, through another means, whether legal or illegal. This may account for the delay in claiming asylum and should not negatively affect credibility. It is important to remember that torture and other persecutory treatment can

---

1   CIRB 1996, section D.
2   *Roble v MEI* [1994] 2d 186 FCTD.
3   *Montenegro, Suleyama v MCA* [1996] FCTD, No IMM-3173–94.

produce a profound shame response which may account for a delay in making an asylum claim. Humiliation and shame are often desired goals of the perpetrator. This shame response may be a major obstacle to disclosures.

Although there are a number of reasons why victims of sexual violence in particular might not be forthcoming with information about their experiences at the outset, their reluctance to report such abuse can clearly have significant implications for the determination of their claims. This is reflected in IAT decisions including *Jamil*,[1] which concerned a divorced Muslim woman from Pakistan subjected to abuse, rape and mental torture at the hands of the Pakistani police and her husband's family. In this case, the Home Office Presenting Officer argued that the timing of the appellant's claim of sexual harassment was important and must undermine her claim. When the appellant had first arrived at Heathrow she made no mention of the violence to which she had been subjected. Experience has shown, however, that incidents may not come to light until refugees have been resettled and seek therapy which may be months or even years later.[2] This has been recognised by the **Australian** Refugee Review Tribunal in the case of a woman from Sri Lanka who was raped by the LTTE and who had not revealed this prior to the hearing:[3]

> 'It is well-documented that cultural norms may lead to the non-disclosure of sexual violence: I accept the applicant's reasons for the tardy mention of this claim – her shame and guilt, the violation of family honour if the matter became public and her fear of being rejected by her husband if he found out. These are common reactions to trauma … The applicant's rejection of the opportunity to have an interpreter at the Tribunal hearing is illustrative of the applicant's great fear that her experiences would become known in the Sri Lankan community. I also note that the delegate [interviewing officer] was male and that he only interviewed the applicant briefly on the same day as her husband. These conditions were not conducive to the disclosure of the applicant's experiences at the interview with the delegate. I consider that the discrepancy in the applicant's claims as to whether initially two or three men came to her home on the night of the rape is explicable. Poor memory, confusion and inability to recall parts of the traumatic event are common symptoms of a traumatic reaction … I find that this discrepancy does not detract from the applicant's general credibility.'

Information disclosed later by the victim should not automatically be disregarded or considered to reflect negatively on the credibility of the applicant. Delay in submitting an application, or in giving a full account of experiences after an initial application, or once a claim has been refused, should not of itself undermine the credibility of a woman's application. However, it is likely, particularly in the current decision-making context, that the Home Office will draw such a conclusion. Representatives should therefore ensure that they can provide an adequate explanation for any delays which may have taken place. It may be necessary for representatives to obtain psychological reports on the mental health status of their female clients to explain the delay in revealing information about gender-specific forms of persecution.

---

1   *Jamil v SSHD* (unreported) 25 June 1996 (13588) (IAT).
2   Turner 1996.
3   RRT V96/05479 29 January 1997.

Both the appellate authorities and the courts in the UK have increasingly recognised that there may be valid reasons for a delay in applying for asylum. The IAT has stated that 'it seems to us entirely understandable that a potential refugee would think it far preferable to obtain admission before applying for asylum when arriving at the airport'. One adjudicator has said illegal entry into the UK should not reflect ill on the applicant's general credibility.[1] Most recently, the High Court in *Adimi*[2] similarly accepted that there were valid reasons for a delay in making an asylum application until after entry had been gained into the UK:

> 'Most asylum seekers who attempt to enter the country before making their claims will do so for reasons suggested by UNHCR rather than with a view to falsifying their claims with the assistance of friends and contacts here. And the premium placed by the benefits system upon refugees claiming asylum on entry rather than after entry already represents a significant sanction against late claims.'

10.4.3 Demeanour

> 'Think of all the fiction you have read; "She looked at him with a steady eye", "Not once did she falter", "She spoke simply from the heart"; or conversely, "She had a shifty, down-at-heel look", "She could not hold my gaze", "She shuffled anxiously and cleared her throat several times". Many of our asylum seekers respond to direct questioning in the latter category, and for the genuine asylum seeker, there are reasons for this. In many authoritarian regimes and cultures, it is impolite, wrong, especially for a woman, to look one's superiors in the eye. The eyes must be cast down. This fact has been beaten into many a torture survivor.'[3]

Insofar as representatives and asylum officers deal with people from a diversity of countries, cultures and backgrounds, cross-cultural sensitivity is required of all those involved in the determination process regardless of the gender of the applicant. Cultural sensitivity should extend to the way in which questions are asked and should be acknowledged when considering a woman's responses to questions. Nowhere is this sensitivity more needed than in assessing credibility and 'demeanour'. By 'demeanour' what is meant is how a person handles herself physically, for example, maintaining eye contact, shifts in posture and hesitations in speech, and trauma may have a significant impact on the ability to present testimony in a manner deemed 'credible'. However, as the extract above suggests, the credibility problem which is associated with demeanour may be exacerbated for female applicants whose culture demands, for example, that they should avert their eyes when speaking to an authority figure as a sign of respect:

> 'In Anglo-American cultures, people who avert their gaze when answering a question, or seem nervous, are perceived as untruthful. In other cultures, however, body language does not convey the same message. In certain Asian cultures, for example, people will avert their eyes when speaking to an authority figure as a sign of

---

1   See ARC 1996a for further information.
2   *R v Uxbridge Magistrates Court ex parte Adimi and Others* [1999] Imm AR 560, INLR 490 (HC).
3   Hinshelwood, G 1997, p 161.

respect. This is a product of culture, not necessarily of credibility'[1] (emphasis added).

In this context, the response of the applicant to questioning should be treated with caution, but representatives and advisers should be aware that demeanour is clearly an important aspect of an adjudicator's assessment of a woman's credibility:

> 'I have watched the appellant giving evidence with very great care indeed and I watched her demeanour. I must say that there were times when she was rather irritating in not answering the questions directly and forthrightly but I am convinced having watched her giving evidence that that was not because she wished to hide anything but it was because of her extreme nervousness.'[2]

> 'I personally believed everything that the appellant told me, she was giving her evidence particularly about the sexual acts under great strain and distress, it was certainly not an act, and at one stage, she said she felt physically sick and I am sure that that was the case, when the horrible memories of the acts which she complained of, were brought back to the forefront of her memory. At times, I wondered whether she would be able to continue with her evidence which she gave in a very flat and unemotional voice.'[3]

> 'We note that the respondent presented herself [to the adjudicator] as being quietly spoken and continually tearful and overwhelmed by distress. That was not the Tribunal's opinion in relation to the evidence she gave. We have found her to be articulate and intelligent ... The Tribunal has given the respondent's claim the most anxious scrutiny and finds that it is fabricated.'[4]

Inferences drawn about the credibility of an application from the applicant's demeanour during a hearing has been addressed in the Canadian context in *MG v MCI*[5] which concerned a woman who had been a victim of domestic violence for more than 20 years. Her asylum claim was initially refused by the CRDD but this decision was based in significant part on conclusions which had been drawn about her credibility based on demeanour. This was subsequently the subject of strong criticism by the courts, which also commented on the failure of the CRDD to adequately take into consideration its own gender guidelines:

> 'In considering a story such as the one the applicant tells and in making a finding of credibility, a decision maker must consider the evidence from the perspective of the teller, and, in particular, give careful consideration to what conduct might be expected of a woman living under the violent conditions described ... the applicant has to tell about her abuse and the action she took, or did not take as a result, is only one part of what is required to substantiate her refugee claim; the other part is the knowledge, understanding and sensitivity that the CRDD must possess in order to properly assess the applicant's story ...'.

In the **UK**, the problem of assessing the demeanour of the applicant has been noted by Bingham J (as he then was):

---

1   INS 1995, p 7.
2   Appeal No HX/6670/96 (unreported) 22 October 1996.
3   Appeal No HX/75889/94 (unreported) 23 November 1995.
4   *M v SSHD* (unreported) 17 August 1999 (16444) (IAT).
5   Appeal No HX/75889/94 (unreported) 23 November 1995.

'If a Turk shows signs of anger when accused of lying, is that to be interpreted as the bluster of a man caught out in deceit or the reaction of an honest man to an insult? If a Greek, similarly challenged, becomes rhetorical and voluble and offers to swear to the truth of what he has said on the lives of his children, what (if any) significance should be attached to that? If a Japanese witness, accused of forging a document, becomes sullen, resentful and hostile, does this suggest that he has done so or he has not? I can only ask these questions, I cannot answer them. And if the answer be given that it all depends on the impression made by the particular witness in the particular case that is in my view no answer. The enigma usually remains. To rely on demeanour is in most cases to attach importance to deviations from a norm when in truth there is no norm.'[1]

In *Daniel*,[2] the Tribunal stressed the requirement for caution in relying upon the demeanour of a witness whose language and culture are different.

Representatives should therefore be aware that cultural and other differences and trauma play an important role in determining demeanour, ie how a woman presents herself physically, for example, whether she maintains eye contact, shifts her posture or hesitates when speaking. The level and type of emotion displayed by a woman during the recounting of her experiences should not adversely affect her credibility. A lack of displayed emotion does not necessarily mean that the woman is not distressed or deeply affected by what has happened. Expert evidence may be useful in cases refused for these reasons.

10.5 SUPPORTING EVIDENCE

The process of verification is critical for the success of an asylum claim because it establishes both that the fear of persecution is well-founded and that the applicant's claim is credible. It is generally accepted that where human rights reports indicate that a risk of harm exists, a genuine fear of persecution in a country is likely to be well-founded.[3] It remains the case, however, that for women in particular this information may simply not be readily available. Because women refugees are frequently subjected to forms of persecution which differ from those of men, they may be unable to document their experiences. For example, they may not be able to provide membership cards or newspaper cuttings relating to their political involvement because they have been indirectly involved through a supporting role or because the political opinion has been imputed to them. Similarly, information about violence within the family or community may be difficult to find. Background reports and country information published by organisations such as Amnesty International and the US State Department have, until very recently, lacked an analysis of the position and status of women and the extent of this analysis remains limited.

Representatives should therefore be aware that information to support a woman's claim may not be readily available and that because women's experiences of persecution frequently differ from those of men, they may be

1   *R v Secretary of State ex parte Dhirubhai* [1986] Imm AR.
2   *Daniel* (unreported) 2 July 1996 (13623) (IAT).
3   Macdonald and Blake 1995, p 382.

unable to document their experiences. The absence of information should not necessarily be taken as an indicator that human rights abuses do not occur. Representatives should make every effort to obtain supporting information which can strengthen the credibility of their client's asylum claim.

10.5.1 Documentary evidence and country reports

'The applicant's statements ... cannot be considered in the abstract, and must be viewed in the context of the relevant background situation. A knowledge of conditions in the applicant's country of origin ... is an important element in assessing the applicant's credibility.'[1]

Information about the human rights situation in the applicant's country of origin, both from the State's own sources and from non-governmental organisations, plays a vital role in refugee status determination. However, information which is relevant to the asylum cases of refugee women may not be readily available. Few refugee documentation centres have information on the position of women in a given country, on the incidence of sexual violence in that country, and on the consequences of returning to the country in question for a woman in the claimant's alleged position. This is an impediment to women whose claim to refugee status is related to their gender status, especially given that, in the absence of information, decision-makers will normally presume that there are no specific problems. Even if women who have fled their countries because of gender-related persecution are willing to reveal their experiences, they often have trouble substantiating them; women's stories may not appear credible and they may have more difficulties than men with comparable claims:

'Where a gender-related claim involves threats of or actual violence at the hands of government authorities (or at the hands of non-state agents of persecution where the state is either unwilling or unable to protect), the claimant may have difficulty in substantiating her claim with any "statistical data" on the incidence of [sexual] violence in her country.'[2]

'It should be noted that violence against women, particularly sexual or domestic violence, tends to be largely under-reported or ignored in many countries. The absence of information on the above topics for any particular country should not necessarily be taken as an indicator that abuses of women's human rights do not occur.'[3]

Given that country reports produced by IND do not always explicitly address gender issues, representatives should, in accordance with the UNHCR's *Guidelines on the Protection of Refugee Women* (1991), make themselves familiar with the status and experiences of women in the country from which their client has fled:

'Adequate research of the claims made in the application and an understanding of the situation in the country of origin of the applicant is important for the full exploration of the person's claims. Where gender-related claims are raised, or

---

1   UNHCR 1979, para 42.
2   CIRB 1996a, section C2.
3   ADIMA 1996, para 3.6.

suspected, an understanding of the role, status and treatment of women in the country of origin is particularly important.'[1]

In addition to examining issues directly related to the claim and the differential application of human rights for women, representatives should consider a number of issues when gathering information:[2]

-   *position of women before the law* including their standing in court, the right to bring a complaint and give evidence, divorce and custody law, the right to own property, reproductive rights, freedom to travel, and the political, social and economic rights referred to below;
-   *political rights of women* including the right to vote, to hold office and belong to a political party;
-   *social and economic rights of women* including the right to marry the person of their choice, the right not to marry and the right to divorce, the right to determine their own sexuality, the right to an education, a career, and a job or remunerated activities, the status of single women, widows or divorcees, and freedom of dress;
-   *consequences for women who refuse to abide by or who challenge social, religious or cultural norms regarding their behaviour* including, for example, norms regarding virginity and pre- or extra-marital sex or pregnancy, norms around the institution of the family including arranged marriages and divorce, and norms about behaviour and dress;
-   *incidence and form of violence against women;*
-   *efficacy of protection available to women* and the sanctions or penalties on those who perpetrate the violence;
-   *consequences that may befall a woman on her return.*

It may also be useful to gather information about the cultural and social mores of the country with regard to the role and status of women, the family, the nature of family relationships, attitudes towards same sex relationships and attitudes towards 'foreign' influences:[3]

> 'In assessing gender-based persecution it is important to research the accepted norms of the relevant societies to determine how they operate both through legislation and in terms of actual practice in order to determine the degree of protection available to women.'

Both representatives and, ultimately, decision-makers need to know about the prevalence of practices such as female infanticide and dowry deaths in different societies. At the same time, they need to be aware of the consequences for those women who fail to conform to mandatory dress codes, or for those who lose their virginity or become pregnant before marriage. The need for evidence regarding the failure of the State to provide protection will be particularly crucial to refugee claims based on experiences such as domestic violence and other types of harm in which the State is not directly implicated.[4] For example, does the State turn a blind eye to the punishment meted out to these women when family honour

---

1   UNHCR 1991, para 73.
2   UNHCR 1995.
3   ADIMA 1996, para 4.11.
4   Stairs and Pope 1990.

might be at stake or is the State able to provide protection to women in urban but not in rural areas? The difficulty, of course, is that limited country-specific material is available through the traditional sources of information for refugee claims. This is in large part due to the failure of many States to consider violence against women to be a serious problem, or one worth the assignment of resources sufficient to provide for the wide dissemination of research.

It may be necessary for advocates to build their own pool of resources through direct contacts with members of government departments, social services and academia. Where no country-specific information about gender-related issues is available, advocates should use general information about such issues to support, by extension, their client's claim. For example, the literature on domestic violence from many different countries makes reference to the inadequacy of police response. Given that, in the absence of such information, it will be very hard to establish the validity of a refugee woman's claim for asylum, a number of different methods can be adopted in order to gather supporting information:

–   researching the position of women in countries of origin from articles, newspapers, studies and reports, including those published by government departments, inter-governmental organisations, non-governmental organisations, women's and community organisations;
–   interviewing other women from the country of origin to verify the material collected in the interview;
–   gathering general information about the position of women in countries of origin from articles, newspapers, recent studies and reports;
–   accessing on-line information available on the Internet (see Sources of Further Information and Support at the back of this book), or sources such as the UNHCR's RefWorld on CD-Rom;
–   contacting specialists and expert witnesses familiar either with the region or the gender issues involved;
–   contacting the Refugee Women's Resource Project (based at Asylum Aid) whose resource centre contains books, materials and research on issues affecting women as asylum seekers.

If an application is refused on grounds relating to the substance of the claim, the use of expert witnesses may prove invaluable at the appeal stage, in addition to documentary evidence relating to the situation of women in a particular country.[1] It is clear from existing determinations that when such efforts are made to obtain information, the woman is more likely to be successful in her application for asylum or in an appeal against a negative decision by the Home Office. The importance of adequate background information about the country of origin can be seen in the case of a woman from Algeria who applied for asylum because of the threat of *mut'a* or temporary pleasure marriage:

> 'Having carefully perused all those documents I have referred to, I have no doubt in my mind that GIA members do select and target single women in Algeria for the purpose of enjoyment marriages ... having carefully studied the background

---

1   See also ILPA 1997b.

information about the country and having studied the current position of Algeria, I am satisfied that the appellant's fear was well-founded.'[1]

Expert evidence submitted can also lead to a reconsideration of the case prior to a hearing.

10.5.2 Medical evidence

The extent to which medical evidence will be useful in supporting a claimant's testimony will depend largely upon the details of each claim, and it should be noted that even in cases of rape or sexual violence, unlike other forms of torture, there is generally no physical evidence unless the rape was a particularly brutal one or the woman was a virgin and has no children. Moreover, torturers and abusers often choose methods precisely because they do not leave marks. Representatives should also be aware that there are cases where medical evidence has been dismissed by the adjudicator, as in the case of an Ethiopian woman who was raped by government soldiers:

> 'It seems reasonable to suggest that they [the scars] could also be compatible with numerous innocent activities. Indeed the examiner appears understandably to have relied rather more on the appellant's emotional responses to examination, which she claims were "definitely those of an abused woman" ... It is my view that the appellant's emotional response to the doctor was calculated and false ... the appellant's rape is a complete fabrication.'[2]

This decision was subsequently overruled by the IAT:

> 'The doctor giving the report is a very highly qualified and experienced psychiatrist retained by the Medical Foundation ... In our view in his evaluation of the medical report [the adjudicator] was so dismissive of the potential weight of the report that it amounts to an error in law to say that it provided no independent support to her claim and that the rape claim was a fabrication.'[3]

Reports from specialist organisations (in addition to GPs) which make an assessment of the refugee woman's physical and mental health can be critical to the successful outcome of refugee women's claims for asylum. In the case of a woman from Zaire, reports by the Black Women's Rape Action Project and Women Against Rape highlighted the traumatic effects on the applicant of an horrific gang rape by soldiers at gunpoint, the threat to her life, and the murder and violence against close members of her family which she witnessed.[4] This report was instrumental in overturning the earlier refusal of the Home Office to accept that, in the light of these experiences, her life would be in danger if she returned to Zaire. If representatives consider that such information would be beneficial to the claims of their female clients they should ensure that a referral is made to the appropriate organisation at the earliest possible opportunity.

---

1   Appeal No HX/66670/96 (unreported) 22 October 1996.
2   Appeal No HX/73584/94 (unreported) (1995).
3   *Gimhedin v SSHD* (unreported) 21 October 1996 (14019) (IAT).
4   *How asylum procedures failed Mrs. X and how the Short Procedure (SP) will lead to a further deterioration of standards* (Hackney Community Law Centre and WAR press release, 1996).

10.6 THE STANDARD OF PROOF

An asylum seeker has to show a 'reasonable degree of likelihood' that she will be persecuted if removed from the UK. According to Hathaway (1991), the 'standard of proof' should be set at the criterion of a 'reasonable possibility' of persecution, and not at more strict criteria such as 'real and substantial danger' of persecution or the occurrence of persecution being 'more likely than not'. In the UK, the standard of proof to be applied to the assessment of the future likelihood of persecution has been laid down by the House of Lords in *Sivakumaran*.[1] That the appellant's fear of persecution is well-founded means that there has to be demonstrated a 'reasonable degree of likelihood' that she would be persecuted for a Refugee Convention reason if returned to her own country:

> 'In my opinion the requirement that an applicant's fear of persecution should be well-founded means that there has to be demonstrated a reasonable degree of likelihood that he will be persecuted for a Convention reason if returned to his own country.'

This approach was subsequently reinforced by *Kaja*:[2]

> 'Where the central feature for assessment is the reasonable likelihood of an event occurring and that event will have extremely grave consequences if it does occur, there is no inherent reason why the estimate must be based on facts more likely than not to have occurred ... In both Sivakumaran and Direk there was reference to the relevance of the past to the estimate of the future. In both the estimate was based on a single estimate of "reasonable likelihood".'

Despite this, there has been considerable debate in recent years as to whether the same standard, namely reasonable likelihood, should be applied when the fact finder is considering historical or existing facts which will to a greater or lesser extent inform the assessment as to what will occur in the future. The IAT re-examined the issue of the standard of proof more recently in *Horvath*,[3] where it was argued by the Home Office that the existing position reflected in *Kaja*[4] was wrong, being contrary to *Jonah*,[5] which was binding on them. However, the Tribunal followed the majority decision in *Kaja*[6] and was of the opinion that the emphasis in status determination should concentrate on protection from prospective risk of persecution, in other words, that it should be forward looking. The Tribunal noted that there had been an unhealthy fixation in the UK on past mistreatment. The Tribunal also noted that this standard has been legislatively approved in para 5(5) of Sch 2 to the Asylum and Immigration Appeals Act 1993 as amended by s 1 of the Asylum and Immigration Act 1996:

> 'For us the matter must remain as laid down by the majority in Kaja until such time as Parliament reconsiders the issue, which it is likely to have an early opportunity of so doing. Until it does so, it is the view of the Tribunal that adjudicators would be well

1   *SSHD v Sivakumaran and Others* [1988] Imm AR 147 (HL).
2   *Kaja v SSHD* [1995] Imm AR 1 (IAT).
3   *Horvarth v SSHD* [1999] INLR 7 (IAT).
4   *Kaja v SSHD* [1995] Imm AR 1 (IAT).
5   *R v IAT ex parte Jonah* [1985] Imm AR 7 (QBD).
6   *Kaja v SSHD* [1995] Imm AR 1 (IAT).

advised to concentrate on considering the whole issue which is before them and to consider on that evidence, whether there is a reasonable degree of likelihood that the appellant has a well-founded fear of persecution for reasons of race, religion, nationality, membership of a particular social group or political opinion.'

This decision was not challenged by the Home Office when *Horvath* went to the Court of Appeal[1] and the approach in *Kaja* still stands.

The standard of proof required in asylum cases in the UK is in recognition of the difficulties asylum seekers face in proving their claim and the serious consequences of a wrong decision. Nonetheless, establishing that the fear of persecution is well-founded remains problematic for many asylum seekers who often have no witness to the acts of violence against them and have no corroborative proof that the acts occurred. For many women this problem may be exacerbated because of the type of activity in which they were involved, or because serious harm has been inflicted within the family or community.

If there is no independent proof available, it will be necessary to rely on the testimony of the applicant alone, in which case it is critical that testimony is obtained which is believable, consistent and sufficiently detailed to provide a plausible and coherent account of the basis for the fear. The problems of reliance upon testimony alone in cases of female applicants highlight the importance of gender-sensitive information gathering. Representatives should make every effort to gather additional evidence and information relating to both the situation for women in the applicant's country of origin and about the applicant's physical and mental health.

It should also be noted that, when an assessment is made by the decision-maker as to whether the fear of persecution is well-founded, this will be based in significant part on general conditions in the applicant's country of origin but may not take into account the particular experiences of women. An assessment should also be made of a woman's particular fear and of whether any changes in country conditions are meaningful and effective enough for her fear of persecution to be no longer well-founded. A change in country circumstances, generally viewed as a positive change, may have no impact, or even a negative impact, on a woman's fear of persecution. As has been suggested throughout this book, harm in many cases occurs at the hands of non-State agents (which includes family and community members) whose actions are ignored or condoned by the authorities. Notwithstanding that changes may have occurred, such agents of persecution are seldom brought to justice and there is no accountability by the State for the acts of persecution inflicted on women:

> 'Many cases of gender-based persecution occur at the hands of non-state agents of persecution whose actions are ignored or condoned by the authorities. Even where changes in the national legislation or other state of affairs have occurred, such agents of persecution are seldom brought to justice and there is no accountability by the state for the acts of persecution inflicted on the applicant.'[2]

In some cases, adjudicators have taken into account the additional likelihood of persecution simply by virtue of the applicant being returned to their country of

---

1   *Horvath v SSHD* [2000] INLR 15 (CA).
2   ADIMA 1996, para 4.20.

origin. The implication is that for women the risk of return is even greater than for their male counterparts:

> 'It also seems to be to be a fair point that the appellant returning to Khartoum by herself is likely to draw attention to herself in the light of the authorities' attitude towards women travelling alone.'[1]

> 'If she were to be returned to Sierra Leone she would be a woman on her own and it appears to me from the documentary evidence I have seen that she, as a women on her own, would be very vulnerable in that country.'[2]

10.7 A NOTE ON THE APPEALS PROCESS

Procedures for asylum determination in the UK are currently undergoing extensive and fast-moving change. This includes the appeals process. Rights of appeal under the Immigration and Asylum Act 1999 are very complex and the implications of the Human Rights Act 1998 are not yet clear. Representatives must ensure that they are up to date with these developments.

Given that a significant number of applications are initially refused by the Home Office, the appeals process has become increasingly important for those seeking asylum in the UK and often represents the first occasion where all the facts of the case are heard. The refusal to grant refugee status to women may be on credibility grounds such as those outlined above, on substantial issues of interpretation or on a combination of the two. Since July 1993, all those whose asylum applications are considered substantively and refused have the right to appeal to a special adjudicator. Those whose appeals are dismissed have the right to apply for leave to appeal to the IAT against the determination, although not those who have been placed in the fast-track, accelerated appeals procedure. Community Legal Service now covers the cost of representation at the appeal hearing itself but is subject to a merits test and a financial eligibility test. Meanwhile, although access to benefits for asylum seekers is complex, all asylum seekers refused since July 1996 will lose benefits. Some asylum seekers awaiting appeal may suffer intense financial hardship for a period of between one and two years because of delays in the appellate process.[3] The situation is compounded by the fact that the Home Office can apply for leave to appeal to the IAT against a determination which is in favour of the asylum seeker. For those who have arrived in the UK with children and who are responsible for their care, usually women, the current system serves only to make them more vulnerable to exploitation and abuse.

Most, if not all, of the procedural problems facing refugee women which have been discussed in this chapter are likely to arise during the appeals process. In addition, however, there is also some evidence to suggest that rather than allowing gender-related cases to reach the courts where precedents could be established, the Home Office have awarded ELR to some female applicants.

---

1   Appeal No HX/75947/94 (unreported) 5 May 1995.
2   Appeal No HX/62851/95 (unreported) 15 October 1996.
3   Refugee Council 1996.

Clearly, rights and benefits associated with ELR are significantly lower than those associated with full refugee status, especially regarding family reunion. In such cases, the representative in consultation with his or her client will need to decide whether to challenge the grant of ELR. Although it is important to develop a body of case-law on the gender-related persecution claims, proceeding with an appeal against a refusal to upgrade should be considered very carefully because of the dangers of curtailment or non-renewal of ELR. Representatives should be especially aware of the potential damage of a negative finding on credibility.

It is also apparent that, for many of the reasons discussed in this chapter, women may be less willing than men to proceed further and may be content to settle for ELR although it limits the possibility of family reunion. There are practical and financial reasons for this reluctance including anxieties about reliving the events as well as fears about publicity. The following testimony from a Middle Eastern woman, forced to undergo hymen reconstruction because she was no longer a virgin, illustrates the concerns of many female asylum seekers:

> 'They [the Home Office] made a deal and told me to take one year Exceptional Leave to Remain ... In the end I accepted it. Had I won this case I would have been the first woman and that's what they wanted to avoid. I really wanted to win my case and open things up but I didn't want to fight anymore. If I carried on I would have been famous but scandalised. A lot of personal problems would come out. All my private life would come out, and names. I would help a lot of women but then I would pay the price ... maybe even a bullet on the street. I care for my friends, my family and my reputation.'[1]

10.8 CAMPAIGNING

In addition to the legal process, campaigning may be essential, and representatives should utilise all available means to fight the removal of their client. Timing of the launch of a campaign is critical and advisers should have a strategy in mind in the early stages of the case. Successful campaign strategies undertaken by representatives have included:

– utilising existing campaign networks and anti-deportation campaigns;
– obtaining resolutions in support of the campaign from branches of political parties, trade unions and anti-racist organisations;
– approaching parliamentarians and prominent individuals for support;
– contacting women's organisations, faith groups and refugee community organisations;
– contacting refugee charities to see if they can support a point of issue;
– raising awareness through public meetings, colleges and workplaces;
– accessing family, school and local community support networks;
– utilising media networks to gain sympathetic coverage.

Southall Black Sisters, a black women's organisation specialising in the needs of Asian women and Women Against Fundamentalism have launched a number of

---

1   Comments made by a Jordanian asylum applicant during an interview with the author, November 1996.

successful campaigns on behalf of refugee women. The following case study is just one example of how campaigning can be extremely effective (see Box 10.2).

Box 10.2

The campaign to prevent the removal of Ms J started in March 1990 when Ms J was suddenly picked up by police and detained in Harmondsworth Detention Centre. She was not with her young children at the time, one of whom was still being breast fed, and was to be removed without them. This was despite the fact that her legal representatives had made representations which were pending a decision. Southall Black Sisters (SBS) and Women Against Fundamentalism (WAF) launched a campaign to obtain her release from detention and prevent her immediate removal. They contacted her solicitor and MP who made representations on her behalf. They also contacted the press, who contacted the Home Office, IND and the detention centre. *The Independent* newspaper covered the story. This pressure led to Ms J's release from detention and she was allowed to remain until a decision had been made in her case. In the meantime, SBS and WAF continued to build up public support and produced a campaign leaflet asking for help. As a result of this campaign Ms J was granted ELR.

APPENDICES

Appendix 1

UNHCR EXCOM RESOLUTIONS ON REFUGEE WOMEN[1]

EXCOM Conclusion No.39 (XXXVI) 1985 – Refugee Women and International Protection:
– stresses the need for UNHCR and host governments to give particular attention to the international protection needs of refugee women
– recommends that States, individually, jointly and in co-operation with UNHCR, redefine and reorient existing programmes, and where necessary, establish new programmes to meet the specific needs of refugee women

EXCOM Conclusion No. 46 (XXXVII) 1987 – General Conclusion on International Protection:
– notes that refugee women had special protection and assistance needs
– recognises the need for reliable information and statistics about refugee women in order to increase awareness of their situation

EXCOM Conclusion No. 54 (XXXIX) 1988 – Refugee Women:
– elaborates on the special vulnerability of refugee women and the particular problems they face

EXCOM Conclusion No. 60 (XL) 1989 – General Conclusion on International Protection:
– reiterates concerns about the physical safety and sexual exploitation of refugee women

EXCOM Conclusion No. 64 (XLI) 1990 – Refugee Women and International Protection:
– urges States and others to ensure that the needs and resources of refugee women are fully understood and integrated
– outlines a number of aims in promoting measures for improving the international protection of refugee women

EXCOM Conclusion No. 73 (XLIV) 1993 – Refugee Protection and Sexual Violence:
– examines the implications of sexual violence for protection
– calls upon states and UNHCR to ensure the equal access of women and men to refugee status determination procedures

---

1   The full texts of the UNHCR's EXCOM Conclusions can be found on the UNHCR's RefWorld on CD-Rom and on-line at http://www.unhcr.ch/refworld/unhcr/excom/xconc/menu.htm.

Appendix 2

CIRB *GUIDELINES ON WOMEN REFUGEE CLAIMANTS FEARING GENDER-RELATED PERSECUTION: UPDATE* (CANADA) (November 1996)

The definition of a Convention refugee in the *Immigration Act* does not include *gender* as an independent enumerated ground for a well-founded fear of persecution warranting the recognition of Convention refugee status. As a developing area of the law, it has been more widely recognised that gender-related persecution is a form of persecution which can and should be assessed by the Refugee Division panel hearing the claim. Where a woman claims to have a gender-related fear of persecution, the central issue is thus the need to determine the linkage between gender, the feared persecution and one or more of the definition grounds.

Most gender-related refugee claims brought forward by women raise four critical issues which these Guidelines seek to address:

1.   To what extent can women making a gender-related claim of fear of persecution successfully rely on any one, or a combination of, the five enumerated grounds of the Convention refugee definition?

2.   Under what circumstances does sexual violence, or a threat thereof, or any other prejudicial treatment of women constitute persecution as that term is jurisprudentially understood?

3.   What are the key evidentiary elements which decision-makers have to look at when considering a gender-related claim?

4.   What special problems do women face when called upon to state their claim at refugee determination hearings particularly when they have had experiences that are difficult and often humiliating to speak about?

A.   DETERMINING THE NATURE AND THE GROUNDS OF THE PERSECUTION

Obviously, not all claims brought forward by women are specifically gender-related. Women frequently claim fear of persecution in common with their male fellow citizens, though not necessarily of the same nature or at the same level of vulnerability, for such reasons as belonging to an ethnic or a linguistic minority, or membership in a political movement, a trade union or a religious denomination.

I.   GENERAL PROPOSITION

Although gender is not specifically enumerated as one of the grounds for establishing Convention refugee status the definition of *Convention refugee* may properly be interpreted as providing protection for women who demonstrate a well-founded fear of gender-related persecution by reason of any one, or a combination of, the enumerated grounds.

Before determining the appropriate ground(s) applicable to the claim, decision makers must first identify the **nature** of the persecution feared by the claimant.

Generally speaking, women refugee claimants may be put into four broad categories, although these categories are not mutually exclusive or exhaustive:

1. **Women who fear persecution on the same Convention grounds, and in similar circumstances, as men. That is, the risk factor is not their sexual status, per se, but rather their particular identity (i.e. racial, national or social) or what they believe in, or are perceived to believe in (i.e. religion or political opinion).** In such claims, the substantive analysis does not vary as a function of the person's gender, although the nature of the harm feared and procedural issues at the hearing may vary as a function of the claimant's gender.

2. **Women who fear persecution solely for reasons pertaining to kinship, i.e. because of status, activities or views of their spouses, parents and siblings, or other family members.** Such cases of 'persecution of kin' typically involve violence or other forms of harassment against women, who are not themselves accused of any antagonistic views or political convictions, in order to pressure them into revealing information about the whereabouts or the political activities of their family members. Women may also have political opinions imputed to them based on the activities of members of their family.

3. **Women who fear persecution resulting from certain circumstances of severe discrimination on grounds of gender or acts of violence either by public authorities or at the hands of private citizens from whose actions the state is unwilling or unable to adequately protect the concerned persons.** In the refugee law context, such discrimination may amount to persecution if it leads to consequences of a substantially prejudicial nature for the claimant and if it is imposed on account of any one, or a combination, of the statutory grounds for persecution. The acts of violence which a woman may fear include violence inflicted in situations of domestic violence and situations of civil war.

4. **Women who fear persecution as the consequence of failing to conform to, or for transgressing, certain gender-discriminating religious or customary laws and practices in their country of origin.** Such laws and practices, by singling out women and placing them in a more vulnerable position than men, may create conditions for the existence of a gender-defined social group. The religious precepts, social traditions or cultural norms which women may be accused of violating can range from choosing their own spouses instead of accepting an arranged marriage, to such matters as the wearing of make-up, the visibility or length of hair, or the type of clothing a woman chooses to wear.

II. GROUNDS OTHER THAN MEMBERSHIP IN A PARTICULAR SOCIAL GROUP

Race:
There may be cases where a woman claims a fear of persecution because of her race and her gender. For example, a woman from a minority race in her country may be persecuted not only for her race, but also for her gender.

Religion:
A woman who, in a theocracy for example, chooses not to subscribe to or follow the precepts of a state religion may be at risk of persecution for reasons of religion. In the context of the Convention refugee definitions, the notion of religion may encompass,

among other freedoms, the freedom to hold a belief system of one's choice or not to hold a particular belief system and the freedom to practise a religion of one's choice or not to practise a prescribed religion. In certain states, the religion assigns certain roles to women; if a woman does not fulfil her assigned role and is punished for that, she may have a well-founded fear of persecution for reasons of religion. A woman may also be perceived as expressing a political view (and have a political opinion imputed to her) because of her attitude and/or behaviour towards religion.

Nationality:

A gender-related claim of fear of persecution may be linked to reasons of nationality in situations where a national law causes a woman to lose her nationality (i.e. citizenship) because of marriage to a foreign national. What would constitute good grounds for fearing persecution is not the fact of losing her nationality as such (notwithstanding that such laws are discriminatory to the extent that they do not apply to men married to foreign nationals), but the consequences she may suffer as a result.

Political Opinion:

A woman who opposes institutionalised discrimination against women, or expresses views of independence from male social/cultural dominance in her society, may be found to fear persecution by reason of her **actual political opinion or a political opinion imputed to her (i.e. she is perceived by the agent of persecution to be expressing politically antagonistic views)**. Two considerations are of paramount importance when interpreting the notion of 'political opinion':

1. In a society where women are 'assigned' a subordinate status and the authority exercised by men over women results in a general oppression of women, their political protest and activism do not always manifest themselves in the same way as those of men.

2. The political nature of oppression of women in the context of religious laws and rituals should be recognised. Where tenets of the governing religion in a given country require certain kinds of behaviour exclusively from women, contrary behaviour may be perceived by the authorities as evidence of an unacceptable political opinion that threatens the basic structure from which their political power flows.

III. MEMBERSHIP IN A PARTICULAR SOCIAL GROUP

In considering the application of the 'membership in a particular social group' ground, decision-makers should refer to the Supreme Court of Canada decision in *Ward*. **The *Ward* decision indicated three possible categories of 'particular social group':**

1) **groups defined by an innate or unchangeable characteristic;**
2) **groups whose members voluntarily associate for reasons so fundamental to their human dignity that they should not be forced to forsake the association; and**
3) **groups associated by a former voluntary status, unalterable due to its historical permanence.**

The Court gave examples of the three categories as follows:

> The first category would embrace individuals fearing persecution on such bases as **gender**, linguistic background and sexual orientation, while the second would encompass, for example, human rights activists. The third branch is included more because of historical intentions, although it is also relevant to the anti-discrimination influences, in that one's past is an immutable part of the person.

Depending on the basis of the claim, women refugee claimants may belong to a group defined in any of these categories.

A further holding of the *Ward* decision is that a particular social group cannot be based solely on the common victimisation of its members. A group is not defined solely by common victimisation if the claimant's fear of persecution is also based on her gender, or on another innate or unchangeable characteristic of the claimant.

Family as a particular social group

There is jurisprudential authority for recognising claims grounded in familial affiliation (i.e. where kinship is the risk factor) as coming within the ambit of the 'membership in a particular social group' category. See, for example, *Al-Busaidy, Talal Ali Said v MEI*,

> ... the [Immigration and Refugee] Board has committed reviewable error in not giving due effect to the applicant's uncontradicted evidence with respect to his membership in a particular social group, namely, his own immediate family.

Gender-defined particular social group

There is increasingly international support for the application of the particular social group ground to the claims of women who allege a fear of persecution solely by reason of their gender. See *Conclusion No. 39 (XXXVI) Refugee Women and International Protection, 1985*, where the Executive Committee of the United Nations High Commissioner for Refugees (UNHCR) ...

> (k) Recognised that States, in the exercise of their sovereignty, are free to adopt the interpretation that women asylum-seekers who face harsh or inhuman treatment due to their having transgressed the social mores of the society in which they live may be considered as a 'particular social group' within the meaning of the Article 2 A(2) of the 1951 United Nations Refugee Convention.

Application of the statutory ground

In evaluating the 'membership in a particular social group' ground for a fear of gender-related persecution, two considerations are necessary:

1. Most of the gender-specific claims involving fear of persecution for transgressing religious or social norms may be determined on **grounds of religion or political opinion**. Such women may be seen by the governing authorities or private citizens as having made a religious or political statement in transgressing those norms of their society, even though UNHCR *Conclusion No. 39*, above, contemplates the use of 'particular social group' as an appropriate ground.

2. **For a woman to establish a well-founded fear of persecution by reasons of her membership in a gender-defined particular social group under the first category in *Ward* (i.e. groups defined by an innate or unchangeable characteristic):**

   - The fact that the particular social group consists of large numbers of the female population in the country concerned is **irrelevant** – race, religion, nationality and political opinion are also characteristics that are shared by large numbers of people.

   - **Gender is an innate characteristic and, therefore, women may form a particular social group within the Convention refugee definition**. The relevant assessment is whether the claimant, as a woman has a well-founded fear of persecution in her country of nationality by reason of her membership of this group.

- **Particular social groups comprised of sub-groups of women may also be an appropriate finding in a case involving gender-related persecution**. These particular social groups can be identified by reference to factors, in addition to gender, which may also be innate or unchangeable characteristics. Examples of other such characteristics are age, race, marital status and economic status. Thus, for example, there may be sub-groups of women identified as old women, indigenous women, single women or poor women. In determining whether these factors are unchangeable, consideration should be given to the cultural and social context in which the woman lives, as well as to the perception of the agents of persecution and those responsible for providing state protection.

- **Because refugee status is an *individual remedy*, the fact that a claim is based on social group membership may not be sufficient in and of itself to give rise to refugee status**. The woman will need to show that she has a genuine fear of harm, that one of the grounds of the definition is the reason for the feared harm, that the harm is sufficiently serious to amount to persecution, that there is a reasonable possibility that the feared persecution would occur if she was to return to her country of origin and that she has no reasonable expectation of adequate national protection.

B. ASSESSING THE FEARED HARM

Claims involving gender-related fear of persecution often fall quite comfortably within one of the five grounds of the Convention refugee definition. The difficulty sometimes lies in establishing whether the various forms of prejudicial treatment or sanctions imposed on women making such claims come within the scope of the concept of 'persecution'.

CONSIDERATIONS

The circumstances which give rise to women's fear of persecution are often unique to women. The existing bank of jurisprudence on the meaning of persecution is based, for the most part, on the experiences of male claimants. Aside from the few cases of rape, the definition has not been widely applied to female-specific experiences, such as infanticide, genital mutilation, bride-burning, forced marriage, domestic violence, forced abortion or compulsory sterilisation.

The fact that violence, including sexual and domestic violence, against women is universal is **irrelevant** when determining whether rape, and other gender-specific crimes constitute forms of persecution. **The real issues are whether the violence – experienced or feared – is a serious violation of a fundamental human right for a Convention ground and in what circumstances can the risk of that violence be said to result from a failure of state protection.**

The social, cultural, traditional and religious norms and the laws affecting women in the claimant's country of origin ought to be assessed **by reference to human rights instruments which provide a framework of international standards for recognising the protection needs of women.** What constitutes permissible conduct by the agent of persecution towards women may be determined, therefore, by reference to international instruments such as:

Universal Declaration of Human Rights

International Covenant on Civil and Political Rights

International Covenant on Economic, Social and Cultural Rights

Convention on the Elimination of All Forms of Discrimination Against Women

Convention on the Political Rights of Women

Convention on the Nationality of Married Women

Convention Against Torture and other Cruel, Inhuman or Degrading Treatment or Punishment

Declaration on the Elimination of Violence Against Women

A woman's claim to Convention refugee status **cannot be based solely on the fact that she is subject to a national policy or law to which she objects**. The claimant will need to establish that:

(a)   the policy or law is inherently persecutory; or
(b)   the policy or law is used as a means of persecution for one of the enumerated reasons; or
(c)   the policy or law, although having legitimate goals, is administered through persecutory means; or
(d)   the penalty for non-compliance with the policy or law is disproportionately severe.

C.   EVIDENTIARY MATTERS

When an assessment of a woman's claim of gender-related fear of persecution is made, the evidence must show that what the claimant genuinely fears is persecution for a Convention reason as distinguished from random violence or random criminal activity perpetrated against her as an individual. The central factor in such an assessment is, of course, the claimant's particular circumstances in relation to both the general human rights record of her country of origin and the experiences of other similarly situated women. Evaluation of the weight and credibility of the claimant's evidence ought to include valuation of the following considerations, among others:

1.   **A gender-related claim cannot be rejected simply because the claimant comes from a country where women face generalised oppression and violence and the claimant's fear of persecution is not identifiable to her on the basis of an individualised set of facts**. This so-called 'particularised evidence rule' was rejected by the Federal Court of Appeal in *Salibian v MEI*, and other decisions.

2.   **Decision-makers should consider evidence indicating a failure of state protection if the state or its agents in the claimant's country of origin are unwilling or unable to provide adequate protection from gender-related persecution.** If the claimant can demonstrate that it was objectively unreasonable for her to seek the protection of her state, then her failure to approach the state for protection will not defeat her claim. Also, the fact that the claimant did or did not seek protection from non-government groups is irrelevant to the assessment of the availability of state protection.

    When considering whether it is objectively unreasonable for the claimant not to have sought the protection of the state, **the decision-maker should consider, among other relevant factors, the social, cultural, religious and economic context in which the claimant finds herself**. If, for example, a woman has suffered gender-related persecution in the form of rape, she may be ostracised from her community for seeking protection from the state. Decision-makers should consider this type of information when determining if the claimant should reasonably have sought state protection.

    In determining whether the state is willing or able to provide protection to a woman fearing gender-related persecution, **decision-makers should consider the fact that the forms of evidence which the claimant might normally provide as 'clear and convincing proof' of state inability to protect, will not always be either available or useful in cases of gender-related persecution**.

For example, where a gender-related claim involves threats of or actual sexual violence at the hands of government authorities (or at the hands of non-state agents of persecution, whether the state is either unwilling or unable to protect), the claimant may have difficulty in substantiating her claim with any 'statistical data' on the incidence of sexual violence in her country.

In cases where the claimant cannot rely on the more standard or typical forms of evidence as 'clear and convincing proof' of failure of state protection, **reference may need to be made to alternative forms of evidence to meet the 'clear and convincing' test**. Such alternative forms of evidence might include the testimony of women in similar situations where there was a failure of state protection, or the testimony of the claimant herself regarding past personal incidents where state protection did not materialise.

3.   **A change in country circumstances, generally viewed as a positive change, may have no impact, or even a negative impact, on a woman's fear of gender-related persecution**. In situations where a woman's fear is related to personal-status laws or where her human rights are being violated by private citizens, a change in country circumstances may not mean a positive change for the woman, as these areas are often the last to change. An assessment should be made of the claimant's particular fear and of whether the changes are meaningful and effective enough for her fear of gender-related persecution to no longer be well-founded.

4.   **In determining the reasonableness of a woman's recourse to an internal flight alternative (IFA), decision-makers should consider the ability of women, because of their gender, to travel safely to the IFA and to stay there without facing undue hardship**. In determining the reasonableness of an IFA, the decision-makers should take into account factors including religious, economic, and cultural factors, and consider whether and how these factors affect women in the IFA.

D.   SPECIAL PROBLEMS AT DETERMINATION HEARINGS

Women refugee claimants face special problems in demonstrating that their claims are credible and trustworthy. Some of the difficulties may arise because of cross-cultural misunderstandings. For example:

1.   Women from societies where the preservation of one's virginity or marital dignity is the cultural norm may be reluctant to disclose their experiences of sexual violence in order to keep their 'shame' to themselves and not dishonour their family or community.

2.   Women from certain cultures where men do not share the details of their political, military or even social activities with their spouses, daughters or mothers may find themselves in a difficult situation when questioned about the experiences of their male relatives.

3.   Women refugee claimants who have suffered sexual violence may exhibit a pattern of symptoms referred to as Rape Trauma Syndrome, and may require extremely sensitive handling. Similarly, women who have been subjected to domestic violence may exhibit a pattern of symptoms referred to as Battered Woman Syndrome and may also be reluctant to testify. In some cases it will be appropriate to consider

whether claimants should be allowed to have the option of providing their testimony outside the hearing room by affidavit or by videotape, or in front of members and refugee claims officers specifically trained in dealing with violence against women. Members should be familiar with the UNHCR Executive Committee *Guidelines on the Protection of Refugee Women.*

FRAMEWORK OF ANALYSIS

1. Assess the harm feared by the claimant. Does the harm feared constitute persecution?

(a) For the treatment to be likely to amount to persecution, it must be a serious form of harm which detracts from the claimant's fundamental human rights
(b) To assist decision-makers in determining what kinds of treatment are considered persecution, an objective standard is provided by international human rights instruments

2. Ascertain whether the claimant's fear of persecution is based on any of the grounds, singly or in combination, enumerated in the Convention refugee definition. Considerations:

– It is necessary to ascertain the characteristic of the claimant which places her or members of her group at risk, and to ascertain the linkage of that characteristic to a Convention ground
– Gender is an innate characteristic and it may form a particular social group
– A subgroup of women may also form a particular social group. Women in these particular social groups have characteristics (innate or unchangeable) additional to gender, which make them fear persecution
– The gender-defined group cannot be defined **solely** by the fact that its members share a common persecution

3. Determine whether the claimant's fear of persecution is well-founded. This includes an assessment of the evidence related to the ability or willingness of the state to protect the claimant and, more generally, the objective basis of the claim. Considerations:

– There may be little or no documentary evidence presented with respect to the inadequacy of state protection as it related to gender-related persecution. There may be a need for greater reliance on evidence of similarly situated women and on the claimant's own experience
– The claimant need not have approached non-state organisations for protection
– Factors including the social, cultural, religious, and economic context in which the claimant finds herself should be considered in determining whether it was objectively unreasonable for the claimant not to have sought state protection
– Where a woman's fear related to personal-status laws or where her human rights are being violated by private citizens, an otherwise positive change in country conditions may have no impact, or even a negative impact, on a woman's fear of gender-related persecution

4. If required, determine whether there is a possibility of an internal flight alternative. Considerations:

– Whether there would be undue hardship for the claimant, both in reaching the location of the IFA and in establishing residence there

Religious, economic, social and cultural factors, among others, may be relevant in determining the reasonableness of an IFA for a woman fearing gender-related persecution.

Appendix 3

RWLG *GENDER GUIDELINES FOR THE DETERMINATION OF ASYLUM CLAIMS IN THE UK* (July 1998)

Contents

SECTION 1

Framework

Why Current Interpretation Fails Women

1.1   The 1951 UN Convention relating to the Status of Refugees and 1967 Protocol (the

'Refugee Convention') has often been approached with a partial perspective and interpreted through a framework of male experiences during the process of asylum determination in the UK.

1.2   Women suffer the same deprivation and harm that is common to all refugees. For example many are targeted because they are political activists, community organisers, members of women's movements or persist in demanding that their rights or those of their relatives or community members are respected.

1.3   The experiences of women in their country of origin often differ significantly from those of men because women's political protest, activism and resistance may manifest itself in different ways. For example:

- Women may hide people, pass messages or provide community services, food, clothing and medical care;
- The authorities in some countries exploit family relationships to intensify harm;
- Women who do not conform to the moral or ethical standards imposed on them may suffer cruel or inhuman treatment;
- Women may be targeted because they are particularly vulnerable, for example, those with caring responsibilities or young women who can easily be sexually abused;
- Women may be persecuted by members of their family and/or community.

1.4   Women are currently unable to benefit equitably from protection under the Refugee Convention. The reasons are two-fold:

- Procedural and evidential barriers prevent women's access to the asylum determination process;
- In interpreting the Refugee Convention, women's experiences have been marginalised. For example, whilst overt expression of a political opinion through conventional means such as involvement in political parties may be considered as a basis for political asylum, less conventional forms of political resistance, such as refusal to abide by discriminatory laws or to follow prescribed rules of conduct, are often wrongly categorised as personal conduct.

1.5   Increased emphasis on the role of gender is intended to ensure that all aspects of a woman's asylum claim are fully and fairly considered. This approach does not alter the meaning or interpretation of the Refugee Convention. Even where gender is not the central issue, giving conscious consideration to gender-related aspects of a case should assist interviewers and decision-makers to fully understand a woman's experiences.

1.6   These Guidelines represent good practice and in many respects are also applicable to the asylum claims of men. Regular training is essential to ensure that procedural and substantive concerns are properly responded to.

1.7   These Guidelines aim to raise awareness of women's experiences of persecution and to enable interviewers and decision-makers to apply the Refugee Convention in a way which embraces the totality of human experiences, to respond to the particular experiences and needs of women, and to assert and affirm the rights of women to effective international protection within the asylum determination process.

Definitions
1.8   There has been a tendency for the term 'gender' to be used synonymously with the term 'sex'. 'Gender' is not the same as 'sex' which is biologically defined. The term 'gender' refers to the social construction of power relations between women and men, and the implications of these relations for women's (and men's) identity, status, roles and responsibilities:

- Gender refers to the social organisation of sexual difference;
- Gender acquires a socially and culturally constructed meaning;
- Gender is a primary way of signifying relations of power.

1.9   Gender relations, and therefore gender differences, are historically, geographically and culturally specific, so that what it means to be a woman or a man varies over place and time. Any analysis of the way in which gender (as opposed to biological sex) shapes the experiences of asylum seeking women, must therefore *contextualise* those experiences.

1.10   Gender is a social relation that enters into, and partly constitutes, all other social relations and identities. Women's experiences of persecution, and of the process of asylum determination, will also be shaped by differences of race, class, sexuality, age, marital status, sexual history and so on. Looking at gender, as opposed to sex enables an approach which can accommodate specificity, diversity and heterogeneity.

1.11   In order to comprehend, and appropriately respond to, the role of gender in shaping women's experiences of persecution, it is important that interviewers and decision-makers understand clearly the relationship between gender and the elements of the refugee definition. The concept of women being persecuted *as* women is not the same as women being persecuted *because* they are women.

1.12   The concept of women being persecuted *as* women addresses *forms of persecution that are gender-specific* including, for example, sexual violence, female genital mutilation, forced abortion and sterilisation and denial of access to contraception. Understanding the ways in which women are violated as women is critical to naming as persecution those forms of harm which only or mostly affect women.

1.13   To say that a woman fears persecution *because* she is a woman addresses the causal relationship between gender (as socially constructed) and persecution. For example, sexual activity outside a socially condoned relationship may result in persecution.

1.14   Gender-specific persecution is therefore a term used to explain 'serious harm' within the meaning of persecution. Gender-related persecution is used to explain the basis of the asylum claim (i.e. the grounds of the persecution). A woman may be persecuted *as* a woman (e.g. raped) for reasons unrelated to gender (e.g. activity in a political party), not persecuted *as* a woman but still *because* of gender (e.g. flogged for refusing to wear a veil), and persecuted *as* and *because* she is a woman (e.g. female genital mutilation).

1.15   Gender-specific violations do not necessarily constitute persecution *because* of gender. For example, if a man's genitals are subjected to electric shocks, he is certainly being tortured in a gender-specific way, but it does not follow that he is being persecuted *because* of his gender.

Structure

1.16   These Guidelines systematically analyse women's asylum claims in relation to the essential elements of the refugee definition in Article 1(A) of the Refugee Convention.[1]

1.17   Within this framework, persecution is defined as '*the sustained or systematic violation of basic human rights demonstrative of a failure of state protection in relation to one of*

---

1   According to Article 1(A) of the 1951 UN Convention Relating to the Status of Refugees, the term 'refugee' shall apply to any person who 'owing to a well-founded fear of being persecuted for reasons of race, religion, nationality, membership of a particular social group or political opinion, is outside [her] country of origin and is unable, or, owing to such fear is unwilling to avail [herself] of the protection of that country; or who, not having a nationality and being outside the country of [her] former habitual residence as a result of such events is unable or, owing to such fear, is unwilling to return to it.'

the core entitlements which have been recognised by the international community.[1] The concept of persecution within the Refugee Convention therefore raises two questions:

- **Is there a violation of human rights which amounts to 'serious harm'?**
  This is addressed in Section 2 of these Guidelines
- **Is the state unable or unwilling to offer effective protection?**
  This is addressed in Section 3 of these Guidelines

'Persecution' = Serious Harm + The Failure of State Protection

---

1.18   Having established whether persecution or a fear of persecution exists, the next step is to establish whether the persecution or fear of persecution is for one of the reasons enumerated in the Refugee Convention. This is addressed in Section 4 of these Guidelines.

1.19   Particular procedural and evidential issues arise in the asylum claims of women. These are addressed in Section 5 of these Guidelines.

The International Framework for Protection

1.20   The Refugee Convention is only one of many international instruments which set minimum human rights standards. These other instruments may be useful tools in interpreting the Refugee Convention and in evaluating a claim to ensure proper protection. These include, but are not limited to:

- The Universal Declaration of Human Rights (UDHR) (1948);
- The 1926 Slavery Convention and Supplementary Convention on the Abolition of Slavery, the Slave Trade and Institutions and Practices Similar to Slavery of 1956;
- The 1949 Geneva Conventions on the Laws of War and the two Additional Protocols of 1977;
- The Convention for the Suppression of the Traffic in Persons and the Exploitation of Prostitution of Others (1949);[2]
- The European Convention on Human Rights (ECHR) (1950);
- The Convention on the Consent to Marriage, Minimum Age for Marriage and Registration of Marriages (1962);
- The Convention on the Elimination of All Forms of Racial Discrimination (1965);
- The International Covenant on Civil and Political Rights (ICCPR) (1966);
- The International Covenant on Economic, Social and Cultural Rights (ICESCR) (1966);
- **The Convention on the Elimination of All Forms of Discrimination Against Women (CEDAW) (1979);**
- The UN Convention Against Torture and Other Cruel, Inhuman or Degrading Treatment or Punishment (UNCAT) (1984);
- The Convention on the Rights of the Child (CROC) (1989);
- **The UN Declaration on the Elimination of Violence Against Women (1993);**
- **The UN Platform for Action (1995).**

1.21   In addition to the *Handbook on Procedures and Criteria for Determining Refugee Status* (1979), the Executive Committee (EXCOM) of the UNHCR has issued a number of notes and conclusions relating specifically to refugee women. The UNHCR has also

---

1   James Hathaway 1991 *The Law of Refugee Status*, Butterworth, 112.
2   This Convention only relates to trafficking for sexual purposes, however there are currently moves at the European level to broaden and update this Convention and its focus.

issued several relevant publications of interest. These include *Guidelines on the Protection of Refugee Women* (1991) and *Sexual Violence Against Refugees; Guidelines on Prevention and Response* (1995).

1.22   The determining authorities in Canada, the United States and Australia have produced Gender Guidelines which alert interviewers and decision-makers to the specific difficulties many women face gaining protection under the Refugee Convention.

1.23   Where a woman is not recognised as a Convention refugee but could be at risk if removed from the UK, or where there are other compassionate or humanitarian circumstances, she should be given permission to remain or leave to enter or remain. This option should not be seen as an alternative to providing proper legal protection in cases where the woman should be recognised as a refugee within the meaning of the Refugee Convention.

1.24   Where a woman is likely to be subjected to torture or to inhuman or degrading treatment or punishment, her removal is prohibited by Article 3 of the European Convention on Human Rights (ECHR).

SECTION 2

The Meaning of 'Serious Harm'

2.1   To be recognised as a Convention refugee an asylum applicant must fear a form of harm which can be characterised as persecution.

2.2   Whether an instance of harm, including harm which is gender-specific, amounts to persecution should be assessed on the basis of internationally recognised human rights standards as set out in Section 1 of these Guidelines.

2.3   Torture or cruel, inhuman or degrading treatment, the threat of execution, slavery, or enforced conformity of belief always constitute 'serious harm' within the meaning of persecution. Similarly the risk of arbitrary arrest or detention, house arrest by family or community members, denial of freedom of movement, opinion, association or privacy, is usually to be equated with 'serious harm'.

2.4   A discriminatory measure, in itself or cumulatively with others – for example, restrictions on rights to earn a livelihood, to practice or not practice a religion, to have access to public places or normally available educational, legal, welfare and health provision – may amount to 'serious harm'.

2.5   The fact that violence against women is universal is irrelevant when determining whether gender-specific forms of harm amount to 'serious harm'.

2.6   There are many forms of harm that are specific to, or more commonly affect women that also constitute torture or cruel, inhuman or degrading treatment. These include, *but are not limited to*, sexual violence and abuse, rape, female genital mutilation, marriage-related harm, violence within the family or community, domestic slavery, forced abortion and forced sterilisation. Gender-specific violence does not differ analytically from beatings, torture or other forms of violence that are commonly held to amount to persecution.

2.7   Sexual violence can include, *but is not limited to*, enforced nakedness; sexually abusive taunts and threats; rape; mechanical or manual stimulation of the erogenous zones; the insertion of objects into the body openings; the forced witnessing of sexual acts; forced masturbation or to be masturbated by others; fellatio and oral sex; a general atmosphere of sexual aggression and threats of the loss of the ability to reproduce and/or enjoyment of sexual relations in the future.

2.8   Sexual violence has serious physical, social and psychological consequences and is a grave violation of the fundamental human right to security of the person including the right not to be subjected to torture or other cruel inhuman or degrading treatment or punishment.

2.9   Sexual violence carries traumatic social repercussions which may be affected by a woman's cultural origins or social status. These may include, *but are not limited to,* rejection by (or of) the spouse and by family or community members, stigmatisation or ostracism by the wider community, and punishment and/or deprivation of education, employment and other types of assistance and protection. Where a victim of sexual violence may have no alternative but to marry her attacker or become a prostitute, these are also human rights violations.

2.10   Forced abortion, sterilisation and female genital mutilation constitute torture and are infringements of the basic right not be treated inhumanely or degradingly, of the right to private and family life, and of the right to marry and have a family.

2.11   'Serious harm' related to marriage includes, *but is not limited to,* forced marriage, 'dowry death' or bride burning, 'honour killings' and 'temporary pleasure marriages'.

2.12   Social and cultural norms regarding appropriate gender roles and behaviour may mean that lesbians face violations of their human rights. Lesbians may experience different forms of 'serious harm' than those characteristically targeted at gay men. For example, many lesbians have effectively been denied the right to sexual orientation because they have been forced into marriage.

2.13   Physical and mental abuse within the family is a wide-spread and often gender-specific form of 'serious harm' and a violation of women's human rights.

2.14   Women may be subjected to discriminatory treatment which is enforced through law or through the imposition of social or religious norms which restrict their opportunities and rights. This can include, *but is not limited to*:

- Family and personal laws;
- Dress codes;
- Employment or education restrictions;
- Restrictions on women's freedom of movement and/or activities.

2.15   Such restrictions may in themselves constitute 'serious harm'. For example, dress codes may violate a woman's right to freedom of conscience, expression or religion, either in themselves or because of the consequences of the refusal, failure or inability to comply.

2.16   A broad range of penalties may be imposed for disobeying restrictions placed on women. Such penalties will often constitute 'serious harm', particularly where the level of punishment for violating discriminatory norms is disproportionately severe.

2.17   Adverse social consequences that constitute 'serious harm' may be associated with, for example, arranged or child marriage, remaining single, mixed marriage, separation, divorce or widowhood, or seeking to obtain any rights in respect of custody of children.

2.18   Decision-makers are reminded that the legal obligation to eliminate all forms of discrimination against women is a fundamental tenet of international human rights law.

SECTION 3

The Failure of State Protection

3.1   In addition to establishing a well-founded fear of 'serious harm', a woman must also show that the state has failed to protect her. A failure of state protection exists in the following situations:

- If 'serious harm' has been inflicted by the authorities or by associated organisations or groups **or**;
- If 'serious harm' has been committed by others and the authorities are *unwilling* to give effective protection **or**;
- If 'serious harm' has been committed by others, and the authorities are *unable* to give effective protection.

3.2   International legal obligations of the state are found in international treaty and customary law and include specific obligations to protect women's human rights.

3.3   State protection must be meaningful, accessible, effective and available to a woman regardless of her race, ethnicity, sexual orientation, disability, religion, class, age, occupation or any other aspect of her identity. In some cases there may be protection in theory, but actual practice must be examined. Corroborative evidence will not always be available.

3.4   Conduct by those associated with the state, including sexual violence, is the responsibility of the state.

3.5   Gender-based discrimination is often enforced through law as well as through social practices. The existence of a law or social policy can itself amount to a failure of state protection, for example, a law or policy could be inherently persecutory, or it may have a 'legitimate' goal but be administered through persecutory means, or the penalty for non-compliance with the law or policy may be disproportionately severe.

3.6   State responsibility includes those instances where social mores dictate gender-related abuse as an acceptable practice and where there are no effective means of legal recourse to prevent, investigate or punish such acts. Where the state fails to provide adequate protection, it does not matter whether this derives from collusion, indifference or impotence; it amounts to official acquiescence.

3.7   The state is liable for human rights violations by private individuals where it refuses or is unable to provide effective protection or redress. State inaction includes, *but is not limited to,* official legislation (for example, marital rape exemptions in law), lack of police response to pleas for assistance and/or a reluctance, refusal or failure to investigate, prosecute or punish individuals. Where a state facilitates, accommodates, tolerates, justifies, or excuses denials of women's rights, there is a failure of state protection.

3.8   A claim should not be rejected simply because a woman comes from a situation where the state is unable to provide protection.

3.9   It is not always reasonable or possible for a woman to alert the authorities to her need for protection, for example, if by doing so she risks violence or harassment, or has reasonable doubts that she will be protected. In such circumstances, the fact that a woman has not alerted the authorities ought not to be held against her.

3.10   The implications of gender in determining the reasonableness of an internal flight alternative must be recognised. For example, financial, logistical, social, cultural and other barriers may significantly affect a woman's ability to travel to another area of the country, and stay there without facing hardship, insecurity or the right to be with her family.

SECTION 4

Convention Grounds

General Proposition

4.1   Although gender is not specifically enumerated as one of the grounds for establishing status within the Refugee Convention, these Guidelines encourage decision-makers to let gender inform their assessment under race, religion, nationality, political opinion or membership of a particular social group. 'Religion' and 'political opinion' in particular need to be properly interpreted to include women's experiences. In some cases 'women' (or some sub-category thereof) may qualify as a 'particular social group'.

4.2   The predominant interpretation of persecution on the grounds of political opinion exemplifies the problem of a definition which has typically been seen in terms of male experience. The archetypal image of a political refugee as someone who is fleeing persecution for direct involvement in conventional political activity, does not always correspond with the reality of many women's experiences.

4.3   It is important to recognise that a woman may face persecution because of a Convention ground which is attributed to her. Where the persecution of women is concerned, an *imputed or attributed* Convention ground may be important.

4.4   It is important to recall that the preamble to the Refugee Convention specifically refers to the intention of the signatories to uphold fundamental rights. When determining the ambit of actual or imputed (attributed) Convention grounds, for example political opinion, it is therefore vital to look to the core human rights instruments in international law as outlined in Section 1 of these Guidelines.

4.5   For some women there may be an additional likelihood of persecution simply by virtue of being returned to her country of origin.

Race

4.6   Whilst actual or attributed racial identity is not specific to women, it may operate in tandem with gender to explain why a woman fears persecution. For example, whilst the destruction of ethnic identity and/or prosperity of a racial group may be through killing, maiming or incarcerating men, women may be viewed as propagating ethnic identity through their reproductive role, and may be persecuted through, for example, sexual violence or control of reproduction.

Nationality

4.7   The term 'nationality' does not only mean 'citizenship'. It can include membership of an ethnic or linguistic group and may overlap with the terms 'race', 'religion' and 'political opinion'.

4.8   Whilst actual or attributed national identity is not specific to women, it may operate in tandem with gender to explain why a woman fears persecution. Persecution for reasons of nationality may result from legal and social practices which deprive a woman of her nationality or citizenship rights in certain situations, for example, through marriage to a 'foreign' national.

Religion

4.9   A woman may face harm for her adherence to or rejection of a religious belief or practice. Religion as the persecution ground may include *but is not limited to*, the freedom to hold a belief system of one's choice or *not to hold* a particular belief system and the freedom to practise a religion of one's choice or *not to practise* a prescribed religion.

4.10   There is often overlap between religious and political persecution. The *political nature* of oppression of women in the context of religious laws and ritualisation must be recognised. Where religious tenets require certain kinds of behaviour from a woman, contrary behaviour may be perceived as evidence of an unacceptable political opinion regardless of what a woman herself actually believes.

4.11   A woman's religious identity may be aligned with that of other members of her family or community. Imputed or attributed religious identity may therefore be important.

Actual or Imputed (Attributed) Political Opinion

4.12   The International Covenant on Civil and Political Rights (ICCPR) recognises that there is a fundamental right for an individual to freely hold an opinion, to freely express opinions and to enjoy freedom of conscience.

4.13   It is important not to underestimate or overlook the political dimensions of a woman's experiences of persecution even though a woman may not regard herself as making a political statement. She may not directly claim, orally or in writing, that she has been persecuted for reasons of political opinion and may find it difficult to explain the reasons for her persecution.

4.14   Many women are visibly active in conventional political activities such as belonging to political parties or other groups/associations/movements, making speeches, attending demonstrations and writing publications. However women are also directly involved in non-conventional forms of political activity. An activity is rendered political by its context. For example, women may hide people, pass messages or provide community services, food, clothing or medical care. All of these political activities put women at risk of harm on the basis of an actual or imputed political opinion.

4.15   Frequently the penalty for political activity in the broadest sense, whether actual or imputed, will be even more severe for women due to the breach of social and cultural norms which preclude women's involvement.

4.16   'Private' issues commonly associated with women are not inherently less political than those taking place in the 'public' sphere. Conflicts concerning the demarcation of privacy (for example, freedom to choose to wear the veil or not, to have an education or undertake certain work, to be sexually active or not, to choose her partner, to be free from male domination and violence, to exercise reproductive rights and to reject female genital mutilation) are conflicts of a political nature.

4.17   A woman who opposes institutionalised discrimination against women or expresses views of independence from the social or cultural norms of society may sustain or fear harm because of her actual political opinion or a political opinion that has been or will be imputed to her. She is perceived within the established political/social structure as expressing politically antagonistic views through her actions or failure to act. If a woman resists gendered oppression, her resistance is political.

4.18   Where a woman does not directly or intentionally challenge institutionalised norms of behaviour she may nonetheless be imputed (i.e. attributed) with a political opinion. This can be seen, for example, in the characterisation of a raped woman as adulterous, in the social ostracism of an unmarried, separated, divorced, widowed or lesbian woman, and in the politicisation of (unintentional) violations of dress codes.

4.19   A woman may suffer harm on the basis of an imputed (attributed) political opinion as a result of the perception that her political views are aligned with those of dominant family or community members (usually male).

4.20   Claims for asylum which are based on sexual orientation are not fundamentally different from other claims for asylum. It should be noted that in some contexts a woman's fear of persecution for her political activities or opinions, may be exacerbated because her choice of sexual orientation, whether actual or attributed, is used as a pretext for persecution.

Membership of a Particular Social Group

4.21   Most women can be protected within the other Convention grounds, i.e. race, religion, nationality and political opinion, whether actual or imputed. However in some cases gender may be a factor in recognising membership of particular social group or an identifying characteristic of such a group.

4.22   Particular social groups can be identified by reference to innate or unchangeable characteristics that a woman should not be expected to change or cannot change for historical reasons. Examples of such characteristics may include, but are not limited to, sex, age, marital status, family and kinship, past economic status/class, occupational history, disability, sexual history and ethnic, tribal or clan affiliation.

4.23   Whether these factors are unchangeable, depends on the cultural and social context in which the woman lives, as well as the perception of the agents of persecution and those responsible for providing state protection. The important principle to consider is whether the persecution suffered or feared is *for reasons of* membership of a particular social group.

4.24   External perception may be a factor in the identification of a 'particular social group'. Persecutory conduct, whilst not in itself creating a 'particular social group', may constitute evidence of such a perception.

4.25   Family or kin associations may define a particular social group. There are cases where women are persecuted solely because of their family or kinship relationships, for example, a woman may be persecuted as a means of demoralising or punishing members of her family or community, or in order to pressurise her into revealing information.

4.26   The fact that the particular social group consists of large numbers of the female population in the country concerned is *irrelevant* – race, religion, nationality and political opinion are also characteristics that are shared by large numbers of people.

SECTION 5

Procedural and Evidential Issues

5.1   Procedures for refugee determination are critical. These have been modelled on the assumption that refugees are *politically active men* who have been persecuted by the state as a result of those activities. The asylum determination process can be made more responsive to the experiences of women if interviewers and decision-makers are aware of, and respond to, the procedural and evidential difficulties that face women.

Access to the Determination Process

5.2   Some women asylum seekers arrive alone. Others arrive as part of a family unit and are sometimes not interviewed or are cursorily interviewed about their experiences even when it is possible that they, rather than, or as well as, their male relatives, have been persecuted. Male relatives or associates may not raise relevant issues because they are unaware of the details or their importance or are ashamed to report them.

5.3   It is important not to assume that a woman's status is derivative; a woman's claim to refugee status may in some cases be as strong as, or stronger than, that of her male relative or associate.

5.4   Where a woman applies for asylum as a dependant, she should be informed *in private,* and in terms she understands, of her right to make an independent application for asylum at any stage, and should be advised to consult a legal representative before doing so. Adverse inferences about her credibility should not be drawn from any delay in making an application.

5.5   Information provided by a woman must not be disclosed or used for any purpose other than a determination of her own asylum claim without her specific written consent.

Interviews

5.6   If a full interview is considered necessary, it should not take place on arrival.

5.7   The purpose of the interview is to enable a woman to describe her experiences. It is the duty of the interviewer to facilitate this process.

5.8   Women face particular difficulties in making their case to the authorities, especially when they have had experiences that are difficult and/or painful to describe. The interview should be non-confrontational and exploratory. This is critical for the full discussion of experiences relating to a woman's claim.

5.9   Women may be stigmatised by the *assumption* that they have been sexually abused if, for example, they have been arrested, detained or involved in conflict. The stigma associated with sexual violence means some women who have *not* been sexually abused, may be unable or unwilling to describe their experiences.

Finding Out About Women's Experiences

5.10   It is important that the interview room and surrounding environment be conducive to open discussion. There must be sufficient time available and there should be no disturbances. Interviewers and decision-makers should be aware of, and take into account, for example, women's responsibilities as carers, distances to be travelled, issues of privacy, the need to provide refreshments and breaks, and the potentially traumatic effects of interviews.

5.11   Interviewers and decision-makers should be aware that any indication that a woman's claim may not be treated as confidential is likely to seriously hinder her willingness to provide full details of her claim, and may even discourage her from making a claim.

5.12   Post-Traumatic Stress Disorder (PTSD), depressive disorders, trauma, anxiety, shame or anger may affect a woman's ability or willingness to describe her experiences.

5.13   Women from societies where, for example, the preservation of virginity or marital dignity is the cultural norm, may be reluctant to disclose certain information relevant to their asylum claim or that of other members of their family. Women do not necessarily understand the importance of disclosing their experiences, particularly those of sexual violence or abuse. There may be good reasons not to tell, which can range from the fact that it is very hard to do, to the fear that her experiences may become known to others and/or lead to her being ostracised from her family and/or community.

5.14   If it becomes apparent that a woman needs additional support of any kind, for example referral to a rape crisis centre or other specialist service, then the offer of a referral should be made before the determination process is concluded.

Presence of Family Members

5.15   Female victims of violence, discrimination and abuse often do not volunteer information about their experiences and may be particularly reluctant to do so in the presence of family or community members.

5.16   Women should be asked *privately* whether they want to be interviewed outside the hearing of other members of their family, especially male family members and children. Whilst the giving of information is a highly stressful experience for anyone, women may only be able to communicate experiences of sexual abuse or other kinds of harm when family members are not present. Sexual violence in particular may be viewed as a failure on the part of the woman to preserve her virginity or marital dignity.

Interviewers and Interpreters

5.17   Interviewers and decision-makers should appreciate the difficulties inherent in speaking through an interpreter.

5.18   The role of the official interpreter is to interpret truly, accurately, fully, distinctly and audibly using appropriate language and emphasis. It is the duty of the interviewer to ensure that this role is fulfilled.

5.19   A woman who has suffered sexual abuse may be reluctant, or may find it difficult or even impossible to talk about her experiences through a male (or even female) interpreter who is a member of her community.

5.20   Many women have been abused by men. Coupled with a fear and distrust of authorities, this fact is likely to seriously inhibit the capacity of a woman to divulge details of her experiences to a male interviewer or through a male interpreter.

5.21   If a woman is interviewed in connection with her asylum claim, she should have access to a woman interviewer and interpreter.

5.22   Merely being female does not guarantee an awareness of gender issues. Regular training on the issues raised in these Guidelines and interview skills training more generally is essential.

Asking the Right Questions

5.23   Interviewers should familiarise themselves with the status and roles of women in the country from which a woman has fled and should refer to paragraphs 5.43 and 5.44 for further information.

5.24   The information revealed during the course of the interview may reflect the ways in which questions are asked. Unless the right questions are asked it is unlikely that a woman will be able to describe her experiences.

5.25   For example, interviewers should not focus their questions on political activities narrowly defined. Political activities also include, *but are not limited to*, community activism, providing food or shelter, message taking, hiding people or refusing to conform to particular social norms. Women may also have a different perception of torture, which may not equate with the types of harm they fear, for example sexual violence, violence within the family, marriage-related harm, female genital mutilation and forced abortion and sterilisation.

2.26   Non-confrontational open and/or indirect questions should be asked in order to establish a woman's reasons for fleeing.

2.27   More direct follow-up questions should be asked to ascertain details of the woman's full experiences. Depending on what a woman says, the following types of questions may be of assistance:

- Why did you leave your country?
- Did you have any problems?
- Were you treated badly?
- Was anyone you know treated badly?
- Why did you think this happened?
- Who was responsible?
- How did you feel?
- What difficulties did these experiences cause you?
- Did you complain to the authorities? If not, why not?
- What would happen to you if you were to return to your country?

This is *not* a prescriptive or sequential list. Interviewers must consider relevant follow-up questions. For example:

- What else happened to you?

Culturally Sensitive Communication

5.28   The failure to appreciate cross-cultural differences may jeopardise the quality of the information revealed by a woman and prevent an effective interview taking place.

5.29   Women may find it difficult to recall painful or sensitive events. Active listening skills play an important part in the flow of the interview. These include:

- Reflective listening (i.e. paraphrasing what has been said by the woman);
- Not talking at the same time as the woman;
- Not making judgmental comments;
- Maintaining composure if the woman gets angry or upset;
- Ensuring minimum interruptions and/or distractions;
- Ensuring the interpreting is an accurate reflection of the woman's testimony (e.g. relative length of translation, reaction from the woman) .

5.30   Body language can be interpreted in many different ways. It is important that interviewers ensure they avoid gestures which may be perceived as intimidating or culturally insensitive or inappropriate and inhibiting.

5.31   Interviewers and decision-makers should be aware that cultural and other differences and trauma play an important role in determining demeanour i.e. how a woman presents herself physically, for example, whether she maintains eye contact, shifts her posture or hesitates when speaking.

5.32   The level and type of emotion displayed by a woman during the recounting of her experiences should not adversely affect her credibility. A lack of displayed emotion does not necessarily mean that the woman is not distressed or deeply affected by what has happened.

Credibility

5.33   Many women face additional problems in demonstrating that their claims are credible.

5.34   A woman's priority is to achieve safety for herself and/or family members. She may not claim asylum whilst she is able to achieve safety, however temporary or illusory, through another means, whether legal or illegal. This may account for the delay in claiming asylum and should not negatively affect credibility.

5.35   An inability to provide information relevant to a claim should not of itself undermine credibility. In many cultures men do not share information about their political, military or even social activities with their female relatives. Gaps in a woman's knowledge should not be construed as lack of credibility.

5.36   When two or more people give an account it is inevitable that differences occur due to recall, emphasis and perspective. This should not necessarily be interpreted as indicating that they are not giving accurate accounts of their experiences.

5.37   Women in particular may not be forthcoming with full information about their experiences if gender-sensitive interviewing procedures are not followed.

5.38   Torture and other persecutory treatment can produce a profound shame response. Humiliation and shame are often desired goals of the perpetrator. This shame response may be a major obstacle to disclosure. Experience has shown, for example, that incidents of sexual abuse may not come to light for months or even years.

5.39   Delay in submitting the application, or in giving a full account of experiences after the initial application, or once a claim has been refused, should not of itself undermine the credibility of a woman's application.

Evidence

5.40   Where human rights reports indicate that a risk of harm exists, a genuine fear of persecution in a country is likely to be well-founded. Conversely, the absence of information should not necessarily be taken as an indicator that human rights abuses do not occur.

5.41   Information to support a woman's claim may not be readily available. Women's experiences of persecution frequently differ from those of men and they may be unable to document their experiences. For example, they may not be able to provide membership cards or newspaper cuttings relating to their political involvement because they have been indirectly involved through a supporting role or because the political opinion has been imputed to them. Similarly, information about violence within the family or community may be difficult to find.

5.42   Background reports and country information often lack analysis of the position and status of women. Statistical data on the incidence of sexual or other violence is often inadequate or lacking.

Documentary Evidence and Country Reports

5.43   Interviewers and decision-makers should familiarise themselves with the role, status and treatment of women in the country from which a woman has fled. It is essential to consider a number of issues when gathering information. These include, *but are not limited to*:

- *Position of women before the law* including their standing in court, the right to bring a complaint and give evidence, divorce and custody law, the right to own property, reproductive rights, freedom to travel, and the political, social and economic rights referred to below;

- *Political rights of women* including the right to vote, to hold office and belong to a political party;
- *Social and economic rights of women* including the right to marry the person of their choice, the right not to marry and the right to divorce, the right to determine their own sexuality, the right to an education, a career, and a job or remunerated activities, the status of single women, widows or divorcees, and freedom of dress;
- *Consequences for women who refuse to abide by or who challenge social, religious or cultural norms regarding their behaviour* including, for example, norms regarding virginity and pre- or extra-marital sex or pregnancy, norms around the institution of the family including arranged marriages and divorce, and norms about behaviour and dress;
- *Incidence and form of violence against women* and the forms it takes (such as, *but not limited to,* violence within the family, sexual abuse, honour killings, bride burning);
- *Efficacy of protection available to women* and the sanctions or penalties on those who perpetrate the violence;
- *Consequences that may befall a woman on her return.*

5.44   Where it is difficult to obtain evidence relevant to a woman's claim, interviewers and decision-makers should consider:

- Researching the position of women in countries of origin from articles, newspapers, studies and reports, including those published by government departments, inter-governmental organisations, non-governmental organisations, women's and community organisations;
- Accessing on-line information available on the Internet or sources such as the UNHCR's RefWorld on CD-Rom;
- Contacting specialists and experts (whether in the UK or elsewhere) who are familiar with the region and/or the gender issues involved.

Medical and Other Evidence

5.45   If an interviewer or decision-maker receives medical, psychological, professional or other related expert evidence at any stage, it should be considered with care and assessed impartially.

5.46   It should be noted that there is frequently no physical evidence in cases involving rape or sexual violence. In addition interviewers and decision-makers should be aware that torturers and abusers often choose methods precisely because they do not leave marks.

The Standard of Proof

5.47   An asylum seeker has to show a 'reasonable degree of likelihood' that she will be persecuted if removed from the UK. This standard of proof is in recognition of the difficulties asylum seekers face in proving their claim and the serious consequences of a wrong decision.

5.48   An assessment as to whether the fear of persecution is well-founded should not simply be based on general conditions in her country of origin but should take into account the particular experiences of women. An assessment should also be made of the claimant's particular fear and of whether any changes in country conditions are meaningful and effective enough for her fear of persecution to be no longer well-founded.

5.49   A change in country circumstances, generally viewed as a positive change, may have no impact, or even a negative impact, on a woman's fear of persecution.

5.50   In many cases harm occurs at the hands of non-state agents (which includes family and community members) whose actions are ignored or condoned by the authorities. Notwithstanding that changes may have occurred, such agents of persecution are seldom brought to justice and there is no accountability by the state for the acts of persecution inflicted on the woman.

5.51   For some women the risk of return may be even greater than for their male counterparts, for example, because of the authorities' and societies' attitude towards women travelling alone.

The Implementation of Guidelines

'UNHCR endorses the principle of gender specific guidelines and recognises the need for such guidelines in the UK. We congratulate the RWLG on compiling such a quality document.'
Hope Hanlan
Representative of the United Nations High Commissioner for Refugees
May 1998

'State parties to the 1951 Refugee Convention are urged to adopt guidelines with respect to gender-related asylum claims.'
Report of the UN Special Rapporteur on Violence against Women
26th January 1998

Calls for the adoption of guidelines with respect to women's asylum claims have also been made by the UN Division for the Advancement of Women (9–12 November 1997). The UN Platform for Action (1995) similarly supports and promotes efforts by states towards the development and application of gender guidelines.[1]

In October 1996 the UK Immigration Appeal Tribunal (IAT) held that gender guidelines 'ensure that vital issues are objectively canvassed in weighing refugee claims where gender is a factor.'[2]

The principle of gender guidelines for the determination of asylum claims in the UK has been advocated and endorsed by a wide spectrum of individuals and organisations including women's organisations, refugee community groups, non-governmental organisations, local authorities, health practitioners, judges, academics and legal practitioners as well as UNHCR.

Simply making women visible is not enough, rather an entirely different approach is needed. Guidelines are a beginning not an end, a process rather than a product. These Guidelines are only a first step towards ensuring that women are able to benefit equitably from protection under the Refugee Convention.

These Guidelines are founded upon the body of experience of women asylum seekers and refugees, refugee community groups, legal practitioners and academics. *We call upon the United Kingdom government to adopt and apply these Guidelines immediately.*

---

1   See for example Article 147.
2   *Gimhedin (Almaz Woldu) v SSHD*, 21 October 1996 (14019) unreported.

Appendix 4

ADIMA *GUIDELINES ON GENDER ISSUES FOR DECISION-MAKERS* (AUSTRALIA) (July 1996)

1 INTRODUCTION

1.1   These guidelines have been developed to help officers in assessing gender based claims by applicants for protection visas in Australia or entry to Australia under the offshore Humanitarian Programme. The purpose of these guidelines is to ensure that applications are dealt with effectively and sensitively.

1.2   In recognising that women may experience persecution and discrimination differently from men, the guidelines provide advice on how decision makers can best approach claims of gender-based persecution. It should be noted that claims of gender based persecution can be made by both men and women. However, the feminine pronoun is used in relation to the applicant throughout the guidelines in recognition of the fact that most gender-based claims are made by female applicants.

1.3   The guidelines provide practical guidance on procedural issues which can influence women applicants and which may affect their ability to present their claims, for example, in relation to receiving applications, managing interviews and ensuring confidentiality of information. They also offer assistance with the interpretation of the regulatory requirements of the various protection, refugee and humanitarian visa classes as they relate to claims put forward by applicants with gender-based claims, with the aim of ensuring that the assessment process is sensitive to gender issues.

1.4   The information provided in this guide should be read in the context of the Department's broader guidelines on refugee and humanitarian decision-making:

- for applications in Australia for protection visa: *Onshore Refugee Procedures Manual,* relevant chapters of the *Procedures Advice Manual (PAM III),* including the *Refugee Law Guidelines;*
- for applications under the offshore Humanitarian Programme: relevant chapters of *the Procedures Advice Manual (PAM III),* including the *Generic Guidelines B Offshore Humanitarian Visas.*

1.5   This document aims to give decision makers an additional level of understanding of the particular needs of women within existing policy frameworks for refugee and humanitarian applications; as such, it does not replace other relevant policy advice, but is intended to complement it.

1.6   These guidelines are designed to apply to officers in Australia and at overseas posts. Accordingly, they acknowledge that often different operational decision making environments exist. The advice contained in these guidelines should be adopted as far as practicable.

2 BACKGROUND

The international protection framework

2.1   The international community's response to refugees is based on the *1951 Convention and 1967 Protocol relating to the law of Refugees* (Refugee Convention) and the principle of non-refoulement. The United Nations High Commissioner for Refugees (UNHCR) is the international body that is responsible for providing international protection to refugees and promoting lasting solutions to their plight.

2.2   There are a number of international instruments in which obligations to protect the human rights of women, including refugee women, may be found. They include:

> *Universal Declaration of Human Rights* (UDHR)
> *International Covenant on CIWI and Political Rights (ICCPR)*
> *International Covenant on Economic, Social and Cultural Rights* (ICESCR)
> *Convention Against Torture and Other Cruel, Inhuman or Degrading Treatment or Punishment (CAT)*
> *Convention on the Elimination of all Forms of Racial Discrimination (CERD)*
> *Convention on the Elimination of all Forms of Discrimination Against Women* (CEDAW)
> *Convention on the Rights of the Child* (CROC)
> *Convention on Consent to Marriage, Minimum Age for Marriage and Registration of Marriages*
> *Convention on the Nationality of married Women*
> *1949 Geneva Conventions on the Laws of War and the two Additional Protocols of 1977*
> *Declaration on the Protection of Women and Children in Emergency and Armed Conflict*
> *Declaration on the Elimination of Violence Against Women*

2.3   The international community has devoted a considerable amount of effort and resources to refugees and displaced people. As a result there now exists a complex, if at times fragile, network of institutions, laws and agreements specifically designed to meet the needs of people who have been forced to leave their homeland. Refugee protection has thus taken a number of forms:

- admission to safety in the country of asylum and observance of the fundamental principle of non-refoulement;
- temporary protection until a lasting solution may be found – this may be (in order of preference) voluntary repatriation, local integration or resettlement in a third country; and
- the development of new strategies on prevention which are designed to address the causes as well as the consequences of forced displacement.

There is also an awareness in the international community that lasting solutions to the problem of human displacement will only be found if a concerted effort is made to protect human rights.

2.4   Recently there has been an increasing awareness and focus on the particular vulnerability of refugee and displaced women.

Recognising the needs of refugee and displaced women

2.5   Women compose the majority of people in vulnerable situations because they have been displaced or are refugees. UNHCR indicate that of an estimated 27 million refugees and displaced people in the world, the vast majority are women and children. Women are often particularly vulnerable – after fleeing persecution and violence they may face new threats of violence and abuse in their country of asylum. In addition, due to social and cultural mores they may not necessarily have the same remedies for state protection as men, or the same opportunities for flight.

2.6   The issue of gender persecution and problems facing women asylum seekers have received attention from the Executive Committee of the United Nations High Commissioner for Refugees' Programme (EXCOM), UNHCR and some governments. UNHCR adopted *Guidelines on the Protection of Refugee Women* in 1991. A number of EXCOM Conclusions have been adopted recommending the development of appropriate guidelines, culminating in 1995 with EXCOM's recommendation that:

> 'In accordance with the principle that women's rights are human rights, these guidelines should recognise as refugees women whose claim to refugee status is based upon well-founded fear of persecution for reasons enumerated in the 1951 Convention and 1967 Protocol, including persecution through sexual violence or other gender-related persecution.'

2.7   International concerns regarding the plight of refugee women have not been confined to the mechanisms surrounding refugee protection. The 1995 World Conference of Women in Beijing drew attention to the violation of women's human rights experienced by refugee women and recommended the development of gender guidelines. The development of this document should be seen in this international context.

Australia's response

2.8   Australia accords a high priority to the promotion and protection of human rights in the international sphere. Australia also has a long-standing commitment to assist international efforts to prevent and alleviate humanitarian crises through diplomatic initiatives, participation in peace-keeping forces, aid, resettlement of refugees and other humanitarian cases through the offshore Humanitarian Programme and the granting of permanent residence to individuals who have been found in need of protection in Australia in accordance with our international obligations under the Refugee Convention.

2.9   Persons requiring resettlement from overseas may apply under the offshore Humanitarian Programme, which is subdivided into the Refugee component, the Special Humanitarian Programme and the Special Assistance Category. Australia has historically recognised some special needs of women via the Woman at Risk visa subclass of the Refugee component, which is specifically targeted at woman refugees or women registered as 'of concern' to the UNHCR who are in danger of victimisation, harassment or serious abuse because of their sex. In addition, overseas staff of the Department who will be assessing applications under the offshore Humanitarian Programme receive cross-cultural and gender sensitivity training prior to taking up their positions overseas. In terms of the processing of applications by women for protection visas in Australia, officers have also received training in cultural and gender sensitisation.

2.10   Whilst women represent the majority of refugees worldwide, they represent a smaller proportion of the refugees who are resettled in Australia under the offshore Humanitarian Programme or granted protection visas in Australia. This may be a result of many factors, including women's inability or lack of resources to travel unaccompanied or the tendency of applications to be made by the male head of the household. Nonetheless, women's vulnerability remains.

2.11   Guidelines for officers which specifically address women's needs are important if women's claims of persecution, including gender-based persecution, are to be properly heard and assessed. When applying for humanitarian visas, women may face particular problems, such as difficulties in making their case to decision makers, especially when they have had experiences which are difficult and painful to describe. There may also be social and cultural barriers to lodging applications and/or pursuing claims related to their own experiences. For example: in families where the male head of household seeks asylum, claims relating to female members of the family unit may not be mentioned, may be ignored or may not be given any weight by either the male head of household, or the decision maker, or the female applicant herself.

2.12   Barriers to accessing the refugee and humanitarian visa system and the failure to fully explore women's claims can be compounded by difficulties in gaining recognition of the particular forms of persecution or discrimination manifested against women.

2.13   Guidelines for decision makers which focus on these gender-related issues assist in promoting a consistent, sensitive approach to women's claims. They are also consistent with international practice and meet the Government's objectives to provide equitable and accessible services.

2.14   The following chapters focus on two main areas where women may face difficulty in gaining recognition of their claims for protection:

• procedural issues; and
• the assessment of claims.

   Focusing attention on gender-related persecution/discrimination will ensure that officers are conscious of forms of harm that may be inflicted on a woman uniquely or more commonly than on a man.

2.15   It should be noted that these guidelines do not advocate gender as an additional ground in the Refugee Convention definition. However, it should be accepted that gender can influence or dictate the type of persecution or harm suffered and the reasons for this treatment. Even where gender is not the central issue, giving conscious consideration to gender-related aspects of a case will assist officers to understand the totality of the environment from which an applicant claims a fear of persecution or abuse of their human rights.

3   PROCEDURES

3.1   The following procedures are primarily focused on women applicants for protection visas in Australia and women applicants applying under the offshore Humanitarian Programme. They may also be applied to male applicants who make claims of gender based persecution. While procedures differ between Australia and overseas posts, reflecting the different criteria for each visa class and decision making environments, there are common elements that can be applied by officers required to examine and process visa applications, regardless of the particular visa class applied for.

3.2   The procedures outlined below should, nonetheless, be read in conjunction with the other instructions relating to specific visa classes. For example, applications for entry into Australian under the offshore Humanitarian Programme should be considered with regard to the *Generic Guidelines B2: Offshore Humanitarian Visas* and guidelines on specific visa classes and subclasses; applications lodged in Australia for protection visas should be considered with regard to the *Onshore Refugee Procedures Manual* and the *Refugee Law Guidelines*.

Preparing the case

Researching Claims

3.3   Adequate research of the claims made in the application and an understanding of the situation in the country of origin of the applicant is important for the full exploration of a person's claims. Where gender related claims are raised, or suspected, an understanding of the role, status and treatment of women in the country of origin is particularly important. Adequate preparation allows a relationship of confidence and trust with the applicant to be developed and allows an interviewer to ask the right questions and deal with any problems that arise during an interview.

Sources of Information

3.4   There are a variety of sources of information available, depending on the location of the decision maker. Officers in Australia have access to the online information databases of the Country Information Service Section of the Department (CISNET). Officers at overseas posts have access to a variety of local sources, including Department of Foreign Affairs and Trade officers, UNHCR and access to CISNET on CD-ROM.

3.5   The types of information which may be relevant in assessing gender-related claims are often similar to that relevant for other types of claims. However, research should also focus on the following areas:

- legal, economic and civil status of women in the country of origin
- the incidence of violence against women in the country of origin, including both sexual and domestic, and the adequacy of state protection afforded to women
- cultural and social mores of the country with respect to such issues as the role and status of women, the family, nature of family relationships, attitudes towards same-sex relationships, attitudes to 'foreign' influences, etc
- respect for and adherence to fundamental human rights including the differential application of human rights for women issues directly related to claims raised in the application

3.6   It should be noted that violence against women, particularly sexual or domestic violence, tends to be largely under-reported or ignored in many countries.

The absence of information on the above topics for any particular country should not necessarily be taken as an indicator that abuses of women's human rights do not occur.

3.7   Identifying these issues will enable an officer to become aware of the cultural sensitivities and differences in a particular country before considering the applicant's claims.

Using the Information

3.8   When assessing a woman's claims of well-founded fear of persecution (for the protection visa class and refugee visa subclasses), the evidence must show that what the woman applicant genuinely fears is persecution for a Convention reason as distinguished from random violence or criminal activity perpetrated against her as an individual. The general human rights record of the country of origin, and the experiences of other women in a similar situation, may indicate the existence of systematic persecution for a Convention reason.

- A more detailed examination of assessing claims and facts against the refugee definition can be found in Part 4 'The Assessment of the Claims', the *Onshore Refugee Procedures Manual, Refugee Law Guidelines* and in *PAM3 Generic Guidelines B2 – Offshore Humanitarian Visas*.

- Only the refugee subclasses of the offshore Humanitarian Programme (subclasses 200, 201, 203 and 204) require applicants to demonstrate that they are subject to persecution (ie for a Convention reason). The other visa classes and subclasses of the offshore Humanitarian Programme refer to criteria where applicants are subject to 'substantial discrimination' or who are in vulnerable situations. Policy advice for interpreting these criteria may be found in *PAM3 Generic Guidelines B2 – Offshore Humanitarian Visas* and the PAM3 guidelines on specific visa classes.

Interviews

3.9   The objective of an interview is to obtain further information from the applicant on her claims and to clarify any details that are uncertain or ambiguous in the application. Interviewing officers should seek to clarify all matters material to the final outcome of the application.

3.10   It is important to identify the person included in an application who has the strongest claims. An application written by, or an interview with, a male head of household may place little or no emphasis on a female family unit member's experience of persecution or discrimination, even though her experiences may carry the most weight. A woman who is included in the application as a member of a family unit should be given the opportunity of a separate interview so that she is able, with appropriate assurances of confidentiality, to outline her experiences.

Interview Process

3.11   Interviewing a woman who has/or may come forward with gender-related claims must be done in a sensitive and sympathetic way, with respect for confidentiality.

3.12   Many women face particular difficulties when discussing gender-related claims which may include rape, or other forms of sexual violence, domestic violence and discrimination. In particular, women may experience difficulty in recounting sexual torture or rape in front of family members. Some women, because of the shame they may feel over what has happened to them, may understandably be reluctant to identify the true extent of persecution they have suffered because of their continuing fear and distrust of people in authority. They may also be afraid to reveal their experiences because they are so traumatised by them or because they fear reprisals from their family and/or community. Female applicants who are survivors of torture and trauma, in particular, require a supportive environment where they can be reassured of the confidentiality of the gender-sensitive claims they are making.

3.13   Officers should be aware that female victims of violence, discrimination and abuse often do not volunteer information about their experiences and may be reluctant to do so in the presence of family members. In particular, during interviews where an interpreter is used, a woman applicant may be reluctant to divulge information for fear that the interpreter may be an informer for the authorities in the country of origin or that they will divulge their story to others in the community. The applicant should be assured of the confidential nature of the interview process.

> In the vast majority of cases women who have experienced torture and/or trauma have suffered these abuses at the hands of men. Coupled with a fear and distrust of authorities, this fact is likely to seriously inhibit the capacity of a female applicant to divulge details of her experiences to a male interviewer.

3.14   It will be a matter of the officer having prior appreciation of women's issues in the country of origin, skilful and sensitive interviewing and an understanding of the psychological effects of torture and trauma that will assist these issues to come forward.

Physical environment

3.15   In order to facilitate discussion of gender-related claims it is important that the interview room and surrounding environment be conducive to open discussion. The interview room should be arranged in such a way as to encourage discussion of the claims, promote confidentiality and to lessen any possibility of perceived power imbalances.

Use of Interpreter

3.16   Before scheduling the interview, ensure that appropriate arrangements have been made for interpreters who are sensitive to any special requirements of the applicant regarding language, dialect or ethno-cultural sensitivities. If an applicant has made claims of a sensitive or traumatic nature every effort should be made to ensure an interpreter and interviewing officer of the same sex.

3.17   Where an officer suspects, as a result of researching the country information relating to the case, that gender-related claims may be raised or discussed, every effort should be made to engage an interpreter of the same sex, with regard to any cultural or religious sensitivities, wherever possible.

3.18   During the interview, both the interviewer and interpreter should be aware of the possible difficulties in interpreting particular words, such as 'rape' or 'assault', which may have different meanings or connotations in the applicant's language.

Establishing rapport

3.19   Establishing good rapport with an applicant is very important and begins with the first contact. At the interview, the interviewer should take the time to introduce him/herself and the interpreter, explain clearly what his/her role is and the exact purpose of the interview. The applicant should be assured that her claims will be treated in an absolutely confidential manner.

3.20   Officers should behave in a culturally and gender sensitive manner throughout the interview. It is essential that the interviewer remain neutral, compassionate and objective during the interview.

3.21   However, it should be remembered that no matter how supportive the interviewing officer and the environment may be, the interview process (because of the imbalance of power between participants) will impact on how women may respond.

Culturally sensitive communication

3.22   Officers are required to deal with a wide range of people and as such they should have a well developed understanding of cultural differences, especially in relation to the way they communicate with others.

3.23   Body language can be interpreted in many different ways. It is therefore important that officers ensure they avoid gestures which may be perceived as intimidating or culturally insensitive or inappropriate. Whilst it is important that officers maintain control of the interview, it is also important to ensure that body language does not inhibit the discussion by making the applicant feel uncomfortable.

3.24   Similarly, an approach which is too relaxed may create the impression that the officer is not listening. The officer should allow the applicant to present her claims with minimal interruption.

Active listening skills play an important part in the flow of the interview and can assist an applicant who may be finding it difficult to recall painful or sensitive events associated with her claims.

3.25   Being aware of cultural sensitivities during the interview may provide the applicant with reassurance. As with most interviews this can most appropriately be demonstrated by attentive listening, including the following:

- reflective listening (ie paraphrasing what has been said by the applicant)

- not talking at the same time as the applicant not making judgemental comments
- maintaining composure if the applicant gets angry or upset
- nodding affirmatively when appropriate
- ensuring minimum interruptions and/or distractions
- ensuring the interpreting is an accurate reflection of the applicant's testimony (eg relative length of translation, reaction from the applicant)

3.26   If an officer feels that a female applicant has further claims of a sensitive nature that have not been discussed during any stage of the interviewing process, the applicant should be encouraged to provide any supplementary information that she feels may support her claims. Alternatively, if an applicant has difficulty in speaking about her persecution, she may be more comfortable putting her claims in writing.

Assessing and handling information

Credibility/Demeanour

3.27   In many societies the stigma attached to victims of sexual assault are such that women cannot bring themselves to discuss such events. In addition, the effects of abuse and trauma may make it difficult for a woman to accurately recall the details and dates of the events when they finally recount their experiences. It may be that a woman is either unable to discuss a particular experience or may not see its relevance to her claims. It is also unlikely that a woman whose written claims are part of an application supplied by other members of her family unit or who is interviewed in the presence of other family members will discuss the circumstances surrounding a sexual assault.

> The fact that a woman failed to raise a gender-related claim of persecution on several occasions should not necessarily cast doubt on her credibility if it is raised at a later date and should not be responded to as if it does. The pertinent issue, of course, is whether or not the claimed event occurred and, in the protection visa class and refugee visa subclasses, whether it was for a Convention reason.

3.28   If such claims are revealed separately from the rest of the family, officers must treat the information provided with great care. This is particularly necessary if the woman has indicated that other members of the family are unaware of her experiences. In some cultures rape and other forms of sexual assault are seen as the woman's failing to preserve her virginity or marital dignity – disclosure of this information to family members may have adverse consequences to the applicant.

3.29   Similarly, the level of emotional distress exhibited by a female applicant during the recounting of her experiences should not automatically add more credibility to her claims than that of another who may be very calm and quiet when describing a similar event. A lack of emotion displayed at interview does not necessarily mean that the applicant is not distressed or deeply affected by what has happened. Cultural differences and trauma can often play an important role in determining demeanor.

3.30   In some circumstances, it may be reasonable to seek, and accept, objective psychological evidence. It is unnecessary to establish the precise details of the sexual assault as opposed to the fact of its occurrence and the motivation of the perpetrator. In some circumstances it should be noted that a woman may not be aware of the reasons for her abuse.

Confidentiality

3.31   Any applicant who has provided gender-related claims should be reassured that the details will not be provided, in any form, to another member of their family unit. All information both written and audio taped should be marked *'Not for release to anyone except with the agreement of the applicant'*.

3.32 All confidential information provided by female applicants, particularly that of a gender-sensitive nature, is protected under the *Freedom of Information Act*. The only circumstances in which another member of a family unit can obtain access to the gender related claims (or indeed any claims) made by a female member of their family is with the written consent of the female applicant concerned.

3.33 If a visa is refused, some applicants who have provided gender-sensitive claims may wish to personally collect their notification letter and copy of the decision record, or nominate a separate address for the letter to be sent. These issues should be discussed with the applicant at the interview stage.

4 THE ASSESSMENT OF CLAIMS

4.1 The following section provides guidance for officers assessing applications for protection visas and applications for entry to Australia, under the offshore Humanitarian Programme, as a refugee (ie under visa class 866 and subclasses 200, 201, 203 and 204). These types of applications centre on the definition of 'refugee' in the *1951 Convention* and *1967 Protocol relating to the Status of Refugees* (Refugee Convention).

- Women outside Australia who are refugees or who are registered as being of concern to UNHCR may also be eligible for entry to Australia under the Woman at Risk (WR) 204 visa subclass of the offshore Humanitarian Programme. This visa reflects Australia's response to the circumstances of certain women outside their home country who are in danger of victimisation, harassment or serious abuse because of their gender. Further policy advice in deciding applications of this visa subclass can be found in *PAM3 Schedule 2 – Permanent Visa (Migrant) Woman At Risk – Visa 204*.

- Under the offshore Humanitarian Programme, applicants who meet the Refugee Convention definition of a refugee must also satisfy the other criteria of the visa subclass before they may be granted a visa.

- Officers should also refer to other sources of guidance for processing these applications, including: *Onshore Refugee Procedures Manual; Refugee Law Guidelines; PAM Generic Guidelines B2: Offshore Humanitarian Visas*.

4.2 The non-refugee components of the offshore Humanitarian Programme (the Special Humanitarian and Special Assistance Categories) are designed for people who do not meet refugee criteria but who, nonetheless:

- are subject to substantial discrimination amounting to serious human rights violations and for whom resettlement in Australia is the appropriate solution; or
- are suffering some form of disadvantage or hardship meriting a humanitarian response and who have close links to Australia.

Although discrimination, disadvantage and hardship constitute lesser tests than persecution, assessment of applications for these visas will also involve an examination of the human rights environment in an applicant's country of origin. Officers should be aware that women may experience not only persecution but also discrimination, disadvantage or hardship in a manner qualitatively different from men as a result of their gender.

The Refugee Convention is intended to provide protection to persons who have a well founded fear of being persecuted on specified grounds. Recognising that treatment or discrimination amounts to persecution is the first step. An officer must also be satisfied that this fear of persecution is 'well-founded' and that it is 'for reasons of' a Convention ground.

Persecution and gender-related persecution

4.3   The types of persecution inflicted on individuals may differ because of their gender. It is important to bear in mind that gender-based persecution is only one of many types of persecution a woman may encounter.

- Accordingly, officers must carefully consider all general claims of persecution before turning to consider gender-related claims, otherwise there is the possibility that a woman's claims of persecution unrelated to gender will be ignored.
  - this will also avoid unnecessary retraumatisation of applicants over their experiences related to sexual violence.

4.4   The process of identifying every abuse of human rights against internationally agreed standards of human rights (the human rights protected in the International Bill of Human Rights which includes the UDHR, ICCPR and ICESCR – see 2.2 above) should allow a decision-maker to properly consider all serious forms of harm a person may face, including those harms that are gender-based.

- the further step of focusing on gender-based persecution will ensure that officers are conscious of forms of harm that may be inflicted on a woman uniquely or more commonly than on a man.
- this emphasis on gender-related persecution, combined with the appropriate techniques and awareness, may assist a decision-maker to elicit such claims which would otherwise have remained untouched.

  Increased emphasis on the role of gender in persecution is not intended to alter the ordinary meaning of persecution. Rather it is intended to ensure that all of the applicant's claims of persecution are fully considered.

4.5   Australian case law has referred to internationally agreed standards of human rights in recognising persecution. Whilst there are areas of uncertainty, it can generally be stated that the more fundamental the right threatened, the more likely that the breach of that right amounts to persecution.

Persecution by torture or cruel, inhuman or degrading punishment or treatment

4.6   Rape and other forms of sexual assault are acts which inflict severe pain and suffering (both mental and physical) and which have been used by many persecutors. Such treatment clearly comes within the bounds of torture as defined by the Convention Against Torture (CAT). Furthermore, sexual violence amounts to a violation of the prohibition against cruel, inhuman or degrading treatment, the right to security of person and in some instances the right to life, as contained in a variety of international instruments. There are many other types of treatment that are specific to women, such as female genital mutilation and forced abortion, that also constitute cruel, inhuman or degrading treatment.

4.7   Rape is often used to punish a woman for her actions or to encourage her to put pressure on others whose activities meet with State disapproval. Systematic rape has also been used as part of 'ethnic cleansing'.

4.8   It should also be remembered that in many nations victims of sexual assault become outcasts or are considered to have committed a criminal offence. This fact can be part of the persecutor's motivation in choosing this form of persecution.

Restrictions imposed by legal, social or religious mores

4.9   The status of women in some societies may be restricted and dictated by legal, social or religious mores. The restrictions will vary from mere inconvenience to oppression. In addition a broad range of penalties may be imposed for disobeying restrictions placed on women. Officers should carefully assess the available country of origin information on those issues.

Possible persecution by violation of thought, conscience and religion

4.10   Gender-based persecution is sometimes more subtle than other forms. It can take the form of restrictions on the way a woman behaves or it can involve forcing her to act in a certain way. It may affect a woman's ability to participate in the public life of a society.

Some examples of gender-based treatment against women which may constitute persecution in particular circumstances are:

- social oppression of women – in some communities the status and behaviour of women has been dictated by a State sanctioned religious hierarchy
- denial of participation by women in the political, civil or economic life
- forced marriage – many societies practice arranged marriage and this in itself may not be a persecutory practice. However, the consequences of defying the wishes of one's family when viewed against the background of the State's failure to protect a person should be carefully considered
- infanticide, forced abortion, female genital mutilation, which has serious impact on a woman's physical and mental health.

Agents of persecution

4.11   A Convention refugee is someone who is at risk because their country of nationality has failed to protect them from persecution. A failure to protect can occur in several ways. It may be that the authorities are themselves the perpetrators of the persecution. However, it may be that the persecutor is another party from whom the authorities do not protect the person either because they are unwilling or unable to do so. Claims of gender-based persecution often involve persecution committed by non-state agents.

In assessing gender-based persecution it is important to research the accepted norms of the relevant societies to determine how they operate both through legislation and in terms of actual practice in order to determine the degree of protection available to women.

4.12   In some societies, particular types of violence against women may be officially condemned or even illegal but in fact be so endemic that local authorities turn a blind eye to its occurrence. Sometimes these forms of abuse are systemic or culturally acceptable so that local authorities may actively participate or be complicit in the harms suffered.

4.13   It is important to remember that the international protection of the Refugee Convention is only available to those who are not able to gain protection from their national authorities. Where a non-state agent of persecution is involved there is a need to establish that the state is 'unwilling or unable' to protect the applicant. Clearly, this is established if the authorities were aware of a person's need for protection (either because of her approach or by some other means) and none was forthcoming.

4.14   It should also be noted that it is not always reasonable or possible for a woman to alert the authorities to her need for protection. State protection should be effective – with provision of mechanisms for dealing with complaints and also assurance that such avenues for redress are realistic and accessible to a woman of her culture and position.

- Officers should investigate why a woman did not seek the protection of the state, as her inability to even request protection may in itself be indicative of a failure of state protection.

Cumulative grounds

4.15   An applicant may put forward accounts of different types of harm, none of which, taken individually, will amount to persecution. In these cases it is necessary to consider the cumulative effect of the individual instances of harm.

4.16   This principle is not gender specific. However, the forms of harm directed against women may be more various and more subtle. This may reflect the fact that the woman may not be the primary focus of the persecutory behaviour, which may be directed primarily at male family members.

Well-founded fear

Past Persecution and the 'changed circumstances' test

4.17   There are two ways that a well-founded fear of persecution can be established:

- there is a 'real chance' of future persecution; or
- a person has been persecuted in the past and the 'changed circumstances' test (set down by the High Court in *Chan* has not been satisfied.

4.18   There is a significant difference between the two. A person who has suffered persecution in the past does not have to prove that there is a 'real chance' of future persecution. Rather, a continuing well-founded fear of persecution should be accepted unless the officer can establish that there has been a substantial and material change in circumstances in the country of origin.

4.19   The application of the 'changed circumstances' test must be carefully applied in cases of gender-related persecution. The subjective state of mind of the applicant has obvious implications for gender-related persecution, especially in cases of sexual assault, where the effects on the victim are long lasting. In addition, an overall understanding of the role and perception of women in the applicant's society will demonstrate the extent of the persecution a woman would face if she were to return.

4.20   Officers must also carefully consider what circumstances, if any, would satisfy the 'changed circumstances' test in cases of gender-related persecution. Many cases of gender-based persecution occur at the hands of non-state agents of persecution whose actions are ignored or condoned by the authorities. Even where changes in the national legislation or other state of affairs have occurred, such agents of persecution are seldom brought to justice and there is no accountability by the state for the acts of persecution inflicted on the applicant.

Relocation

4.21   An important consideration in gender-related persecution, as with other persecution, is whether the persecution occurs nationwide or whether it is regionalised. It may be for example that a person is able to access protection in urbanised parts of the country where there is a real chance of persecution in the rural areas. If so, officers should consider whether the applicant could reasonably be expected to relocate within her own country.

In considering the issue of relocation the relevant issue is whether the applicant could safely live in another part of the country. Officers must carefully consider gender-related issues when applying this test. Financial, logistical, social, cultural and other barriers to reaching internal safety may significantly affect persons of one gender over another. In addition, gender bases persecution may be systemic and no protection may be available from the authorities in any part of the country.

Convention grounds

4.22   There are five Convention grounds: race, religion, nationality, membership of a particular social group and political opinion. In addition to actual membership of a Convention ground, a well-founded fear of persecution may be for reasons of an *imputed* Convention ground. A woman's claims for refugee status may rest on one or more grounds of the Convention even where the persecution is gender-based.

4.23   Where the persecution of women is concerned, it should be recognised that an *imputed* Convention ground is an important aspect to consider. Women in many societies are forced into a subordinate role in many areas of life. Therefore, the opportunities to assume a publicly recognisable profile do not occur frequently and women are often aligned with the views of their male relatives.

4.24   The added difficulty is that, in many societies women have little or no information on the activities of their male relatives and may find it difficult to explain the reasons for their persecution. They may not realise that the authorities, for example, impute a political opinion to them because of their association (by marriage, family links etc) with others who have attracted the authorities' attention.

Political opinion

4.25   In some societies, overt demonstration of political opinion by women may not be possible as women are not allowed to formally participate in political life. However, there may be country information about the existence of covert political organisations involving women or about the suspicions of authorities that such organisations exist. Furthermore, the fact that a woman may challenge particular social conventions about the manner in which women should behave may be considered political by the authorities and may attract persecutory treatment on this basis.

> In some societies an organisation of women who are not seeking a public or political profile but who may, for example, possess a feminist ideology, may be viewed as espousing a political opinion hostile to the current administration and persecuted for that reason.

4.26   In many cases there is a societal assumption that women defer to men on all significant issues and that their political views are aligned with those of the dominant members of their family (usually husbands, fathers or brothers). They may thus experience persecution for this reason, ie imputed political opinion.

4.27   There are also cases where persecutors are aware that a woman possesses no political opinion but persecute her as a means of demoralising the rest of her family or community who do hold a political opinion hostile to the current administration.

4.28   The difficulty in assessing claims of imputed political opinion, of course, is that the woman may not be aware of the reasons why she has been persecuted. Officers faced with unexplained instances of persecution should look to whether the explanation may be traced to her family's political opinion or another Convention ground.

Race

4.29   Race is a Convention ground based on readily identifiable characteristics. In general racism knows no gender, however persecution may be expressed in different ways against men and women. For example the persecutor may choose to destroy the ethnic identity and/or prosperity of a racial group by killing, maiming or incarcerating the men whilst the women may be viewed as capable of propagating the ethnic identity and persecuted in a different way, such as through sexual violence.

Religion
4.30   In certain societies, the role ascribed to women may be attributable to the requirements of the state or official religion. The failure of women to conform to this role or model of behaviour may then be perceived by the authorities or other agents of persecution as the failure to practise or to hold certain religious beliefs and as such an attempt to corrupt the society or even as a threat to the religion's continued power. This may be the case even though the woman actually holds the official religious faith but it is not outwardly evidenced by her behaviour.

Nationality
4.31   Gender-based persecution for reasons of nationality may have its genesis in laws which deprive a woman of her citizenship in certain situations (eg marriage to a foreign national). Alternatively, a woman who has married a foreign national may not be able to live with him in her country of nationality. Rather than the loss of citizenship itself, officers should enquire into what harm results from this loss. For example, whether it leads to loss of right of residence or loss of other privileges or benefits.

Membership of a Particular Social Group
4.32   The Australian Federal Court has laid down some essential principles in the interpretation of the particular social group ground. Those principles are summarised as follows:

- the claimed particular social group must be cognisable
    - a group is cognisable if there is a common unifying element binding the members of the group because of shared common social characteristics and/or shared interest or experience in common *(Morato's case)*;
    - cognisability does not require a voluntary association amongst the members of the group *(Morato's case)*;
    - a group is not cognisable where the sole criterion defining the group is a common act although it is possible that, over a period of time, individuals who engage in similar actions may form a particular social group *(Morato's case)*;
    - the group is not defined solely by the persecution feared *(Morato's case)*.
- the nexus between the particular social group and the fear of persecution must be established. That is, there is a well-founded fear of persecution *'for reasons of'* membership of that group *(Morato's case)*; and
- the individual is (or is perceived to be) a member of that group, i.e. there is a common unifying element binding members together *(A & B's case)*.

4.33   While 'gender' of itself is not a Convention ground, it may, be a significant factor in recognising a particular social group or an identifying characteristic of such a group. Officers should bear in mind that there is no Australian jurisprudence on the issue of women as a 'particular social group'. The Refugee Review Tribunal has found that whilst being a broad category, women nonetheless have both immutable characteristics and shared common social characteristics which may make them cognisable as a group and which may attract persecution. In addition, gender may be combined with certain other characteristics which could define a particular social group in situations where there is evidence that this group suffers or fears to suffer severe discrimination or harsh and inhuman treatment that is distinguished from the situation of others of the same gender.

The important principle to consider is whether the persecution suffered or feared is for reasons of membership of a particular social group.

Officers should consider this Convention ground on a case by case basis which takes account of the totality of an applicant's claims and the situation in the applicant's country of origin.

Appendix 5

EUROPEAN CONVENTION ON HUMAN RIGHTS (ECHR) (4 November 1950)[1]

Article 2   Right to life

Article 3   'No one shall be subjected to torture or to inhuman or degrading treatment or punishment'

Article 4   Prohibition of forced or compulsory labour

Article 5   Deprivation of liberty

Article 6   Right to a fair and impartial hearing 'within a reasonable time'

Article 8   Respect for private and family life

Article 9   Right to freedom of thought, conscience and religion

Article 10   Right to freedom of expression

Article 11   Freedom of association

Article 12   Right to marry and found a family

Article 13   Right to the grant of an effective remedy before a national authority

---

1   Full text available in UNHCR's *Collection of International Instruments Concerning Refugees*, Geneva 1990 and numerous other sources.

Appendix 6

IAA *ASYLUM GENDER GUIDELINES*
(November 2000)

Contents

Section 1   Framework

Why Guidelines?

1.1   The 1951 Convention Relating to the Status of Refugees and the 1967 Protocol Relating to the Status of Refugees (together hereafter referred to as the 'Refugee Convention') applies both to men and women. It is often assumed that men and women therefore benefit equally from the international protection granted by the Refugee Convention. However, since the drafting of the Refugee Convention, the dominant conception of the refugee in Western jurisprudence has been of a man and today, women may not benefit equitably from its protections.

The reasons are twofold:

1. because the jurisprudence has not, to date, fully considered the specific issues raised by women's asylum claims and/or has tended to consider them from a framework of male experiences;
2. because the procedural and evidential requirements of the domestic asylum determination process are not equally accessible to both women and men.

1.2   To correct this imbalance States have been urged to adopt guidelines with respect to women's asylum claims by the UN Special *Rapporteur* on Violence Against Women,[1] the UN Division for the Advancement of Women,[2] the UN Platform for Action (1995 – see Art 147).

1.3   Gender guidelines have been introduced by Canada, Australia, the USA and UNHCR. In the UK the IAT has commended the use of the Canadian guidelines [see *Almaz Woldu Gimedhin* (IAT) (14019)]. In the UK *Gender Guidelines for the Determination of Asylum Claims in the UK* addressed to first instance decision makers in the Home Office, have been published by the Refugee Women's Legal Group in July 1998, drawing on the guidelines existing in other countries.

1.4   Most of these guidelines are applicable to the asylum claims of both men and women. They address the role of gender in the asylum determination process rather than simply the position of women asylum seekers or the role of biological sex.

1.5   In these guidelines, the terms 'women', 'woman', 'she' and 'her' apply equally to men. They are used to acknowledge that it is often women who have difficulties in relation to gender aspects of their asylum claims. Women, by virtue of their gender, may have specific protection needs and concerns.

1.6   Women refugees suffer the same deprivation and harm that is common to all refugees and they are frequently persecuted for reasons which are the same or similar to their male counterparts.

1.7   The experiences of women in their country of origin often differ from those of men, for example women's political protest, activism and resistance may manifest itself in different ways. This may alter the nature of their asylum claims, their ability to produce evidence relating to their claim, both oral and documentary, and the appropriate procedures to be used in determining their asylum claims.

For example:

- women may hide people, pass messages or provide community services, food, clothing and medical care;

---

1   Report of the UN Special Rapporteur on Violence Against Women, 26 January 1998.
2   Expert Group Meeting on Gender-Based Persecution December 1997.

- women who fail or refuse to conform to behavioural norms ('social mores') imposed on them by the state or society may suffer ill-treatment;
- women may be perceived as sharing the same political, religious, national, racial or other affiliations as their male relatives and have the affiliation and beliefs of their male relatives attributed or imputed to them;
- women may be unable, or less able, for example for legal,[1] economic or social (including economic) reasons to travel freely or to live on their own, or without family members thus limiting their ability to relocate within their country of origin. Women's child care responsibilities may affect their ability to relocate;
- women may be targeted because they are vulnerable, especially young women who can easily be sexually abused or mothers who will do anything to protect their children;[2]
- women may be targeted as a means of attracting or contacting or pressurising their male relatives or a whole community;
- women may be persecuted by members of their own family and/or community;
- women may be victims of domestic violence;
- women may be persecuted because of their choice of sexual partners including same-sex partners; and
- women may be victims of forced prostitution.

Aims

1.8 These guidelines aim to provide the judiciary of the IAA with the tools to enable them to fully and effectively consider and decide the asylum claims under the Refugee Convention. Specific focus on the role of gender is intended to ensure that all aspects of asylum claims are fully and fairly considered.

In particular they have the following aims:

- Jurisprudence – to ensure that women's asylum claims are fully considered under the Refugee Convention so that jurisprudence properly reflects the experience of both female and male refugees.
- Procedures – to ensure that the asylum determination process is accessible to both women and men and that the procedures used do not prejudice women asylum seekers or make it more difficult for them to present their asylum claims.[3]
- Evidential Requirements – to ensure that the judiciary are aware of the particular evidential problems which may be faced by women asylum seekers and that appropriate steps are taken to overcome them.

---

1   For example Kenyan married women are legally required to obtain the consent of their husbands before obtaining a national identity card or passport and Nigerian women are required by law to obtain permission from a male family member before having an application for a passport processed: see US Department of State, *1999 Country Reports on Human Rights Practices* (February 2000). Egyptian women must have permission from their fathers to obtain a passport if they are unmarried or under the age of 21; married women must obtain the same permission from their husbands: see US Department of State, *1999 Country Reports on Human Rights Practices* (February 2000).
2   'Particularly vulnerable were young women between fourteen and eighteen who were sought after and targeted for being virgins. The rebels often entered houses and compounds asking specifically for virgin girls. There are documented cases of girls as young as eight being abused.' Human Rights Watch, *Sierra Leone: Getting Away with Murder, Mutilation, Rape, New Testimony from Sierra Leone,* July 1999.
3   See UN Platform for Action (1995).

1.9   Even where gender is not a central issue in an asylum claim, giving consideration to gender-related aspects of a case will assist in fully understanding and determining the whole of an asylum claim.

1.10   The examples given in these guidelines are illustrative and not exhaustive.

Definitions

1.11   Terms relating to gender and the elements of the refugee definition are not always used very clearly. This section defines some of the important terms relating to gender issues in asylum claims.

Gender

1.12   Gender is not the same as biological sex. Gender refers to the socially and culturally constructed experience of being a woman or a man and the *power relations* between women and men. It affects both women's and men's social identity, status, roles and responsibilities. Gender relations and gender differences are historically, geographically and culturally specific – what it means to be a woman or a man may vary over time and place and may be affected by other factors such as race, age, class and marital status.

Gender specific forms of harm

1.13   Certain forms of harm are more frequently or only used against women or affect women in a manner which is different from men. These include, but are not limited to, for example, sexual violence, societal and legal discrimination, forced prostitution, trafficking, refusal of access to contraception, bride burning, forced marriage, forced sterilisation, forced abortion and (forced) female genital mutilation, enforced nakedness/sexual humiliation.

Gender related persecution

1.14   The terms *gender related persecution* and *gender persecution*[1] relate to the causal relationship between the persecution and the reason for the persecution – i.e. the reason for the persecution. Where it occurs a woman may be persecuted *because* of her gender (e.g. where she is persecuted because she refuses or fails to comply with social/religious/cultural behaviour expected from a woman). Gender-related persecution is not necessarily the same as persecution on the basis of biological sex. It does not simply refer to persons being persecuted because they are biologically male or female, but to them being persecuted because they fail or refuse to comply with the social requirements of being a man or a woman.

1.15   Thus, an asylum seeker may be persecuted in a *gender specific manner* for reasons unrelated to gender (e.g. raped because of her membership in a political party), she may be persecuted in a *non-gender specific manner,* but because of her gender (e.g. flogged for refusing to wear a veil), and persecuted in a *gender specific manner* and *because of her gender* (female genital mutilation or the honour killing of an adulterous woman).

Gender blind

1.16   Where, on its face, a provision or policy, etc. makes no distinction between men and women.

Gender neutral

1.17   Where, in practice, a provision or policy, etc. provides equally for men and women. In order to achieve *gender neutrality* it may be necessary to recognise that men and women

---

1   This term is often, incorrectly, used to cover the asylum claims of women in general or is confused with gender specific harm.

have different experiences and may thus have different fears, needs, concerns and priorities.

The International Protection Framework

1.18 The 1951 Refugee Convention is part of an international legal framework of protection. This framework is contained in international human rights law, including both international treaties and international customary law (which is effective in UK common law).

IAA judiciary should bear in mind that the Refugee Convention comprises part of this larger international legal protection framework for a number of reasons.

These include:

- That international human rights law instruments (and customary law) should be referred to for guidance in construing the Refugee Convention under principles of international treaty interpretation [see Annex II to these Guidelines and IAA Legal Factsheet *'Principles of Interpretation'*, May 1999].
- Some of the UK's domestic asylum law has specifically been introduced to comply with international human rights treaties in addition to the Refugee Convention.[1]
- The IAA's obligations in relation to the European Convention on Human Rights ('ECHR').[2]
- There are a number of international human rights instruments (in addition to the Refugee Convention) which specifically prohibit expulsion of non-citizens (and *refoulement*) on human rights grounds.[3]

---

1   See Schedule 2, para 5(5) to Asylum and Immigration Act 1996 and UN Convention Against Torture ('UNCAT') – '[w]e are determined to honour our obligations under the 1951 United Nations Convention on Refugees and the 1981 [UN] Convention on Torture and Cruel or Inhuman Treatment. Those are the principles underlying this Bill [Asylum and Immigration Bill 1995/6]'. Minister of State Home Office, Baroness Blatch, HL Second Reading 14/2/96, Hansard Col. 959. Thus, following *Pepper v Hart* [1993] 1 All ER 42, they should arguably be interpreted consistently.

2   Following entry into force of the Human Rights Act 1998, the IAA will be obliged to apply the ECHR and, since the case of *R v Secretary of State for the Home Department ex parte Danaei* [1998] INLR 124 (CA), have been able to make findings of fact in relation to the ECHR which are binding on the Secretary of State:
    'Often, of course, the Secretary of State will not have the benefit of the adjudicator's findings in Art. 3 [ECHR] cases, and this court alone [the Court of Appeal] will then have the role of exercising "independent scrutiny" of the claim. When, however, as here, the adjudicator has made findings, then, even if he has enjoyed no particular advantage over the Secretary of State in reaching his conclusions the ECHR may perhaps be expected to take exception to a Secretary of State's decision which merely disagrees [with the adjudicator's factual findings].' [*R v SSHD ex parte Danaei* (CA) [1998] INLR 124, [1998] Imm AR 84].
    'If the Secretary of State is to set aside or ignore a finding on a factual issue which has been considered and evaluated at an oral hearing by the special Adjudicator he should explain why he has done so and he should not do so unless the relevant factual conclusion could itself be impugned on Wednesbury principles, or has been reconsidered in the light of further evidence, or is of limited or negligible significance to the ultimate decision for which he is responsible.' [*R v SSHD ex parte Danaei* (CA) [1998] INLR 124, [1998] Imm AR 84. For further information on ECHR see *IAA Legal Fact Sheets*].

3   These include: UNCAT 1984 and the International Convention on Civil and Political Rights (ICCPR) 1966 (for more on this see General Comment 15 1986). UNCAT 1984 defines torture as follows:
    'Article 1

1.19   International Human Rights instruments and customary international law provide a wide range of rights and obligations which are binding on the United Kingdom and form part of the international protection framework.

1.20   A list of some of the relevant international treaties is in Annex II to these Guidelines.

Section 2   Persecution – Serious Harm and Failure of State Protection

2.1   To be recognised as a refugee an asylum applicant must fear a form of harm which constitutes 'persecution' within the meaning of the Refugee Convention.

Definition of Persecution

2.2   The Refugee Convention contains no definition of persecution; guidance is given in the *UNHCR Handbook on Procedures and Criteria for Determining Refugee Status 1988*, re-edited 1992 ('UNHCR Handbook'),[1] caselaw and by academic writers.

2.3   The term 'persecution' is linked to violations of human rights as set out in the international human rights instruments and international customary law:

Persecution is: '*the sustained or systemic violation of basic human rights demonstrative of a failure of state protection in relation to one of the core entitlements which has been recognised by the international community.*'[2]

'*. . . comprehensive analysis requires the general notion of persecution to be related to developments within the broad field of human rights.*'[3]

2.4   It will be necessary to consider whether the fear is of persecution from an agent of the state (for example a police or army member) or a non state agent (for example an

---

1) For the purposes of this Convention, the term "torture" means any act by which severe pain or suffering, whether physical or mental, is intentionally inflicted on a person for such purposes as obtaining from him or a third person information or a confession, punishing him for an act he or a third person has committed or is suspected of having committed, or intimidating or coercing him or a third person, or for any reason based on discrimination of any kind, when such pain or suffering is inflicted by or at the instigation of or with the consent or acquiescence of a public official or other person acting in an official capacity. It does not include pain or suffering arising only from, inherent in or incidental to lawful sanctions.
2) This article is without prejudice to any international instrument or national legislation which does or may contain provisions of wider application.'
– With reference to Art 1(1) the case of *Elmi v Australia* Communication No 120/1998 noted that UNCAT would prevent expulsion of a Somali national who feared torture by the Hawiye clan. The UN Committee Against Torture considered that warring factions in Somalia would fall 'within the phrase "public officials or other persons acting in an official capacity"; case available at
http://www.unhchr.ch/tbs/doc.nsf/. . .6c278025679a003c37ec?Opendocument – With reference to Art 1(2) where 'torture' is referred to in UK statutory materials regard should be had to the ordinary dictionary definition of the term in keeping with UK principles of statutory interpretation. The *Concise Oxford Dictionary* defines torture as:
'1) the infliction of severe bodily pain especially as a punishment or means of persuasion, 2) severe physical or mental suffering.' *Concise Oxford Dictionary*, Ninth Edition, Clarendon Press (1995) at page 247.

1   Paragraphs 51–60 and 65 *UNHCR Handbook*, Geneva (1992).
2   Hathaway, J., *The Law of Refugee Status*, Butterworths Canada (1991) at page 114 (referred to in these guidelines as 'Hathaway'), see also Home Office Asylum Directorate Instructions Chapter 1, Paragraph 8.1.
3   Goodwin-Gill, G., *The Refugee in International Law*, 2nd Edition, Oxford University Press (1996).

opposition group) since this will affect the approach taken to deciding whether the feared treatment is 'persecution' within the meaning of the Refugee Convention.[1]

State Agents

The term 'persecution' covers ill-treatment which is of sufficient seriousness.

Non State Agents

The term 'persecution' under the Refugee Convention includes two factors:

1. serious harm or ill-treatment from non-state agents; and
2. inability or unwillingness of the State to protect the victim from such harm or ill-treatment.[2]

2.5 The term 'persecution' is thus considered in these Guidelines in the form of two questions:

1. Is there a violation of human rights/harm which amounts to 'serious harm'? This is addressed in Section 2A of these Guidelines
2. Is the state unable or unwilling to offer effective protection? This is addressed in Section 2B of these Guidelines

Section 2A   The Meaning of Serious Harm

2A.1 Whether harm, including gender-specific harm, amounts to persecution should be assessed on the basis of internationally recognised human rights standards.[3]

> *'In our considered opinion, the term "persecution" should be defined by reference to human rights standards. In this respect we agree with the academic commentators, in particular Goodwin-Gill and Hathaway, and we associate ourselves with the view expressed in [the IAT decision of] Gashi [1997] INLR 96] that decision-makers should look in particular at the preamble to the 1951 [Refugee] Convention.'*[4] [*Horvath v SSHD* (IAT) [1999] INLR 7, [1999] Imm AR 121]

---

1   Important UK cases on the meaning of persecution include:
    R v IAT ex parte Jonah (QBD) [1985] Imm AR 7;
    Gashi v Nikshiqi (IAT) [1997] INLR 96;
    Horvath v SSHD (HL) [2000] 3 WLR 379;
    Horvath v SSHD (CA) [2000] INLR 15, [2000] Imm AR 205;
    Horvath v SSHD (IAT) [1999] INLR 7, [1999] Imm AR 121;
    Faraj v SSHD (CA) [1999] INLR 451;
    Demirkaya v SSHD (CA) [1999] INLR 441, [1999] Imm AR 498;
    Ravichandran v IAT (CA) [1996] Imm AR 97;
    Kagema v SSHD (CA) [1997] Imm AR 137.
2   *Horvath v SSHD* (HL) [2000] 3 WLR 379.
3   See also paragraphs 1.18 and section 2 above; for an earlier approach in UK caselaw see *R v IAT ex parte Jonah* (QBD) [1985] Imm AR 7: the term 'persecution' 'should be given its ordinary, dictionary definition' – the definition in the *Shorter Oxford English Dictionary* was 'to pursue, hunt, drive ... to pursue with malignancy or injurious action; esp. to oppress for holding a heretical opinion or belief'.
4   The Preamble to the Refugee Convention states, *inter alia*: 'Considering that the Charter of the United Nations and the Universal Declaration of Human Rights approved on 10 December 1948 by the General Assembly have affirmed the principle that human beings shall enjoy fundamental rights and freedoms without discrimination, Considering that the United Nations has, on various occasions, manifested its profound concern for refugees and endeavoured to assure refugees the widest possible exercise of these fundamental rights and freedoms'.

2A.2 Only 'serious harm' will constitute 'persecution' within the meaning of the Refugee Convention. Not all harm or violations of human rights standards will amount to 'serious harm'.

> *'The denial of human rights is not the same as persecution, which involves the infliction of serious harm.'* [*Islam v Secretary of State for the Home Department, R v IAT ex parte Shah* (HL) [1999] INLR 144,[1] [1999] Imm AR 283]

> *'Persecution may involve physical or mental ill-treatment. Torture is such ill-treatment carried to extremes. But persecution, unlike torture, always involves a persistent course of conduct . . . It involves an element of sustained or systematic failure of protection towards the person or group[2] the object of such persecution, as distinct from casual or random acts of violence inflicted on citizens at large . . . an incident of torture of a person which is the sole incident affecting that person may amount to persecution if there are other incidents affecting a group[3] of which that person is a member.'* [*Faraj v SSHD* (CA) [1999] INLR 451]

> *'. . . what conduct may amount to persecution is a question of degree. At one end of the scale there may be arbitrary deprivation of life, torture and cruel, inhumane and degrading punishment or treatment. In such a case the conduct may be so extreme that one instance is sufficient. But less serious conduct may not amount to persecution unless it is persistent.'*[4] [*Demirkaya v SSHD* (CA) [1999] INLR 441, [1999] Imm AR 498]

2A.3 Hathaway's approach to the meaning of persecution, within the Refugee Convention, is frequently referred to. He states:

> Persecution is: '*the sustained or systemic violation of basic human rights demonstrative of a failure of state protection in relation to one of the core entitlements which has been recognised by the international community. The types of harm to be protected against include the breach of any right within the first category, a discriminatory or non-emergency abrogation of a right within the second category, or the failure to implement a right within the third category which is either discriminatory or not grounded in the absolute lack of resources*'.[5]

2A.4 Hathaway refers above to three levels of human rights and the situations in which their breach may constitute serious harm.[6] The three levels of human rights are:

Level One Rights:

Rights stated in the Universal Declaration of Human Rights 1948 (UDHR) and the International Covenant on Civil and Political Rights 1966 (ICCPR) which countries may not derogate from even in times of compelling national emergency. They include:

- freedom from arbitrary deprivation of life (Art 6 ICCPR);
- freedom from torture, cruel, inhuman or degrading punishment or treatment (Art 7 ICCPR);
- freedom from slavery and servitude (Art 8 ICCPR);

---

1   See also *Horvath v SSHD* (IAT) [1999] INLR 7 at page 28E, 30E and *Horvath v SSHD* (HL) [2000] 3 WLR 379.
2   Note – this is not specifically referring to a 'particular social group' within the meaning of the Refugee Convention.
3   See footnote 2.
4   With regard to persistence of the harm see also *Ravichandran v IAT* (CA) [1996] Imm AR 97: 'Persecution must at least be persistent and serious ill-treatment without just cause by the state, or from which the state can provide protection but chooses not to do so.'
5   Hathaway, J., page 114, see also Home Office Asylum Directorate Instructions Chapter 1, Paragraph 8.1.
6   See Hathaway, pp 109–112.

- freedom from imprisonment for inability to fulfil a contractual obligation (Art 11 ICCPR);
- protection from retroactive criminal prosecution (Art 15 ICCPR);
- right to be recognised as a person in law (Art 16 ICCPR); and
- freedom of thought, conscience and religion (Art 18 ICCPR).

According to Hathaway failure of the state of origin to ensure these 'first level' rights will, under any circumstances, 'be tantamount to persecution'.[1]

Level Two Rights:

Rights stated in the UDHR and in the ICCPR from which states may derogate during a state of emergency which has been officially proclaimed. These rights include:

- freedom from arbitrary arrest and/or detention (Art 9 ICCPR);
- right to equal protection for all (Art 26 ICCPR);
- rights, in criminal hearings, to a fair and public hearing and a presumption of innocence (Art 14 ICCPR);
- protection of family and privacy (Art 17 ICCPR);
- right to freedom of movement inside a country and to choice of residence (Art 12 ICCPR);
- freedom to leave and return to one's country of origin (Art 12 ICCPR);
- liberty of opinion, expression, assembly and association (Arts 19, 21, 22 ICCPR);
- right to form and join trade unions (Art 22 ICCPR);
- right and opportunity to take part in the conduct of public affairs, and vote in periodic and genuine elections (Art 25 ICCPR); and
- right to have access to public employment without discrimination (Art 25 ICCPR).

A failure to ensure these rights will generally be a violation of a state's basic duty of protection of its nationals unless 1) the government's derogation was strictly required by the problems of a real emergency situation, and 2) the derogations are not applied in a discriminatory way and 3) that the derogation was not inconsistent with other aspects of international law.

> *'Where, for example, the failure to respect a basic right in this category goes beyond that which is strictly required to respond to the emergency (in terms of scope or duration), or where the derogation impacts disproportionately on certain subgroups of the population, a finding of persecution is warranted.'*[2]

Level Three Rights:

Rights in the UDHR and carried forward in the International Covenant on Economic, Social and Cultural Rights 1966 (ICESCR).[3] The state will be in breach if it secures the rights in a discriminatory manner or where it takes no steps to ensure the rights despite having adequate finances to do so. These rights include:

- right to work, including just and favourable conditions of employment, remuneration and rest (Arts 6 and 7 ICESCR);

---

1   Hathaway at page 109.
2   Hathaway at page 110.
3   Generally the ICESCR does not demand immediate compliance, but rather demands that States 'take steps to the maximum of [their] available resources' to 'achieve progressively the full realisation of the rights' without 'discrimination of any kind as to race, colour, sex, language, religion, political or other opinion, national or social origin, property, birth or other status.'

- right to an adequate standard of living including: food, clothing, housing (Art 11 ICESCR);
- right to enjoyment of highest attainable standard of health (Art 12 ICESCR);
- right to education (Arts 13 and 14 ICESCR);
- protection of the family, especially children and mothers (Art 10 ICESCR); and
- right to engage in and benefit from cultural, scientific, literary and artistic expression (Art 15).

According to Hathaway 'a state is in breach of its basic obligations where it either ignores these interests notwithstanding the fiscal ability to respond or where it excludes a minority of its population from their enjoyment. Moreover, the deprivation of certain of the socio-economic rights, such as the ability to earn a living, or the entitlement to food, shelter, or health care will at an extreme level be tantamount to the deprivation of life or cruel, inhuman or degrading treatment, and hence unquestionably constitute persecution.'[1]

Discrimination

2A.5   Protection from persecution based on discrimination is an important purpose of the Refugee Convention and the elimination of discrimination based on sex is a fundamental tenet of international human rights law (e.g. Art 2 ICCPR, Art 3 ICESCR 1966, Convention on the Elimination of All Forms of Discrimination Against Women 1979 ('CEDAW').

> '*The relevance of the preambles [to the Refugee Convention] is twofold. First, they expressly show that a premise of the Convention was that all human beings shall enjoy fundamental rights and freedoms. Secondly, and more pertinently, they show that counteracting discrimination, which is referred to in the first preamble, was a fundamental purpose of the Convention.*' [Lord Steyn, *Islam v Secretary of State for the Home Department, R v IAT ex parte Shah* (HL) [1999] INLR 144, [1999] Imm AR 283]

> '*In my opinion, the concept of discrimination in matters affecting fundamental rights and freedoms is central to an understanding of the [Refugee] Convention*' [Lord Hoffmann, *Islam v Secretary of State for the Home Department, R v IAT ex parte Shah* (HL) [1999] INLR 144, [1999] Imm AR 283]

2A.6   Definition of discrimination:

> The Refugee Convention is concerned '*with persecution which is based on discrimination. And in the context of a human rights instrument, discrimination means making distinctions which principles of fundamental human rights regard as inconsistent with the right of every human being to equal treatment and respect.*' [Lord Hoffmann, *Islam v Secretary of State for the Home Department, R v IAT ex parte Shah* (HL) [1999] INLR 144, [1999] Imm AR 283]

> To discriminate is: to '*make a distinction in the treatment of different categories of people or things esp. unjustly or prejudicially against people on grounds of race, colour, sex, social status, age, etc.*' [*The New Shorter Oxford English Dictionary*, Oxford University Press (1993)]

2A.7   Discrimination (and discriminatory treatment) may:

---

1   Hathaway at page 111.

- amount to 'serious harm' within the meaning of the Refugee Convention;
- be the/a factor which turns 'harm' into 'serious harm' and a breach of human rights (for example – discriminatory access to police protection or education); and
- be a factor in failure of state protection in the Refugee Convention (thus the State may protect some groups in society and not others).

2A.8 The state may discriminate in relation to a wide range of harm and all levels of human rights. For example:

- The State and its agents may themselves discriminate directly – e.g. through discriminatory laws and the application of laws in a manner which impacts disproportionately against certain groups or individuals.
- Non-state agents may carry out discriminatory activities or social/cultural/ religious discriminatory norms may exist and the State and its agents may support, be unwilling, or unable to take serious action to combat the discrimination.[1]

2A.9 Discrimination against women may include (but is not limited to):

- political rights – e.g. women may be discriminated against in relation to voting or being able to be involved in mainstream or grassroots politics or to be publicly involved;
- economic rights – e.g. there may be legal and or social/cultural restrictions on women taking paid employment or employment outside the home;
- professional – e.g. women may be barred from certain types of employment or restricted in their ability to undertake them;
- education – e.g. women may be discriminated against in their access to education including basic literacy;
- health care – e.g. women may be discriminated against in their access to health care including birth control of their choice;
- marriage rights – e.g. women may not be free to choose their own partner due to legal and/or social/cultural/religious restrictions;
- property rights – e.g. women may not be allowed to own or inherit property (or not equally with men);
- child custody rights – e.g. women may not be entitled to custody of their children on divorce;
- freedom of movement – e.g. women may be restricted in their freedom of movement including their ability to move outside the home, to travel or to travel alone or to travel without the consent of a male relative; and
- equal protection of the law – e.g. violence most often suffered by women may not be illegal or prosecuted or subject to evidential restraints, women's evidence may not be considered equal to men's.

2A.10 A discriminatory measure, in itself or cumulatively with others, may be 'serious harm' in some circumstances, for example:

---

1 See for example the views of Lord Steyn regarding the position of women in Pakistan as expressed in *Islam v SSHD; R v IAT ex parte Shah* [1999] INLR 144 (HL): *'The distinctive feature of this case is that in Pakistan women are unprotected by the State: discrimination against women in Pakistan is partly tolerated by the State and partly sanctioned by the State'*. In relation to the same issue Neal, D. states: *'Some nations officially condemn sex discrimination, but fail for cultural reasons to protect women in particular instances, Others actively proscribe sex discrimination or guarantee women's rights, but are unsuccessful in adequately enforcing such prohibitions and safeguards – often because social traditions or religious laws eviscerate progressive legislation.'* [in 'Women as a Social Group: Recognising Sex-Based Persecution as Grounds for Asylum' Columbia Human Rights Law Review [Vol 20:1 1988] 203].

- if the discrimination has consequences of a substantially prejudicial nature for the person concerned (see further at paragraph 2A.11), for example, serious restrictions on right to earn a livelihood, to practise or not practise the religion of their choice, restrictions on freedom of movement such as forced seclusion or lack of access to normally available education, legal, welfare and health provision; and
- if the discriminatory measures, irrespective of how serious they are, lead the person concerned to feel apprehensive and insecure as regards their future existence.[1]

'New Zealand refugee jurisprudence accepts [Hathaway's view] that refugee law ought to concern itself with actions which deny human dignity in any key way and that the sustained or systemic denial of core human rights is the appropriate standard various acts of discrimination, in their cumulative effect, can deny human dignity in key ways and should properly be recognised as persecution for the purposes of the Convention.' [*Re MN* Refugee Appeal No 2039/93, 12 February 1996, Chairman: R. Haines, New Zealand Refugee Status Appeals Authority]

'Although we did not hear full argument on the point, my preliminary view is that breach of third category rights [i.e. socio-economic rights] cannot be said as a matter of law to amount to persecution just as it cannot be said as a matter of law that breach of these rights could never amount to persecution. It is a matter of fact and degree and judgement in the individual case.' [*Horvath v SSHD* (CA) [2000] INLR 15, [2000] Imm AR 205]

2A.11   Discriminatory restrictions on women may in themselves constitute serious harm if they have consequences of a substantially prejudicial nature for the women concerned: for example, compelling a woman to wear the veil will violate her right to freedom of conscience and religion if she has deep beliefs regarding this.

'the concept of persecution is broad enough to include governmental measures that compel an individual to engage in conduct that is not physically painful or harmful but is abhorrent to that individual's deepest beliefs.' [*Fatin v INS* 12F. 3d 1233 (3rd Cir. 1993), also approved in *Fisher v INS* 37 F.3d 1371, 1379–1381 (9th Cir.1994) and *Re MN* Refugee Appeal No 2039/93, 12 February 1996, Chairman: R. Haines, New Zealand Refugee Status Appeals Authority]

'... the Fisher decision is ... important for the recognition it has given to the significance of being required to comply with codes and requirements fundamentally at odds with one's own conscience and beliefs or deeply held convictions, or to engage in conduct that is abhorrent to one's own beliefs.' [*Re MN* Refugee Appeal No 2039/93, 12 February 1996, Chairman: R. Haines, New Zealand Refugee Status Appeals Authority]

2A.12   A wide range of penalties may be imposed on women for disobeying restrictions placed on women (including cultural, social and legal restrictions). Such penalties will often constitute serious harm. Where restrictions are placed on both men and women, the punishment for breaching those restrictions may be greater for women than men. Where a woman will receive heavier punishment than will a man then this will constitute serious harm.

2A.13   Restrictions on women may have social, medical or other consequences for women which constitute 'serious harm'. For example, consequences for women in mixed marriages or child or arranged marriages, and on separation, divorce or widowhood.[2]

---

1   See paragraphs 53, 54 & 55 UNHCR Handbook.
2   Human Rights Watch World Report 1996 reported as follows: 'In late 1994 the Women's Rights Project [Nigeria] and Human Rights Watch/Africa sent research teams to Nigeria to investigate discrimination against widows in the south and forced child marriage in the north. In some areas of the south, we found that widows were forced to endure humiliating

Violence Against Women

2A.14 The fact that violence and/or discrimination against women occurs in every country is *irrelevant* when determining whether gender-specific forms of harm[1] amount to 'serious harm'.

2A.15 The fact that, within a particular country, violence and/or discrimination against women is endemic and/or socially/culturally accepted is *irrelevant* when determining whether gender-specific forms of harm amount to 'serious harm'.

Whether particular treatment amounts to 'serious harm' should be decided on the basis of international human rights standards. [See e.g. Lord Hoffmann, *obiter* in *Islam v SSHD; R v IAT ex parte Shah* [1999] INLR 144 (HL), [1999] Imm AR 283]

2A.16 Gender-specific harm does not differ analytically from other forms of ill-treatment and violence that are commonly held to amount to persecution and may constitute torture or cruel inhuman or degrading treatment or punishment.

2A.17 Gender-specific harm may include *but is not limited to* sexual violence and abuse, female genital mutilation, marriage-related harm, violence within the family, forced sterilisation and forced abortion.[2] For further details see Definitions Section of these Guidelines.

---

rituals when their husbands died and that they were denied inherited property under discriminatory customary law. In five northern states that we visited, we found that girls are customarily forced by their families into marriage, frequently before puberty, despite the girls' express objections or attempts to run away. Many child brides are compelled to engage in sexual relations as soon as they are married and, as a consequence, they become pregnant and give birth before they are physically mature. *This can not only increase their risk of death in childbirth, but also cause serious medical complications due to early pregnancy, including obstetric or vesico-vaginal fistula ... Girls suffering from their complications smell from the constant leakage of urine, and many are abandoned by their husbands and families.*' In Nigeria '[a]lthough women are not barred legally from owning land, in some customary land tenure systems only men can own land, and women can only gain access to land only through marriage or family. In addition many customary practices do not recognise a woman's right to inherit her husband's property and many widows were rendered destitute when their in-laws took virtually all of the deceased husband's property. Widows are subjected to unfavourable conditions as a result of discriminatory traditional customs and economic deprivation. "Confinement" is the most common rite of deprivation to which widows are subjected, and it occurs predominately in eastern Nigeria. Confined widows are under restrictions for as long as 1 year and usually are required to shave their heads and dress in black garments. In other areas, a widow is considered a part of her husband's property, to be "inherited" by his family.' – US Department of State, *1999 Country Reports on Human Rights Practices*, February 2000. – For more information concerning the particular problems which occur as a result of widowhood see Owen, M, *A World of Widows*, Zed Books (1996).

1 See definitions at para. 1.11–1.17.

2 'We would regard enforced abortion as torture, as we would enforced mutilation or sterilisation. I can undertake to put the guidance in instructions to caseworkers and to make that guidance available to the House': Minister of State Home Office Ann Widdecombe MP, HC Consideration of Lords Amendments to the Asylum and Immigration Bill 1995/6, 15/7/96, Hansard Col 842. 'I stress that both personally and as a Minister I utterly accept that forcible abortion, sterilisation, genital mutilation and allied practices would almost always constitute torture. In fact, they would probably always constitute torture. There is no doubt in my mind that anyone making a case to us on those grounds would have an extremely good case for asylum.' Minister of State Home Office Ann Widdecombe MP, HC Consideration of Lords Amendments to the Asylum and Immigration Bill 1995/6, 15/7/96, Hansard Col 844. 'Rape and other forms of sexual violence clearly amount to persecution in the same way as do other acts of serious physical abuse.' Minister of State Home Office, Baroness Blatch, HL Committee 20/4/96, Hansard Cols 1485–1486.

2A.18   Sexual violence can include, *but is not limited to,* rape;[1] enforced nakedness, mechanical or manual stimulation of the erogenous zones; the insertion of objects into the body openings; the forced witnessing or commission of sexual acts; forced masturbation; fellatio and oral coitus; a general atmosphere of sexual aggression, the loss of the ability to reproduce plus threats of the above: sexual violence is a form of aggression.

> *'... rape is a form of aggression and ... the central elements of the crime of rape cannot be captured in a mechanical description of objects and body parts. ...'* [*Prosecutor v Jean-Paul Akayesu* (ICTR) Case No. ICTR-96-4-T, 2 September 1998[2]]

> *'We want to kill the myth that rape is sexually motivated – it is usually intended to inflict violence and humiliation.'* [Deputy Assistant Commissioner Wyn Jones of the Metropolitan Police[3]]

2A.19   Sexual violence may be a violation of the right not to be subjected to torture or cruel inhuman or degrading treatment or punishment and may be a crime against humanity.[4]

> *'the deliberate ill-treatment inflicted on [the applicant] by being beaten, being placed in a tyre and hosed with pressurised water, combined with the humiliation of being stripped naked, fell clearly within the scope of the prohibition of Article 3 [ECHR]. The Commission also found that rape committed by an official or person in authority on a detainee must be regarded as treatment or punishment of an especially severe kind. Such an offence struck at the heart of the victim's physical and moral integrity and had to be characterised as a particularly cruel form of ill-treatment involving acute physical and psychological suffering. 79. The Commission found that the applicant had been the victim of torture at the*

---

1   Rape has now been defined in international law. The International Criminal Tribunal for Former Yugoslavia has defined rape as: (i) the sexual penetration, however slight: (a) of the vagina or anus of the victim by the penis of the perpetrator or any other object used by the perpetrator; *or* (b) of the mouth of the victim by the penis of the perpetrator; (ii) by coercion or force or threat of force against the victim or a third person. See *Prosecutor v Anto Furundzira,* (ICTY) Case No. IT-95-17/1-T, 10 December 1998. The International Criminal Tribunal for Rwanda defines rape as 'physical invasion of a sexual nature committed on a person under circumstances which are coercive' and defines 'sexual violence, which includes rape, as any act of a sexual nature which is committed on a person under circumstances which are coercive. Sexual violence is not limited to physical invasion of the human body and may include acts which do not involve penetration or even physical contact ... [such as the incident] in which the Accused ordered the Interahamwe to undress a student and force her to do gymnastics naked in the public courtyard of the bureau communal, in front of a crowd'. See *Prosecutor v Jean-Paul Akayesu* (ICTR) Case No. ICTR-96-4-T, 2 September 1998. (http://www.un.org/ictr/english/judgements/akayesu.html)

2   International Criminal Tribunal for Rwanda, case available at: http://www.un.org/ictr/english/judgements/akayesu.html

3   *The Guardian,* January, 1985, reported in Temkin, J., *Rape and the Legal Process,* Sweet and Maxwell (1987) at page 161.

4   Rape is listed as a crime against humanity in the Statutes of the International Tribunals for Former Yugoslavia and Rwanda. The Rome Statute of the International Criminal Court lists as crimes against humanity 'rape, sexual slavery, enforced prostitution, forced pregnancy, enforced sterilisation, or any other form of sexual violence of comparable gravity'. Protocol II to the Geneva Convention 1949 and Relating to the Protection of Victims of Non-International Armed Conflicts lists acts which are prohibited against non-combatants or former combatants including 'outrages upon personal dignity, in particular humiliating and degrading treatment, rape, enforced prostitution and any form of indecent assault'. A 1995 report of the Inter-American Commission on Human Rights on Haiti concluded that rape as a weapon of terror against women is a crime against humanity in peacetime.

hands of officials in violation of Article 3' – [*Aydin v Turkey* (ECHR) (1997) 25 EHRR 251]

2A.20 Sexual violence may have serious *physical, psychological* and social consequences for both male[1] and female victims.

'... *while being held in detention the applicant was raped by a person whose identity has still to be determined. Rape of a detainee by an official of the State must be considered to be an especially grave and abhorrent form of ill-treatment given the ease with which the offender can exploit the vulnerability and weakened resistance of his victim. Furthermore, rape leaves deep psychological scars on the victim which do not respond to the passage of time as quickly as other forms of physical and mental violence. The applicant also experienced the acute physical pain of forced penetration, which must have left her feeling debased and violated both physically and emotionally ... 86. The [European] Court [of Human Rights] is satisfied that the accumulation of acts of physical and mental violence inflicted on the applicant and the especially cruel act of rape to which she was subjected [by Turkish gendarme officers while in detention]amounted to torture in breach of Article 3 of the Convention [ECHR]. Indeed the Court would have reached this conclusion on either of these grounds taken separately.'* [*Aydin v Turkey* (ECHR) (1997) 25 EHRR 251]

2A.21 Sexual violence may have traumatic *social* repercussions for the victim.[2] These may be affected by the victim's cultural origins and/or social status. Such social

---

1   Sexual violence may have severe consequences for male victims and, in the UK, men are said to be reluctant to admit to having been forced into sex, see report of research carried out at the Royal Free and University College Medical School, London – *The Guardian*, 26 March 1999. In relation to the physical consequences where the victim is young see, *for example,* footnote 2 at p 281. In relation to the psychological effects of rape: 'Rape commonly results in severe and long-lasting psychological sequelae that are complex and shaped by the social and cultural context in which the rape occurs. Most of the data on the psychological effect of rape come from studies of adult Western women in peacetime who have suffered a single episode of rape. They describe both short term and long term effects. Commonly reported feelings at the time of the rape include shock, a fear of injury or death that can be paralysing, and a sense of profound loss of control over one's life. Longer-term effects can include persistent fears, avoidance of situations that trigger memories of the violation, profound feelings of shame, difficulty remembering events, intrusive thoughts of the abuse, decreased ability to respond to life generally, and difficulty re-establishing intimate relationships. In any culture women may not voice their distress in "psychological" terms. For example in the study of 107 Ugandan women raped during war, only two presented with what could be called psychological symptoms (nightmares and loss of libido). Fifty-three percent described their distress in physical complaints (headaches, chest pain and rashes) and 57% in gynaecological symptoms. The persistence of perceived infestation in this group often despite multiple treatment for symptoms (approximately two thirds had no clinical findings of infection) reflects a common sequel to rape of feeling dirty and infected. For Ugandan women, the experience of rape disrupted their sense of community: keeping this aspect of their lives secret alienated them from other people. These women often expressed the fear that they would be rejected by their partners and the rest of the community.' Swiss, S. and Giller J.E., 'Rape as a Crime of War: A Medical Perspective' in *The Journal of the American Medical Association* August 4 1992 Vol 470.
2   For example, in Kosovo ethnic Albanian women consider that '[rape] is the worst possible thing ... they would rather die than be raped, especially the unmarried, whose life is then essentially over.' Indeed the subject is so fraught that counsellors and doctors have great problems in finding out who the victims are: 'They cannot come and admit that they have been raped', according to the humanitarian medical agency, *Medecins sans Frontieres,* reported in *The Guardian*, 19 October 1999 *Kosovo's Wounded Women find no peace*. In relation to Uganda 'Rape commonly results in severe and long-lasting psychological sequelae that are complex and shaped by the social and cultural context in which the rape occurs ... In a study of 107 Ugandan women who had been raped by soldiers, only half had

repercussions may include, but are not limited to, rejection by (or of) the spouse and by family members, stigmatisation or ostracism by the wider community, and punishment and/or deprivation of education, employment and other types of assistance and protection. Where a victim of sexual violence has no alternative but to marry her attacker or become a prostitute, these are also human rights violations.

> *'Rape causes physical and mental suffering in the victim. In addition to the violence suffered at the time it is committed ... [it] also causes a psychological trauma that results on the one hand from having been humiliated and victimised, and on the other, from suffering the condemnation of the members of their community if they report what has been done to them.'*
> [*Raquel Marti de Mejia v Peru*, Case 10.970, Report No. 5/96, Inter-American Commission on Human Rights, March 1 1996]

2A.22   Forcible abortion, sterilisation or acts involving genital mutilation are infringements of the right to freedom from torture, inhuman and degrading treatment or punishment,[1] of the right to private and family life[2] and may be crimes against humanity and, as such, will constitute 'serious harm'.[3]

> *Rome Statute of the International Criminal Court*
> *Art 7 – Crimes against humanity*
>   *1. For the purpose of this statute 'crime against humanity' means any of the following acts when committed as part of a widespread or systematic attack directed against any civilian population, with knowledge of the attack: ...*
>   *g) Rape, sexual slavery, enforced prostitution, forced pregnancy, enforced sterilisation, or any other form of sexual violence of comparable gravity*

Harm Within Family Life

2A.23   Physical and mental violence and ill-treatment within the family is a wide-spread and often gender-specific form of harm. The fact that such treatment occurs within the

---

told anyone about the rape incident as many as 7 years after the rape, despite the fact that all still had problems related to the rape when they finally spoke of it.' and 'For Ugandan women, the experience of rape disrupted their sense of community; keeping this aspect of their lives secret alienated them from other people. These women often expressed the fear that they would be rejected by their partners and the rest of the community.' Giller, JE, *War, Women and Rape*, London University 1995. Thesis; quoted in Swiss, S and Giller JE, 'Rape as a Crime of War: A Medical Perspective' in *The Journal of the American Medical Association* August 4 1992 Vol 470.

1   Right to freedom from torture, inhuman and degrading treatment and punishment: ECHR 1950 Art. 3, ICCPR 1966 Art. 7; CAT 1984, UDHR 1948 Art. 5.

2   Right to private and family life: ECHR 1950 Art. 8; ICCPR 1966 Art 17, UDHR Art. 12.

3   'We would regard enforced abortion as torture, as we would enforced mutilation or sterilisation.' 'I stress that both personally and as a Minister I utterly accept that forcible abortion, sterilisation, genital mutilation and allied practices would almost always constitute torture. In fact, they would probably always constitute torture. There is no doubt in my mind that anyone making a case to us on those grounds would have an extremely good case for asylum.' – Ann Widdecombe MP, Minister of State for the Home Office, House of Commons Consideration of Lords Amendments to the Asylum and Immigration Bill 1995/6(?), *Hansard* Col. 842–844.

   'Caseworkers are reminded that the following acts, when committed or sanctioned by officials, would probably always constitute torture: forcible abortion, forcible sterilisation, or acts involving genital mutilation and allied practices.' Home Office Asylum Directorate Instructions July 1998, Chap. 3, para 2.1.

family context does not mean that it will not constitute 'serious harm' – treatment which would constitute 'serious harm' if it occurred outside the family will also constitute 'serious harm' if it occurs within a family context. As with other forms of harm whether it constitutes 'serious harm' within the meaning of the Refugee Convention should be assessed on the basis of internationally recognised human rights standards.

2A.24   Harm within family life and marriage-related harm includes, *but is not limited to*:

- *forced marriage* – marriage of a person without their free consent;[1]
- *domestic violence*;[2]
- *'dowry death'* or *bride burning* – where a woman is subject to bullying, mental and physical harm and may be murdered or driven to suicide by her husband and/or in-laws who are dissatisfied with the dowry given by the bride's family or in order to obtain further payments of dowry from the bride's family;[3]
- *'honour killings'* – where a woman is killed in order to retain the 'honour' of her family; for example, this may occur where a woman has a sexual relationship, including a marriage relationship, with someone not approved of by the family, or is in some other manner considered to have affected the honour of the family;[4]

---

1   Art. 23(3) ICCPR: 'No marriage shall be entered into without the free and full consent of the intending spouses.'; Art. 12 ECHR: 'Men and women of marriageable age have the right to marry and to found a family, according to the national laws governing the exercise of this right'.

2   For example in Turkey '[s]pousal abuse is serious and widespread. According to the Family Research Institute in the Prime Minister's Office, beating in the home is one of the most frequent forms of violence against women.' Spousal abuse was only made illegal in 1998 and 'is still considered an extremely private matter, involving societal notions of family honour. Few women go to the police, who in any case are reluctant to intervene in domestic disputes and frequently advise women to return to their husbands.' In Nigeria '[r]eports of spousal abuse are common, especially those of wife beating in polygamous families. Police normally do not intervene in domestic disputes, which seldom are discussed publicly. The Penal Code permits husbands to use physical means to chastise their wives as long as it does not result in "grievous harm" which is defined as loss of sight, hearing, power of speech, facial disfigurement, or other life threatening injuries.' – US Department of State, *1999 Country Reports on Human Rights Practices*, February 2000.

3   In Pakistan these deaths are often associated with burns caused by explosions in defective and dangerous ovens, see Canadian IRB Human Rights Briefs: *Women in Pakistan*, June 1994, see also 'The Agony of Pakistan's Stove-burnt brides', *The Guardian*, 3 August 1998. In India the 1993 census notes that approximately 5,000 dowry-related deaths, including suicides, were reported in eight states plus the capital, Delhi although it is officially illegal to demand dowry from the bride's family (see Dowry Prohibition Act 1961 and Dowry Prohibition (Amendment) Act 1984). Husband's families 'commonly demand more dowry after the wedding. Brides often become victims of mental and physical abuse when they fail to meet these demands. In a large number of cases the abuse culminates in suicide or murder', see Canadian IRB Human Rights Brief: *Women in India*, September 1995.

4   In Brazil '[m]en who commit crimes against women, including sexual assault and murder, are unlikely to be brought to trial. Although the Supreme Court in 1991 struck down the archaic concept of "defence of honour" as a justification for killing one's wife, courts are still reluctant to prosecute and convict men who claim that they attacked their wives for infidelity.' – US Department of State, *1999 Country Report on Human Rights Practices in Brazil* (February 2000). With reference to honour killings in Pakistan see Amnesty Report September 1999, *Pakistan, Honour killings of girls and women*. The report states that, according to the non-governmental Human Rights Commission of Pakistan, 286 women were reported to have been killed for reasons of honour in 1998 in Punjab province alone. (pages 3–4 of the report). In Iran the killing will normally be carried out by the family of the woman herself, rather than that of her husband. See Sana al-Khayyat *Honour and Shame:*

- *Sati* – a Hindu practice whereby a widow 'attains virtue' by burning herself alive on her [late] husband's funeral pyre;[1] and

- *Mut'a/sigheh* or temporary pleasure marriage – a 'temporary' form of marriage; it may be, in effect, a form of legal prostitution[2] or even rape.[3]

Homosexuals/Sexual Life

2A.25   Social and cultural norms regarding appropriate gender roles and behaviour may mean that homosexuals face violations of their human rights and suffer persecution. Restrictions on the ability to freely choose and practice their sexual orientation may be a breach of the right to respect for private life. Social, cultural and other restrictions which oblige homosexuals to marry persons of the opposite sex may violate the right to marry only with full and free consent[4] and the right to respect for private life.

'There can be no doubt that sexual orientation and activity concern an intimate aspect of private life' under Article 8 ECHR [*Laskey, Jaggard and Brown* (ECHR) (1997) 24 EHRR 39[5]]

'. . . it seems to me there is now a broad international consensus that everyone has a right of respect for his private life. A person's private life includes his sexual life, which thus deserves respect. Of course no person has a right to engage in interpersonal sexual activity. His right in this field is primarily not to be interfered with by the state in relation to what he does in private at home, and to an effort by the state to protect him from interference by others. That is the core right. There are permissible grounds for state interference with some persons' sexual life – e.g. those who most easily express their sexual desires in sexual activity with small children, or those who wish to engage in sexual activities in the unwilling presence of others. However the position has now been reached that criminalisation of homosexual activity between consenting adults in private is not regarded by the international community at large as acceptable. If a person wishes to engage in such activity and lives in a state which enforces a criminal law prohibiting such activity, he may be able to bring himself

---

Women in Modern Iraq (1990) pages 21–22 quoted in *Re MN* Refugee Appeal No 2039/93, 12 February 1996, Chairman: R. Haines, New Zealand Refugee Status Appeals Authority.

1   In India *sati* is illegal (Abolition of Sati Act 1829, Commission of Sati (Prevention) Act 1987), however the practice is said to continue, see *Human Rights Brief: Women in India*, Canadian DIRB September 1995; see also Owen, M. *World of Widows*, Zed Books (1996) pp 18–19.

2   See *The Status of Women Under Islamic Law*, Nasir, J. Graham & Trotman 1990; *Outlines of Muhammadan Law*, Fyzee, A. Oxford University Press, 1974. In Iran under article 1075 of the civil code, 'temporary marriage, is limited by a period of time, normally specified in the marriage contract. This period may vary from one hour to a maximum of 99 years. The husband may terminate the marriage at any time. He has no obligation to provide financial support, and neither husband nor wife are permitted to inherit from the other. In Iran a man may have an unlimited number of temporary wives': para 2.6.1 *Human Rights Briefs: Women in the Islamic Republic of Iran*, Canadian DIRB, June 1994. see *The Status of Women Under Islamic Law*, Nasir, J. Graham & Trotman 1990; *Outlines of Muhammadan Law*, Fyzee, A. Oxford University Press, 1974.

3   'In Algeria, reports suggest that armed groups have abducted women and girls for forced, temporary "marriages" in which the captive women and girls are raped, sexually abused and often mutilated and killed'. Report of the UN Rapporteur on Contemporary Forms of Slavery, 22 June 1998. (http://www.hri.ca/fortherecord1998/documentation/commission/e-cn4-sub2-1998-13.htm).

4   Art. 23(3) ICCPR: 'No marriage shall be entered into without the free and full consent of the intending spouses.'; Art. 12 ECHR: 'Men and women of marriageable age have the right to marry and to found a family, according to the national laws governing the exercise of this right'.

5   See also, among other ECHR cases, *Dudgeon v UK* (ECHR) (1981) 4 EHRR 39.

within the definition of a refugee.' [*Jain v SSHD* (CA) [2000] Imm AR 82, [2000] INLR 71]

2A.26 Where a case involves a homosexual asylum applicant who is in a stable relationship in the UK IAA judiciary should also bear in mind the Home Office concession policy on same sex relationships.[1]

Section 2B The Failure of State Protection

2B.1 Where an asylum applicant fears persecution from non-state agents, in addition to establishing a well-founded fear of 'serious harm', she must also show that the state has failed or would fail to protect her.[2] A failure of state protection may exist in the following situations:[3]

- If 'serious harm' has been committed by non-state agents and the authorities are *unwilling* to give effective protection; or
- If 'serious harm' has been committed by non-state agents and the authorities are *unable* to give effective protection.

If 'serious harm' has been inflicted *by the State or its agents* (associated organisations or groups) it follows that there is a 'failure of state protection'.[4]

2B.2 The State of origin is not expected to provide a guarantee against all risk of persecution, rather the level of protection to be expected is a practical standard in keeping with every state's primary duty to provide protection to those within its jurisdiction.

> *'The primary duty* [to protect] *lies with the home state. It is its duty to establish and to operate a system of protection against the persecution of its own nationals.*[5] *If that system is lacking the protection of the international community is available as a substitute. But the application of the surrogacy principle rests upon the assumption that, just as the substitute cannot achieve complete protection against isolated and random attacks, so also complete protection against such attacks is not to be expected of the home state. The standard to be applied is therefore not that which would eliminate all risk and would thus amount to a guarantee of protection in the home state. Rather it is a practical standard, which takes proper account of the duty which the state owes to all its own nationals.'* [*Horvath v SSHD* (HL) [2000] 3 WLR 379]

2B.3 The actual practice in the country of origin should be considered rather than theory. In some cases state protection may exist in theory, but not in actual practice.[6]

---

1   Home Office Concession Policy on unmarried couples (including same-sex relationships) announced by Immigration Minister on 10 October 1997 (implemented 13 October 1997), and amended on 16 June 1999.

2   *Horvath v SSHD* (HL) [2000] 3 WLR 379.

3   See para 65 UNHCR Handbook, see also *Horvath v SSHD* (HL) [2000] 3 WLR 379 'There must be in place a system of domestic protection and machinery for the detection, prosecution and punishment of actings contrary to the purposes which the [Refugee] Convention requires to have protected. More importantly there must be an ability and a readiness to operate that machinery'.

4   'In a case where the allegation is of persecution by the state or its own agents the problem [of whether there is state protection and/or a need for surrogate international protection] does not, of course, arise. There is a clear case for surrogate protection by the international community.' *Horvath v SSHD* (HL) [2000] 3 WLR 379.

5   In fact the duty of the state would appear to be owed not just to nationals, but to all within its jurisdiction. See, for example, General Comment 15 on the position of aliens under the ICCPR available at http://www.unhchr.ch/tbs/doc.nsf/...d86ec12563ed004aaa1b? Opendocument

6   For example – in Brazil, men who commit crimes against women, including sexual assault and murder, are unlikely to be brought to trial, courts are reluctant to prosecute and convict

Where state protection exists it must be meaningful, accessible, effective and available to a woman regardless of her culture and position. It should be borne in mind that documentary evidence may not always be available.[1]

2B.4   A woman may be unwilling or unable to alert the authorities of her country of origin to her need for protection, for example, where doing so may put her at risk of violence, harassment, shame, rejection by her society or even prosecution.[2]

2B.5   The legal duties of home states include specific obligations to protect women's human rights, for example:

- *Art. 3 ICCPR:* 'The State Parties to the present Covenant undertake to ensure the equal right of men and women to the enjoyment of all civil and political rights set forth in the present Covenant';
- *Art. 3 ICESCR:* 'The States Parties to the present Covenant undertake to ensure the equal rights for men and women to the enjoyment of all economic, social and cultural rights set forth in the present Covenant';
- *Art. 2 UDHR:* 'Everyone is entitled to all the rights and freedoms set forth in this Declaration without distinction of any kind, such as race, colour, sex . . .'; and
- *Art. 2 CEDAW:* 'States Parties condemn discrimination against women in all its forms, agree to pursue by all appropriate means and without delay a policy of eliminating discrimination against women . . .'.

'Serious harm' inflicted by the State or those associated with it

2B.6   'Serious harm' inflicted by the State and/or by those associated with the state, including sexual violence, is the responsibility of that state regardless of its formal attitude or public position in relation to such conduct.[3]

---

men who claim that they attacked their wives for infidelity and preliminary results from a study by the Catholic Pontifical University of Sao Paulo indicate that about 70% of criminal complaints regarding domestic violence against women are suspended without a conclusion and only 2% of criminal complaints of violence against women lead to convictions – see US Department of State, *1999 Country Reports on Human Rights Practices in Brazil* (February 2000). In Ecuador the law does not allow a person to lay a complaint against a member of their own family thus women who are victims of domestic violence must be accompanied to visit the police authorities by a third party who will file the complaint on their behalf. It is reported that police officers and judges 'tend to look upon domestic violence as a problem between man and wife which should be resolved privately, namely within the family, and they perceive women who are victims of such violence as having asked for it and deserving the blame for it'. Further 'in, general, women who approach the police meet with little but indifference and humiliation. As soon as a woman enters the police station, she is reminded that she cannot file a complaint against her husband, and the person who is accompanying her to lay the charge is often intimidated'. See Research Directorate Canadian Documentation, Information and Research Branch Immigration & Refugee Board, *Human Rights Brief: Domestic Violence Against Women in Ecuador*, December 1994.

1   UNHCR Handbook at paragraphs 196, 197, 203, 204.

2   'In cases where the alleged perpetrator is acquitted, which happens frequently, the rape charge can be converted into an adultery or fornication charge applying not only to the accused but to the rape victim as well. Moreover, medical evidence given by the victim in support of a rape charge can be used against her as proof of adultery or fornication. . . . Even if the victim is cleared of all charges, she must nevertheless bear the shame of an act to which it is believed she consented and which is considered unacceptable in Pakistani society.' paragraph 2.3.2 Canadian IRB Human Rights Briefs: Women in Pakistan June 1994.

3   Even where a state has taken action to prosecute employees for wrong-doing it may still be considered to have acted in breach of human rights – see *Selmouni v France* (ECHR) (1999) 29 EHRR 403. The legal doctrine of 'command responsibility' provides that commanders, superiors and other authorities are liable for crimes perpetrated by their subordinates. 'Any

Under the ECHR State authorities *'are strictly liable for the conduct of their subordinates; they are under a duty to impose their will on subordinates and cannot shelter behind their inability to ensure that it is respected.'* [*Ireland v the UK* (ECHR) (1978) 2 ECHR) 25]

'Current international law establishes that sexual abuse committed by members of security forces, whether as a result of a deliberate practice promoted by the State or as a result of failure by the State to prevent the occurrence of this crime, constitutes a violation of the victims' human rights, especially the right to physical and mental integrity.' [*Raquel Marti de Mejia v Peru*, Case 10.970, Report No. 5/96, – Inter-American Commission on Human Rights, March 1 1996[1]]

'International human rights law which deals with State responsibility rather than individual criminal responsibility, bans torture both in armed conflict and in time of peace. By these human rights treaties, States have committed themselves to refrain from committing torture (through their agents), and to prohibit and punish this crime. With regard to the latter obligation, States have accepted the compulsory jurisdiction to investigate, prosecute and punish perpetrators.' Prosecutor v Anto Furundzija [(ICTY) Case No. IT-95-17/1-T, 10 December 1998[2]]

'Whatever the outcome of the domestic [criminal] proceedings [against police officers alleged to have ill-treated Mr Selmouni while in custody], the police officers' conviction or acquittal does not absolve the respondent State from its responsibility under the [European] Convention [on Human Rights].' [*Selmouni v France* (ECHR) (1999) 29 EHRR 403]

State Law, Policy and Practices

2B.7 The existence of particular laws or social policies or social practices (including traditions and cultural practices) or the manner in which they are implemented may themselves constitute or involve a failure of state protection. Thus, for example:

- a law, policy or practice may be inherently persecutory;
- it may have a 'legitimate' goal but be administered unfairly, in a discriminatory fashion or through persecutory means; and
- the penalty for non-compliance with the law, policy or practice may be disproportionately severe against certain persons/groups.

For example in Pakistan the legal requirements to prove rape are extremely stringent, including a requirement that the victim must supply 'extraordinary conclusive proof' and:

'in cases where the alleged perpetrator is acquitted, which happens frequently, the rape charge can be converted into an adultery or fornication charge applying not only to the

---

commander or other responsible authority who orders a subordinate to commit acts of sexual slavery or sexual violence, *or who otherwise knew or should have known that such acts were likely to be committed and failed to take steps to prevent them,* may be held responsible for the commission of the international crimes which those acts constitute. *The law of command responsibility relates to acts of rape and sexual violence as it does to all other serious violations of international criminal law.'* Persons who are in command may include political leaders, government officials and civilian authorities. Where acts of sexual violence are occurring on a 'widespread or notorious basis' superiors will be presumed to have knowledge of the acts – Report of the UN Special Rapporteur, Ms Gay McDougall, on Contemporary Forms of Slavery 22 June 1998 (http://www.hri.ca/fortherecord1998/documentation/commission/e-cn4-sub2-1998-13.htm)

1   The Inter-American Commission on Human Rights found that the rape, and threat to rape again, by a member of the Peruvian security forces constituted torture under the American Convention on Human Rights.

2   Available at http://www.un.org/icty/Supplement/supp1-e/furundzija.htm

accused but to the rape victim as well. Moreover, medical evidence given by the victim in support of a rape charge can be used against her as proof of adultery or fornication.

... Even if the victim is cleared of all charges, she must nevertheless bear the shame of an act to which it is believed she consented and which is considered unacceptable in Pakistani society.' [para. 2.3.2, Research Directorate, Documentation, Information and Research Branch, Immigration & Refugee Board Canada, *Human Rights Briefs: Women in Pakistan,* June 1994]

Non-State Agents[1]

2B.8   There may be a failure of state protection in relation to 'serious harm' inflicted by non-state actors. Protection may exist in theory, but not in practice. Even where the official policy is to provide protection, no protection may exist in practice.

Such failure of state protection may occur through, *but is not limited to*

- legal provisions or absence of legal provisions (for example, marital rape exemptions in law);
- lack of access to justice and police protection;
- lack of police response to pleas for assistance and/or a reluctance, refusal or failure to investigate, prosecute or punish individuals; and
- encouragement or toleration of particular social/religious/customary laws, practices and behavioural norms or an unwillingness or inability to take action against them.

'... in Pakistan there is widespread discrimination against women. Despite the fact that the constitution prohibits discrimination on grounds of sex, an investigation by Amnesty International at the end of 1995 reported that government attempts to improve the position of women had made little headway against strongly entrenched cultural and religious attitudes. Women who were victims of rape or domestic violence often found it difficult to obtain protection from the police or a fair hearing in the courts. In matters of sexual conduct, laws which discriminated against women and carried severe penalties remained upon the statute book. The International Bar Association reported in December 1998 that its mission to Pakistan earlier in the year heard and saw much evidence that women in Pakistan are discriminated against and have particular problems in gaining access to justice ...

... Domestic violence such as was suffered by Mrs Islam and Mrs Shah in Pakistan is regrettably by no means unknown in the UK. It would not however be regarded as persecution within the meaning of the Convention. This is because the victims of violence would be entitled to the protection of the State. The perpetrators could be prosecuted in the criminal courts and the women could obtain orders restraining further molestation or excluding their husbands from the home under the Domestic Violence and Matrimonial Proceedings Act 1976. What makes it persecution in Pakistan is the fact that according to evidence which was accepted by the special adjudicator in Mrs Islam's case and formed the basis of findings which have not been challenged, the State was unwilling or unable to offer her any protection.' [Lord Hoffmann in *Islam v SSHD; R v IAT ex parte Shah* (HL) [1999] INLR 144, pp 158–159, [1999] Imm AR 283, pp 296–297].

'The line between discrimination and persecution may be crossed when the State becomes involved ... or where the state does not provide "a sufficiency of protection" for its citizens against the most blatant forms of discrimination by sections of the populace.' [*Horvath v SSHD* (IAT) [1999] INLR 7, [1999] Imm AR 121]

---

1   On meaning of 'persecution' and 'failure of state protection' in relation to fear of non-state agents see generally *Horvath v SSHD* (HL) [2000] 3 WLR 379.

'Serious Harm' and Social/Religious norms, practices and traditions

2B.9 Social, cultural and religious behavioural requirements, traditions and norms may consider gender-related harm to be acceptable practice. In such circumstances there will be a failure of state protection where the state is unwilling or unable to give protection.[1] It is irrelevant whether such failure is due to state approval of such social/religious/cultural behavioural norms/practices and traditions, state indifference or impotence.

Failure of state protection may exist through (this list is illustrative not exhaustive):

- legal provisions or absence of legal provisions;
- official legislation;
- lack of access to justice and police protection; and
- lack of police, or other appropriate, response to pleas for assistance and/or a reluctance, refusal or failure to investigate, prosecute or punish individuals.

'and, in particular, the use of tribal social values as well as Islamic ideology to control women . . . Shahrzad Mojab in 'Women from Iran' . . .

In this context, it can be readily understood that the rejection by a woman of such teachings and of the state power used to enforce those teachings will have consequences at both the religious as well as the political levels. . .

. . . we agree with the conclusion reached by Ann Mayor in Islam and Human Rights: Tradition and Politics (2nd ed., 1995) 112 that the evidence overwhelmingly establishes that Islamic principles, Islamic law, and Islamic morality has been interpreted in Iran [by the State] to justify depriving women of any semblance of equality with men, subjecting them to a wide range of discriminatory laws and treatment, and effectively confining them to serving their husbands, performing domestic tasks, and bearing and raising children. Because the religious and political imperatives which operate at state level are intended to operate and in fact operate at the domestic or family level as well, we see no distinction on these facts between persecution by the state and persecution by male family members.' [Re *MN* Refugee Appeal No 2039/93, 12 February 1996, Chairman: R. Haines, New Zealand Refugee Status Appeals Authority]

'What makes [domestic violence against women] persecution in Pakistan is the fact that according to evidence which was accepted by the special adjudicator in Mrs Islam's case and formed the basis of findings which have not been challenged the State was unwilling or unable to offer her any protection. The adjudicator found it was useless for Mrs Islam, as a woman, to complain to the police or the courts about her husband's conduct. On the contrary, the police were likely to accept her husband's allegations of infidelity and arrest her instead. The evidence of men was always deemed more credible than that of women. If she was convicted of infidelity, the penalties could be severe. Even if she was not prosecuted, as a women separated from her husband she would be socially ostracised and vulnerable to

---

1   See for example domestic violence in Kenya: 'Beaten wives challenge custom' *The Guardian* 31 December 1998 – Ms Mwau of the Kenyan Federation of Women Lawyers is reported as saying 'There is a wall of silence surrounding the issue of domestic violence even though it is so widespread' she said, adding that matters were made worse by an institutionalised reluctance on the part of the police and judiciary to tackle the issue.' Kenyan law *'carries penalties of up to life imprisonment for rape, although actual sentences are usually no more than 10 years. The rate of prosecution remains low because of cultural inhibitions against publicly discussing sex, fear of retribution, disinclination of police to intervene in domestic disputes, and unavailability of doctors who otherwise might provide the necessary evidence for conviction. Moreover, wife beating is prevalent and largely condoned by much of society. Traditional culture permits a man to discipline his wife by physical means and is ambivalent about the seriousness of spousal rape. There is no law specifically prohibiting spousal rape.'* – US Department of State, *1999 Country Reports on Human Rights Practices* (February 2000).

attack, even murder, at the instigation of her husband or his political associates.' [*Islam v SSHD; R v IAT ex parte Shah* (HL) [1999] INLR 144, [1999] Imm AR 283]

Internal Relocation/Flight

2B.10   Where an asylum seeker has a well-founded fear of persecution in one part of their country of origin or habitual residence, but it is *reasonable* to expect them to relocate to another part of that country then they will not be entitled to refugee status,[1] [see *Robinson v Secretary of State for the Home Department & IAT* (CA) [1997] Imm AR 568.[2]]

2B.11   The question to be asked in deciding whether it is reasonable to expect an asylum seeker to relocate is: would it be unduly harsh for the asylum seeker to relocate within their country of origin [see *Karanakaran v SSHD* (CA) [2000] INLR 122, [2000] Imm AR 271].

2B.12   An asylum seeker's gender must be taken into consideration when deciding whether internal relocation is reasonable or unduly harsh. Financial, logistical, social, cultural, legal[3] and other barriers may significantly affect a woman's ability to travel to another area of the country, and to stay there without facing hardship.[4]

2B.13   An internal relocation alternative must offer reasonable longevity and be a substantive durable alternative to international protection through asylum. An asylum seeker must not be 'punished' for not choosing internal relocation in the past. There is no duty upon an asylum seeker to 'run and hide' (*Ahmed* 1993 FCJ 718 Canada FCA 1993, p 31 Hathaway).

---

1   The issue of internal relocation falls to be considered only once it has been decided that a woman has a well-founded fear of persecution in one area of country of origin/habitual residence, see *Sharef* (IAT) (15858).

2   'Where it appears that persecution is confined to a specific part of a country's territory the decision-maker should ask: can the claimant find effective protection in another part of his own territory to which he or she may reasonably be expected to move? We have set out in paras 18 and 19 of this judgement appropriate factors to be taken into account in deciding what is reasonable in this context. We consider the test suggested by Linden JA – "would it be unduly harsh to expect this person to move to another less hostile part of the country?" – to be a particularly helpful one.' The factors set out in paras 18–19 are: 'all the circumstances of the case, against the backcloth that the issue is whether the claimant is entitled to the status of refugee. Various tests have been suggested. For example (a) if as a practical matter (whether for financial, logistical or other good reason) the "safe" part of the country is not reasonably accessible; (b) if the claimant is required to encounter great physical danger in travelling there or staying there; (c) if he or she is required to undergo undue hardship in travelling there or staying there; (d) if the quality of the internal protection fails to meet basic norms of civil, political and socio-economic rights.' *Robinson v Secretary of State for the Home Department & IAT* (CA) [1997] Imm AR 568 – see also para 91 UNHCR Handbook.

3   For example Kenyan married women are legally required to obtain the consent of their husbands before obtaining a national identity card or passport and, in Egypt, unmarried women require the consent of their fathers to obtain passports and travel whereas married women require the consent of their husbands; women in Saudi Arabia are not legally allowed to drive motor vehicles and, if they ride in a vehicle driven by a man who is not an employee or a close male relative, risk arrest. See US Department of State, *1999 Country Reports on Human Rights Practices* (February 2000).

4   For example, in Sudan, 'Violence against women continues to be a problem ... In particular displaced women from the South were vulnerable to harassment, rape, and sexual abuse. The Government did not address the problem of violence against women, nor was it discussed publicly.' US Department of State, *1999 Country Reports on Human Rights Practices* (February 2000).

Section 3   Convention Grounds

General Proposition

3.1   The Refugee Convention exists to provide protection to both men and women. The Convention should thus be interpreted in a manner which reflects the experiences of both men and women. This is important when considering whether the asylum claim fits into one, or more, of the Convention grounds. 'Religion' and 'political opinion' in particular should be properly interpreted to include women's experiences.

3.2   In interpreting the Refugee Convention grounds (i.e. race, religion, nationality, political opinion, membership of a particular social group) it is important to bear in mind that the preamble to the Refugee Convention expresses the intention of the drafters to uphold fundamental rights. Guidance should therefore be sought from international human rights law.[1]

3.3   Women may face persecution because of a Refugee Convention ground which is attributed or imputed to them. In many societies a woman's political views, race, nationality, religion and social affiliations are often seen as aligned with relatives or associates or with those of her community. It is therefore important to consider whether a woman is persecuted because of a Convention ground which has been attributed or imputed to her.[2]

3.4   Causation – the Refugee Convention requires that a person must have been persecuted 'for reasons of' one of the Convention grounds. It is not necessary that all members of the group be persecuted. The criteria will be satisfied either where the 'serious harm' was inflicted for a Convention ground or there is a failure of State protection for a Convention ground [see *Islam v SSHD; R v IAT ex parte Shah* (HL) [1999] INLR 144, [1999] Imm AR 283.[3]]

---

1   See Annex III to these Guidelines and the *IAA Factsheet on Treaty Interpretation*. 'The relevance of the preambles [to the Refugee Convention] is twofold. First, they expressly show that a premise of the Convention was that all human beings shall enjoy fundamental rights and freedoms. Secondly, and more pertinently, they show that counteracting discrimination, which is referred to in the first preamble, was a fundamental purpose of the Convention.' Lord Steyn, *Islam v Secretary of State for the Home Department; R v IAT ex parte Shah* [1999] INLR 144, [1999] Imm AR 283 (HL).

2   *Danian v SSHD* (CA) [2000] Imm AR 96, [1999] INLR 533: '... The following propositions are elementary, but need to be restated to assist in identifying the issues in this case: 1. On any view, the Geneva Convention ... only applies in a case where the applicant has a well-founded fear of persecution in the country to which it is proposed to send him by reason of, inter alia, political opinion. 2. That political opinion maybe one imputed to him by the authorities of the country in question, even if it is not in fact held by him...'

3   'Suppose that the Nazi government in those early days did not actively organise violence against Jews, but pursued a policy of not giving any protection to Jews subjected to violence by neighbours. A Jewish shopkeeper is attacked by a gang organised by an Aryan competitor who smash his shop, beat him up and threaten to do it again if he remains in business. The competitor and his gang are motivated by business rivalry and a desire to settle old personal scores, but they would not have done what they did unless they knew that the authorities would allow them to act with impunity. And the ground upon which they enjoyed impunity was that the victim was a Jew. Is he being persecuted on grounds of race? Again, in my opinion, he is. An essential element in the persecution, the failure of the authorities to provide protection, is based upon race. It is true that one answer to the question "Why was he attacked?" would be "because a competitor wanted to drive him out of business". But another answer, and in my view the right answer in the context of the [Refugee] Convention, would be "he was attacked by a competitor who knew that he would receive no protection because he was a Jew".' Lord Hoffmann, *Islam v Secretary of State for the Home Department, R v IAT ex parte Shah*, (HL) [1999] INLR 144, [1999] Imm AR 283.

3.5   In some cases a woman may be placed at risk of persecution simply by removing her to her country of origin from a country where she has been residing. The risk of return for women may be even greater than for men, for example, where women face difficulties in travelling alone or without a male escort.

'*Amnesty International has stated that at the border [of Turkey] the names of all those entering and leaving Turkey are checked against computer records of wanted political suspects. Given the high profile of her family members' involvement, and the history of her own activities, we have concluded that the appellant in this case falls within the category of those persons with a well founded fear of persecution for her perceived political opinion.*' [*Bulut v SSHD* (IAT) (19241)[1]]

Race

3.6   Both men and women may be persecuted on the basis of their race. Women may be targeted, not simply because of their own race, but also because they are perceived as propagating a racial group or ethnic identity through their reproductive role. This may also affect the form which persecution on the grounds of race takes, for example, sexual violence or control of reproduction. Moreover humiliation of women may be used as a method of humiliating an entire community[2] and mass rape may be a means of genocide. (For example the rape of Kosova Albanian women by Serbs in the Federal Republic of Yugoslavia;[3] the rape of ethnic Chinese women in Indonesia;[4] the rape of Tutsi women in Rwanda;[5] the use of forcible mixed marriage.[6]) Rape and sexual abuse in such circumstances will be crimes against humanity in international humanitarian law relating to both internal and international conflicts.[7]

---

1   See also *Senga* (IAT) (12842).
2   'The [RUF] rebels sought not only to control and degrade their victims but also to undermine and degrade the authority of the family and community. The victims described feeling terror, humiliation, and shame, and their parents, husbands, and community elders described feeling powerless at their inability to protect them.' Human Rights Watch, *Sierra Leone: Getting Away with Murder, Mutilation, Rape, New Testimony from Sierra Leone,* July 1999.
3   *The Guardian,* 14 April 1999: 'Serb forces pick off young women as a way of asserting their power and of attacking the ethnic Albanian population by impregnating women with a Serbian child'.
4   *The Guardian,* 15 July 1998 'Raped for the "crime" of being Chinese': 'The sexual terrorism of the Chinese community ... began in early May [1998] when riots broke out after several protests against the then president, Suharto. While the lootings and burnings of Chinese properties stopped after a week, the rape of women of the minority that is hated and envied for its economic success has continued [i.e. the Chinese community]'. *The Times,* 23 June 1998: 'Rape victims relive Jakarta riot horror': 'Horrifying stories of gang rape and racist violence are emerging after the rioting that shook Jakarta [Indonesia] last month. Like the looting itself, these attacks appear to have been specifically targeted – this time against Chinese women, many of whom are said to be still in hiding out of shame'.
5   See *Prosecutor v Jean-Paul Akayesu* (ICTR) Case No. ICTR-96-4-T available at http://www.un.org/ictr/english/judgements/akeyesu.html
6   Human Rights Briefs: Women in Bangladesh, Canadian DIRB, December 1993, para 5.2: 'The CHTC [Chittagong Hill Tracts Commission] has also documented cases of forced marriage of tribal women to Muslim men. According to the CHTC "forced intermarriage is one way in which women are used as an instrument to integrate the [tribal] hill peoples into Bengali society and to change the demographic balance in the area"'.
7   Rape and sexual assault fall within the acts prohibited by common Article 3 of the Geneva Conventions (which applies to internal conflicts) and are specifically outlawed by Protocol II (which applies to internal conflicts). Rape (which is broadly defined and includes sexual assaults, see the international law definitions of rape at footnote 1 at p 283) is specified to be a crime against humanity in the Statutes of the International Criminal Tribunals for

'Moreover, rape is considered to be a method of psychological torture because its objective, in many cases, is not just to humiliate the victim but also her family or community.' [*Raquel Marti de Mejia v Peru*, Case 10.970, Report No. 5/96, Inter-American Commission on Human Rights, March 1 1996]

3.7 A woman's racial identity may be perceived to be linked with that of other members of her family or community. Her racial identity or loyalty may thus be called into question where she has married into or taken a partner of another racial group. A woman may thus be persecuted either because of the racial identity of her birth or upbringing or the racial identity of the family and/or community that she has married into.

Nationality

3.8 Both men and women may be persecuted on the basis of their nationality. Nationality should be understood, not simply as citizenship but, in its broadest sense, to include ethnic, religious and cultural and linguistic communities.[1]

3.9 Women may be deprived of full citizenship rights in certain circumstances – for example if they marry a foreign national. In such circumstances it may be necessary to consider what harm results from this loss and whether it may amount to 'serious harm' and persecution on the basis of nationality.

3.10 A woman's nationality may be aligned, or perceived as being aligned, with that of other members of her family or community, including the family or community that she has entered into through marriage. Imputed or attributed nationality may therefore be an important reason for persecution of a woman.

Religion

3.11 A woman may face harm for her adherence to, or rejection of, a religious belief or practice.

3.12 Religion as a Convention ground includes *but is not limited to*:

- the freedom to **hold** a belief system of one's choice or **not to hold** a particular belief system and; and
- the freedom to **practice** a religion of one's choice or **not to practice** a prescribed religion.[2]

Rwanda and Former Yugoslavia and in the Rome Statute of the International Criminal Court.

1   See Goodwin-Gill, G. *The Refugee in International Law*, Clarendon Paperbacks(1996), page 45.

2   Freedom of religion as defined in the major international human rights conventions makes this clear.
    Art. 18 ICCPR:
    'Everyone shall have the right to freedom of thought, conscience and religion. This right shall include freedom to have or to adopt a religion or belief of his choice, and freedom, either individually or in community with others and in public or private, to manifest his religion or belief in worship, observance, practice and teaching.'
    Art. 18 UDHR:
    'Everyone has the right to freedom of thought, conscience and religion; this right includes freedom to change his religion or belief, and freedom, either alone or in community with others and in public or private, to manifest his religion or belief in teaching, practice, worship and observance.'
    Art 9 ECHR:
    'Everyone has the right to freedom of thought, conscience and religion: this right includes freedom to change his religion or belief, and freedom either alone or in community with others and in public or private, to manifest his religion or belief, in worship, teaching, practice and observance.'

'[freedom of religion is] one of the most vital elements that go to make up the identity of believers and their conception of life, but it is also a precious asset for atheists, agnostics, sceptics and the unconcerned. The pluralism indissociable from a democratic society, which has been dearly won over the centuries depends on it.' [Kokkinakis v Greece (ECHR) (1993) 17 EHRR 397]

'[freedom of religion] also implies, inter alia, freedom to "manifest [one's] religion". Bearing witness in words and deeds is bound up with the existence of religious conviction.'[1] [Kokikinakis v Greece (ECHR) (1993) 17 EHRR 397]

3.13 Where the religion assigns particular roles or behavioural codes to women; a woman who refuses or fails to fulfil her assigned role or abide by the codes may have a well-founded fear of persecution on the ground of religion.

3.14 Failure to abide by the behavioural codes set out for women may be perceived as evidence that a woman holds unacceptable religious opinions regardless of what she actually believes about religion.

3.15 There may be considerable overlap between religious and political persecution. Examples of this overlap may occur, *but are not limited to*, where:

- the state is a theocracy;
- the state supports or favours a particular religious persuasion (including atheism/secularism[2]);
- political activities are undertaken by religious groups; or
- political groups have a religious agenda;
- the state tolerates or otherwise fails to provide protection against the activities and/or social practices of non-state agents who are supporters of a particular religious persuasion (regardless of the state's formal attitude to such activities and/or social practices).

In such circumstances the asylum claim should be considered under the Convention grounds of 'political opinion' and 'religion'.

'It is clear that in Iran there is no clear and defined boundary to political opinion. Autocratic states pass tyrannous laws and frequently do so under the guise of religion. It is not possible in our view to make a sweeping statement that the breach of so-called Islamic precepts does not involve also the expression of political opinion. It may not necessarily do so but it can and often does. A woman who is westernised must we think have considerable difficulty in concealing it. If she reveals it in our view it is perceived in Iran to be the expression of a political opinion contrary to the state. It is not merely transgression of Islamic mores it is transgression of an Islamic mora as interpreted by this particular regime and the two are

---

1   Thus, in this case, the European Court of Human Rights found that a Greek law making proselytising an offence was in breach of the right to freedom of religion under Art 9 ECHR. See also *Iftikhar Ahmed v SSHD* (CA) [2000] INLR 1.

2   For example, in Turkey there is a ban 'on the wearing of religious head garments in government offices and other state-run facilities. Hundreds of women who wear head coverings have lost their jobs in the public sector as nurses and teachers. During the year 312 teachers, including 180 student teachers, lost their jobs for wearing head coverings. Women who wear head coverings also have been prohibited from registering for university courses since 1998, and 47 professors and university administrators were dismissed for wearing or supporting the wearing of head garments. The armed forces regularly dismiss individuals whose official files reflect participation in Islamist fundamentalist activities.' By contrast, in Sudan, a 'number of government directives require that women in public places and female students and teachers conform to what the Government deeded an Islamic dress code.' US Department of State, *1999 Country Reports on Human Rights Practices*, February 2000.

indistinguishable. We are not going so far as to say that every woman can say that she will not abide by the dress laws and by so doing bring herself within the Convention, it depends on the circumstances, but in this case . . . the perception will be that she is making a political statement and therefore the persecution will be for a Convention reason on that basis.' [*Fathi and Ahmady* (IAT) (14264)]

'Given the theocratic nature of the current regime in Iran, the appellant's opposition, both to the patriarchal society comprising her extended Arab family and to the male domination of women in Iranian society at large, is conveniently addressed under both the "religion" and "political opinion" grounds.' [*Re MN*, Refugee Appeal No 2039/93, 12 February 1996, Chairman: R. Haines, New Zealand Refugee Status Appeals Authority]

'the Islamic principle of inferiority of women is now the basis of the policy of a despotic state that uses extreme forms of violence in order to regulate male/female relations on the basis of Islamic dogmas. The Islamic state uses without any restraint the enormous state power in order to regulate the life of women from the moment they are born to the last stage in the burial ceremonies. Every moment in the life of women is regulated in one way or another by the powerful state machinery.'

In this context, it can be readily understood that the rejection by a woman of such teachings and of the state power used to enforce those teachings will have consequences at both the religious as well as the political levels.

'. . . we agree with the conclusion reached by Ann Mayor in Islam and Human Rights: Tradition and Politics (2nd ed., 1995) 112 that the evidence overwhelmingly establishes that Islamic principles, Islamic law, and Islamic morality has been interpreted in Iran [by the State] to justify depriving women of any semblance of equality with men, subjecting them to a wide range of discriminatory laws and treatment, and effectively confining them to serving their husbands, performing domestic tasks, and bearing and raising children. Because the religious and political imperatives which operate at state level are intended to operate and in fact operate at the domestic or family level as well, we see no distinction on these facts between persecution by the state and persecution by male family members.' [*Re MN* Refugee Appeal No 2039/93, 12 February 1996, Chairman: R. Haines, New Zealand Refugee Status Appeals Authority]

3.16 A woman's religious identity may be perceived to be aligned with that of other members of her community and/or family. Her religious beliefs and/or loyalty may be called into question where she has married into another religious group and indeed she may even lose her religious identity.[1] Imputed or attributed religious identity should therefore be considered in a woman's asylum claim.

Political Opinion

3.17 The Refugee Convention does not provide a definition of persecution, but guidance may be sought from international human rights law, the views of academics and the UNHCR Handbook[2] as well as from caselaw.

'In the 1951 Convention, 'political opinion' should be understood in the broad sense, to incorporate, within substantive limitations now developing generally in the field of human rights, any opinion on any matter in which the machinery of State, government, and policy may be engaged.' [Goodwin-Gill, G. *The Refugee in International Law*, Oxford University Press (1996) page 49]

---

1   See Pearl, D. and Menski, W., *Muslim Family Law*, Sweet & Maxwell (1998), paras 6–23, 6–31.

2   UNHCR Handbook paras 80–86.

'The notion of persecution on account of political opinion was conceived in liberal terms [by the drafters of the Refugee Convention] . . . protection on the ground of political opinion was to be extended not only to those with identifiable political affiliations or roles, but also to other persons at risk from political forces within their home community.' [Hathaway, J, *The Law of Refugee Status*, Butterworths Canada (1991), page 149]

3.18 What makes an action or opinion political or non-political is the social structure and social context of the asylum-seeker's country of origin.[1] This point is considered further at paragraph 3.22.

3.19 The Convention ground 'political opinion' covers both the holding of the opinion itself and the expression of that opinion.[2]

'. . . there is merit in [the] submissions that it would be wrong to deny this appellant the protection afforded by the Convention on the basis that the authorities may leave him alone if he refrains from expressing any political opinion whatsoever.' [*Bakor* (IAT) (13793)]

'[the adjudicator drew a distinction between actions and political beliefs], a distinction which we find to be of limited value in asylum law, with great respect to the Special Adjudicator.' [The Home Office Presenting Officer] *'properly in our view, accepts that this was a misdirection of law. A political belief or affiliation may be manifested in more than one way. An intellectual might pen a tract or a pamphlet, a cinematographer might make a propaganda film, a political activist might campaign for his or her party in an election, or someone may simply go to fight for a cause in which they believe.'* [*Orlov* (IAT) (18505)]

3.20 It is important not to underestimate or overlook the political reasons for a woman's persecution even though she may not regard herself as acting politically. She may not directly claim, orally or in writing, that she has been persecuted for reasons of political opinion and may find it difficult to explain the reasons for her persecution.[3]

---

1   See letter from Patrick Tigere, Legal Adviser Standards and Legal Advice Section, Department of International Protection UNHCR Geneva to IAA dated 20 February 2000: 'What makes an action or opinion political or non-political is the social structure and therefore depends on the social context within which the action in question is deemed to take place. This concept has been well-established in refugee studies and needs to be applied in considering female asylum claims in a gender sensitive way'.

2   See for example UNHCR Handbook paras 80–86:
Article 19 of the ICCPR also links opinions and the expression of those opinions:
'1) Everyone shall have the right to hold opinions without interference.
2) Everyone shall have the right to freedom of expression; this right shall include freedom to seek, receive and impart information and ideas of all kinds, regardless of frontiers, either orally, in writing or in print, in the form of art, or through any other media of his choice.'
Article 10 ECHR:
'1. Everyone has the right to freedom of expression. This right shall include freedom to hold opinions and to receive and impart information and ideas without interference by public authority and regardless of frontiers.'
Article 11 ECHR:
'1. Everyone has the right to freedom of peaceful assembly and to freedom of association with others, including the right to form and to join trade unions for the protection of his interests.'

3   UNHCR Handbook para 67: 'It is for the examiner, when investigating the facts of the case, to ascertain the reason or reasons for the persecution feared and to decide whether the definition in the 1951 [Refugee] Convention is met with in this respect.' Also para 66: 'Often the applicant [for asylum] himself may not be aware of the reasons for the persecution feared. It is not, however, his duty to analyse his case to such an extent as to identify the reasons in detail'.

Mainstream and Grassroots Politics and Political Activity

3.21 Both women and men are visibly active in conventional politics and political activities such as, *but not limited to,* belonging to political parties, trade unions or other groups/associations/movements, making speeches, attending demonstrations and writing publications.

3.22 Women's role in society means that they may be more active in forms of political activity seen more often as being within women's domain or in keeping with women's roles. It is necessary to ensure that 'political opinion' is interpreted to include women's political activities.

3.23 Political activities often undertaken by women (as well as by men) may include (but are not limited to): providing community services, food, clothing, medical care, hiding people and passing messages from one person to another. The context in which these activities are performed makes them political, regardless of whether they are inherently political. For example posting posters is not inherently political, but will be if, for example, they support a particular party or cause; cooking food is not inherently political, but will be if, for example, it is part of or supportive of Trade Union activities. Such political activities may put women at risk of persecution on the basis of an actual or imputed political opinion.

3.24 The penalty for engaging in political activity, whether actual or imputed, may be more severe for women than men if engaging in such activities also involves breaching social and cultural norms precluding women's involvement in such matters. For example women may both receive punishment from the state for their activities and be socially ostracised.

Opposition to discrimination against women

3.25 Involvement in the women's movement with the aim of improving women's position within society is political activity.

> there is *'little doubt that feminism qualifies as a political opinion'* [*Fatin v INS* [1993] 12 F.3d 1233 (3rd Circuit)[1]]

Non-compliance with Societal/Religious Codes of Behaviour for Women

3.26 Opinions and conflicts concerning the role of women within society and women's behaviour are conflicts of a political nature. Thus where a woman is persecuted as a result of her opposition to, or refusal to comply with, the prescribed role of women in her country of origin such persecution will be on the basis of her political opinion.[2] There may also be overlaps with persecution on other grounds.

3.27 In many countries clear social roles and behaviour are prescribed for women.[3] They may be:

- prescribed by the state through law, legal structures and social policies;

---

1   US Court of Appeals, Third Circuit.
2   Spijkerboer, Thomas, *Women and refugee status: Beyond the public/private distinction,* Emancipation Council (1994) 'women who fear persecution because they transgress social mores in general are not persecuted because they are women. They are persecuted because they refuse to be "proper" women. When seen in its context one cannot but consider such an act of defiance as being both political and religious'.
3   Note: roles and behaviour may also be prescribed for men.

- prescribed by society, or individuals or groups within society, and upheld or tolerated by the state; and
- prescribed by society, or individuals or groups within society, and the state may or be unable, or otherwise fail, to protect those who refuse or fail to conform.

Such social roles and behaviour may be extremely wide ranging, including, for example: restrictions on ability to vote, to access education, to control reproduction through contraception, to drive a car, to travel alone, to leave the home, to choose a marriage partner, to take employment or to practice certain professions, to dress without adherence to dress codes, to live without male protection, to apply for a passport or identity card, to choose a lesbian sexual partner, and to reject female genital mutilation.

'The Islamic state [of Iran] uses without any restraint the enormous state power in order to regulate the life of women from the moment they are born to the last stage in the burial ceremonies. Every moment in the life of women is regulated in one way or another by the powerful state machinery.' [*Re MN*, Refugee Appeal No 2039/93, 12 February 1996, Chairman: R. Haines, New Zealand Refugee Status Appeals Authority]

3.28 Women may also be persecuted under this head where they do not intentionally or openly oppose or reject the prescribed social roles and behaviour, but do so inadvertently, accidentally or are perceived to do so.[1]

'The 9th Circuit in Fisher … held that [in order to prove that she would be persecuted if returned to her country of origin] the refugee claimant did not have to show that she would take conscious steps to violate the moral codes to discharge this burden. Recognition had to be given to the fact that violation of the codes could occur inadvertently … [in relation to this case] the relentless pressure and harassment to which the appellant was subjected drove her to breaking point and led others to observe that she was likely to explode at the slightest provocation. Given who she is and given her deeply held beliefs, we find it would be highly likely that before long she would be driven to the same point. [*Re MN* Refugee Appeal No 2039/93, 12 February 1996, Chairman: R. Haines, New Zealand Refugee Status Appeals Authority]

'Furthermore, it was not necessary for a claimant to intend to make her views known to the Iranian regime. Martyrdom is not required. [for an asylum seeker to prove persecution].' [*Re MN* Refugee Appeal No 2039/93, 12 February 1996, Chairman: R. Haines, New Zealand Refugee Status Appeals Authority]

3.29 A woman who opposes discrimination against women may be perceived as also holding particular other political views and thus may be persecuted for political opinions attributed to her, regardless of whether she does actually hold those views.

3.30 A woman who expresses views of independence from or refuses or fails to conform to the legal, social or cultural norms of society regarding women's behaviour may be perceived as holding certain political views and thus persecuted on the basis of political opinions attributed to her, regardless of whether she does actually hold those views.[2] [See *Fathi and Ahmady* (IAT) (14264) at paragraph 3.15 above].

---

1   See also UNHCR Handbook paragraphs 82 and 83.
2   Women's dress may be seen as symbolising particular political views, thus in Turkey attempts were taken to prevent an elected female politician from taking her seat on the basis that she wore a headscarf, viewed by Turkey's secular elite as a symbol of political Islam and fundamentalism (*The Guardian*, 'Headscarf MP warns off army' 4 May 1999) and women are barred from wearing religious head coverings in government offices and other state-run facilities – see footnote 2 at p 297.

Sexual Orientation

3.31 A woman's choice of sexual orientation may itself be, or may be perceived as, an expression of political opinion.[1]

Imputed/Attributed Political Opinion – Family and Community

3.32 A woman may suffer harm on the basis of an imputed political opinion as a result of the perception that her political views are aligned with those of dominant community or family members including both her own birth family and community and that which she has married into.

> '*Mr Hurst [the HOPO] in his submissions before us submitted that if we were to find that the second appellant had been raped and tortured then we should conclude that this had nothing to do with the husband's political activities and views. We have to say that this suggestion is not an attractive argument, and that the whole story is really linked to the husband's activities. In her evidence before us, the second appellant specifically said that she was questioned about her husband and that the authorities were concerned to find out about him. We reject Mr Hurst's submission and find as a fact that the detentions, tortures and rape arose as a result of her husband's political activities.*' [*Findik* (17029), (IAT)]

> '*The [European] Commission [of Human Rights] found it established that during her custody in the Derik gendarmarie station [in Turkey]: "... the applicant [a 17 year old Kurdish woman] was blindfolded, beaten, stripped, placed inside a tyre and sprayed with high pressure water, and raped. It would appear probable that the applicant was subjected to such treatment on the basis of suspicion of collaboration by herself or members of her family with members of the PKK, the purpose being to gain information and/or to deter her family and other villagers from becoming implicated in terrorist activities."*' [*Aydin v Turkey* (ECHR) (1997) 25 EHRR 251]

3.33 A woman may be harmed not simply for her own political views or those attributed/imputed to her but also to harm an entire family or community for its political views or affiliations.

> In Sierra Leone the '*RUF forces perpetrated systematic, organised and widespread sexual violence against girls and women including individual and gang-rape, sexual assault with objects such as sticks and firewood, and sexual slavery. These sexual crimes were most often characterised by extraordinary brutality and frequently preceded or followed by violent acts against other family members...*

> *The motive of the attackers, according to what they told the victims, was both to be rewarded for having endured hardship in the bush and to punish their victims for supporting the current government or having sexually accommodated ECOMOG soldiers...*

> *The rebels sought not only to control and degrade their victims but also to undermine and degrade the authority of the family and community. The victims described feeling terror, humiliation, and shame, and their parents, husbands, and community elders described feeling powerless at their inability to protect them.*' [Human Rights Watch, *Sierra Leone: Getting Away with Murder, Mutilation, Rape, New Testimony from Sierra Leone*, July 1999]

Membership of a Particular Social Group

Brief Framework of Analysis

3.34 The three questions to be asked in this framework of analysis are set out below and then referred to in detail.

---

1   For example, this may be the situation where laws, policies or society prescribe a sole or primary role for women as wives and mothers.

In considering whether an appellant is a member of a 'particular social group' it may be useful for decision-makers to ask:

1. what is the 'particular social group' in question – is the group definable? *and 2 or 3*

2. does the 'particular social group' have an identity in the country of origin in the eyes of (a) the community at large or (b) the persecutors; *or*

3. do the members of the 'particular social group' have a 'shared immutable characteristic' i.e. one which either (a) is beyond the ability of the appellant to change either because it is innate and unchangeable or because it is a former characteristic of the appellant which cannot now be changed (e.g. previous membership of the army) or (b) is so fundamental to their identity, their human dignity or conscience that they ought not to be required to change. [See *Re ZWD*, Refugee Appeal No 3/91 (New Zealand Refugee Review Board) [1]]

The existence of discrimination against the group in question may have a particular role in determining whether the group is a particular social group under the Refugee Convention [see *Islam v SSHD; R v IAT ex parte Shah* (HL) [1999] INLR 144, [1999] Imm AR 283].

Identity in the country of origin

3.35 A particular social group will exist where a group of individuals with a particular characteristic are recognised by society as being different from others in the society.

A 'particular social group may either be "voluntary and self-generating" or may, in effect, be created by society where the individuals who form part of the "particular social group" have been set apart by the norms of customs of that society, so that all people who have their particular characteristic are recognised as being different from all others in that society.' [*Islam v SSHD; R v IAT ex parte Shah* (HL) [1999] INLR 144, [1999] Imm AR 283]

3.36 Whether they do so will depend on the evidence and the factual situation in the particular country of origin. Persons who may constitute a 'particular social group' in one country or at one point in history may not in another country or at another point in history.

'To identify a social group, one must first identify the society of which it forms a part.' [per Lord Hoffmann, *Islam v SSHD; R v IAT ex parte Shah* (HL) [1999] INLR 144, [1999] Imm AR 283]

'As social customs and social attitudes differ from one country to another, the context for the [enquiry as to whether particular individuals are "members of a particular social group"] is the country of the person's nationality. The phrase can thus accommodate particular social groups which may be recognisable as such in one country but not in others or which, in any given country, have not previously been recognised.' [per Lord Hope, *Islam v SSHD; R v IAT ex parte Shah* (HL) [1999] INLR 144, [1999] Imm AR 283]

'It is generally agreed that the [particular social] group must constitute a cognisable group sharing common characteristics which set its members apart from society at large and for which they are jointly condemned by their persecutors. What constitutes a cognisable group is in my opinion a function of the particular society in which it exists. Westernised women may be cognisable as a distinct social group in an Islamic country in the Middle East but not in Israel; just as landowners were such a group in pre-Revolutionary Russia but would not be in England today.' [per Lord Millet, *Islam v SSHD; R v IAT ex parte Shah* (HL) [1999] INLR 144, [1999] Imm AR 283]

---

1   Other important cases on particular social group include: *SSHD v Savchenkov* (CA) [1996] Imm AR 28; *Re ZWD*, Refugee Appeal No. 3/91 (New Zealand Refugee Review Board); *Re GJ* [1998] INLR 387 (NZRSAA); *A v MIAH* [1998] INLR 1, 30 G (Aust HC); *Re Acosta* (1985) 19 I & N 211 (US BIA); *Canada (AG) v Ward* [1997] INLR 42.

3.37 The society of a country of origin, the acts of persecutors and other external factors have a role in defining a 'particular social group'.

> *'In general terms a social group may be said to exist when a group of people with a particular characteristic is recognised as a distinct group by society. The concept of a group means that we are dealing here with people who are grouped together because they share a characteristic not shared by others, not with individuals. The word "social" means that we are being asked to identify a group of people which is recognised as a particular group by society. As social customs and social attitudes differ from one country to another, the context for this inquiry is the country of the person's nationality.'* [per Lord Hope, *Islam v SSHD; R v IAT ex parte Shah* (HL) [1999] INLR 144, [1999] Imm AR 283]

3.38 The actions of the persecutors may identify or even cause the creation of a 'particular social group'.

- – see *A v Miah* [1998] INLR 1, 30 G (High Court of Australia)
- – per Lord Steyn, *Islam v SSHD; R v IAT ex parte Shah* (HL) [1999] INLR 144, [1999] Imm AR 283

Shared immutable characteristics

3.39 Particular social groups can be identified by reference to innate or unchangeable characteristics or characteristics that a woman should not be expected to change. Examples of such characteristics are gender, age, race, marital status, family and kinship ties, sexual orientation, economic status and tribal or clan affiliation. Whether these factors are unchangeable, depends on the cultural and social context in which the woman lives, as well as the perception of the agents of persecution and those responsible for providing state protection.

3.40 *Ejusdem Generis* ('of the same kind') approach to 'particular social group' This approach stresses the characteristics of the individual members of the 'particular social group'.

> *'Applying the doctrine of ejusdem generis, we interpret the phrase "persecution on account of membership in a 'particular social group'" to mean persecution that is directed toward an individual who is a member of a group of persons all of whom share a common, immutable characteristic. The shared characteristic might be an innate one such as sex, colour, or kinship ties or in some circumstances it might be a shared past experience such as former military leadership or land ownership. The particular kind of group characteristic that will qualify under this construction remains to be determined on a case-by-case basis'* [*Re Acosta* (1985) 19 I & N 211, quoted with approval in *Islam v SSHD; R v IAT ex parte Shah* (HL) [1999] INLR 144, [1999] Imm AR 283]

3.41 Discrimination – in identifying whether a group will constitute a 'particular social group' the existence of discrimination against that group will be of importance.

> *'In 1951 the draftsmen of Art 1A of the Convention explicitly listed the most apparent forms of discrimination then known, namely the large groups covered by race, religion, and political opinion. It would have been remarkable if the draftsmen had overlooked other forms of discrimination. After all, in 1948 the Universal Declaration [on Human Rights] had condemned discrimination on the grounds of colour and sex. Accordingly, the draftsmen of the Convention provided that membership of a particular social group would be a further category.'* [per Lord Steyn, *Islam v SSHD; R v IAT ex parte Shah* (HL) [1999] INLR 144, [1999] Imm AR 283]

> *'In my opinion, the concept of discrimination in matters affecting fundamental rights and freedoms is central to an understanding of the [Refugee] Convention. It is concerned not with all cases of persecution, even if they involve denials of human rights, but with*

persecution which is based on discrimination. The obvious examples, based on the experience of the persecutions in Europe which would have been in the minds of the delegates in 1951, were race, religion, nationality and political opinion. But the inclusion of "particular social group" recognised that there might be different criteria for discrimination, in pari materiae with discrimination on the other grounds, which would be equally offensive to principles of human rights. **In choosing to use the general term 'particular social group' rather than an enumeration of specific social groups, the framers of the Convention were in my opinion intending to include whatever groups might be regarded as coming within the anti-discriminatory objectives of the *[Refugee]* Convention.'** [per Lord Hoffmann, *Islam v SSHD; R v IAT ex parte Shah* (HL) [1999] INLR 144, [1999] Imm AR 283]

Cohesiveness

3.42 There is no legal requirement that a 'particular social group' will only exist if the members of the group are cohesive or known to each other.

'... I cannot accept the view ... that the expression "particular social group" connotes a number of people joined together in a group with some degree of cohesiveness, co-operation or interdependence. It would exclude the victims of persecution on the ground of birth or social or economic class which was precisely the kind of persecution which the framers of the 1951 [Refugee] Convention are most likely to have had in contemplation. The requirement appears to have originated in the decision of the US Court of Appeals (Ninth Circuit) in Sanchez-Trujillo v Immigration and Naturalisation Service (1986) 801 F 2d 1571 but the decision has not been followed in other circuits in the US Department of State, and the requirement has been rejected in both Canada and Australia. In my opinion it should be rejected here also. The presence of such a factor may demonstrate that a distinct social group exists; its absence does not demonstrate the contrary.' [per Lord Millett, *Islam v SSHD; R v IAT ex parte Shah* [1999] INLR 144 (HL), [1999] Imm AR 283 – see also per Lord Steyn and per Lord Hoffmann]

Existence separately of persecution

3.43 A 'particular social group' must exist independently of the feared persecution. [*Islam v SSHD; R v IAT ex parte Shah* [1999] INLR 144, [1999] Imm AR 283]

Family or kin association

Family or kin associations may define a particular social group. There are cases where women are persecuted solely because of their family or kinship relationships, for example, a woman may be persecuted as a means of demoralising or punishing members of her family or community, or in order to pressurise her into revealing information. [See, for example, *Quijano v Secretary of State for the Home Department* (CA) [1997] Imm AR 227[1]]

Size of the group

3.45 The fact that the particular social group consists of large numbers of the female population in the country concerned is *irrelevant* – race, religion, nationality and political opinion are also characteristics that are shared by large numbers of people.

Section 4   Well-founded fear

4.1 Determination as to whether the asylum applicant has a 'well-founded' fear will include:

- determining whether the applicant has a subjective fear of return; *and*

---

1   See also the discussion of this issue in Crawley, H, *Women as Asylum Seekers: A Legal Handbook*, ILPA (1997) and in Hathaway, J *The Law of Refugee Status*, Butterworths (1991).

- determining whether that fear is objectively 'well-founded'.[1]

Both involve an assessment of *all* the evidence including oral and documentary evidence. Issues of credibility should be considered in light of *all* of the evidence including the documentary evidence about the asylum applicant's country of origin.[2]

> 'It is our view that credibility findings can only really be made on the basis of a complete understanding of the entire picture. It is our view that one cannot assess a claim without placing that claim into the context of the background information of the country of origin.'
> [*Horvath v SSHD* (IAT) [1999] Imm AR 121, [1999] INLR 7]

> '... the adjudicator's credibility finding cannot stand in the light of the lack of reference to any part of the documentary evidence submitted to him. An adjudicator need not refer to each and every part of the evidence. However it is essential that there is reference to a sufficient part of the documentary evidence to indicate that conclusions are based on the evidence as a whole, and, in particular, that any consideration of credibility takes place with an appreciation of the appellant's country of origin'. [*Tharmalingam* (IAT) (18452)]

> '... the probative value of an asylum seeker's evidence must be evaluated in light of what is known about the conditions in the country of origin. If a Special Adjudicator fails to relate an appellant's story to the background evidence on the appellant's country, he has necessarily applied the wrong approach in the case.' [*Jeyakumar* (IAT) (18779)]

> 'An adjudicator must remind himself about the background material and reach his findings on credibility in the light of all the documentary evidence before him. He cannot make a finding on credibility in a vacuum.' [*Acero Garces* (IAT) (14675)]

4.2 The nature and quality of the evidence presented at a hearing will be affected by the evidential and procedural requirements adopted both before the hearing and *at the hearing*. These may cause particular problems for women asylum seekers. All factors within Section 5 on evidential and procedural issues should thus be considered.

4.3 Country of origin information – An assessment as to whether a woman's fear of persecution is credible and well-founded should not be simply based on general conditions in the applicant's country of origin but should take into account the particular experiences of women in that country.

Section 5 Procedural and Evidential Issues

5.1 Particular procedural and evidential issues may arise in relation to the asylum claims of women.

5.2 Women's approach to pursuing their asylum claims may well be different than that of some men.

> 'The first and foremost preoccupation [of victims of torture] is with their asylum claim. There is a noticeable difference between men and women in the manifestation of this anxiety, with exceptions, of course. Men are often much more vocal and active in their anxiety, they change solicitors, seek letters, reports, ask to be brought forward in the queue. They cannot settle. Most women I have seen [over 9 years of therapeutic work with survivors of torture] have just melted into the background after their arrival especially if they have no children, or have left their children behind. They are frequently "befriended"

1   See UNHCR Handbook paragraphs 37–50 and *SSHD v Sivakumaran et al* (HL) [1988] Imm AR 147.
2   *R v IAT ex parte Sardar Ahmed* [1999] INLR 473 (QBD), *Horvath v SSHD* (IAT) [1999] Imm AR 121, [1999] INLR 7.

by a lawyer who does nothing and they stay in the room allocated to them for weeks, months on end, just putting time and distance between themselves and their shame.' [Hinchelwood, G. Dr.,[1] *Gender-based Persecution: Report to the UN Expert Group Meeting on Gender-based Persecution,* November 1997]

Procedures and Requirements – Application/Pre-Appeal Stage

5.3 The procedures and evidential standards/requirements adopted before the hearing by representatives and the Home Office[2] will all affect the nature and quality of the Home Office decision and the evidence presented on appeal. For example, if a woman has been interviewed in the presence of her family members she may not have disclosed certain facts relevant to her claim for asylum[3] and where a woman has not been able to check the contents of her Home Office interview this may affect the reliability of that record (currently the Home Office 'interviewing officers will no longer offer a read over of the written notes after an asylum interview' – letter from the Asylum Policy Unit of the Home Office to the Immigration Law Practitioners Association dated 23 June 2000).

Procedures and Requirements at the Appeal Stage

5.4 The nature and quality of the evidence given at a hearing may be affected by the procedures adopted at the IAA, for example those adopted during the course of the hearing. Thus judiciary should consider whether the procedures which they adopt facilitate and encourage full disclosure by the asylum seeker.

5.5 Women's asylum claims will be more appropriately considered if interviewer, representative and decision-makers, including judiciary, are aware of the particular procedural and evidential difficulties that women asylum seekers face.

At the hearing

5.6 IAA judiciary may regulate the procedure to be followed at hearings; see Rule 30 Immigration and Asylum Appeals (Procedure) Rules 2000. Thus consideration should be given to:

1. provision of a female interpreter;
2. provision of an all female panel (Adjudicator, HOPO, interpreter);[4]
3. hearing the appeal in a more informal environment such as that adopted by the family courts, with the parties sitting around a table rather than a formal court setting;
4. hearing the case 'in chambers' (see Rule 40 Immigration and Asylum Appeals (Procedure) Rules 2000);
5. excluding family members, and/or others, from the hearing room (see Rule 40 Immigration and Asylum Appeals (Procedure) Rules 2000);

---

1 Medical Foundation for the Care of Victims of Torture.
2 For information generally on the conduct of Home Office asylum interviews at ports see Crawley, H., *Breaking Down the Barriers: A report on the conduct of asylum interviews at ports,* ILPA (1999).
3 'Provide women the opportunity to be questioned by themselves, out of the hearing of other members of their family. Victims of sexual abuse may not feel comfortable recounting their experiences in front of their fathers, husbands, brothers or children' UNHCR Gender-Sensitive Techniques for Interviewing Women Refugees, (1991).
4 See for example *Tiganov* (IAT) (11193), *Akyol* (IAT) (14745). See also para. 28 European Union Minimum Guarantees on Asylum Procedures: 'Member States must endeavour to involve skilled female employees and female interpreters in the asylum procedure here necessary, particularly where female asylum-seekers find it difficult to present the grounds for their application in a comprehensive manner owing to the experiences they have undergone or to their cultural origin.'

6. making the determination anonymous (i.e. not including the appellant's name or other facts identifying the appellant); and

7. requesting that evidence regarding sexual assaults be given in writing[1] or through video link. Consideration should be given to the above even where not requested to do so by an appellant or their representative.

Access to the Determination Process

5.7 Female asylum seekers' access to the asylum determination process may be hampered by a variety of factors and this may affect their asylum claims.

5.8 Women who arrive as part of a family unit are sometimes not interviewed or are cursorily interviewed about their experiences by either the Home Office or the representatives. In such circumstances full details of women's asylum claims are unlikely to be disclosed;[2] even where it is the woman, rather than the man, who has the stronger claim for asylum. Male relatives may fail to raise relevant issues because they are unaware of the details or their importance or ashamed to report them. For example, where the woman is not questioned herself, no evidence may have been given that a woman has been subjected to sexual violence, threats or harassment by police as a result of her own political opinions or those of her family. Further no evidence may have been given concerning persecution of the woman from within the family itself.

5.9 Even where women are invited to make independent claims for asylum (and/or are warned by the Home Office about the potential risks of not making an independent claim) women may still have particular difficulties in accessing the asylum determination process.

5.10 The Home Office, representatives, *and women themselves*, often assume that their asylum claims are derivative of male relatives' claims. A woman's claim for refugee status is not necessarily derivative and may be as strong or stronger than that of her male relative.

5.11 Women asylum seekers may not put themselves forward for interview or to claim refugee status independently of their family.[3] There are various reasons for this which may include (but are not limited to):

---

1   Australian Department of Immigration and Multicultural Affairs Guidelines on Gender Issues for Decision Makers ('ADIMA Guidelines') at 3.26, Immigration and Refugee Board of Canada Gender Guidelines ('Canadian Guidelines') D3.

2   'Provide women the opportunity to be questioned by themselves, out of the hearing of other members of their family. Victims of sexual abuse may not feel comfortable recounting their experiences in front of their fathers, husbands, brothers or children' UNHCR Gender-Sensitive Techniques for Interviewing Women Refugees (1991), see also ADIMA Guidelines 3.10, 3.27.

3   Women's approach to pursuing their asylum claims may well be more passive than that of some men. See Hinchelwood, G. Dr. (Medical Foundation for the Care of Victims of Torture), 'Gender-based Persecution: Report to the UN Expert Group Meeting on Gender-based Persecution' 9–14 November 1997: 'The first and foremost preoccupation [of victims of torture] is with their asylum claim. There is a noticeable difference between men and women in the manifestation of this anxiety, with exceptions, of course. Men are often much more vocal and active in their anxiety, they change solicitors, seek letters, reports, ask to be brought forward in the queue. They cannot settle. Most women I have seen [over 9 years of therapeutic work with survivors of torture] have just melted into the background after their arrival especially if they have no children, or have left their children behind. They are frequently "befriended" by a lawyer who does nothing and they stay in the room allocated to them for weeks, months on end, just putting time and distance between themselves and their shame.'

- that official matters are generally dealt with by the man in the family;
- a concern not to offend their husband or male associate(s)/relative(s) by acting independently;
- fear of disclosing information which will bring them into disrepute;
- fear that details of the interview may be disclosed to others;
- fear of dealing with officials;
- a belief that she may achieve safety in other ways; and
- the fact that accepting that one is an exile may be very difficult (see further at 5.43).

5.12   Women may be extremely concerned that the details of the claim and/or the fact that they have claimed asylum be kept secret.[1] Where an asylum interview or questioning is not confidential this is likely to affect an asylum seeker's disclosure of information and may discourage the making of an asylum claim.

5.13   When women apply for asylum as a dependant, they are not necessarily informed *in private*, or in terms and language they understand, of their right to make an independent application for asylum at any stage, or to obtain legal advice on the benefits of doing so. This may affect the number of women making independent claims for asylum and may lead to delay in their making claims – as they will only make the claims having obtained advice or where there is no other option for the family. Thus delay in making an asylum application should not necessarily affect the credibility of a woman's asylum claim (see further at 5.43).

5.14   Not all female asylum seekers enter the UK as part of a family, or other group. Women who enter and seek asylum on their own may also be affected by the matters raised above.

Obtaining Oral Evidence

General

5.15   Women face particular difficulties in making their case to the authorities, especially when they have had experiences which are difficult and painful to describe.[2]

5.16   In the light of some of the particular difficulties which women may face the *judiciary* may wish to consider the procedures which *they* adopt during the hearing and note the options set out at 5.6 above. Adjudicators conducting first hearings may wish to raise these issues at a pre-hearing stage.

5.17   A non-confrontational exploratory interview is critical to allow for the full discussion of past experiences relating to a woman's claim and to facilitate the giving of all evidence which may be relevant to her claim. Where such an interview has not taken place this may affect the nature and quality of the evidence presented at appeal.[3]

---

1   ADIMA Guidelines 3.28.
2   See *R v SSHD ex parte Ejon* (QBD) [1998] INLR 195 a case in which the asylum seeker was unable to disclose her past experiences of sexual violence. See also ADIMA Guidelines at 3.12 and 3.13, Hinchelwood, Dr. G. (Medical Foundation for the Care of Victims of Torture), 'Interviewing Female Asylum Seekers' Paper delivered at UNHCR Symposium on Gender-Based Persecution 23 February 1998 and UNHCR Gender-Sensitive Techniques for Interviewing Women Refugees, 1991.
3   Goodwin-Gill, G., *The Refugee in International Law*, Oxford University Press (1996), page 355: 'Research shows that errors in testimony increase dramatically in response to specific questions (25%–33% more errors) by comparison with spontaneous testimony given in the form of a free report. Such free reports also tend to be sketchy and incomplete, however, and can be most effectively filled out by using "open", rather than "closed" questions.'

5.18 It is necessary to be aware that the manner in which the Home Office interview(s) was conducted and the manner in which the hearing is conducted may affect the evidence given. Evidence may be best obtained if during an asylum interview of a female asylum seeker the interview room and surrounding environment are conducive to open discussion, including providing ample time and ensuring that there are no disturbances[1] and if interviewers and decision makers are aware of, and take into account, for example, women's childcare responsibilities and schedules, distances to be travelled and issues of privacy. Failure to pay attention to such issues may affect the nature and quality of the evidence given.[2]

5.19 Even where the interviewer and the interviewing environment have been supportive of an asylum seeker and good practice has been followed, the interview process itself will impact on the manner in which an asylum seeker gives her testimony and the information which she reveals.[3]

5.20 Any indication that a woman's claim may not be treated as confidential is likely to seriously hinder her ability to provide full details of her claim and may discourage her from making a claim.[4]

5.21 Emotional trauma and depression are likely to affect a woman's ability to give testimony,[5] her demeanour and the nature of the evidence which she gives.

5.22 Women may not realise that it is essential to disclose certain information. Where there are factors which would cause women not to disclose such information, they are unlikely to do so unless clearly asked about such experiences.

Effective Communication

5.23 The failure to appreciate cross-cultural differences may jeopardise the quality of the information revealed by a woman and prevent an effective interview taking place. For example the terms 'rape', 'assault', 'detain', 'charge', 'arrest', 'court' and 'hearing' may have different meanings or different connotations in different countries.[6]

---

1   ADIMA Guidelines 3.15.
2   See UNHCR Gender-Sensitive Techniques for Interviewing Women Refugees, 1991: 'Be patient with female applicants to overcome inhibitions, particularly regarding sexual abuse. Questions may need to be asked in a number of different ways before victims of rape and other abuses feel able to tell their stories. Enough time should be allowed during the interviewing process to permit the female applicant to build a rapport with the interviewer so she is able to recount her experiences. Do not ask for details of the sexual abuse; the important thing in establishing a well-founded fear of persecution is to establish that some form has occurred.'
3   ADIMA Guidelines 3.21.
4   ADIMA Guidelines 3.13.
5   See *R v SSHD ex parte Ejon,* (QBD) [1998] INLR 195 in which it was accepted by the High Court that the applicant had been unable to disclose evidence because of psychological damage. See also Bremner et al 'Deficits in Short-Term Memory in Post Traumatic Stress Disorder', *Am J Psychiatry* 150:7, July 1993 – alterations and impairment of memory may be linked to post traumatic stress. Among the literature on the psychological effects of migration, war, etc. see Bathai P, 'Stress in Exile', *Issues in Social Work Education* Vol 12.2, Summerfield and Toser, ' "Low Intensity" War and Mental Trauma in Nicaragua', *Medicine and War* Vol 7, 84–99 (1991), Summerfield D, 'Addressing Human Response to War and Atrocity' in *Beyond Trauma* (Kleber RJ, ed. 1995). See also the discussion of these issues in *Prosecutor v Jean-Paul Akayesu* (ICTR) Case No. ICTR-96-4-T, 2 September 1988. See also UNHCR Gender-Sensitive Techniques for Interviewing Women Refugees, 1991.
6   ADIMA Guidelines 3.18. See also the discussion of this issue in *Prosecutor v Jean-Paul Akayesu* (ICTR) Case No. ICTR-96-4-T, 2 September 1998. See also UNHCR Gender-Sensitive Techniques for Interviewing Women Refugees, 1991.

5.24   Cultural and other differences and trauma play an important role in determining demeanour, i.e. how a woman presents herself physically, for example, whether she maintains eye contact, shifts her posture or hesitates when speaking.[1]

5.25   Body language can be interpreted in many different ways. It is important that interviewers ensure they avoid gestures which may be perceived as intimidating or culturally insensitive or inappropriate and therefore inhibit discussion.[2]

Obtaining Oral Evidence: Presence of Family Members
5.26   Female victims of violence, discrimination and abuse often do not volunteer information about their experiences and may be particularly reluctant to do so in the presence of family members or members of their community.[3]

5.27   Women from all societies and especially from societies where the preservation of privacy in sexual or marital matters is important may be very reluctant to disclose certain information relevant to their asylum claim or that of other members of their family particularly where that information relates to sexual or family matters.[4] There are good reasons for women not to disclose information about their experiences of sexual violence. These can range from the fact that it is very hard to do due to the fear that her experiences may become known to others and lead to her being ostracised from her family and/or

1   ADIMA Guidelines 3.29. See also UNHCR Gender-Sensitive Techniques for Interviewing Women Refugees, 1991: 'Be aware of gender differences in communication, particularly non-verbal communications. As an interviewer avoid intimidating gestures that inhibit responses. In assessing the credibility of the female applicant, for example, do not judge it on the basis of such Western cultural values as the ability to maintain eye contact.' See also the discussion of this issue in *Prosecutor v Jean-Paul Akayesu* (ICTR) Case No. ICTR-96-4-T, 2 September 1998: '... it is a particular feature of the Rwandan culture that people are not always direct in answering questions, especially if the question is delicate. In such cases, the answers given will very often have to be "decoded" in order to be understood correctly. This interpretation will rely on the context, the particular speech community, the identity of and the relation between the orator and the listener, and the subject matter of the question.'

2   ADIMA Guidelines 3.23.

3   ADIMA Guidelines 3.12, 3.13, 3.27. See also UNHCR Gender-Sensitive Techniques for Interviewing Women Refugees, 1991.

4   The International Criminal Tribunal for Rwanda has noted 'the cultural sensitivities involved in public discussion of intimate matters and recalls the painful reluctance and inability of [Rwandan] witness to disclose graphic anatomical details of sexual violence they endured.' See *Prosecutor v Jean-Paul Akayesu* (ICTR) Case No ICTR-96-4-T, 2 September 1998. Moreover the reporting of rape to authorities is very low even in Western countries. Temkin, J., Rape and the Legal Process, 1987, Sweet & Maxwell discusses rape reporting rates in the UK, USA and New Zealand in some detail – see pages 8–16 and notes the very low reporting of rape in those countries. She records a number of surveys including: USA: United States National Crime Survey 1979 estimated that 50% of forcible rapes were reported to the police, a survey by Diana Russell of sexual assault in the San Francisco area in 1978 found that only 1 in 10 rapes (excluding marital rape) were reported to the police. New Zealand: it has been estimated, in 1982, that four out of five 'rape offences' are not reported. Britain: The British Crime Survey: Scotland (published by the Scottish Office 1984) noted that 92% of sexual offences were not reported to the police; in England and Wales the British Crime Survey (published by the Home Office 1982) estimated that only 46% of rape and indecent assault offences were recorded. A survey conducted by *Women's Own* magazine in 1986 found that 76% of women who claimed to have been raped did not report it to the police; according to the London Rape Crisis Centre 75% of women who reported sexual assault to them between 1976–80 did not report the offence to the police. In the UK the police have concluded that special interviewing techniques and procedures are necessary when dealing with the alleged victims of sexual violence. These initiatives are

community.[1] Further 'some women cannot bear to believe the facts of their having been raped and therefore not only deny it to outsiders but even deny their experience to themselves.'[2]

5.28 If family or community members are present during the giving of evidence/ interviewing this may affect the nature and quality of the evidence given.[3] Good interviewing practice includes asking asylum seekers *privately* whether they want to be interviewed outside the hearing of other members of the family, especially male family members and children.

5.29 These factors apply to pre-hearing interviews and also to the giving of directions and the hearing of a woman's asylum appeal at the IAA.

Obtaining Oral Evidence: Interpreters, Interviewers and Appeals

5.30 A woman may be reluctant, or find it difficult, to talk about her experiences through a male (or even female) interpreter or one who is a member of her community especially where these experiences relate to sexual or family issues.[4]

5.31 Many women have been abused by men. Coupled with a fear and distrust of authorities, this fact is likely to seriously inhibit the capacity of a woman to divulge details of her experiences to a man or through a male interpreter.[5]

5.32 The asylum applicant should be asked whether she would like a female interviewer and/or interpreter. The European Union Minimum Guarantees on Asylum Procedures state that: 'Member States must endeavour to involve skilled female employees and female interpreters in the asylum procedure where necessary, particularly where female asylum-seekers find it difficult to present the grounds for their application in a

---

reported at pages 159–164 of Temkin, J., *Rape and the Legal Process*, 1987, Sweet & Maxwell and include special training for police officers dealing with alleged victims of sexual violence, rape suites, the use of female staff. Note also the pronouncements of the then Deputy Assistant Commissioner Jones of the Metropolitan Police (*The Guardian*, January, 1985) 'We want to kill the myth that rape is sexually motivated – it is usually intended to inflict violence and humiliation.' In relation to Uganda 'in a study of 107 Ugandan women who had been raped by soldiers, only half had told anyone about the rape incident as many as 7 years after the rape, despite the fact that all still had problems related to the rape when they finally spoke of it.' Also 'For Ugandan women, the experience of rape disrupted their sense of community; keeping this aspect of their lives secret alienated them from other people. These women often expressed the fear that they would be rejected by their partners and the rest of the community.' Giller, JE, War, 'Women and Rape', London University 1995. Thesis; quoted in Swiss, S and Giller, JE, 'Rape as a Crime of War: A Medical Perspective' in *The Journal of the American Medical Association* August 4 1992 Vol 470.

1   In Kosovo ethnic Albanian women consider that '[rape] is the worst possible thing . . . They would rather die than be raped, especially the unmarried, whose life is then essentially over.' Indeed the subject is so fraught that counsellors and doctors have great problems in finding out who the victims are: 'They cannot come and admit that they have been raped', according to the humanitarian medical agency, Medecins sans Frontieres, reported in *The Guardian*, 19 October 1999 'Kosovo's Wounded Women find no peace'; ADIMA Guidelines 3.12, 3.13, 3.28, 4.8.

2   Dr Hinchelwood (Medical Foundation for the Care of Victims of Torture), see letter from Medical Foundation for the Care of Victims of Torture to the IAA dated 21 February 2000.

3   ADIMA Guidelines 3.12, 3.13.

4   ADIMA Guidelines 3.13. See also UNHCR Gender-Sensitive Techniques for Interviewing Women Refugees, 1991: 'The recruitment and training of female interpreters is a precondition for the most effective interviewing.'

5   ADIMA Guidelines 3.13, 60. See also UNHCR Guidelines on the Protection of Refugee Women ('UNHCR Guidelines').

comprehensive manner owing to the experiences they have undergone or to their cultural origin.'[1]

5.33 Merely being a female does *not* guarantee an awareness of gender issues[2] and even where the interviewer/interpreters have been female an asylum seeker may still not have fully disclosed all important features of her asylum claim.[3]

5.34 These factors may also apply to the giving of directions and the hearing of a woman's asylum appeal at the IAA.

Obtaining Oral Evidence: Interviews and Appeals: Asking the Right Questions

5.35 The information revealed by an asylum seeker will reflect the ways in which questions are asked.[4] Unless the correct questions are asked it is unlikely that full disclosure will be made either at interview or during the appeal hearing. The use of interpreters exacerbates this problem – unless clear and precise questions are asked they may be interpreted with a different meaning or nuance.[5]

5.36 Some knowledge about the status and roles of women in the country from which the applicant has fled may assist the questioner in asking the right questions.[6]

5.37 Questions asked during asylum interviews and hearings sometimes reflect the dominant conception that a refugee is generally a man involved in conventional politics.[7] It is important to ensure that the questions asked encompass the problems often faced by women. For example:

a)   Questions about political activities should not focus only on political activities as narrowly defined, such as office holding, but should be wider ranging as political activities may also include *but are not limited to* providing food or shelter, message taking, hiding people or refusing to conform to particular social norms.

b)   Where questions are asked about 'persecution' or 'torture' female asylum seekers may not give information about the particular ill-treatment which they have suffered. This may occur because the asylum seeker does not herself understand that the terms 'torture' or 'persecution' may include sexual violence, violence within the family, marriage-related harm, abortion and other forms of harm often suffered by women. A different approach might include asking whether an applicant had been, and feared being, 'treated badly'.[8]

---

1   See European Union Minimum Guarantees on Asylum Procedures, para 28.

2   In Sierra Leone '[v]ictims of sexual abuse frequently reported female rebels having taken part in rounding up operations [for rape and sexual abuse] and often singling out girls and women for their commanders.' Human Rights Watch, *Sierra Leone: Getting Away with Murder, Mutilation, Rape, New Testimony from Sierra Leone*, July 1999.

3   ADIMA Guidelines 3.21.

4   For information on the conduct of Home Office asylum interviews see Crawley, H., *Breaking Down the Barriers: A report on the conduct of asylum interviews at ports*, ILPA (1999).

5   ADIMA Guidelines 3.18.

6   ADIMA Guidelines 3.14.

7   Crawley, H. ,*Women as Asylum Seekers: A legal handbook*, ILPA (1997) paragraph 2.2.4 at p 24 and also Crawley, H., *Breaking Down the Barriers: A report on the conduct of asylum interviews at ports*, ILPA (1999).

8   Crawley, H., *Women as Asylum Seekers: A legal handbook*, ILPA (1997).

5.38 Non-confrontational open and/or indirect questions allow the questioner to establish the applicant's reasons for fleeing and to obtain indications about whether gender-related harm has occurred.[1]

5.39 More direct follow-up questions should be asked to ascertain details of the woman's full experiences. It should be remembered that a woman may not know what information is relevant to her claim and the questioner must use their skills to ensure that the correct information is disclosed.[2] Moreover the questioner may not be aware of what information is relevant until the end of the interview. In such circumstances steps should be taken to ensure that a woman is questioned about these issues.

> '... while the burden of proof in principle rests on the [asylum] applicant, the duty to ascertain and evaluate all the relevant facts is shared between the applicant and the examiner. Indeed, in some cases, it may be for the examiner to use all the means at his disposal to produce the necessary evidence in support of the application...' [paragraph 195, UNHCR, *Handbook on Procedures and Criteria for Determining Refugee Status*, Geneva (re-edited 1992)]

> 'While an initial interview should normally suffice to bring an applicant's story to light, it may be necessary for the examiner to clarify any apparent inconsistencies and to resolve any contradictions in a further interview, and to find an explanation for any misrepresentation or concealment of material facts. Untrue statements by themselves are not a reason for refusal of refugee status and it is the examiner's responsibility to evaluate such statements in the light of all the circumstances of the case.' [paragraph 199, UNHCR, *Handbook on Procedures and Criteria for Determining Refugee Status*, Geneva (re-edited 1992)]

Credibility

5.40 Women may face additional problems in demonstrating that their claims are credible.[3] Information to support a woman's claim may not be readily available and the nature of women's experiences and position in society may make it difficult or impossible for them to document their claims or provide evidence.

Absence of Documentary Evidence

5.41 In many circumstances refugees do not have documentary evidence relating to events which have taken place or their fears of future persecution.[4] The nature of women's activities and place within society may lead them to have particular problems.[5]

The following are some examples (this list is not exhaustive):

    a)   an asylum seeker who has been persecuted because she consistently refuses to wear the veil in protest against Islamisation is unlikely to have a document to show this;

    b)   an asylum seeker who has been persecuted on the basis of her husband's membership of a political party may not herself hold a party membership card and may be unable to produce her husband's card or evidence of their relationship;

    c)   an asylum seeker who has been persecuted on the basis of political activities such as running a soup kitchen for trade unionists, or providing shelter for politicians may not hold a party membership card;

---

1   See footnote 2 at p 293 above.

2   ADIMA Guidelines 3.27.

3   Immigration and Refugee Board of Canada Gender Guidelines ('Canadian Guidelines') D.

4   See, for example, UNHCR Handbook paragraphs 196–197, 203.

5   Canadian Guidelines C2: '... decision-makers should consider the fact that the forms of evidence which the claimant might normally provide ... of state inability to protect, will not always be either available or useful in cases of gender-related persecution.'

d)   an asylum seeker who has been persecuted because of her sexual orientation is unlikely to have documentary evidence of her sexual orientation;[1]

e)   reports regarding circumstances in the asylum seeker's country of origin may fail to document or address particular issues relating to women, even where a sub-section of the report pertains to women.

Corroboration

5.42   In many cases evidence given by an asylum seeker will not be corroborated; absence of corroboration does not mean that the account given is not credible. It is an error of law to require corroborative evidence in an asylum case.[2]

Delay

5.43   Delay in claiming asylum or revealing full details of an asylum claim will not necessarily be due to the lack of credibility of a particular asylum claim or claimant.

- *A woman's priority is to achieve safety and security* (for herself and/or family members). She may not claim asylum whilst she is able to achieve safety, however temporary or illusory, through other means, whether legal or illegal. This may account for the delay in claiming asylum.

- Accepting that one is an exile is very difficult especially if it means leaving loved ones at home. This difficulty may be expressed as ambivalence about enduring exile; this is not an uncommon phenomena among women asylum seekers.[3]

- Torture, sexual violence and other persecutory treatment produce feelings of profound shame.[4] This 'shame response' is a major obstacle to disclosure. Many victims will never speak about sexual violence or will remain silent about it for many years.[5]

- Delay in claiming asylum and/or in revealing full details about an asylum claim may also be validly occasioned by other factors including many procedural and evidential factors outlined in these guidelines (see, for example, access by women to the asylum determination process at paragraphs 5.7–5.14 above).

Demeanour

5.44   The level and type of emotion displayed by a woman during the recounting of her experiences should play a limited role in assessing her credibility. Individual, cultural and other differences and trauma[6] all play an important role in determining demeanour and make it difficult to assess credibility.

---

1   Such cases may be considered either under the Convention ground of 'particular social group' (see paras 3.34–3.38 above) or political opinion (see paras 3.17–3.33).

2   Ackah IAT (10953) 'By making a general finding of lack of credibility and following that with a recording of statements made by the appellant with no reason as to why these should not be credible, apart from lack of substantiation, leaves open the distinct possibility that the reason for the lack of credibility was the lack of substantiation ... an appellant is entitled to know why an adjudicator disbelieves him or her, be it that the statements are inherently improbable, the evidence is contradictory or inconsistent, or the witness' demeanour and the way in which evidence is given. In this determination (apart from the lack of substantiation) there is no reason.' Kasolo (IAT) (13190) 'It is a misdirection, in our view, to imply that corroboration is necessary.'

3   Dr Hinchelwood, Letter from Medical Foundation for the Care of Victims of Torture to the IAA dated 21 February 2000.

4   Dr Hinchelwood, G. (Medical Foundation for the Care of Victims of Torture), Report to UN Experts Committee, 6 November 1997.

5   See, for example, Guler, J et al, *Uganda: War, Women and Rape, The Lancet* Vol 337, 9 March 9 1991 set out in full at footnote 2 at p 284.

6   See, for example, Swiss, S. and Guler, J., 'Rape as a Crime of War, A Medical Perspective', in *The Journal of the American Medical Association*, see footnotes 1 and 2 at p 284 above.

A lack of displayed emotion does not necessarily mean that the woman is not distressed or deeply affected by what has happened.[1] Assessing demeanour of a witness may be particularly difficult where she is from a different country, is giving evidence either through an interpreter or in English which is not their first language.

'*as Bingham MR said at various point of his article in "Current Legal Problems" 1985 Volume 38 at page 14:*

"*A second note of caution must also be sounded. An English judge may have, or think that he has, a shrewd idea of how a Lloyds Broker or a Bristol wholesaler, or a Norfolk farmer, might react in some situation which is canvassed in the course of a case but he may, and I think should, feel very much more uncertain about the reactions of a Nigerian merchant, or an Indian ships' engineer, or a Yugoslav banker. Or even, to take a more homely example, a Sikh shopkeeper trading in Bradford. No judge worth his salt could possibly assume that men of different nationalities, education, trades, experience, creeds and temperaments would act as he might think he would have done or even – which may be quite different – in accordance with his concept of what a reasonable man would have done.*"

'*There is then the further source of unreliability arising principally from the fallibility of human memory. Recollections are known to fade and to be recalled. Evidence from a witness who belongs to some other nationality giving evidence in a language other than English and through an interpreter . . . again are a cause of uncertainty: a matter which an adjudicator should properly take into account in assessing credibility . . . it is generally considered as central to the adjudicator's task that there is an assessment of credibility. In a cross-cultural situation, frequently through interpreters this is a formidable task.*' [*Kasolo* (IAT) (13190)]

'*I cite, for the purpose of adopting it as an expression of my own view, a passage from "The Judge as Juror: The Judicial Determination of Factual Issues", a lecture given by Bingham J at University College, London, on 7 February 1985 and published in Current Legal Problems, 1985, page 1. ". . . To rely on demeanour is in most cases to attach importance to deviations from a norm when there is in truth no norm."*' [*R v SSHD ex parte Patel* (QBD) [1986] Imm AR 208].

'*In assessing the credibility of the female applicant, for example, do not judge it on the basis of such Western cultural values as the ability to maintain eye contact.*' [UNHCR, *Gender-Sensitive Techniques for Interviewing Women Refugees* (1991)]

Evidence where persecution grounds are attributed/imputed and persecution as a family member

5.45 In some circumstances women may not be able to give full details of the reasons for their ill-treatment. This may be a particular problem where women are persecuted for an imputed/attributed convention reason or where they are persecuted because they are a member of a family. Women may not know details of the activities of the relatives, community members whose views/identity are imputed or attributed to them. In many cultures men do not share information about their political, military or even social activities with their female relatives, communities or associates.[2]

---

1   ADIMA Guidelines 3.29.
2   Canadian Guidelines D2; UNHCR, Gender-Sensitive Techniques for Interviewing Women Refugees (1991): 'Understand that women in many societies do not have specific information about the activities of men in their families. Gaps in their knowledge should not be construed as lack of credibility unless there is other evidence of such lack of credibility.'

Oral Evidence – discrepancies

5.46 When two (or more) people give separate accounts of the same set of circumstances it is inevitable that differences occur due to recall, emphasis and perspective. Such differences do not necessarily indicate that the witnesses are not giving a truthful account to the best of their recollection and belief.

Oral Evidence

5.47 There are many reasons, some of which are referred to above, why women in particular are not forthcoming with full information about their experiences which will be exacerbated if gender-sensitive interviewing procedures are not followed. Special care must be taken in relation to evidence pertaining to sexual violence; care must be taken before drawing any adverse inferences where an appellant, or other witness, has earlier described a rape as an attempted rape or as touching, beating or other ill-treatment or even as pain or illness.[1]

Country of Origin Information

Country Information

5.48 Even where a woman does not say that she fears (or has experienced) gender-related persecution[2] or gender-specific harm[3] her asylum claim may well be affected by the position of women in her country of origin. An assessment as to whether the fear of persecution is well-founded should not be simply based on general conditions in the applicant's country of origin but should take into account the particular experiences of women in that country.

5.49 Women's fear of persecution may be influenced by many factors which include, *but are not limited to*: *the position of women before the law (including customary/religious law)* including their standing in court, the right to lay a complaint and give evidence, the weight of the evidence of women,[4] divorce and custody law, the right to own property and to access contraception; *the formal political rights of women* including the right to vote, to hold office and belong to a political party; *women's rights in respect of marriage, family and private life* to marry the person of their choice, or not to marry, and to determine her own sexual orientation, the right to an education, a career, and a job or remunerated activities, the status of widows and divorcees, and freedom of dress:

---

1   '... of 107 Ugandan women raped during war, only two presented with what could be called psychological symptoms (nightmares and loss of libido). Fifty-three percent described their distress in physical complaints (headaches, chest pain and rashes) and 57% in gynaecological symptoms. The persistence of perceived infestation in this group often despite multiple treatment for symptoms (approximately two thirds had no clinical findings of infection) reflects a common sequel to rape of feeling dirty and infected. For Ugandan women, the experience of rape disrupted their sense of community: keeping this aspect of their lives secret alienated them from other people. These women often expressed the fear that they would be rejected by their partners and the rest of the community.' Swiss, S. and Giller J.E., 'Rape as a Crime of War: A Medical Perspective' in *The Journal of the American Medical Association* 4 August 1992 Vol 470.

2   See definitions section at paras 1.11–1.17 above.

3   See definitions at paras 1.11–1.17 above.

4   For example in Ecuador women can only bring proceedings for rape or domestic violence if they have a witness and in Pakistan a woman's evidence is of less weight than a man's – US State Department, *1999 Country Reports,* February 2000, see also Research Directorate Documentation, Information and Research Branch, Immigration and Refugee Board Canada, *Human Rights Briefs: Women in Pakistan,* June 1994.

- *the consequences for women who refuse to abide by or challenge social norms regarding their behaviour* including, for example, norms regarding sexual activity and pregnancy, norms around the institution of marriage including arranged marriages and divorce and norms about behaviour and dress;
- *the incidence and form of violence against women* and the forms it takes (such as violence within the family, sexual abuse, honour killings, bride burning);
- *the efficacy or protection available to women* and the sanctions or penalties on those who perpetrate the violence; and
- *the consequences that may befall a woman on her return.*

Country Information: Documentary Evidence

5.50 There may be limited documentary evidence about the position of women in the country of origin. Background reports and country information often lack adequate information about the problems faced by women.

5.51 Information regarding women may be found from, among other sources:

- the Legal & Research Unit of the IAA;
- mainstream newspapers;
- human rights organisations and institutions including those with a particular concern with women;
- economic development and humanitarian organisations and institutions;[1]
- organisations, institutions and journals specifically concerned with women;
- the Internet or CD-Rom (such as UNHCR's Refworld);
- specialist and expert witnesses familiar with the region and/or the gender issues involved;
- Home Office bulletins as well as reports produced by CIPU; and[2]
- The Women's Legal & Resource Centre, Asylum Aid.

Changes in the country of origin

5.52 The effect of changes in a country of origin must be considered in each particular case and whether they affect the existence and/or well-foundedness of the appellant's fears of persecution. Changes in circumstances in a country of origin which appear positive may, in fact, be irrelevant to an asylum claim, or strengthen a woman's fear of persecution, for example – where a woman fears domestic violence from family members a change of political leadership in her country of origin may be irrelevant to her asylum claim.[3]

5.53 Where refugee status should have been granted at the time of the application, but was not, the burden will be upon the Secretary of State to show that the circumstances have changed in the country of origin sufficiently to result in the fear no longer being well-founded.[4]

5.54 Where circumstances have improved in the asylum seeker's country of origin since the asylum seeker left the question will still be: is there is a well-founded fear of persecution? Any changes which may affect this question must be durable before it can be said that the basis for the fear of persecution no longer exists.[5]

---

1 Economic development organisations and institutions – such as Oxfam, Concern, and the Department for Overseas Development (DFID) are often particularly concerned with the position of women.
2 The Country Information and Policy Unit of the Home Office.
3 Immigration and Refugee Board of Canada Guidelines, C3.
4 *Mohamed Arif v SSHD* (CA) [1999] INLR 327, [1999] Imm AR 271.
5 In relation to the application of the cessation clause (Refugee Convention (Art 1C95)) a 'change of circumstances' in the country of origin must be one which is a 'fundamental' change 'which can be assumed to remove the basis of the fear of persecution. A mere – possibly transitory – change in the facts surrounding the individual refugee's fear, which

5.55   Changes in the country of origin – fear of non-state agents of persecution. Feared non-state agents of persecution may remain in existence and a danger to the asylum applicant regardless of other changes in the country of origin. The decision-maker should ask – do the changes mean that the particular fears of persecution in the particular case are not well founded at the date of determination?

Expert Evidence (including medical evidence)

5.56   If an interviewer or decision-maker receives medical, psychological, professional or other related expert evidence at any stage, it should be considered with care and assessed impartially.[1]

> *'In my judgement it was completely wrong for the tribunal in the present case to dismiss considerations put forward by experts of the quality who wrote opinions [about the situation in the asylum seeker's country of origin] on this case as "pure speculation"'* [per Lord Justice Sedley in *Karanakaran v SSHD* (CA) [2000] Imm AR 271, [2000] INLR 122]

> *'Any medical report or psychiatric report deserves careful and specific consideration, bearing in mind, particularly, that there may be psychological consequences from ill-treatment which may affect the evidence which is given by the applicant. In the tribunal's view, it is incumbent upon the adjudicator to indicate in the determination that careful attention has been given to each and every aspect of medical reports, particularly given that these are matters of expert evidence which cannot be dismissed out of hand.'* [*Mohamed* (IAT) (12412)[2]]

5.57   It should be noted that there is often no physical evidence following rape or sexual violence.

Annex I   UNHCR Gender-Sensitive Techniques for Interviewing Women Refugees

part of UNHCR Guidelines on the Protection of Refugee Women 1991

It may be necessary to use a variety of gender-sensitive techniques to obtain information from women during the status-determination process. The recruitment and training of female interpreters is a precondition for the most effective interviewing:

- Be aware of gender differences in communication, particularly non-verbal communication. As an interviewer avoid intimidating gestures that inhibit responses. In assessing the credibility of the female applicant, for example, do not judge it on the basis of such Western cultural values as the ability to maintain eye contact.

- Be patient with female applicants to overcome inhibitions, particularly regarding sexual abuse. Questions may need to be asked in a number of different ways before victims of rape and other abuses feel able to tell their stories. Enough time should be allowed during the interviewing process to permit the female applicant to build a rapport with the interviewer so she is able to recount her experiences. Do not ask for details of the sexual abuse; the important thing in establishing a well-founded fear of persecution is to establish that some form has occurred.

---

does not entail such major changes of circumstances, is not sufficient to make this clause applicable.' UNHCR Handbook paragraph 135. See also paragraph 136: 'It is frequently recognised that a person who – or whose family – has suffered under atrocious forms of persecution should not be expected to repatriate. Even though there has been a change of regime in his country, this may not always produce a complete change in the attitude of the population, nor, in view of his past experiences, in the mind of the refugee.'

1   In addition to these cases, see also *Zaitz v SSHD* (CA) IATRF 99/0760/4, 28 January 2000.
2   See also *Ibrahim* (IAT) (17270), upholding the case of *Mohamed* (IAT)(12412).

- Recognise that women who have been sexually assaulted exhibit a pattern of symptoms that are described as Rape Trauma Syndrome. These symptoms include persistent fear, a loss of self-confidence and self-esteem, difficulty in concentration, an attitude of self-blame, a pervasive feeling of loss of control, and memory loss or distortion. These symptoms will influence how a woman applicant responds during the interview. If misunderstood, they may wrongly be seen as discrediting her testimony.

- Understand that women in many societies do not have specific information about the activities of men in their families. Gaps in their knowledge should not be construed as lack of credibility unless there is other evidence of such lack of credibility.

- Provide women the opportunity to be questioned by themselves, out of the hearing of other members of their family. Victims of sexual abuse may not feel comfortable recounting their experiences in front of their fathers, husbands, brothers or children.

Annex II Relevant International Conventions

Relevant international conventions include the following:

- The Geneva Convention on the Status of Refugees 1951 and the 1967 Protocol;
- The Universal Declaration of Human Rights (UDHR) (1948);
- The International Covenant on Civil and Political Rights (ICCPR) (1966);
- The International Covenant on Economic, Social and Cultural Rights (ICESCR) (1966);
- The European Convention on Human Rights (ECHR) (1950);
- The 1946 Slavery Convention and Supplementary Convention on the Abolition of Slavery, the Slave Trade and Institutions and Practices Similar to Slavery of 1956;
- 1949 Refugee Conventions on the Laws of War and two additional Protocols of 1977;
- Convention for the Suppression of the Traffic in Persons and the Exploitation of Prostitution of Others (1949);
- The Convention on the Consent to Marriage, Minimum Age for Marriage and Registration of Marriages (1964);
- The Convention on the Elimination of All Forms of Racial Discrimination (1965);
- The Convention on the Elimination of All Forms of Discrimination Against Women (CEDAW) (1979);
- The UN Convention Against Torture and Other Cruel, Inhuman or Degrading Treatment or Punishment (UNCAT) (1984);
- The Convention on the Rights of the Child (CROC) (1989);
- The UN Declaration on the Elimination of Violence Against Women (1993); and
- The UN Platform for Action (1993).

International human rights instruments may be found in/at:

Colombey J-P (ed), *Collection of International Instruments and other Legal Texts Concerning Refugees and Displaced Persons,* UNHCR (1995)

Ghandhi, P.R., *International Human Rights Documents,* Blackstone Press Ltd (1995)

Plender R., *Basic Documents on International Migration Law,* Martinus Nijhoff Publishers (1997)

On the website of the UN High Commissioner for Human Rights:
http://www.unhchr.ch/html/intlist.htm
http://www.unhchr.ch/test/home/inner04.htm

320 *Refugees and Gender: Law and Process*

Annex III Principles of International Treaty Interpretation

In interpreting the terms of Refugee Convention, regard should be had to the objects and purposes of the Treaty (see Vienna Convention on the Law of Treaties 1969,[1] Part III, Arts 31 and 32). Further information about Principles of International Treaty Interpretation can be found in the May 1999 IAA Legal Factsheet 'Principles of Interpretation'.

The Refugee Convention should be interpreted:

In good faith in accordance with the ordinary meaning to be given to the terms of the treaty in their context and in the light of its object and purpose. The context, for the purpose of treaty interpretation, comprises, specifically includes the preamble and annexes of the treaty; see Vienna Convention on the Law of Treaties Art 31.

> '*I return to the argument on construction [of the Refugee Convention]. Mr Pannick points out that we are here concerned with the meaning of an international Convention .... I agree. It follows that one is more likely to arrive at the true construction of Art 1A(2) by seeking a meaning which makes sense in the light of the convention as a whole, and the purposes which the framers of the Convention were seeking to achieve, rather than by concentrating exclusively on the language. A broad approach is what is needed, rather than a narrow linguistic approach.*' [*SSHD v Adan* (HL) [1998] INLR 325, [1998] Imm AR 338 per Lord Lloyd of Berwick]

Principles of Interpretation

1. Where necessary to prevent ambiguity or a manifestly absurd or unreasonable interpretation, recourse may also be had to supplementary means of interpretation including the *traveaux preparatoires* and subsequent agreement between the parties as to the interpretation of the treaty; see Vienna Convention on the Law of Treaties Art 32.

    > '*It is a long-established principle of international law that it is legitimate, when interpreting a Treaty, to take into account not only the context in which it was made but also any subsequent practice in the application of the Treaty which established the agreement of the parties regarding its interpretation. This principle has been formalised in Art 31(3)(b) of the Vienna Convention on the Law of Treaties [which codifies the pre-existing public international law].*' [*Robinson v SSHD & IAT* (CA) [1997] Imm AR 568]

2. The views of academic writers will be of assistance in interpreting the Refugee Convention:

    > '*Of equal and perhaps of greater importance [than the caselaw] are the views of academic writers, since it is academic writers who provide the best hope of reaching international consensus on the meaning of the [Refugee] Convention.*' [per Lord Lloyd of Berwick, *SSHD v Adan* (HL) [1998] INLR 325, Imm AR 338]

3. Consistently with the way in which the Convention is interpreted in other countries.

    > '*As a general rule it is desirable that international treaties should be interpreted by the courts of all the states parties uniformly*'. [*Islam v SSHD; R v ex parte Shah* (HL) [1999] INLR 144, [1999] Imm AR 283]

    > '*In a case concerning an international convention it is obviously desirable that decisions in different jurisdictions should, so far [as] possible, be kept in line with each other.*' [*T v SSHD* (HL) [1996] Imm AR 443]

---

1   In force January 1980. See for example *Horvath v SSHD* (HL) [2000] 3 WLR 379, *SSHD v Adan* (HL) [1998] INLR 325, [1998] Imm AR 338, *Robinson v SSHD & IAT* (CA) [1997] Imm AR 568.

Preamble to the Refugee Convention
Includes the following:

> '*Considering* that the Charter of the United Nations and the Universal Declaration of Human Rights approved on 10 December 1948 by the General Assembly have affirmed the principle that human beings shall enjoy fundamental rights and freedoms without discrimination.
>
> *Considering* that the United Nations has, on various occasions, manifested its profound concern for refugees and endeavoured to assure refugees the widest possible exercise of these fundamental rights and freedoms.'

> '*The relevance of the preambles [to the Refugee Convention] is twofold. First, they expressly show that a premise of the Convention was that all human beings shall enjoy fundamental rights and freedoms. Secondly, and more pertinently, they show that counteracting discrimination, which is referred to in the first preamble, was a fundamental purpose of the Convention.*' [Lord Steyn, *Islam v SSHD; R v IAT ex parte Shah* (HL) [1999] INLR 144, [1999] Imm AR 283]

Vienna Convention on the Law of Treaties 1969
Article 31 General rule of interpretation

1. A Treaty shall be interpreted in good faith in accordance with the ordinary meaning to be given to the terms of the Treaty in their context and in light of its object and purpose.

2. The context for the purpose of the interpretation of the treaty shall comprise, in addition to the text, including its preamble and annexes:
   (a) any agreement relating to the treaty which was made between all the parties in connection with the conclusion of the treaty; and
   (b) any instrument which was made by one or more parties in connection with the conclusion of the treaty and accepted by the other parties as an instrument related to the treaty.

3. There shall be taken into account, together with the context:
   (a) any subsequent agreement between the parties regarding the interpretation of the treaty or the application of its provisions;
   (b) any subsequent practice in the application of the treaty which establishes the agreement of the parties regarding its interpretation;
   (c) any relevant rules of international law applicable in the relations between the parties.

4. A special meaning shall be given to the term if it is established that the parties so intended.

Article 32 Supplementary means of interpretation
Recourse may be had to supplementary means of interpretation, including the preparatory work of the treaty and the circumstances of its conclusion, in order to confirm the meaning resulting from the application of article 31, or to determine the meaning when the interpretation according to article 31:

(a) leaves the meaning ambiguous or obscure; or
(b) leads to a result which is manifestly absurd or unreasonable.

Appendix 7

INTERNATIONAL INSTRUMENTS AND WHERE TO OBTAIN THEM

- **Universal Declaration of Human Rights** (UDHR) (1948) in *Basic Documents on Human Rights*, Brownlie 3rd Edition 1992, 24★

- **1949 Geneva Conventions on the Laws of War and the two Additional Protocols of 1977**, excerpts in Mulamba Mbuyi (ed) *Refugees and International Law* 1993, 239 Thompson Canada Ltd

- **European Convention on the Protection of Human Rights** (ECHR) (1950) in UNHCR *Collection of International Instruments Concerning Refugees*, Geneva 1990

- **Convention on Consent to Marriage, Minimum Age for Marriage and Registration of Marriages** (1962)★

- **Convention on the Elimination of All Forms of Racial Discrimination** (1965)★

- **International Covenant on Civil and Political Rights** (ICCPR) (1966) in *Basic Documents on Human Rights*, Brownlie 3rd Edition 1992, 125★

- **International Covenant on Economic, Social and Cultural Rights** (1966)★

- **Convention on the Elimination of All Forms of Discrimination Against Women** (CEDAW) (1979)★

- **UN Convention Against Torture and Other Cruel, Inhuman or Degrading Treatment or Punishment** (UNCAT) (1984) in *Basic Documents on Human Rights*, Brownlie 3rd Edition 1992, 38★

- **Convention on the Rights of the Child** (CROC) (1989) in *Basic Documents on Human Rights* Brownlie 3rd Edition 1992, 182★

- **UN Declaration on the Elimination of Violence Against Women** (1993)★

- **UN Platform for Action** (1995)★

★ Full texts can be found in Refworld, UNHCR CD-Rom. Details from:
Case Postale 2500
CH-1211 Geneva Depot 2,
SWITZERLAND   Internet: http://www.unicc.org/unhcr

Appendix 8

RELEVANT EXTRACTS FROM THE CONVENTION ON THE ELIMINATION OF ALL FORMS OF DISCRIMINATION AGAINST WOMEN (CEDAW), THE UN DECLARATION ON THE ELIMINATION OF VIOLENCE AGAINST WOMEN AND THE UN PLATFORM FOR ACTION

I. Convention on the Elimination of All Forms of Discrimination Against Women (CEDAW) (1979)[1]

Article 1

For the purposes of the present Convention, the term 'discrimination against women' shall mean any distinction, exclusion or restriction made on the basis of sex which has the effect or purpose of impairing or nullifying the recognition, enjoyment or exercise by women, irrespective of their marital status, on a basis of equality of men and women, of human rights and fundamental freedoms in the political, economic, social, cultural, civil and any other field.

Article 2

States Parties condemn discrimination against women in all its forms, agree to pursue by all appropriate means and without delay a policy of eliminating discrimination against women and, to this end, undertake:

(a) to embody the principle of the equality of men and women in their national constitutions or other appropriate legislation if not yet incorporated therein and to ensure, through law and other appropriate means, the practical realization of this principle;

(b) to adopt appropriate legislative and other measures, including sanctions where appropriate, prohibiting all discrimination against women;

(c) to establish legal protection of the rights of women on an equal basis with men and to ensure through competent national tribunals and other public institutions the effective protection of women against any act of discrimination;

(d) to refrain from engaging in any act or practice of discrimination against women and to ensure that public authorities and institutions shall act in conformity with this obligation;

(e) to take all appropriate measures to eliminate discrimination against women by any person, organization or enterprise;

(f) to take all appropriate measures, including legislation, to modify or abolish existing laws, regulations, customs and practices which constitute discrimination against women;

(g) to repeal all national penal provisions which constitute discrimination against women.

---

1   Full text available on the UNHCR's RefWorld on CD-Rom.

Article 3

States Parties shall take in all fields, in particular in the political, social, economic and cultural fields, all appropriate measures, including legislation, to ensure the full development and advancement of women, for the purpose of guaranteeing them the exercise and enjoyment of human rights and fundamental freedoms on a basis of equality with men.

Other Relevant Articles

Article 4   Equality of Opportunity
Article 6   Traffic in Women and Prostitution
Article 7   Political Participation
Article 9   Nationality
Article 10 Access to Education
Article 11 Employment Rights
Article 12 Health and Family Planning
Article 14 Rural Women
Article 15 Equality in and Before the Law
Article 16 Marriage and Child Custody

II.   UN Declaration on the Elimination of Violence Against Women (UN General Assembly Resolution 48/104) (1994)[1]

Article 1

For the purposes of this Declaration, the term 'violence against women' means any act of gender-based violence that results in, or is likely to result in, physical, sexual or psychological harm or suffering to women, including threats of such acts, coercion or arbitrary deprivation of liberty, whether occurring in public or in private life.

Article 2

Violence against women shall be understood to encompass, but not be limited to, the following:

(a)   physical, sexual and psychological violence occurring in the family, including battering, sexual abuse of female children in the household, dowry-related violence, marital rape, female genital mutilation and other traditional practices harmful to women, non-spousal violence and violence related to exploitation;
(b)   physical, sexual and psychological violence occurring within the general community, including rape, sexual abuse, sexual harassment and intimidation at work, in educational institutions and elsewhere, trafficking in women and forced prostitution;
(c)   physical, sexual and psychological violence perpetrated or condoned by the State, wherever it occurs.

Article 3

Women are entitled to the equal enjoyment and protection of all human rights and fundamental freedoms in the political, economic, social, cultural, civil or any other field. These rights include, inter alia:

(a)   the right to life;
(b)   the right to equality;
(c)   the right to liberty and security of person;

---

1   Full text available on-line at gopher://gopher.un.org:70/00/ga/recs/48/104.

(d) the right to equal protection under the law;
(e) the right to be free from all forms of discrimination;
(f) the right to the highest standard attainable of physical and mental health;
(g) the right to just and favourable conditions of work;
(h) the right not to be subjected to torture, or other cruel, inhuman or degrading treatment or punishment.

Article 4

States should condemn violence against women and should not invoke any custom, tradition or religious consideration to avoid their obligations with respect to its elimination. States should pursue by all appropriate means and without delay a policy of eliminating violence against women and, to this end, should:

(a) consider, where they have not yet done so, ratifying or to the Convention on the Elimination of All Forms of Discrimination against Women or withdrawing reservations to that Convention;
(b) refrain from engaging in violence against women;
(c) exercise due diligence to prevent, investigate and, in accordance with national legislation, punish acts of violence against women, whether those acts are perpetrated by the State or by private persons;
(d) develop penal, civil, labour and administrative sanctions in domestic legislation to punish and redress the wrongs caused to women who are subjected to violence; women who are subjected to violence should be provided with access to the mechanisms of justice and, as provided for by national legislation, to just and effective remedies for the harm that they have suffered; States should also inform women of their rights in seeking redress through such mechanisms;
(e) consider the possibility of developing national plans of action to promote the protection of women against any form of violence, or to include provisions for that purpose in plans already existing, taking into account, as appropriate, such cooperation as can be provided by non-governmental organizations, particularly those concerned with the issue of violence against women;
(f) develop, in a comprehensive way, preventive approaches and all those measures of a legal, political, administrative and cultural nature that promote the protection of women against any form of violence, and ensure that the re-victimization of women does not occur because of laws insensitive to gender considerations, enforcement practices or other interventions;
(g) work to ensure, to the maximum extent feasible in the light of their available resources and, where needed, within the framework of international cooperation, that women subjected to violence and, where appropriate, their children have specialized assistance, such as rehabilitation, assistance in child care and mainten-ance, treatment, counselling, and health and social services, facilities and pro-grammes, as well as support structures, and should take all other appropriate measures to promote their safety and physical and psychological rehabilitation;
(h) include in government budgets adequate resources for their activities related to the elimination of violence against women;
(i) take measures to ensure that law enforcement officers and public officials responsible for implementing policies to prevent, investigate and punish violence against women receive training to sensitize them to the needs of women;
(j) adopt all appropriate measures, especially in the field of education, to modify the social and cultural patterns of conduct of men and women and to eliminate prejudices, customary practices and all other practices based on the idea of the inferiority or superiority of either of the sexes and on stereotyped roles for men and women;

(k)   promote research, collect data and compile statistics, especially concerning domestic violence, relating to the prevalence of different forms of violence against women and encourage research on the causes, nature, seriousness and consequences of violence against women and on the effectiveness of measures implemented to prevent and redress violence against women; those statistics and findings of the research will be made public;

(l)   adopt measures directed towards the elimination of violence against women who are especially vulnerable to violence;

(m)   include, in submitting reports as required under relevant human rights instruments of the United Nations, information pertaining to violence against women and measures taken to implement the present Declaration;

(n)   encourage the development of appropriate guidelines to assist the implementation of the principles set forth in the present Declaration;

(o)   recognize the important role of the women's movement and non-governmental organizations world wide in raising awareness and alleviating the problem of violence against women;

(p)   facilitate and enhance the work of the women's movement and non-governmental organizations and cooperate with them at local, national and regional levels;

(q)   encourage intergovernmental regional organizations of which they are members to include the elimination of violence against women in their programmes, as appropriate.

III.   UN Platform for Action (1995)[1]

Article 113

The term 'violence against women' means any act of gender-based violence that results in, or is likely to result in, physical, sexual or psychological harm or suffering to women, including threats of such acts, coercion or arbitrary deprivation of liberty, whether occurring in public or private life. Accordingly, violence against women encompasses but is not limited to the following:

(a)   physical, sexual and psychological violence occurring in the family, including battering, sexual abuse of female children in the household, dowry-related violence, marital rape, female genital mutilation and other traditional practices harmful to women, non-spousal violence and violence related to exploitation;

(b)   physical, sexual and psychological violence occurring within the general community, including rape, sexual abuse, sexual harassment and intimidation at work, in educational institutions and elsewhere, trafficking in women and forced prostitution;

(c)   physical, sexual and psychological violence perpetrated or condoned by the State, wherever it occurs.

Article 114

Other acts of violence against women include violation of the human rights of women in situations of armed conflict, in particular murder, systematic rape, sexual slavery and forced pregnancy.

Article 115

Acts of violence against women also include forced sterilisation and forced abortion, coercive/forced use of contraceptives, female infanticide and prenatal sex selection.

---

1   The full text of the Platform for Action can be found on the UNHCR's RefWorld on CD-Rom.

Article 117

Acts or threats of violence, whether occurring within the home or in the community, or perpetrated or condoned by the State, instil fear and insecurity in women's lives and are obstacles to the achievement of equality and for development and peace. The fear of violence, including harassment, is a permanent constraint on the mobility of women and limits their access to resources and basic activities. High social, health and economic costs to the individual and society are associated with violence against women. Violence against women is one of the crucial social mechanisms by which women are forced into a subordinate position compared with men. In many cases, violence against women and girls occurs in the family or within the home, where violence is often tolerated. The neglect, physical and sexual abuse, and rape of girl children and women by family members and other members of the household, as well as incidences of spousal and non-spousal abuse, often go unreported and are thus difficult to detect. Even when such violence is reported, there is often a failure to protect victims or punish perpetrators.

Article 118

Violence against women is a manifestation of the historically unequal power relations between men and women, which have led to domination over and discrimination against women by men and to the prevention of women's full advancement. Violence against women throughout the life cycle derives essentially from cultural patterns, in particular the harmful effects of certain traditional or customary practices and all acts of extremism linked to race, sex, language or religion that perpetuate the lower status accorded to women in the family, the workplace, the community and society. Violence against women is exacerbated by social pressures, notably the shame of denouncing certain acts that have been perpetrated against women; women's lack of access to legal information, aid or protection; the lack of laws that effectively prohibit violence against women; failure to reform existing laws; inadequate efforts on the part of public authorities to promote awareness of and enforce existing laws; and the absence of educational and other means to address the causes and consequences of violence. Images in the media of violence against women, in particular those that depict rape or sexual slavery as well as the use of women and girls as sex objects, including pornography, are factors contributing to the continued prevalence of such violence, adversely influencing the community at large, in particular children and young people.

Strategic objective D.1. Take integrated measures to prevent and eliminate violence against women

Article 124

Action to be taken by Governments:

(a) condemn violence against women and refrain from invoking any custom, tradition or religious consideration to avoid their obligations with respect to its elimination as set out in the Declaration on the Elimination of Violence against Women;

(b) refrain from engaging in violence against women and exercise due diligence to prevent, investigate and, in accordance with national legislation, punish acts of violence against women, whether those acts are perpetrated by the State or by private persons;

(c) enact and/or reinforce penal, civil, labour and administrative sanctions in domestic legislation to punish and redress the wrongs done to women and girls who are subjected to any form of violence, whether in the home, the workplace, the community or society;

(d) adopt and/or implement and periodically review and analyse legislation to ensure its effectiveness in eliminating violence against women, emphasizing the prevention of violence and the prosecution of offenders; take measures to ensure the protection of women subjected to violence, access to just and effective remedies, including compensation and indemnification and healing of victims, and rehabilitation of perpetrators.

Article 135

While entire communities suffer the consequences of armed conflict and terrorism, women and girls are particularly affected because of their status in society and their sex. Parties to conflict often rape women with impunity, sometimes using systematic rape as a tactic of war and terrorism. The impact of violence against women and violation of the human rights of women in such situations is experienced by women of all ages, who suffer displacement, loss of home and property, loss or involuntary disappearance of close relatives, poverty and family separation and disintegration, and who are victims of acts of murder, terrorism, torture, involuntary disappearance, sexual slavery, rape, sexual abuse and forced pregnancy in situations of armed conflict, especially as a result of policies of ethnic cleansing and other new and emerging forms of violence. This is compounded by the life-long social, economic and psychologically traumatic consequences of armed conflict and foreign occupation and alien domination.

Article 136

Women and children constitute some 80 per cent of the world's millions of refugees and other displaced persons, including internally displaced persons. They are threatened by deprivation of property, goods and services and deprivation of their right to return to their homes of origin as well as by violence and insecurity. Particular attention should be paid to sexual violence against uprooted women and girls employed as a method of persecution in systematic campaigns of terror and intimidation and forcing members of a particular ethnic, cultural or religious group to flee their homes. Women may also be forced to flee as a result of a well-founded fear of persecution for reasons enumerated in the 1951 Convention relating to the Status of Refugees and the 1967 Protocol, including persecution through sexual violence or other gender-related persecution, and they continue to be vulnerable to violence and exploitation while in flight, in countries of asylum and resettlement and during and after repatriation. Women often experience difficulty in some countries of asylum in being recognised as refugees when the claim is based on such persecution.

Strategic objective E.5. Provide protection, assistance and training to refugee women, other displaced women in need of protection and displaced women

Article 147

Actions to be taken by Governments, intergovernmental and non-governmental organizations and other institutions involved in providing protection, assistance and training to refugee women, other displaced women in need of international protection and internally displaced women, including the Office of the United Nations High Commissioner for Refugees and the World Food Programme as appropriate:

(a) take steps to ensure that women are fully involved in the planning, design, implementation, monitoring and evaluation of all short-term and long-term projects and programmes providing assistance to refugee women, other displaced women in need of international protection and internally displaced women, including the management of refugee camps and resources; ensure that refugee and displaced women and girls have direct access to the services provided;

(b) offer adequate protection and assistance to women and children displaced within their country and find solutions to the root causes of their displacement with a view to preventing it and, when appropriate, facilitate their return or resettlement;

(c) take steps to protect the safety and physical integrity of refugee women, other displaced women in need of international protection and internally displaced women during their displacement and upon their return to their communities of origin, including programmes of rehabilitation; take effective measures to protect from violence women who are refugees or displaced; hold an impartial and thorough investigation of any such violations and bring those responsible to justice;

(d) while fully respecting and strictly observing the principle of non-refoulement of refugees, take all the necessary steps to ensure the right of refugee and displaced women to return voluntarily to their place of origin in safety and with dignity, and their right to protection after their return;

(e) take measures, at the national level with international cooperation, as appropriate, in accordance with the Charter of the United Nations, to find lasting solutions to questions related to internally displaced women, including their right to voluntary and safe return to their home of origin;

(f) ensure that the international community and its international organizations provide financial and other resources for emergency relief and other longer-term assistance that takes into account the specific needs, resources and potentials of refugee women, other displaced women in need of international protection and internally displaced women; in the provision of protection and assistance, take all appropriate measures to eliminate discrimination against women and girls in order to ensure equal access to appropriate and adequate food, water and shelter, education, and social and health services, including reproductive health care and maternity care and services to combat tropical diseases;

(g) facilitate the availability of educational materials in the appropriate language – in emergency situations also – in order to minimize disruption of schooling among refugee and displaced children;

(h) apply international norms to ensure equal access and equal treatment of women and men in refugee determination procedures and the granting of asylum, including full respect and strict observation of the principle of non-refoulement through, inter alia, bringing national immigration regulations into conformity with relevant inter-national instruments, and consider recognizing as refugees those women whose claim to refugee status is based upon the well-founded fear of persecution for reasons enumerated in the 1951 Convention and the 1967 Protocol relating to the Status of Refugees, including persecution through sexual violence or other gender-related persecution, and provide access to specially trained officers, including female officers, to interview women regarding sensitive or painful experiences, such as sexual assault;

(i) support and promote efforts by States towards the development of criteria and guidelines on responses to persecution specifically aimed at women, by sharing information on States' initiatives to develop such criteria and guidelines and by monitoring to ensure their fair and consistent application;

(j) promote the self-reliant capacities of refugee women, other displaced women in need of international protection and internally displaced women and provide programmes for women, particularly young women, in leadership and decision-making within refugee and returnee communities;

(k) ensure that the human rights of refugee and displaced women are protected and that refugee and displaced women are made aware of these rights; ensure that the vital importance of family reunification is recognized;

(l) provide, as appropriate, women who have been determined refugees with access to vocational/professional training programmes, including language training, small-scale enterprise development training and planning and counselling on all forms of violence against women, which should include rehabilitation programmes for victims of torture and trauma; Governments and other donors should contribute adequately to assistance programmes for refugee women, other displaced women in need of international protection and internally displaced women, taking into account in particular the effects on the host countries of the increasing requirements of large refugee populations and the need to widen the donor base and to achieve greater burden-sharing;

(m) raise public awareness of the contribution made by refugee women to their countries of resettlement, promote understanding of their human rights and of their needs and abilities and encourage mutual understanding and acceptance through educational programmes promoting cross-cultural and interracial harmony;

(n) provide basic and support services to women who are displaced from their place of origin as a result of terrorism, violence, drug trafficking or other reasons linked to violence situations

Article 148
Actions to be taken by Governments;

(a) disseminate and implement the UNHCR Guidelines on the Protection of Refugee Women and the UNHCR Guidelines on Evaluation and Care of Victims of Trauma and Violence, or provide similar guidance, in close co-operation with refugee women and in all sectors of refugee programmes;

(b) protect women and children who migrate as family members from abuse or denial of their human rights by sponsors and consider extending their stay, should the family relationship dissolve, within the limits of national legislation.

Article 224
Violence against women both violates and impairs or nullifies the enjoyment by women of human rights and fundamental freedoms. Taking into account the Declaration on the Elimination of Violence against Women and the work of Special Rapporteurs, gender-based violence, such as battering and other domestic violence, sexual abuse, sexual slavery and exploitation, and international trafficking in women and children, forced prostitution and sexual harassment, as well as violence against women, resulting from cultural prejudice, racism and racial discrimination, xenophobia, pornography, ethnic cleansing, armed conflict, foreign occupation, religious and anti-religious extremism and terrorism are incompatible with the dignity and the worth of the human person and must be combated and eliminated. Any harmful aspect of certain traditional, customary or modern practices that violates the rights of women should be prohibited and eliminated. Governments should take urgent action to combat and eliminate all forms of violence against women in private and public life, whether perpetrated or tolerated by the State or private persons.

Appendix 9

THE MICHIGAN GUIDELINES ON THE INTERNATIONAL PROTECTION ALTERNATIVE
(April 1999)

In many jurisdictions around the world, 'internal flight' or 'internal relocation' rules are increasingly relied upon to deny refugee status to persons at risk of persecution for a Convention reason in part, but not all, of their country of origin. In this, as in so many areas of refugee law and policy, the viability of a universal commitment to protection is challenged by divergence in state practice. These Guidelines seek to define the ways in which international refugee law should inform what the authors believe is more accurately described as the 'internal protection alternative.' It is the product of collective study of relevant norms and state practice, debated and refined at the First Colloquium on Challenges in International Refugee Law, in April 1999.

The analytical framework

1. The essence of the refugee definition set out in Art. 1(A)(2) of the 1951 Convention relating to the Status of Refugees ('Refugee Convention') is the identification of persons who are entitled to claim protection in a contracting state against the risk of persecution in their own country. This duty of state parties to provide surrogate protection arises only in relation to persons who are either unable to benefit from the protection of their own state, or who are unwilling to accept that state's protection because of a well-founded fear of persecution.

2. It therefore follows that to the extent meaningful protection against the risk of persecution is genuinely available to an asylum-seeker, Convention refugee status need not be recognized.

3. Both the risk of persecution and availability of countervailing protection were traditionally assessed simply in relation to an asylum-seeker's place of origin. The implicit operating assumption was that evidence of a sufficiently serious risk in one part of the state of origin could be said to give rise to a well-founded fear of persecution in the asylum-seeker's 'country.' Contemporary practice in most developed states of asylum has, however, evolved to take account of regionalized variations of risk within countries of origin. Under the rubric of so-called 'internal flight' or 'internal relocation' rules, states increasingly decline to recognize as Convention refugees persons acknowledged to be at risk in one locality on the grounds that protection should have been, or could be, sought elsewhere inside the state of origin.

4. In some circumstances, meaningful protection against the risk of persecution can be provided inside the boundaries of an asylum-seeker's state of origin. Where a careful inquiry determines that a particular asylum-seeker has an 'internal protection alternative,' it is lawful to deny recognition of Convention refugee status.

5. A lawful inquiry into the existence of an 'internal protection alternative' is not, however, simply an examination of whether an asylum-seeker might have avoided departure from her or his country of origin ('internal flight'). Nor is it only an assessment of whether the risk of persecution can presently be avoided somewhere inside the asylum-seeker's country of origin ('internal relocation'). Instead, 'internal protection

alternative' analysis should be directed to the identification of asylum-seekers who do not require international protection against the risk of persecution in their own country because they can presently access meaningful protection in a part of their own country. So conceived, internal protection analysis can be carried out in full conformity with the requirements of the Refugee Convention.

6.   We set out below a summary of our understanding of the circumstances under which refugee protection may lawfully be denied by a putative asylum state on the grounds that an asylum-seeker is able to avail himself or herself of an 'internal protection alternative.' Our analysis is based on the requirements of the Refugee Convention, and is informed primarily by the jurisprudence of leading developed states of asylum. No attempt is made here to address the additional limitations on removal of asylum-seekers from a state's territory that may follow from other international legal obligations, or from a given state's domestic laws. In particular, state parties to the Organization of African Unity's Convention governing the specific aspects of refugee problems in Africa have obligated themselves to protect not only Convention refugees, but also persons at risk due to '. . . external aggression, occupation, foreign domination or events seriously disturbing public order in either part or the whole of [the] country of origin or nationality . . . (emphasis added).'

7.   More generally, state parties are under no duty to decline recognition of refugee status to asylum-seekers who are able to avail themselves of an 'internal protection alternative.' Because refugee status is evaluated in relation to conditions in the asylum-seeker's country of nationality or former habitual residence, and because no express provision is made for the exclusion from Convention refugee status of persons able to avail themselves of meaningful internal protection, state parties remain entitled to recognize the refugee status of persons who fear persecution in only one part of their country of origin.

General nature and requirements of 'internal protection alternative' analysis

8.   There is no justification in international law to refuse recognition of refugee status on the basis of a purely retrospective assessment of conditions at the time of an asylum-seeker's departure from the home state. The duty of protection under the Refugee Convention is explicitly premised on a prospective evaluation of risk. That is, an individual is a Convention refugee only if she or he would presently be at risk of persecution in the state of origin, whatever the circumstances at the time of departure from the home state. Internal protection analysis informs this inquiry only if directed to the identification of a present possibility of meaningful protection within the boundaries of the home state.

9.   Because this prospective analysis of internal protection occurs at a point in time when the asylum-seeker has already left his or her home state, a present possibility of meaningful protection inside the home state exists only if the asylum-seeker can be returned to the internal region adjudged to satisfy the 'internal protection alternative' criteria. A refugee claim should not be denied on internal protection grounds unless the putative asylum state is in fact able safely and practically to return the asylum-seeker to the site of internal protection.

10.   Legally relevant internal protection should ordinarily be provided by the national government of the state of origin, whether directly or by lawful delegation to a regional or local government. In keeping with the basic commitment of the Refugee Convention to respond to the fundamental breakdown of state protection by establishing surrogate state protection through an interstate treaty, return on internal protection grounds to a region controlled by a non-state entity should be contemplated only where there is compelling evidence of that entity's ability to deliver durable protection, as described below at paras. 15–22.

11.   The evaluation of internal protection is inherent in the Convention's requirement that a refugee not only have a well-founded fear of being persecuted, but also be 'unable or, owing to such fear, [be] unwilling to avail himself of the protection of [her or his] country.'

12.   The first question to be considered is therefore whether the asylum-seeker faces a well-founded fear of persecution for a Convention reason in at least some part of his or her country of origin. This primary inquiry should be completed before consideration is given to the availability of an 'internal protection alternative.' The reality of internal protection can only be adequately measured on the basis of an understanding of the precise risk faced by an asylum-seeker.

13.   Assessed against the backdrop of an ascertained risk of persecution for a Convention reason in at least one part of the country, the second question is whether the asylum-seeker has access to meaningful internal protection against the risk of persecution. This inquiry may, in turn, be broken down into three parts:

(a)   Does the proposed site of internal protection afford the asylum-seeker a meaningful 'antidote' to the identified risk of persecution?

(b)   Is the proposed site of internal protection free from other risks which either amount to, or are tantamount to, a risk of persecution?

(c)   Do local conditions in the proposed site of internal protection at least meet the Refugee Convention's minimalist conceptualization of 'protection'?

14.   Because this inquiry into the existence of an 'internal protection alternative' is predicated on the existence of a well-founded fear of persecution for a Convention reason in at least one region of the asylum-seeker's state of origin, and hence on a presumptive entitlement to Convention refugee status, the burden of proof to establish the existence of countervailing internal protection as described in para. 13 should in all cases be on the government of the putative asylum state.

The first requirement: an 'antidote' to the primary risk of persecution
15.   First, the 'internal protection alternative' must be a place in which the asylum-seeker no longer faces the well-founded fear of persecution for a Convention reason which gave rise to her or his presumptive need for protection against the risk in one region of the country of origin. It is not enough simply to find that the original agent or author of persecution has not yet established a presence in the proposed site of internal protection. There must be reason to believe that the reach of the agent or author of persecution is likely to remain localized outside the designated place of internal protection.

16.   There should therefore be a strong presumption against finding an 'internal protection alternative' where the agent or author of the original risk of persecution is, or is sponsored by, the national government.

The second requirement: no additional risk of, or equivalent to, persecution
17.   A meaningful understanding of internal protection from the risk of persecution requires consideration of more than just the existence of an 'antidote' to the risk identified in one part of the country of origin. If a distinct risk of even generalized serious harm exists in the proposed site of internal protection, the request for recognition of refugee status may not be denied on internal protection grounds. This requirement may be justified in either of two ways.

18.   First, the asylum-seeker may have an independent refugee claim in relation to the proposed site of internal protection. If the harm feared is of sufficient gravity to fall within

the ambit of persecution, the requirement to show a nexus to a Convention reason is arguably satisfied as well. This is so since but for the fear of persecution in one part of the country of origin for a Convention reason, the asylum-seeker would not now be exposed to the risk in the proposed site of internal protection.

19.   Second, the legal duty to avoid exposing the asylum-seeker to serious risk in the place of internal protection may be derived by reference to the Refugee Convention's Art. 33(1), which requires state parties to avoid the return of a refugee '... in any manner whatsoever to the frontiers of territories where his life or freedom would be threatened...' for a Convention reason. Where the intensity of the harms specific to the proposed site of internal protection (such as, for example, famine or sustained conflict) rises to a particularly high level, even if not amounting to a risk of persecution, an asylum-seeker may in practice feel compelled to abandon the proposed site of protection, even if the only alternative is return to a known risk of persecution for a Convention reason elsewhere in the country of origin.

The third requirement: existence of a minimalist commitment to affirmative protection

20.   The denial of refugee status is predicated not simply on the absence of a risk of persecution in some part of the state of origin, but on a finding that the asylum-seeker can access internal protection there. This understanding follows from the prima facie need for international refugee protection of all asylum-seekers whose cases are subjected to internal protection analysis. If recognition of refugee status is to be denied to such persons on the grounds that the protection to which they are presumptively entitled can in fact be accessed within their own state, then the sufficiency of that internal protection is logically measured by reference to the scope of the protection which refugee law guarantees.

21.   Good reasons may be advanced to refer to a range of widely recognized international human rights in defining the irreducible core content of affirmative protection in the proposed site of internal protection. In particular, one might rely on the reference in the Refugee Convention's Preamble to the importance of '... the principle that human beings shall enjoy fundamental rights and freedoms without discrimination.' Yet the Refugee Convention itself does not establish a duty on state parties to guarantee all such rights and freedoms to refugees. Instead, Arts. 2–33 establish an endogenous definition of the rights and freedoms viewed as requisite to '... revise and consolidate previous international agreements relating to the status of refugees and to extend the scope of and the protection accorded by such instruments ....' These rights are for the most part framed in relative terms, effectively mandating a general duty of non-discrimination as between refugees and others.

22.   At a minimum, therefore, conditions in the proposed site of internal protection ought to satisfy the affirmative, yet relative, standards set by this textually explicit definition of the content of protection. The relevant measure is the treatment of other persons in the proposed site of internal protection, not in the putative asylum country. Thus, internal protection requires not only protection against the risk of persecution, but also the assimilation of the asylum-seeker with others in the site of internal protection for purposes of access to, for example, employment, public welfare, and education.

'Reasonableness'

23.   Most states that presently rely on either 'internal flight' or 'internal relocation' analysis also require decision-makers to consider whether, generally or in light of a particular asylum-seeker's circumstances, it would be 'reasonable' to require return to the proposed site of internal protection. If the careful approach to identification and assessment of an 'internal protection alternative' proposed here is followed, there is no

additional duty under international refugee law to assess the 'reasonableness' of return to the region identified as able to protect the asylum-seeker.

24. Assessment of the 'reasonableness' of return may nonetheless be viewed as consistent with the spirit of Recommendation E of the Conference of Plenipotentiaries, that the Refugee Convention '. . . have value as an example exceeding its contractual scope and that all nations . . . be guided by it in granting so far as possible to persons in their territory as refugees and who would not be covered by the terms of the Convention, the treatment for which it provides.'

Procedural safeguards

25. Because the viability of an 'internal protection alternative' can only be assessed with full knowledge of the risks in other regions of the state of origin (see paras. 15–16), internal protection analysis should never be included as a criterion for denial of refugee status under an accelerated or manifestly unfounded claims procedure.

26. To ensure that assessment of the viability of an 'internal protection alternative' meets the standards set by international refugee law, it is important that the putative asylum state clearly discloses to the asylum-seeker that internal protection is under consideration, as well as the information upon which it relies to advance this contention. The decision-maker must in all cases act fairly, and in particular ensure that no information regarding the availability of an 'internal protection alternative' is considered unless the asylum-seeker has an opportunity to respond to that information, and to present other relevant information to the decision-maker.

These Guidelines reflect the consensus of all the participants at the First Colloquium on Challenges in International Refugees Law, held at Ann Arbor, Michigan, USA, on April 9–11, 1999.

Appendix 10

ASYLUM DIRECTORATE INSTRUCTIONS ON THE MEANING OF 'PARTICULAR SOCIAL GROUP'

The interpretation of the phrase 'particular social group' for the purposes of the 1951 UN Convention was set out by the House of Lords in *Shah* and *Islam* (1999). In *Shah* and *Islam*, the House of Lords found that:

(i) members of a social group have to have in common an immutable characteristic which is either beyond the power of an individual to change, or is so fundamental to his identity or conscience that it ought not to be required to be changed;

(ii) whilst [the] social group must exist independently of persecution, discrimination against the group could be *taken into account* in identifying it as a social group i.e. discrimination against the group could be a factor contributing to the identity of a social group

The Lords rejected the notion previously held by the Court of Appeal that for a social group to exist there had to be a degree of cohesion.

In applying their definition of social group to the individual cases of *Shah* and *Islam*, the Lords held that in the particular context of Pakistani society women are a social group and that Mrs Shah and Mrs Islam were persecuted by reason of their membership of that group. The persecution comprised violence from their husbands, which the state was unable or unwilling to prevent (and even encouraged).

This means that in the context of a society in which women are subject to serious discrimination *of the kind and severity that their Lordships found to exist in Pakistan,* women are a social group (being singled out by society as shown by the discrimination); and that those who fear or receive violence at the hands of their husbands will be able to show persecution if they can show that the state is unable or unwilling to protect them.

The effect of widening the interpretation of social group is that those applicants, like Mrs Shah and Mrs Islam, *who might formerly have been granted exceptional leave to remain, will now be granted asylum.*

Furthermore, in the light of the judgement we can no longer argue that homosexuals (or other persons defined by sexual orientation) are not capable of being a social group. Discrimination against homosexuals in a society *may be such as to single them out as a social group depending on the factual circumstances in the country concerned.*

When considering whether the issue of social group arises by virtue of alleged discrimination against a member of a group with an immutable characteristic, case-workers should take into account any up-to-date information provided by the Country Information Policy Unit (CIPU) about conditions in the relevant country. Whether an individual is a member of a social group will depend upon the evidence, in particular as to the extent of the discrimination they suffer.

Each case will need to be considered individually on its merits. To qualify for asylum, a member of a social group would also have to show a well founded fear of persecution and that the authorities were unable or unwilling to offer protection and that persecution was *because of* ('for reasons of') their social group.

Appendix 11

ADDRESSING CLAIMS BASED ON SEXUAL ORIENTATION (CCR)[1]

– **There may be a delay in making a claim or in referring to sexual orientation because of bad advice or fears resulting from past experiences**

– **For gay men and lesbians who have come out only since their arrival in Canada, there are often particular difficulties in substantiating the claim, since documentation (often scarce) from the country of origin must be relied upon**

– **The universality of homophobia is sometimes used as an argument against accepting gay men and lesbians as refugees**

– **The implication of laws on homosexuality is not necessarily self-evident**

    – Laws prohibiting homosexuality are *prima facie* evidence of persecution but are sometimes used as a basis for arguing claimants are being prosecuted rather than persecuted

    – Laws which do not directly refer to homosexual activity may be used against gay men and lesbians (eg China's law on hooliganism)

    – Laws which are not being enforced may still have significant impact because their existence gives an air of illegality to the lives of gay men and lesbians, with the consequence that state agencies may refuse protection to gay men and lesbians

– **Gay men, lesbians and bisexuals may enter into heterosexual marriages as a cover to hide their sexual orientation. Gay men and lesbians may also have been in genuine marriages before they came to terms with their sexual orientation**

– **Documentation on human rights violations against members of sexual minorities is inadequate for a number of reasons**

    – Many gay men and lesbians do not report human rights violations they have suffered because the authorities condone or participate in the abuses. In fact reporting abuses may lead to further victimisation

    – In some countries some associations of sexual minorities will not speak out on abuses or will even deny that they occur because of fears for the consequences

    – Few human rights organisations have a well-established tradition of reporting on abuses suffered by sexual minorities and some organisations actually refuse to report these abuses or recognise them as significant human rights violations. Amnesty International included sexual orientation in its mandate only recently. Gay men and lesbians may not have sufficient trust of such organisations to report abuses to them

---

1   Canadian Council for Refugees (CCR) *Addressing Claims Based on Sexual Orientation*, August 1995. Available on-line at http://www.web.net/~ccr/fronteng.htm

- – The experiences of members of sexual minorities may differ significantly between socio-economic classes. In many cases there may be better documentation on the realities of the upper classes, who are likely to be less vulnerable to persecution

- – **There are significant differences between the ways in which gay men and lesbians are treated. For example, in some countries forced psychiatric 'treatment' is used against lesbians in particular, while in some countries sodomy laws are directed against men rather than women**

- – **Board Members may be uncertain about how to test a person's claim that he or she is a member of a sexual minority**

- – **Board Members' personal values and beliefs or discomfort with the issues discussed may compromise gay and lesbian claimants' right to a fair hearing**

Appendix 12

GENDER-SENSITIVE TECHNIQUES FOR INTERVIEWING WOMEN REFUGEES (UNHCR)[1]

It may be necessary to use a variety of gender-sensitive techniques to obtain information from women during the status-determination process. The recruitment and training of female interpreters is a precondition for the most effective interviewing:

- Be aware of gender differences in communication, particularly non-verbal communications. As an interviewer avoid intimidating gestures that inhibit responses. In assessing the credibility of the female applicant, for example, do not judge it on the basis of such Western cultural values as the ability to maintain eye contact

- Be patient with female applicants to overcome inhibitions, particularly regarding sexual abuse. Questions may need to be asked in a number of different ways before victims of rape and other abuses feel able to tell their stories. Enough time should be allowed during the interviewing process to permit the female applicant to build a rapport with the interviewer so she is able to recount her experiences. Do not ask for details of the sexual abuse; the important thing in establishing a well-founded fear of persecution is to establish that some form has occurred

- Recognise that women who have been sexually assaulted exhibit a pattern of symptoms that are described as Rape Trauma Syndrome. These symptoms include persistent fear, a loss of self-confidence and self-esteem, difficulty in concentration, an attitude of self-blame, a pervasive feeling of loss of control, and memory loss or distortion. These symptoms will influence how a woman applicant responds during the interview. If misunderstood, they may wrongly be seen as discrediting her testimony

- Understand that women in many societies do not have specific information about the activities of men in their families. Gaps in their knowledge should not be construed as lack of credibility unless there is other evidence of such lack of credibility

- Provide women the opportunity to be questioned by themselves, out of the hearing of other members of their family. Victims of sexual abuse may not feel comfortable recounting their experiences in front of their fathers, husbands, brothers or children

---

1   UNHCR *Guidelines on the Protection of Refugee Women* 1991, pp 41–42.

USEFUL ADDRESSES AND CONTACT INFORMATION

General

Immigration Law Practitioners' Association (ILPA)
Lindsey House
40–42 Charterhouse Street
London EC1M 6JH   Tel: 020 7251 8383

Refugee Action
240a Clapham Road
Stockwell
London SW9 0PZ   Tel: 020 7735 5361

European Legal Network on Asylum (ELENA)
c/o ECRE
Bondway House
3 Bondway
London SW8 1SJ   Tel: 020 7820 1156

Refugee Council
3 Bondway
London SW8 1SJ   Tel: 020 7582 6922

AIRE Centre (Advice on Individual Rights in Europe)
74 Eurolink Business Centre
49 Effra Road
London SW2 1B2   Tel: 020 7924 0297

Medical

Medical Foundation for the Care of Victims of Torture
96–98 Grafton Road
London NW5 3EJ   Tel: 020 7813 7777

Refugee Support Centre
47 South Lambeth Road
London SW8 1RH   Tel: 020 7820 3606

Foundation for Women's Health Research and Development (FORWARD)
The Africa Centre
King Street
London WC2 8JT   Tel: 020 7379 6889

Traumatic Stress Clinic
73 Charlotte Street
London W1P 1LP   Tel: 020 7530 3666

Women Against Rape/Black Women's Rape Action Project
PO Box 287
London NW6 5QU   Tel: 020 7482 2496

Welfare and Housing
Child Poverty Action Group (CPAG)
1–5 Bath Street
London EC1V 9QA   Tel: 020 7253 3406

London Advice Services Alliance (LASA)
Universal House
88–94 Wentworth Street
London E1 7SA   Tel: 020 7377 2738

National Association of Citizen Advice Bureaux (NACAB)
Middleton House
115–123 Pentonville Road
London N1 9LZ   Tel: 020 7833 2181

Shelter
88 Old Street
London EC1V   Tel: 020 7404 7447

Supporting Information
See ILPA *Directory of Experts on Countries of Origin and Transit of Asylum Seekers* (1997, 2nd edn) and JCWI *European Directory of Migrant and Ethnic Minority Organisations* (1996, JCWI and European Research Centre for Migration and Ethnic Relations).

Representatives should develop their own expert networks through universities, consultants, specialist journals, newspapers, the Foreign and Commonwealth Office, community associations and the following organisations:

Amnesty International
99–109 Rosebery Avenue
London EC1R 4RE   Tel: 020 7413 5500

Human Rights Watch
33 Islington High Street
London N1 9LN   Tel: 020 7713 1995

Migration News Sheet
172–174 rue Joseph 11
B-1000 Brussels   Tel: 0032 2 230 3750

Refugee Studies Centre
Queen Elizabeth House
21 St Giles
Oxford OX1 3LA   Tel: 01865 270722

Refugee Women's Association
The Print House
18 Ashwin Street
London E8 3DL   Tel: 020 7923 2412

Southall Black Sisters (SBS)
52 Norwood Road
Southall
Middlesex
UB2 4DW   Tel: 020 8571 9595

UNHCR
21st Floor, Millbank Tower
21–24 Millbank
London SW1P 4QP   Tel: 020 7828 9191

SOURCES OF INFORMATION AND SUPPORT ON THE INTERNET

AAAS Directory of Human Rights Resources on the Internet
http://shr.aaas.org/dhr.htm

The AAAS Directory of Human Rights Resources on the Internet is an initiative of the Science and Human Rights Program of the American Association for the Advancement of Science. The Directory provides descriptions and links to hundreds of human rights organisations worldwide on the Internet.

Amnesty International
http://www.amnesty.org

Amnesty International is a worldwide campaigning movement that works to promote all the human rights enshrined in the Universal Declaration of Human Rights and other international standards. In particular, Amnesty International campaigns to free all prisoners of conscience; ensure fair and prompt trials for political prisoners; abolish the death penalty, torture and other cruel treatment of prisoners; end political killings and 'disappearances'; and oppose human rights abuses by opposition groups. The Amnesty International website provides access to current news releases, campaigns, links, and on-line library. Amnesty International's annual reports, which document human rights issues of concern to Amnesty International can be downloaded free of charge. Amnesty International also has a series of documents on efforts to prevent FGM http://www.2.amnesty.se including a Human Rights Information Pack on Female Genital Mutilation (1998) which is available on-line at http://www.amnesty.org/ailib/intcam/femgen

Asylumlaw.org
http://www.asylumlaw.org

Asylumlaw.org was founded in March 1999 with the sole purpose of using the Internet to help lawyers worldwide prepare the best asylum cases they can. The site provides documents and collaborating information that can support claims, country conditions reports, legal tools, including tutorials, summaries and recent decisions on all aspects of asylum law and links to other web based resources. There is a particular focus on claims based on gender and sexual orientation.

Australian Refugee Review Tribunal Database
http://www.rrt.gov.au

The Australian Refugee Review Tribunal Database provides on-line access to the full text of all decisions of the Refugee Review Tribunal and currently contains over 8,000 decisions. The data is provided by the Tribunal on a weekly basis.

Bora Laskin Law Library
http://www.law-lib.utoronto.ca

The Bora Laskin Law Library at the University of Toronto has an extensive bibliographic database on all aspects of women's human rights and links to authoritative and diverse information on women's international human rights law. The subjects covered include: reproductive rights and sexual health; female genital mutilation, political rights and participation, nationality and citizenship, refugee/immigration law, sexual orientation, violence against women, slavery and trafficking and marriage and family life. Each subject is divided into:

– articles: annotated bibliographic references to scholarly articles with links to full text where available
– documents: annotated references to conventions and UN Reports, NGO reports, case-law and legislation with links to full text where available
– links to other websites with annotation

British Colombia Institute against Family Violence
http://www.bcifv.org

Established in 1989 as a private, non-profit organisation the Institute works to increase public awareness and understanding of family violence through education and dissemination of information. The Institute provides continuing education for professionals, conducts research, and develops and distributes resources to community organisations. The website provides an on-line library catalogue and access to other web resources.

Canadian Immigration and Refugee Board (CIRB)
http://www.irb.gc.ca

This site provides access to extensive country of origin information including CIRB reports and has a searchable database of Canadian case law. It also provides links to other sites.

Center for the Prevention of Sexual and Domestic Violence
http://www.cpsdv.org

The Center for the Prevention of Sexual and Domestic Violence is a non-profit organisation based in Washington and describes itself as an inter-religious educational resource addressing issues of sexual and domestic violence. Its goal is to engage religious leaders in the task of ending abuse and to serve as a bridge between religious and secular communities. The emphasis is on education and prevention.

Center for Gender and Refugee Studies
http://www.uchastings.edu/cgrs

The Center for Gender and Refugee Studies (part of the Center for Human Rights and International Justice at the University of California, Hastings College of the Law) seeks to enhance the protection of women's human rights by providing expertise and resources in the cases of women asylum seekers. The objective of the Center is to enhance the protection of individual asylum seekers and to advance the development of the law and policy in this very important area. Towards this objective, the Center provides expertise to representatives handling the claims of women asylum seekers, and seeks to educate decision makers on relevant legal and factual norms and to contribute to the formulation of national and international policy and practice. A huge range of information is available through the Centre's website including:

– factual and legal summaries of gender asylum cases
– gender asylum case law including decisions of immigration judges and the BIA

- documents and information about their domestic violence asylum campaign
- information on potential expert witnesses
- a bibliography of the Centre's library of supporting materials
- links to significant related websites

Centre for Reproductive Law and Policy (CRLP)
http://www.crlp.org

The Centre for Reproductive Law and Policy (CRLP) is a non-profit legal and policy advocacy organisation dedicated to promoting women's reproductive rights. The Centre has information on reproductive rights worldwide. It also has a list of publications and press releases on reproductive rights in the refugee context. CRLP's domestic and international programs engage in litigation, policy analysis, legal research, and public education seeking to achieve women's equality in society and ensure that all women have access to appropriate and freely chosen reproductive health services. CRLP works to broaden the use of a rights-based approach to reproductive health, and to recast the discussion of women's reproductive rights in terms of human rights. It lobbies at international, regional and national levels about the manner in which reproductive rights fit within the human rights framework, monitors laws and policies that affect reproductive rights and health and undertakes independent fact-finding missions in different countries in collaboration with national-level organisations.

Domestic Violence and Incest Resource Centre (DVIRC)
http://www.vicnet.au/⁓dvirc

The Centre is based in Australia and was established in 1986 as a state-wide resource for information on domestic violence and child sexual assault. It provides resources and education to professionals and to those who have experienced domestic violence or sexual assault. The website provides access to a range of resources, including pamphlets, booklets for those who have experienced abuse or violence, manuals and other publications. There are links to other websites with information on domestic violence and child sexual abuse. DVIRC also produces a quarterly Newsletter which contains legal updates, lists of current support groups for survivors in Victoria, articles on current issues and lists of new resources and books. The Centre has a specialist reference library focusing on domestic violence, incest and child sexual abuse.

Electronic Immigration Network (EIN)
http://www.ein.org.uk

The Electronic Immigration Network (EIN) aims to link major information providers with advice workers and practitioners dealing with all issues relating to immigration, refugee and nationality law and practice in the UK. It is possible to access case law through the site for a subscription fee. The site also provides an extensive list of links to other relevant organisations.

European Court of Human Rights
http://www.echr.coe.int

Female Genital Mutilation Research Homepage
http://www.hollyfeld.org/fgm

This website contains a complete review of FGM, including US and international laws, films and other reference material, lists of anti-FGM groups, and many hyperlinks. The site also has estimates of the numbers of mutilations in various countries.

Foundation for Women's Health, Research and Development (FORWARD)
http://www.forward.dircon.co.uk

FORWARD is the leading voluntary organisation in the UK working to eliminate FGM. The organisation offers a range of training fora on its activities in relation to FGM and has a list of publications available for purchase as well as details of other materials and links to other sites.

FGM Education and Networking Project
http://www.fgmnetwork.org

This project has information on British and Canadian legislation and a FGM and women's reproduction bibliography. The website contains general introductory material, articles of interest and links to educational, medical and legal resources. There is contact information for several FGM advocacy and discussion groups and the official statements of various international organisations.

Global Reproductive Health Forum
http://www.hsph.harvard.edu/Organizations/healthnet

This site provides extensive information on research on reproductive rights, discussion forums and a search engine.

House of Lords
http://www.parliament.the-stationery-office.co.uk/pa/ld/ldhome.htm

Human Rights Documentation Exchange
http://www.hrde.org

The Human Rights Documentation Exchange defends immigrant survivors of human rights abuses by providing information critical to their claims for refuge in the US, advancing public awareness of human rights abuses, and encouraging public policy development. The Exchange can provide client-specific documentation and will research country conditions and human rights information to corroborate an individual claim for asylum (a fee is charged). It also has a women's documentation project with a country list and bibliography which can be down-loaded on-line.

Human Rights Internet
http://www.hri.ca

Founded in 1976, Human Rights Internet (HRI) is a world leader in the exchange of information within the worldwide human rights community. Launched in the US, HRI has its headquarters in Ottawa, Canada. From Ottawa, HRI communicates by phone, fax, mail and the information highway with more than 5,000 organisations and individuals around the world working for the advancement of human rights. A key objective of the organisation is to support the work of the global non-governmental community in its struggle to obtain human rights for all. To this end, HRI promotes human rights education, stimulates research, encourages the sharing of information, and builds international solidarity among those committed to the principles enshrined in the International Bill of Human Rights. On the premise that accurate information is a precondition for the effective protection of human rights, HRI's primary role is to serve the information needs of international scholars, human rights activists, asylum lawyers, and other organisations via an extensive documentation centre and computerised databases. HRI's databases include information on thousands of human rights organisations, bibliographic abstracts of the literature, bodies which fund human rights work, human rights awards, education programs on human rights, and children's rights information. There is also an on-line guide to the international women's human rights movement.

Human Rights Information and Documentation Network
http://www.huridocs.org

HURIDOCS is an open-ended network where organisations can participate in various ways: Task Forces, training courses etc. HURIDOCS does not have a formal membership structure, but it has contacts with organisations in more than 150 countries. The main focus of HURIDOCS is to strengthen the information handling capacities of organisations in developing countries.

Human Rights Watch
http://www.hrw.org

Human Rights Watch is dedicated to protecting the human rights of people around the world. The organisation investigates and exposes human rights violations and challenges governments and those who hold power to end abusive practices and respect international human rights law. Their website provides information on breaking news, HRW publications and current campaigns.

Human Rights Web
http://www.hrweb.org

The Human Rights Web provides background information on human rights, access to human rights legal and political documents and human rights issues, debates and discussions. It also provides access to other human rights websites and discussion groups.

Immigration Appellate Authority
http://www.courtservice.gov.uk/tribunals/iaa/index.html

International Lesbian and Gay Association
http://www.ilga.org

ILGA's aim is to work for the equality of lesbians, gay men, bisexuals and transgendered people and their liberation from all forms of discrimination. It seeks to achieve this aim through the worldwide co-operation and mutual support of its members. The organisation focuses public and government attention on cases of discrimination against lesbians, gay men, bisexuals and transgendered people by supporting programs and protest actions, asserting diplomatic pressure, providing information and working with international organisations and the international media. The ILGA website provides information on discrimination against lesbians and gay men around the world.

International Gay and Lesbian Human Rights Commission (IGLHRC)
http://www.iglhrc.org/asylum/index.html

The IGLHRC's mission is to protect and advance the human rights of all people and communities subject to discrimination or abuse on the basis of sexual orientation, gender identity or HIV status. A US based non-profit, non-governmental organisation (NGO), IGLHRC responds to such human rights violations around the world through documentation, advocacy, coalition building, public education, and technical assistance. It has an Asylum Project which supports claims for asylum made by those who fear persecution because of their sexual orientation, gender identity or HIV status. It provides documentation of human rights abuses perpetrated against lesbians, gay men, bisexuals, the transgendered and people with HIV/AIDS to clients' lawyers, the media, persons considering an asylum claim and other interested parties. For more information contact asylum@iglhrc.org. The organisation has produced an important guide *Asylum Based on Sexual Orientation: A Resource Guide* to assist asylum seekers in the US, particularly those who have been persecuted on the basis of sexual orientation, gender identity or HIV status. The aim of this resource, which brings together court decisions, legal articles and referral information, is to help lawyers and their clients better prepare their cases. The 500-page Asylum Guide contains articles from nationally renowned lawyers and legal advocates detailing their work, court decisions and relevant legislation from all over the world, including Australia, Canada, Germany, Ireland, New Zealand, the UK and the US, as well as supporting documents from United Nations commissions and the US Justice Department. The Guide is available from the IGLHRC, 1360 Mission Street, Suite 200, San Francisco, CA 94103.

Other resources available from IGLHRC include:

- country files containing documentation of persecution due to sexual orientation or HIV status
- written decisions (US and foreign tribunals) from successful cases
- authoritative declarations on the human rights status of sexual minorities in a particular country
- advisory opinions from UNHCR
- referral to an international network of lawyers who have represented asylum cases based on sexual orientation of HIV status
- contacts with grassroots gay, lesbian and bisexual liberation organisations and/or AIDS non-governmental organisations in over 130 countries worldwide
- Other IGLHRC publications available include: *The Rights of Lesbians and Gay Men in the Russian Federation* (1994); *Unspoken Rules: Sexual Orientation and Women's Human Rights* (1995); *No Human Being is Disposable: Social Cleansing, Human Rights and Sexual Orientation in Colombia* (1995); *Epidemic of Hate: Violation of Human Rights of Gay Men, Lesbians and Transvestites in Brazil* (forthcoming)

International Planned Parenthood Federation
http://www.ippf.org

The IPPF is the largest voluntary organisation in the field of sexual and reproductive health including family planning and is represented in over 180 countries worldwide. It has produced a Charter on Sexual and Reproductive Rights. The website has resources, links, country profiles and a search engine.

Ipas
http://www.ipas.org

Ipas works globally to improve women's lives through a focus on reproductive health. Its work is based on the principle that every woman has a right to the highest attainable standard of health, to safe reproductive choices, and to high quality health care. Its website has a Reproductive Health Gateway which provides a one-stop search facility of over two dozen reproductive health sites

Legal Resources for UK Asylum Lawyers
http://www.asylumlaw.co.uk

This site is a collection of web links, news sources and documents that may be useful in preparing and presenting asylum appeals before UK Immigration adjudicators. There is an emphasis on the Human Rights Act 1998.

Lesbian and Gay Immigration Rights Task Force
http://www.lgirtf.org

The Lesbian and Gay Immigration Rights Task Force is a non-profit organisation addressing the widespread discriminatory impact of immigration laws on the lives of lesbians and gay men and people with HIV through education, outreach, advocacy and the maintenance of a nationwide resource and support network. Site contains various links to information about asylum claims in the US based on sexual orientation. It produces newsletters which give world news in brief outlining the legal, political and social situation in a number of countries worldwide. The organisation has also produced a Handbook for advocates and practitioners entitled *Preparing Sexual-Orientation Based Asylum Claim: A Handbook for Advocates and Asylum Seekers* which is available from the Heartland Alliance for Human Needs and Human Rights, 208 S. La Salle St., Suite 1818, Chicago, IL 60604 or on-line at http://www.lgirtf.org/html/order.html

Raising Daughters Aware (RDA)
http://www.fgm.org

RDA is based in Oakland, California and provides free information and services for FGM affected women, their physicians, and other health care providers, social workers, counsellors and attorneys. The site contains useful background materials and links to other sites.

Refugee Law Center (United States)
http://www.refugeelawcenter.org

The Refugee Law Center (RLC) in the US is a non-profit organisation established in 1994, devoted to strengthening the human rights of refugees and immigrants through legal representation, research, educational initiatives and policy development. Working in collaboration with other human rights and refugee policy representation organisations in the United States and other countries, the RLC produces analytic papers, publishes books and files briefs on issues concerning refugee protection. It also participates in training and provides legal representation in specific cases. The RLC has placed particular emphasis on the development of theories and the advancement of legal doctrine for women immigrants applying for asylum and related protection. The RLC provides representation, as well as research, legal analysis, and training relating to gender violence and human rights violations of women around the world. It maintains a database of gender asylum claims and decisions from the US and other countries.

Refugee Women's Legal Group
http://www.rwlg.org.uk

The RWLG website has information about the group and provides direct access to the websites of relevant organisations which are listed in this book.

Refugee Women's Resource Project
http://www.asylumaid.org.uk

The Refugee Women's Resource Project aims to assist women fleeing serious human rights violations to gain protection in the UK. It has a number of project staff including a caseworker providing expert advice and representation to women seeking asylum, an outreach worker making links with community groups, and a research team producing reports on issues affecting women asylum seekers.

Refworld
http://www.unhcr.ch/refworld

Refworld is a collection of full-text databases representing the most comprehensive and reliable refugee information resource available, drawn from the most current and authoritative sources. The site provides on-line access to UNHCR official documents, country information, legal information, bibliographic information and reference material.

RefNZ
http://www.knowledge-basket.co.nz/refugee/welcome.html

RefNZ provides a searchable database of all the decisions of New Zealand's Refugee Status Appeals Authority (RSAA), the full-text of leading decisions and Practice Notes of the RSAA. Abstracts of New Zealand High Court and Court of Appeal cases dealing with refugee issues are separately provided. Links to leading refugee law decisions from other countries are also available. RefNZ coverage additionally includes papers on New Zealand refugee jurisprudence, and there is a dedicated forum for comment on current refugee issues. RefNews notes recent news and developments in New Zealand refugee law while RefStatistics provides key New Zealand refugee statistics. Links to other refugee-related web sites have also been provided.

Stonewall Immigration Group
http://www.stonewall.org.uk

Stonewall is a lobbying and advocacy group based in London. Stonewall works for change by influencing public opinion, and the opinions of parliament. The group provides regular summaries of any determinations or judgments that may be of assistance to group members and their advisers.

UK Court Service
http://www.courtservice.gov.uk

United States Immigration and Nationality Service
http://www.ins.usdoj.gov/graphics/index.htm

United Nations Human Rights Commission
http://www.un.org/rights/

This site has general information on the UN and human rights including regional and international instruments. There is also information on women and violence and cultural diversity and human rights.

United States Department of State Country Reports on Human Rights Practices
http://www.usis.usemb.se/human/index.html

University of Michigan Law School Refugee Caselaw Site
http://www.refugeecaselaw.org/Refugee/index.htm

The purpose of this site is to promote transnational analysis of refugee law by advocates, decision-makers, and policy-makers committed to the effective implementation of international standards. The site currently collects, indexes, and publishes selected recent court decisions that interpret the legal definition of a 'refugee'. It presently contains cases from the highest national courts of Australia, Austria, Canada, Germany, New Zealand, Switzerland, the UK, and the US.

Women's Commission for Refugee Women and Children
http://www.intrescom.org/wcrwc.html

The Women's Commission for Refugee Women and Children is one of the leading advocacy and expert resource organisations speaking out on behalf of refugee and displaced women and children around the world. The Women's Commission is working to further its goals through four major projects:

– promoting the participation and protection of refugee women
– promoting protection and care of refugee children and adolescents
– promoting the fair treatment of asylum seekers
– promoting access to reproductive health care

Women and Law
http://www.wld.org

Women and Law is a Gopher site containing information on women and international law, as well as on women and the law in specific countries. The Women and Law archive consists of legal documents, news reports, and official statements by governments and NGOs.

Women's Human Rights Net
http://www.oneworld.org/whrnet

whrNET is a collaborative Information & Communication Technology (ICT) project developed by an international coalition of women's organisations. whrNET aims to strengthen advocacy for women's human rights through the effective utilisation of information and communication technologies. The sponsoring organisations are part of a global movement for women's human rights that has grown steadily since the World Conference of Human Rights (Vienna, 1993) and the Fourth World Conference on Women (Beijing, 1995). whrNET is jointly sponsored and supported by its partner organisations and is governed by an elected International Executive Committee. whrNET links partner organisations and women's human rights advocates worldwide via the Internet.

Women's Human Rights Resources Website
http://www.law-lib.utoronto.ca/Diana

The Women's Human Rights Resources web site is a project of the Bora Laskin Law Library at the University of Toronto, Faculty of Law. The site is produced by the Women's Human Rights Resources group in consultation and collaboration with law librarians, lawyers, students, researchers, activists and human rights experts around the world. The site was introduced in 1995 following the publication of Professor Rebecca Cook and Valerie Oosterveld of the University of Toronto 'A Select Bibliography of Women's Human Rights' *America University Law Review* April 1995. The main goal of the Women's Human Rights Resources site is to assist individuals and organisations in using international women's human rights law to promote women's rights. This includes:

- community groups so that they can train, lobby and advocate for women's human rights
- lawyers so that they can seek the effective enforcement of women's human rights at the national and international level
- governments so that they can understand and implement their obligations under international human rights law
- judges so that they can incorporate international human rights law into their decision-making
- activists and advocates so that they can promote women's human rights through international law
- scholars and researchers so that they can ensure full and effective analysis of women's human rights issues
- women who want to know their rights

WomenWatch

http://www.un.org/womenwatch

WomenWatch is a joint initiative of DAW, UNIFEM and INSTRAW. Its website features conventions and declarations of particular importance to women's rights. It also has regional and country information.

World Organisation Against Torture (WOAT)

The World Organisation Against Torture has looked at use of the Convention Against Torture (CAT) to protect victims of persecution on the basis of sexual orientation. The organisation has prepared an information pack on CAT protections and procedures that includes sample petitions, legal briefs and question-and-answer forms. The pack is available on-line at http://www.omct.org/woatusa

World Health Organisation (WHO)

http://www.who.int

The World Health Organisation provides classification and definitions of FGM, information about WHO activities against FGM, an information package (WHO/FRH/WHD/96.26) and a bibliographic database which includes information about research carried out about FGM in a wide range of countries.

BIBLIOGRAPHY

There are numerous publications available which are of interest and relevance to those working with refugee women seeking asylum in the UK, a small number of which are detailed below. It is well worth browsing the shelves of good bookshops (especially in the legal, gender and international relations sections) for further sources of information.

Abrams P (1996) 'Reservations about women: population policy and reproduction rights' *Cornell International Law Journal* vol 29, no 1, pp 1–42

ADIMA (1996) *Refugee and Humanitarian Visa Applications: Guidelines on Gender Issues for Decision-makers* (Australian Department of Immigration and Multicultural Affairs)

Afkhami E (ed) (1994) *Faith and Freedom: Women's Rights in the Muslim World* (IB Taurus & Co, London)

Afkhami M and Friedl E (eds) (1994) *In the Eye of the Storm: Women in Post-Revolutionary Iran* (Tarius, London)

Afshar H (ed) (1996) *Women and Politics in the Third World* (Routledge, London)

Afshari R (1994) 'An essay on Islamic cultural relativism in the discourse of human rights' *Human Rights Quarterly* vol 16, pp 235–276

Agger I (1989) 'Sexual torture of political prisoners: an overview', *Journal of Traumatic Stress* 2(3), 305–318

Agger I (1992) *The Blue Room: Trauma and Testimony Among Refugee Women – A Psycho-Social Exploration* (Zed Books, London)

Ahmed L (1992) *Women and Gender in Islam: Historical Roots of a Modern Debate* (Yale University Press, London)

Althaus F (1997) 'Female circumcision: rite of passge or violation of rights?' *International Family Planning Perspectives* vol 23, no 3, pp 130–133

Amnesty International (1991) *Women on the Front Line: Human Rights Violations Against Women* (Amnesty International, London)

Amnesty International (1993) *Bosnia-Herzegovina: Rape and Sexual Abuse by Armed Forces* (Amnesty International, London) (EUR 63/01/93)

Amnesty International (1994) *Bangladesh: Fundamental Rights of Women Violated with Virtual Impunity* (Amnesty International, London)

Amnesty International (1995) *Women in Prison – imprisoned and abused for dissent* (Amnesty International, London)

Amnesty International (1997a) *Breaking the Silence: Human Rights Violations Based on Sexual Orientation* (Amnesty International, London)

Amnesty International (1997b) *Female Genital Mutilation: A Human Rights Information Pack* (Amnesty International, London) (ACT 77/05/97)

Amnesty International (1999) *Annual Report 1999* (Amnesty International, London)

Anderson B (1983) *Imagined Communities* (Verso, London)

Anker D (1999) *The Law of Asylum in the United States* (Refugee Law Centre, Boston)

Anthias F and Yuval-Davis N (eds) (1989) *Women – Nation – State* (Macmillan, London)

Asylum Rights Campaign (1996a) *The Short Procedure: An Analysis of the Home Office Scheme for Rapid Initial Decisions in Asylum Cases* (ARC, London)

Asylum Rights Campaign (1996b) *The Risks of Getting it Wrong: The Asylum and Immigration Bill Session 1995/6 and the Determination of Special Ajudicators* (ARC, London)

Atoki M (1995) 'Should female circumcision continue to be banned?' *Feminist Legal Studies* vol 3, no 2, pp 223–235

Baron B (1993) 'The construction of national honour in Egypt' *Gender and History* vol 5, no 2, pp 244–255

Bartlett KT and Kennedy R (eds) (1993) *Feminist Legal Theory: Readings in Law and Gender* (Westview Press, Boulder)

Bekker M et al (1996) 'Reconstructing hymens or constructing sexual inequality? Service provision to Islamic young women coping with the demand to be a virgin *Journal of Community and Applied Social Psychology* vol 6, no 5, pp 329–334

Bennett O et al (eds) (1995) *Arms to Fight, Arms to Protect: Women Speak Out About Conflict* (Panos, London)

Bhabha J (1993) 'Legal problems of women refugees' *Women: A Cultural Review* vol 4, no 3, pp 240–249

Bhabha J (1996) 'Embodied rights: gender persecution, state sovereignty and refugees' *Public Culture* vol 9, pp 3–32

Bhabha J and Shutter S (1994) *Women's Movement: Women Under Immigration Nationality and Refugee Law* (JCWI, London)

Binion G (1995) 'Human rights: a feminist perspective' *Human Rights Quarterly* vol 17, pp 509–526

Blondet C 'Out of the kitchens and into the streets: women's activism in Peru' in Basu A (ed) (1995) *The Challenge of Local Feminisms: Women's Movements in Global Perspective* (Westview Press, Boulder)

Boland R (1995) 'Population policies, human rights and legal change' *American University Law Review* vol 44, pp 1257–1278

Boulware-Miller K (1985) 'Female circumcision: challenges to the practice as a human rights violation' *Harvard Women's Law Journal* vol 8, pp 155–177

Bourque S and Grossholz J (1998) 'Politics as an unnatural practice: political science looks at female participation' in Philips A *Feminism and Politics* (OUP, Oxford)

Brennan K (1989) 'The influence of cultural relativism on international human rights law: female circumcision as a case study' *Law and Inequality* vol 7, pp 367–398

Brown W (1988) *Manhood and Politics: A Feminist Reading in Political Theory* (Rowman and Littlefield, New Jersey)

Buijs G (ed) (1993) *Migrant Women: Crossing Boundaries and Changing Identities* (Berg, Oxford)

Bunch C (1990) 'Women's rights as human rights: towards a re-vision of human rights' *Humanitarian Rights Quarterly* vol 12, no 4, pp 486–498

Bunch C (1995) 'Transforming human rights from a feminine perspective' in Peters J and Wolper A (eds) *Women's Rights, Human Rights: International Feminist Perspectives* (Routledge, London)

Bunting A (1993) 'Theorising women's cultural diversity in feminist international human rights strategies' *Journal of Law and Society* vol 20, no 1, pp 6–22

Caldeira T (1990) 'Women, daily life and politics' in Jelin E (ed) *Women and Social Change in Latin America* (Zed Press, London)

Camino LA and Krulfeld RM (eds) (1994) *Reconstructing Lives, Recapturing Meaning: Refugee Identity, Gender and Culture Change* (Gordon and Breach, Basel)

Camus-Jacques G (1989) 'Refugee women: the forgotten majority' in Loescher G and Monahan L (eds) *Refugees and International Relations*

Castel JR (1992) 'Rape, sexual assault and the meaning of persecution' *International Journal of Refugee Law* vol 4, no 1, pp 39–56

Cerny-Smith R (1992) 'Female circumcision: bringing women's perspectives into the international debate' *Southern California Law Review* vol 65, pp 2449–2504

CIRB (1993) *Women in China* (CIRB, Ottawa)

CIRB (1996a) *Guidelines on Women Refugee Claimants Fearing Gender-Related Persecution* (CIRB, Ottawa)

CIRB (1996b) *Guidelines on Women Refugee Claimants Fearing Gender-Related Persecution: UPDATE* (CIRB, Ottawa)

CIRB (June 1999) *China: One-child Policy Update* (CIRB, Ottawa) also available on-line at http://www.irb.gc.ca/

Charles N (1995) 'Feminist politics, domestic violence and the state' *Sociological Review* vol 43, no 4, pp 617–640

Charlesworth H et al (1991) 'Feminist approaches to international law' *American Journal of International Law* vol 85, pp 613–664

Chessler A (1997) 'Justifying the unjustifiable: rite v wrong' *Buffalo Law Review* vol 45, pp 555–613

Cipriani L (1993) 'Gender and persecution: protecting women under international law' *Georgetown Immigration Law Journal*, pp 511–548

Cisse BP (1997) 'International law sources applicable to female genital mutilation: a guide to adjudicators of refugee claims based on fear of female genital mutilation' *Columbia Journal of Transnational Law* vol 35, no 2, pp 429–451

Cook R (1992) 'International protection of women's reproductive rights' *New York University Journal of International Law and Policy* vol 24, pp 645–728

Cook R (1993a) 'Women's international human rights law: the way forward' *Human Rights Quarterly* vol 15, pp 230–261

Cook R (1993b) 'Accountability in international law for violations of women's rights by non-state actors' in Dallmeyer DG (ed) *Reconceiving Reality: Women and International Law* (American Society of International Law, Washington DC) Studies in Transnational Legal Policy No 25

Cook R (1994) 'State accountability under the Convention on the Elimination of All Forms of Discrimination Against Women' in Cook R (ed) *Human Rights of Women: National and International Perspectives* (University of Pennsylvania Press, Philadelphia)

Cook R (1995a) 'International human rights and women's reproductive health' in Peters J and Wolper A (eds) *Women's Rights, Human Rights: International Feminist Perspectives* (Routledge, London)

Cook R (1995b) 'Human rights and reproductive self-determination' *American University Law Review* vol 44, pp 975–1016

Cook R (ed) (1994) *Human Rights of Women: National and International Perspectives* (University of Pennsylvania Press, Philadelphia)

Cook R (1999) 'Gender, health and human rights' in Mann J et al (eds) *Health and Human Rights* (Routledge, London)

Cooke M and Wollacott A (eds) (1993) *Gendering War Talk* (Princetown University Press, New Jersey)

Copelon R (1994a) 'Surfacing gender: re-engraving crimes against women in humanitarian law' *Hastings Women's Law Journal* vol 5, no 2, pp 243–266

Copelon R (1994b) 'Intimate terror: understanding domestic violence as torture' in Cook R (ed) *Human Rights of Women: National and International Perspectives* (University of Pennsylvania Press, Philadelphia)

Copelon R (1995) 'Gendered war crimes: reconceptualising rape in times of war' in Peters J and Wolper A (eds) *Women's Rights, Human Rights: International Feminist Perspectives* (Routledge, London)

Crawley H (1997) *Women as Asylum Seekers: A Legal Handbook* (RWLG, ILPA, Refugee Action, London)

Crawley H (1999) 'Women and refugee status: beyond the public/private dichotomy in UK asylum policy' in Indra D (ed) *Engendering Forced Migration: Theory and Practice* (Berghahn Books, Oxford)

Dalby S (1994) 'Gender and critical geopolitics: reading security discourse in the new world disorder' *Environment and Planning: Society and Space* vol 12, pp 595–612

Dallmeyer DG (ed) (1993) *Reconceiving Reality: Women and International Law* (American Society of International Law, Washington DC (Studies in Transnational Legal Policy No 25))

De Groot J (1993) 'The dialectics of gender: women, men and political discourses in Iran c. 1890–1930' *Gender and History* vol 5, no 2, pp 256–268

Decker D (1998) 'A broken promise: virginity control exams' *Buffalo Human Rights Law Review* vol 4, pp 317–340

Dixon-Mueller R (1993) *Population Policy and Women's Rights: Transforming Reproductive Choice* (Praeger, London)

Dorkenoo E (1994) *Cutting the Rose: The Practice and its Prevention* (Minority Rights Group (MRG), London)

Duncan N (ed) (1996) *Body Space: Destabilizing Geographies of Gender and Sexuality* (Routledge, London)

Dutch Refugee Council (1994) *Female Asylum Seekers: A Comparative Study Concerning Policy and Jurisprudence in the Netherlands, Germany, France, and the United Kingdom* (Dutch Refugee Council, Amsterdam)

ECRE (1993) *Asylum in Europe: An Introduction* (ECRE, London)

ECRE (1997) *Position Paper on Asylum Seeking and Refugee Women* (ECRE, London)

El Saadawi (1997) *The Nawal El Saadawi Reader* (Zed Books, London)

Elshtain JB (1981) *Public Man, Private Woman: Women in Social and Political Thought* (Martin Robertson, Oxford)

Feijoo MC and Gogna M (1990) 'Women in the transition to democracy' in Jelin E (ed) *Women and Social Change in Latin America* (Zed Books, London)

Fisher J (1993) *Out of the Shadows: Women, Resistance and Politics in South America* (Latin American Bureau, London)

Forbes-Martin S (1991) *Refugee Women* (Zed Books, London)

Freedman L and Isaacs ? (1993) 'Human rights and reproductive choice' *Studies in Family Planning* vol 24, pp 18–30

Freedman L (1998) 'Reflections on emerging frameworks of health and human rights' *Health and Human Rights* vol 1, no 4, pp 315–348

Freeman MA (1995) 'The human rights of women in the family: issues and recommendations for the implementation of the women's convention' in J Peters and A Wolper (eds) *Womens Rights, Human Rights: International Feminist Perspectives* (Routledge, London)

Fullerton M (1993) 'A comparative look at refugee status based on persecution due to membership in a particular social group' *Cornell International Law Journal* vol 26, no 3, pp 505–564

Gerami S (1996) *Women and Fundamentalism: Islam and Christianity* (Gorland Publishing, London)

Gilbert L (1995) 'Rights, refugee women and reproductive health' *American University Law Review* vol 44, pp 1213–1252

Ginsberg F and Rapp R (1991) 'The politics of reproduction' *Annual Review of Anthropology* vol 10, pp 311–343

Gocek F and Balaghi S (eds) (1994) *Reconstructing Gender in the Middle East: Tradition, Power and Identity* (Colombia University Press, New York)

Goldberg P (1993) 'Anyplace but home: asylum in the United States for women fleeing intimate violence' *Cornell International Law Journal* vol 26, no 3, pp 565–604

Goldberg P (1995) 'Where in the world is there safety for me: a safe haven for women fleeing gender-based persecution' in Peters J and Wolper A (eds) *Women's Rights, Human Rights: International Feminist Perspectives* (Routledge, London)

Goldberg P and Kelly N (1993) 'International human rights and violence against women: recent developments' *Harvard Humanitarian Rights Journal* vol 6, pp 195–209

Goodman R (1995) 'The incorporation of international human rights standards into sexual orientation asylum claims: cases of involuntary "medical" intervention' *Yale Law Journal* vol 105, pp 255–290

Goodwin J (1994) *Price of Honour: Muslim Women Lift the Veil of Silence on the Islamic World* (Warner Books, London)

Goodwin-Gill G (1983) *The Refugee in International Law* (Clarendon Press, Oxford)

Grahl-Madsen A (1966) *The Status of Refugees in International Law* (Sijthoff, Leyden)

Greatbach J (1989) 'The gender difference: feminist critiques of refugee discourse' *International Journal of Refugee Law* vol 3, no 3, pp 585–605

Gruenbaum E (1996) 'The cultural debate over female circumcision: the Sudanese are arguing this one out for themselves' *Medical Anthropology Quarterly* vol 10, no 4, pp 455–475

Guild E (1996) *The Developing Immigration and Asylum Policies of the European Union* (Kluwer Law International)

HRIC *Caught Between Tradition and the State: Violations of the Human Rights of Chinese Women* available on-line at http://www.igc.apc.org/hric/crf/english/95fall/e9.html

Hall C et al (1993) 'Introduction' *Gender and History* (Special Issue on Gender, Nationalism and National Identities) vol 5, no 2, pp 159–164

Handwerker P (1990) *Birth and Power: Social Change and the Politics of Reproduction* (Westview Press, Boulder)

Hartman B (1987) *Reproductive Rights and Wrongs: The Global Politics of Population Control and Contraceptive Choice* (Harper and Row, New York)

Hathaway J (5 December 1990) 'Gender-specific claims to refugee status and membership in a special social group' (paper presented at a workshop of the Toronto Convention Refugee Determination Division (CRDD) Working Group on Refugee Women Claimants (unpublished)

Hathaway J (1991) *The Law of Refugee Status* (Butterworths, Toronto)

Heise L (1995) 'Freedom close to home: the impact of violence against women on reproductive rights' in Peters J and Wolper A (eds) *Women's Rights, Human Rights: International Feminist Perspectives* (Routledge, London)

Helton AC (1983) 'Persecution on account of membership in a social group as a basis for refugee status' *Colombia Human Rights Law Review* vol 15, no 1, pp 39–67

Hernandes B (1991) 'To bear or not to bear: reproductive freedom as an international human right' *Brooklyn Journal of International Law* vol 18, pp 309–358

Hinshelwood G (1997) 'Interviewing female asylum seekers' *International Journal of Refugee Law* (Special Issue) Autumn

Hirschmann NJ (1996) 'Domestic violence and the theoretical discourse of freedom' *Frontiers* vol 16, no 1, pp 126–151

Hollander NC (1996) 'The gendering of human rights: Women and the Latin American terrorist state' *Feminist Studies* 22(1), 41–80

Human Rights Watch (1992) *Double Jeopardy: Police Abuse of Women in Pakistan* (Human Rights Watch, London)

Human Rights Watch (1999) *Crime or Custom? Violence Against Women in Pakistan* (London) available on-line at http://www.hrw.org/reports/1999/pakistan

ILPA (1992) *Best Practice Guide to the Preparation of Asylum Applications from Arrival to First Interview* (ILPA, London)

ILPA (1996) *The Asylum and Immigration Act 1996: A compilation of ministerial statements made on behalf of the government during the Bill's passage through Parliament* (ILPA, London)

ILPA (1997a) *Best Practice Guide to Asylum Appeals* (ILPA, Law Society, Refugee Legal Group, London)

ILPA (1997b) *Directory of Experts on Conditions in Countries of Origin and Transit* (ILPA, London, 2nd ed)

ILPA (1999) *Breaking Down the Barriers: A Report on the Conduct of Asylum Interviews at Ports* (ILPA, London)

INS (1995) *Consideration for Asylum Officers Adjudicating Asylum Claims From Women* (Immigration and Naturalisation Service)

Indra DM (1987) 'Gender: a key dimension of the refugee experience' *Refuge* vol 6, no 3, pp 3–4

Indra DM (1989) 'Ethnic human rights and gender differences: gender implications for refugee studies and practice' *Journal of Refugee Studies* vol 2, no 2, pp 221–242

Indra DM (1993) 'Some feminist contributions to refugee studies' (paper presented at a joint plenary session of Gender Issues and Refugees: Development Implications and Exploring Knowledge, Power and Practice in Society (CASCA Annual Meetings, York University, Toronto) 9–11 May (unpublished)

Indra D (1999) 'Not a "room of one's own": engendering forced migration knowledge and practice' in Indra D (ed) *Engendering Forced Migration: Theory and Practice* (Berghahn Books, Oxford)

Indra D (ed) (1999) *Engendering Forced Migration: Theory and Practice* (Berghahn Books, Oxford)

James SA (1994) 'Reconciling international human rights and cultural relativism: the case of female circumcision' *Bioethics* vol 8, no 1, pp 1–26

Jaquette JS (ed) (1989) *The Women's Movement in Latin America: Feminism and the Transition to Democracy* (Unwin Hyman, Boston)

Jayawardena K (1986) *Feminism and Nationalism in the Third World* (Zed Books, London)

Jelin E (ed) (1990) *Women and Social Change in Latin America* (Zed Books, London)

Johnsson AB (1989) 'International protection of women refugees: a summary of principal problems and issues' *International Journal of Refugee Law* vol 1, no 2, pp 221–232

Jones A (1996) 'Does "gender" make the world go round? Feminist critiques of international relations' *Review of International Studies* vol 22, no 4, pp 405–430

Jones KB and Jonasdottir AG (eds) (1988) *The Political Interests of Gender: Developing Theory and Research with a Feminist Face* (Sage, London)

Justice, ILPA and ARC (1997) *Providing Protection: Towards Fair and Effective Asylum Procedures* (Justice, ILPA and ARC, London)

Kandiyoti D (ed) (1991) *Women, Islam and the State* (Macmillan, London)

Kelly N (1989) *Working with Refugee Women: A Practical Guide* (NGO Working Group on Refugee Women, Geneva)

Kelly N (1993) 'Gender-related persecution: assessing the asylum claims of women' *Cornell International Law Journal* vol 26, no 3, pp 625–674

Kelly N (1994) 'Guidelines for women's asylum claims' *International Journal of Refugee Law* vol 6, no 4, pp 517–534

Kelson G (1995) 'Granting political asylum to potential victims of female circumcision' *Michigan Journal of Gender and Law* vol 3, pp 257–298

Kelson G (1998) 'Female circumcision in the modern age: should female circumcision now be considered grounds for asylum in the United States?' *Buffalo Human Rights Law Review* vol 4, pp 185–209

Koblinkshy M et al (eds) (1994) *The Health of Women: A Global Perspective* (Westview Press, Boulder)

Kofman E and Peake L (1990) 'Into the 1990s: a gendered agenda for political geography' *Political Geography Quarterly* vol 9, no 4, pp 313–336

Lai S and Ralph RE (1995) 'Female sexual autonomy and human rights' *Harvard Human Rights Journal* pp 201–227

Laurie N et al (1997) 'In and out of bounds and resisting boundaries: feminist geographies of space and place' in Women and Geography Study Group *Feminist Geographies: Explorations in Diversity and Difference* (Longman, London)

Macdonald AI and Blake NJ (1998) *Macdonald's Immigration Law and Practice in the United Kingdom* 4th edn (Butterworths, London)

Mackie G (1996) 'Ending footbinding and infibulation: a convention account' *American Sociological Review* vol 61, no 6, pp 999–1017

MacKinnon C (1993) 'Feminism, Marxism, method and the state: toward feminist jurisprudence' in Bartlett KT and Kennedy R (eds) *Feminist Legal Theory: Readings in Law and Gender* (Westview Press, Boulder)

Macklin A (1995) 'Refugee women and the imperative of categories' *Human Rights Quarterly* vol 17, pp 213–277

Mawani N (1993) 'Introduction to the Immigration and Refugee Board Guidelines on gender-related persecution' *International Journal of Refugee Law* vol 5, no 2, pp 240–247

Mayer AE (1995) *Islam and Human Rights: Tradition and Politics* (Westview Press, Boulder)

Mayer R (1996) 'Female genital mutilation: the modern day struggle to eradicate a tortuous rite of passage' *Human Rights* vol 23, no 4

McClure H et al (1999) *Preparing Sexual-Orientation Based Asylum Claim: A Handbook for Advocates and Asylum Seekers* (Heartland Alliance, Chicago)

McClintock A (1993) 'Family feuds: gender, nationalism and the family' *Feminist Review* pp 61–80

McDowell L and Sharp JP (eds) (1997) *Space, Gender, Knowledge: Feminist Readings* (Arnold, London)

Mertus J (1995) 'State discriminatory family law and customary abuses' in Peters J and Wolper A (eds) *Women's Rights, Human Rights: International Feminist Perspectives* (Routledge, London)

Miller A et al (1999) 'Health, human rights and lesbian existence' in Mann J et al (eds) *Health and Human Rights* (Routledge, London)

Miller-Bashir L (1997) 'Female genital mutilation: balancing intolerance of the practice with tolerance of culture' *Journal of Women's Health* vol 6, no 1, pp 11–14

Minority Rights Group (1992) *Female Genital Mutilation: Proposals for Change* (MRG, London)

Minter S (1996) 'Lesbians and asylum: overcoming barriers to access' in Levy S (ed) *Asylum Based on Sexual orientation: A Resource Guide* (International Gay and Lesbian Human Rights Commission, London Legal Defence and Education Fund, London)

Moghadam VM (ed) (1994a) *Gender and National Identity: Women and Politics in Muslim Societies* (Zed Books, London)

Moghadam VM (ed) (1994b) *Identity Politics and Women: Cultural Reassertions and Feminisms in International Perspective* (Westview Press, Oxford)

Mohanty C et al (eds) (1991) *Third World Women and the Politics of Feminism* (Indiana University Press, Bloomington)

Moussa H (1993) *Storm and Sanctuary: The Journey of Ethiopian and Eritrean Women* (Artemis Enterprises, Ontario)

Mulligan M (1990) 'Obtaining political asylum: classifying rape as a well-founded fear of persecution on the grounds of political opinion' *Boston College Third World Journal* vol 10, pp 355–380

Naim AAA (1992) *Human Rights in Cross-Culture Perspective: A Quest for Consensus* (University of Pennsylvania Press, Philadelphia)

Neal DL (1988) 'Women as a social group: recognising sex-based persecution as grounds for asylum' *Colombia Human Rights Law Review* vol 20, no 1, pp 203–257

Niarchos CN (1995) 'Women, war and rape: challenges facing the international tribunal for the former Yugoslavia' *Human Rights Quarterly* vol 17, pp 649–690

Nzomo M (1997) 'Kenyan women in politics and public decision-making' in Mikell G (ed) *African Feminism: The Politics of Survival in Sub-Saharan Africa* (University of Pennsylvania Press, Philadelphia)

O'Donovan K (1985) *Sexual Divisions in Law* (Weidenfeld and Nicolson, London)

Okin SM (1998) 'Gender, the public and the private' in Philips A (ed) *Feminism and Politics* (OUP, Oxford)

Overall C (1987) *Ethics and Human Reproduction: A Feminist Analysis* (Allen and Unwin, Boston)

Paidar P (1995) *Women and the Political Process in Twentieth Century Iran* (Cambridge University Press, Cambridge)

Parpart VL (1993) 'Who is the "other": a postmodern feminist critique of women and development theory' *Development and Change* vol 24, pp 439–464

Passade Cisse B (1997) 'International law sources applicable to female genital mutilation: a guide to adjudicators of refugee claims based on fear of female genital mutilation' *Colombia Journal of Transnational Law* vol 35, pp 380–451

Perry MJ (1997) 'Are human rights universal? The relativist challenge and related matters' *Human Rights Quarterly* vol 19, no 3, pp 461–509

Peters J and Wolper A (eds) (1995) *Women's Rights, Human Rights: International Feminist Perspectives* (Routledge, London)

Peterson VS (ed) (1992) *Gendered States: Feminist (Re)Visions of International Relations Theory* (Lynne Reinner, Boulder)

Peterson VS (1996) 'The politics of identification in the context of globalisation' *Women's Studies International Forum* vol 19, no 1/2, pp 1–15

Peterson VS and Runyan A (1993) *Global Gender Issues* (Westview Press, Boulder)

Pettman JJ (1996) *Worlding Women: A Feminist International Politics* (Routledge, London)

Philips A (ed) (1998) *Feminism and Politics* (OUP, Oxford)

Radcliffe SA (1993) 'Women's place/el lugar de mujeres: Latin America and the politics of gender identity' in Keith M and Pile S (eds) *Place and the Politics of Identity* (Routledge, London)

Rai S (1996) 'Women and the state in the Third World: some issues for debate' in Rai S and Lievesley G (eds) *Women and the State: International Perspectives* (Taylor and Francis, London)

Randall V (1987) *Women and Politics: An International Perspective* (Macmillan, London)

Refugee Council (1996) *The State of Asylum: A Critique of Asylum Policy in the UK* (Refugee Council, London)

Refugee Legal Centre (1997) *Reviewing the Asylum Determination Procedure – A Casework Study (Parts 1 and 2)* (Refugee Legal Centre, London)

Refugee Women's Legal Group (1998) *Gender Guidelines for the Determination of Asylum Claims in the UK* (RWLG, London)

Ridd R (1986) 'Powers of the powerless' in Ridd R and Callaway H (eds) *Caught Up in Conflict: Women's Responses to Political Strife* (Macmillan, Basingstoke)

Roach Anleu SL (1992) 'Critiquing the law: themes and dilemmas in Anglo-American feminist legal theory' *Journal of Law and Society* vol 19, no 4, pp 423–440

Romany C (1993) 'Women as aliens: a feminist critique of the public/private distinction in human rights law' *Harvard Humanitarian Rights Journal* vol 6, pp 87–106

Romany C (1994) 'State responsibility goes private: a feminist critique of the public/private distinction in international human rights law' in Cook R (ed) *Human Rights of Women: National and International Perspectives* (University of Pennsylvania Press, Philadelphia)

Root NA and Tejani SA (1994) 'Undocumented: the roles of women in immigration law' *Georgetown Law Journal* vol 83, no 2, pp 605–634

Roth K (1994) 'Domestic violence as an international human rights issue' in Cook R (ed) *Human Rights of Women: National and International Perspectives* (University of Pennsylvania Press, Philadelphia)

Sarmer K (1999) *European Human Rights Law: The Human Rights Act 1998 and the ECHR* (LAG, London)

Saunders D (1996) 'Getting lesbian and gay issues on the international human rights agenda' *Human Rights Quarterly* vol 18, no 1, pp 67–106

Schilders N et al (1988) *Sexual Violence: 'You Have Hardly Any Future Left'* (Dutch Refugee Council, Amsterdam)

Seith PA (1997) 'Escaping domestic violence: asylum as a means of protection for battered women' *Colombia Law Review* vol 97, no 6, pp 1804–1843

Shahidian H (1996) 'Iranian exiles and sexual politics: issues of gender relations and identity' *Journal of Refugee Studies* vol 9, no 1, pp 41–72

Sharp JP (1996) 'Gendering nationhood: a feminist engagement with national identity' in Duncan N (ed) *Body Space: Destabilizing Geographies of Gender and Sexuality* (Routledge, London)

Siemens M (1988) 'Protection of women refugees' *Refugees* vol 56, pp 21–22

Siltanen J and Stanworth M (1984) 'The politics of private woman and public man' *Theory and Society* vol 13, no 1, pp 91–118

Slack A (1988) 'Female circumcision: a critical appraisal' *Human Rights Quarterly* vol 10, pp 437–448

Southall Black Sisters (1996) *Domestic Violence and Asian Women: A Collection of Reports and Briefings* (SBS, Southall)

Spijkerboer T (1994) *Women and Refugee Status: Beyond the Public/Private Distinction* (Emancipation Council, The Hague)

Stairs F and Pope L (1990) 'No place like home: assaulted migrant women's claims to refugee status and landings on humanitarian and compassionate grounds' *Journal of Law and Social Policy* vol 6, pp 148–225

Stanley A and Tennant V (1998) 'Women asylum seekers: an alternative approach' *Tolley's Immigration and Nationality Law and Practice* vol 12, no 2, pp 54–59

Strizhak E and Harries C (1993) *Sex, Lies and International Law* (Women's Commission for Refugee Women and Children, New York)

Thomas DQ and Beasley ME (1993) 'Domestic violence as a human rights issue' *Human Rights Quarterly* vol 15, pp 36–62

Thompkins TL (1995) 'Prosecuting rape as a war crime: speaking the unspeakable' *Notre Dame Law Review* vol 70, no 4, pp 845–890

Tickner JA (1992) *Gender in International Relations: Feminist Perspectives on Achieving Global Security* (Colombia University Press, New York)

Tomasevski K (1993) *Women and Human Rights* (Zed Books, London)

Toubia N (1995a) 'Female genital mutilation' in Peters J and Wolper A (eds) *Women's Rights, Human Rights: International Feminist Perspectives* (Routledge, London)

Toubia N (1995b) *Female Genital Mutilation: A Call for Global Action* (RAINBO, New York)

Toubia N (1997) 'Female genital mutilation as grounds for refugee determination' *INSCAN* vol 1, no 1, pp 5–15

Turner S (1996) *Discrepancies and Delays in Histories Presented by Asylum Seekers: Implications for Assessment* (unpublished)

UNHCR (1979) *Handbook on Procedures and Criteria for determining Refugee Status* (UNHCR, Geneva)

UNHCR (1991) *Guidelines on the Protection of Refugee Women* (UNHCR, Geneva)

UNHCR (1995a) *Sexual Violence Against Refugees: Guidelines on Prevention and Response* (UNHCR, Geneva)

UNHCR (1995b) *An Overview of Protection Issues in Western Europe: Legislative Trends and Positions Taken by UNHCR* (UNHCR, European Series No 3, Geneva)

UNHCR (1997) *The State of the World's Refugees* (OUP, Oxford)

Vickers J (1993) *Women and War* (Zed Books, London)

Warwick D (1982) *Bitter Pills: Population Policies and their Implementation in Eight Developing Countries* (CUP, Cambridge)

Waylen G (1992) 'Rethinking women's political participation and protest: Chile 1970–1990' *Political Studies* vol 15, pp 299–314

Waylen G (1994) 'Women and democratisation: conceptualising gender relations in transition politics' *World Politics* vol 46, pp 327–354

Waylen G (1996a) *Gender in Third World Politics* (Open University Press, Birmingham)

Waylen G (1996b) 'Analysing women in the politics of the Third World' in Afshar H (ed) *Women and Politics in the Third World* (Routledge, London)

Winter B (1994) 'Women, the law and cultural relativism in France: the case of excision' *Signs* vol 19, no 4, pp 939–974

Women and Geography Study Group (1997) *Feminist Geographies: Explorations in Diversity and Difference* (Longman, London)

Yamin A (1996) 'Defining questions: situating issues of power in the formulation of a right to health under international law' *Human Rights Quarterly* vol 18, pp 398–438

Yuval-Davis N (1993) 'Gender and nation' *Ethnic and Racial Studies* vol 16, no 4, pp 621–632

Yuval-Davis N (1994) 'Identity politics and women's ethnicity' in Moghadan VM (ed) *Identity Politics and Women: Cultural Reassertions and Feminisms in International Perspective* (Westview Press, Oxford)

Yuval-Davis N (1997) *Gender and Nation* (Sage, London)

INDEX

References are to paragraph numbers and Appendices.

Taliban, *see* Afghanistan
Tamils
  discrimination against, rejected
    argument   3.4.4
  no internal flight alternative, case
    3.4.6
  political opinion
    family member (rape/
      harassment)   4.4.4
  social group membership, persecution
    for   3.5.5, 4.4.5
Temporary pleasure marriage   3.4.5,
  5.2.3, 5.3
  background knowledge required for
    case   10.5.1
Togo
  FGM
    criminalisation of   9.4
    Islam invoked for   9.5.2
    refugee status of woman   9.2,
      9.5.5
  internal flight option, and size of
    9.4
Tonga
  family violence case   6.3
Torture
  see also Rape; Sexual abuse/violence
  Convention against   *App 7*
  FGM as   7.2, 9.3
  freedom from, human right   3.3,
    App 5
  human rights breach   4.2
  psychological effect on claimant
    10.4.2, 10.4.3
  State condoned family violence
    (Congo)   6.4.1
  sterilisation, abortion, FGM etc, as
    7.2
  World Organisation Against Torture
    8.5
Trade union
  membership   4.1.1
Transsexual
  Lebanon   8.3, 8.4.1
Turkey
  homosexuals, whether 'social
    group'   8.4.1

Uganda
  FGM in   9.1.1
United Kingdom
  European Convention on Human
    Rights incorporation   1.6.6

exceptional leave to remain, *see*
  Exceptional leave to remain
FGM, approach to   9.3
family violence cases
  frequent dismissal of   6.3
  'social group' ground cases   6.4.2
Guidelines, Gender   1.6, 1.6.6
Home Office approach to   1.6.6
internal protection alternative,
  interpretation of   3.4.6
procedure for claim in   10.1 *et seq,*
  see also Procedure
reproductive rights violation, cases
  7.4.2
sexual violence, sufficiency for refugee
  status   4.2
social group membership   6.4.2
  Asylum Directorate Instructions
    3.5.5, 8.4.1, *App 10*
  homosexuals, whether constitute
    8.4.1
  limitations of ground in   5.4.3
  standard of proof, HL case   10.6
  UNHCR questionnaire response
    1.6.6
United Nations Declarations, etc   6.3,
  Apps 7, 8
United Nations High Commission for
  Refugees   1.6, 1.6.1, *App 1*
  EXCOM Resolutions on Refugee
    women   *App 1*
  *Gender-Sensitive Techniques for
    Interviewing Women Refugees*
    10.3, *App 12*
  Geneva, Symposium in   1.6.5
  guidelines addressing gender-related
    persecution   1.6.1, 3.3.1, 3.3.2,
    4.3, 5.2.2
  *Handbook on Procedures etc for
    Determining Refugee Status*   3.2
  questionnaire   1.6.5, 1.6.6
  research in to situation in country of
    origin required   10.5.1
Universal Declaration of Human
  Rights   *App 7*

Veil
  compulsory wearing of   3.3.2
  persecution fear for failure   5.2.1
  State punishment for failure
    5.2.1
  politics of   4.1.3, 4.4.3